In the Strength of the Lord

In the Strength of the Lord

THE LIFE AND TEACHINGS
OF JAMES E. FAUST

BY JAMES P. BELL

DESERET BOOK COMPANY
SALT LAKE CITY, UTAH

Library of Congress Cataloging-in-Publication Data

Bell, James P., 1952–
    In the strength of the Lord : the life and teachings of James E. Faust / James P. Bell.
        p.   cm.
    Includes bibliographical references.
    ISBN 1-57345-580-6
    1. Faust, James E., 1920–   . 2. Church of Jesus Christ of Latter-day Saints Biography. 3. Church of Jesus Christ of Latter-day Saints—Doctrines. I. Title.
    BX8695.F38B45   1999
    289.3'092—dc21
    [B]   99-43364
                                                                        CIP

Printed in the United States of America   18961-6405

10   9   8   7   6   5   4   3   2   1

*"In the strength of the Lord
did we go forth . . ."*

MOSIAH 9:17

CONTENTS

PREFACE

In early 1997, I received a telephone call one Saturday morning from my father, who lives in another state. Unlike most of our conversations, which deal with family updates and the like, he began this call with a rather firm declaration. "I know what your next book should be," he said. I had recently completed a book with two dear friends, the late Rex E. Lee and his wife, Janet—and I responded that I did not have plans to write another book. He continued, undeterred, "No, you need to write a biography of James E. Faust."

Though still half asleep, I knew immediately that he was right, but I asked him anyway why he would make this suggestion. His answer was simple: "Because he's a good man, and the members of the Church don't know enough about him."

Not knowing President Faust, but feeling a need to act on my father's suggestion, I passed the idea along to Sheri Dew, who is the vice-president of publishing at Deseret Book and a long-time friend. She, in turn, discussed it with Ron Millett, president of Deseret Book, and the two of them arranged to meet with President Faust and discuss the idea with him.

He listened politely and said he would consider their proposal and then let them know of his decision. Having read, some months later, his journal entry for that day, I know that his initial reaction was a preference that such a book not be done. But after several weeks of discussion with his wife, family members, and a few close associates, he informed Ron and Sheri that he would agree to have a book done—but with two conditions: First, that the biography be brief; and, second, that a selection of his teachings be included in the same volume.

Soon after the three of them visited for the second time, I was asked to meet with President Faust to discuss the possibility of our working together. To say that I drove to that appointment with trepidation would be something of an understatement, but as I was shown into his office, I learned the first of many things I did not know about President James E. Faust. As he stood and took my hand in his, he said, "Jim, how are you?"

In an instant, I decided not to begin our discussion with a deception, and so I replied, "I'm a little nervous."

With his warm smile and a characteristic wave of his hand, he said, "Oh, don't be," and with that any concern I had over meeting a man I so greatly admired simply vanished.

Beyond learning in that moment of his graciousness and warmth, I learned during the subsequent hour of his humility, his discomfort with public recognition, his thoughtful and soft-spoken manner, his humor, and his desire to stand behind— rather than in front of—the messages and sermons he has shared with millions during his ministry as a General Authority. But even with an expressed reluctance to have a book written on his life, President Faust indicated that if sharing something of his life would provide greater insight into his ministry and teachings, he would be willing to work with me on this book.

Over the next year, we met together for an hour almost every Monday morning and discussed his life. Coupled with those interviews, I reviewed the journals he has kept since his call to the Quorum of the Twelve, studied his talks, pored over his scrapbooks, and interviewed Sister Ruth Faust, each of their five children and spouses, several grandchildren, two of his brothers, and several friends and associates. In addition, I conducted interviews with several of his associates among the General Authorities.

The first time we met, President Faust indicated he thought

the biographical portion of this book ought to be about 150 pages, but as we began our interviews and I tried to envision his life broken up into chapters, I felt that about 200 pages would be needed. With his acquiescence, I worked to distill a long and full life into a very brief sketch that, on the one hand, does not do justice to a great man who has made significant—and generally unheralded—contributions to his family, his community, his profession, and The Church of Jesus Christ of Latter-day Saints, but that, on the other hand, is in keeping with his lifelong desire to be, in his words, "a workhorse, not a showhorse."

The limitations on length created challenges in deciding what in President Faust's life to cover and what to leave out. Those decisions were mine alone, and he gave me absolute freedom to write the book as I deemed appropriate. The biography is arranged chronologically, up until President Faust's call to the Twelve, at which point, I opted to deal with his life more thematically—trying to provide enough information on selected topics to give the reader an insight into this man. As a result, vast portions of his life and ministry have not been treated, but that is always the case with biographies, no matter how long or exhaustive they may be. In addition, his absolute adherence to the confidentialities surrounding most of the work in which he is involved precluded my delving into much of what he has done as a General Authority.

These same limitations on length also seemed to dictate that I not interview many of those who know President Faust well, for had I done so I could not possibly have used any significant portion of what I would have gleaned from these interviews. As a result, there were many family members, friends, and Church leaders—both local and general—whom I did not interview, all of whom could have shared significant insights into President Faust's life and ministry. Many, no doubt, would have welcomed the opportunity to talk about a man they know so well and love so much, and I apologize that more of his associates could not have been included.

As for the collection of President Faust's teachings presented herein, these, too, represent a fraction of the countless messages he has shared throughout the world. Most of the talks he has given, unfortunately, have not been formally prepared or recorded, and so I drew from those for which a manuscript existed. Every general conference talk he has given is represented, as well as numerous talks given at firesides, devotionals, funerals, leadership meetings, and community events. My hope in preparing the two sections of this book has been that each would complement the other—that as the reader understands more of President Faust's life, he or she will have greater insight into his teachings, and vice-versa. If there is a lack of cohesiveness between the two sections, the failure is mine alone.

In the course of writing this book, I have amassed a lengthy list of those have helped me in one way or another—but in all cases significantly.

First of all, I thank my wife, Kristi, for her ongoing love, support, encouragement, humor, and friendship. These are very tangible traits, and without them I could not have undertaken this project, nor would I have ever finished it. I also thank my children—Laura (and her husband, Trevor), Shannon, Dianna, Lindsay, Stephanie, and Dana—for their patience and their willingness to share in a marvelous opportunity. I also express gratitude to my father and mother, Preston and Frances Bell, for all they have done to teach and encourage me, as well as to my four sisters and two brothers.

I appreciate the warm and gracious way in which the Faust family has welcomed me into their homes and their lives. Though neither Sister Faust nor any of the Fausts' children—Jim, Janna, Marcus, Lisa, and Robert—enjoys the very public nature of President Faust's calling any more than he does, they all (together with their spouses), were more than happy to help in any way they could. That support was invaluable during the preparation of this book. In addition, several grandchildren (and, in the case of those who are married, their spouses) shared valuable insights into their grandparents.

At one point, I asked President Faust for his advice on who among the General Authorities I should interview, and his response was, "Oh, they're all such busy men; they certainly don't need to spend their time talking about me." Despite his protestations, each of the General Authorities I called immediately agreed to meet and gave generously of his time. To President Gordon B. Hinckley and President Thomas S. Monson of the First Presidency, as well as Elder L. Tom Perry, Elder Neal A. Maxwell, Elder Joseph B. Wirthlin, and Elder Jeffrey R. Holland of the Twelve, I express sincere appreciation for their time and their insight into a man they all regard as a beloved colleague. In addition, Elder and Sister Wm. Grant Bangerter and Elder Albert Choules, Jr., emeritus members of the Seventy, gave generously of their time. Many others took time to be interviewed, including Augustus Faust, Rex Faust, Newell and Fran Stevenson, Justice Richard C. Howe, Bruce Olsen, Steve Coltrin, Bonner Ritchie, and David Galbraith. After the interviews were completed, as I then worked to bring form and shape to a rather substantial amount of material, I sought advice from several friends, including Lee Perry and Steve Brown. To each I express my thanks.

From the outset of this project, President Faust's two secretaries, Margaret Bury and Sheila Kartchner, have been invaluable in scheduling appointments, providing access to materials, and sharing insights into a man they have each come to know in a most unique way. In addition, they have provided much-needed and on-going friendship and support.

During the course of preparing this book, I have attempted to juggle my writing with my full-time responsibilities at KBYU, the public television and public radio stations affiliated with Brigham Young University. In the process, I no doubt dropped more balls than I should have, and I appreciate the understanding and support of all my colleagues at KBYU, particularly John Reim, Sterling Van Wagenen, Derek Marquis,

Cathy Leifson, Duane Roberts, Anna Hirst, Sandy Ewing, Ruston Jones, Christine Nokleby, Chris Twitty, Mike Walker, and Jane Wilson. In addition, I express appreciation to Elder Merrill J. Bateman, who serves as president of BYU, for encouragement and insight given at the outset of this project.

There are numerous individuals (some unknown to me) at Deseret Book who have worked under challenging deadlines to make this book a reality. I thank Ron Millett and Sheri Dew for affording me the opportunity to work on this book. I also express my gratitude to Jay Parry and Linda Gundry for their thoughtful and thorough editing, to Kent Ware for various forms of guidance and support, to Richard Erickson and Michelle Eckersley for their tasteful and inviting design, to Patty Parkinson for her expert typography, to Anne Sheffield for overseeing the many aspects of the production process, and to Keith Hunter and his staff for helping make the public aware of the book's existence.

Finally, I express, inadequately, my appreciation to President James Esdras Faust and his wife, Ruth Wright Faust, for the opportunity to learn of and then share something of his life, which is inextricably tied to hers, with readers throughout the Church. My father was right: President Faust is a good man, and most members of the Church don't know enough about him. I knew that instinctively when my father first made the comment; I know it of a surety now. My hope is that, in some small way, this book will help to change that as it portrays a life well lived and then excerpts the teachings of one who has, throughout his life, focused his every ability on helping each of God's children come to know—and follow—their Savior more fully.

PART I

THE LIFE
OF
JAMES E. FAUST

I

FAITHFUL
FOREFATHERS

On a hot Saturday evening in 1938, Jim Faust went with two of his friends to a county fair near their home in Cottonwood, Utah. As the threesome tried their hands at various games and competitions, one of the group won a carnival strength test by swinging a hammer with enough force to ring the bell atop a tower. The prize for this feat was a cigar, and because there were three in the group, the hawker gave one to each boy.

Two of the three decided to give theirs a try, as eighteen-year-old Jim looked on in silence. Then, after a moment's contemplation, he said gently, "How are you going to feel tomorrow when you sit at the sacrament table?"[1]

Some sixty years later, as James E. Faust serves as second counselor in the First Presidency of The Church of Jesus Christ of Latter-day Saints, Marcus Faust says of his father: "Dad has an inbred, ingrained sense of right and wrong that has always guided everything he has done. There has never been any compromise within him whatsoever, when it comes to issues of right and wrong."

Those who meet James E. Faust inevitably seem to sense that part of his goodness is innate—that it has been with him from birth. In fact, one of the friends who accompanied him to the county fair recalls, "He was always a mature kid, spiritually, even at a very young age. And he did a lot to remind us of who we were and what we were."

Also evident, though, is the fact that his heritage instilled within him many of the characteristics for which he is known today.

Like many Latter-day Saints of his generation, James Esdras Faust comes from pioneer stock. He was born on Saturday, July 31, 1920, in Delta, Utah, a small desert town some 150 miles southwest of Salt Lake City. His mother had prepared a noonday meal for her sister, Angie, and other family members when she began "having pains enough to make her squirm." The only doctor in town was sent for, but he was busy delivering a cousin (who died at birth), so a midwife came and delivered the second of the five sons that would be born to George Augustus and Amy Finlinson Faust. Amy's youngest sister, Angie, who had married George's best friend and who was pregnant with her first child, later described Jim's birth: "You were thin and looked like a wrinkled little old man with not much meat on your bones. As we looked you over and wondered what name to give you, Uncle Willis said, 'James Esdras, for his two uncles,' and it stuck."

No doubt as Amy held her little boy that day, her mind went back to a blessing she had received a few months earlier, as she and Angie had traveled to the Manti Temple and while there had sought blessings from the temple president. Among other things, he had told her that she would bear a son and that he would be a comfort to her throughout her entire life.

Young Jim Faust was surrounded by grandparents, great-grandparents, aunts, uncles, and cousins who lived in the towns of Delta and neighboring Oak City. And though he moved with his parents to Salt Lake City when he was three years of age, the family returned often to Oak City, where Jim heard countless stories of those faithful progenitors, on both his father's and mother's sides, who had converted to Mormonism, crossed the plains, and helped settle Utah.

The first of his maternal ancestors to join the Church was Edward Partridge, who met Parley P. Pratt, Oliver Cowdery, Peter Whitmer Jr., and Ziba Peterson in the fall of 1830. He did not immediately accept their message, but he did study the Book of Mormon and then sought out the Prophet Joseph

Smith, who baptized him on December 11, 1830, in the Seneca River in the township of Fayette, New York.

In February 1831, Edward was called to be the first bishop of the Church, when, in a revelation given to Joseph Smith, the Lord directed the Prophet to select Edward Partridge, "and this because his heart is pure before me, for he is like unto Nathanael of old, in whom there is no guile" (D&C 41:11).

In July of 1833, while attending to his frail wife, who had recently given birth, Bishop Partridge was forced from his home by enemies of the Church bent on driving the Saints from Jackson County, Missouri. Then, after he and Charles Allen refused to renounce their faith, the two were tarred and feathered at the hands of a mob some five hundred strong. He continued to serve faithfully and to stand firm in his testimony, yet on May 27, 1840, Edward Partridge died an untimely death at the age of forty-six in Nauvoo, Illinois.

On that same day, the Prophet Joseph recorded in his journal, "He lost his life in consequence of the Missouri persecutions, and he is one of that number whose blood will be required at their hands."[2] Years later, President James E. Faust would write of the first of his many ancestors who embraced the restored gospel:

> Grandfather was so tortured, humiliated, and suffered so much in his calling from lawless mobs, and was still so steadfast and faithful, that he could not possibly have doubted the genuineness of the revelation that appointed him. Like others who were close to the Prophet, he knew Joseph's heart and soul. Grandfather could not have been deceived. I believe his life and death both prove that he did not lie. His devotion, suffering, and sacrifice eloquently testify that he had implicit faith in Joseph as an inspired servant of God.[3]

Among the five daughters and two sons born to Edward and Lydia Partridge was Caroline Ely, who was born in Ohio and later lived in Joseph and Emma Smith's home in Nauvoo. There she tended the Smiths' children as she watched Joseph go about his daily duties, which led her to pass on to her posterity a sure testimony of the prophetic office and calling of Joseph Smith. Two of the many who heard her testimony before her death in 1908 were Jim's mother and his Aunt Angie, who shared their great-grandmother's convictions frequently with him, his brothers, and their cousins as they were growing up.

In September of 1844, Caroline married Amasa Mason Lyman, who had been serving as a counselor to the Prophet Joseph Smith at the time of his martyrdom. Despite the urging of some who felt he had a legitimate claim to become the leader of the Church, Amasa supported the leadership of the Twelve after the death of Joseph, stating: "I do not rise to electioneer. I am gratified with the open, frank and plain exposition of President Young. . . .

" . . . I believe there is no power, or officer, or means wanted to carry on the work, but what is in the Twelve. I am satisfied that no man can carry on the work, but the power that is in the Twelve. . . .

" . . . I have been at the back of Joseph Smith, and will be at the back of the Twelve forever, and then we will be saved."[4]

Four days later, Amasa Lyman was ordained an apostle and set apart as a member of the Twelve. He accompanied Brigham Young to the Salt Lake Valley in 1847 and helped to settle Fillmore, Utah.

On her paternal side, Amy Finlinson Faust's grandfather was George Finlinson, who, upon accepting the gospel, left his home in Thursby, England, to cross an ocean and half a continent to settle in the desert town of Fillmore, Utah. But leaving the lushly green Lake District of England for the harsh environs of Utah was not his greatest sacrifice.

At the time of his conversion, George was married to Anne Emerson, and the couple had a baby daughter. Anne, however, could not accept her husband's newfound faith and became bitter toward him and his fellow believers. When the call came in the mid-1860s for the Saints in Thursby to gather to Zion, George was determined to obey, even as Anne refused to leave her homeland. So he set sail without her or his daughter, knowing he would never see them again but feeling the obligation to heed a prophet's call.

The two did correspond for some time, and in one letter Anne expressed her concern over not knowing whether she was "a wife or a widow." George wrote back, expressing his concern for her and their daughter but telling her, "You are just any thing you have a mind to call yourself. I told you a long time ago if you want your freedom, you had it from me, and if you wanted to be my wife, you had the privilege to be so. What more could any person desire?" He then shared his convictions with her in these words:

> When a man knows a road, who can persuade him it is wrong? Can any person persuade you to go around by Crofton Tole Bart to Thursby that it was the direct and nearest road, you would tell them they were mistaken. They might talk from now till twenty years from now and I will bet a dollar that they could never persuade you it was the nearest road to Thursby. It is hard for anyone to persuade a person a thing is different from what they know a thing for a certainty themselves. It is the same way with me today about Mormonism as when I left England. I told you it was true when I left England, and I will tell you it is true today. And as for you not having your freedom, you have it just as much as ever. . . . I am now a man calculated to live by true principles, which if you live by would lead you to comfort in this life and happiness in the next life. . . .
>
> Give my love to your mother and father. I respect her yet and your father for all their kindness, and give my daughter a kiss for me.[5]

Soon after his arrival in Utah, George became reacquainted with the Trimble family, who had joined the Church in Thursby and then introduced George to the gospel. Among their children was a daughter, Susan, whom George began to court and soon took as his wife. Like George, Susan had experienced something of the hostility family and friends often heaped upon those who converted to Mormonism. Before her family left their home in Thursby, she received a lengthy letter from "a sincere well-wisher and friend" who told her, in part:

Consider, Susan, the awful and terrible dangers of a long sea voyage. O what a change for you all, to be tossed on the wide, wide ocean far away from all you love, at the mercy of the wind and waves and terrible storms.

Your poor mother, what will become of her, think you—frail, feeble, and delicate as you know she is. It will be an awful, tremendous trial for her, poor woman. Indeed, it is generally thought by those who know her, that she will not be able to stand the fearful hardships of the sea. . . .

Then consider your younger brothers and sisters—what terrible distress and trouble you are going to bring upon them, poor things. O what will you think when you see those innocent children suffering from the awful pains of seasickness, and then how terrible will your condition be, and that of your mother and children, when the waves rage around your ship and threaten to dash you to pieces every moment. . . .

But if you even did get to the Salt Lake, would you be happy then? Not at all. The laws there are very bad, and murders and all sorts of crimes are common. Your money will be taken from you and you will be entirely in the power of those wicked men who are so cruelly but successfully enticing you away. They keep bloodhounds to prevent people from escaping.

It is foolish to suppose that you will be purified and saved by going to a wicked place like the Salt Lake. You know very well, Susan, that people can be good and holy in old England without leaving it.

If you believe in the Bible, you must know that God never says that he wants people to leave their quiet, comfortable homes. No, no. We are to love and serve him on our native land. What sort of men are Brigham Young and all the others of the Salt Lake, that you should be led away by them from England?[6]

Brought to the restored gospel—and to the gathering place of Utah—by their faith, George and Susan drew frequently on that same source of strength as they created a new life for themselves. They settled in Fillmore, where Jim Faust's maternal grandfather, George Edward Finlinson, was born. George Edward, when he grew to maturity, met and married Mary Caroline Roper, who descended from Edward Partridge. George Edward and Mary lived in Oak City, Utah, a town some twelve miles east of Delta, and it was there that their daughter, Amy Finlinson, was born and reared. In addition to the many other characteristics the Finlinson immigrants passed on to their progeny, they passed on what Sister Ruth Faust, wife of President Faust, refers to as "the believing blood of the Finlinsons."

The lineage of Jim's father likewise had its roots in the earliest days of the Church. In fact, in the April 1997 general conference, President Faust told of his paternal ancestry as he spoke of the importance of temples and covenants:

> On February 3, 1846, it was a bitter cold day in Nauvoo, Illinois. That day, President Brigham Young recorded in his diary:
>
> "Notwithstanding that I had announced that we would not attend to the administration of the ordinances, the House of the Lord was thronged all day. . . . I also informed the brethren that I was going to get my wagons started and be off. I walked some distance from the Temple supposing the crowd would disperse, but on returning I found the house filled to overflowing.
>
> "Looking upon the multitude and knowing their anxiety, as they were thirsting and hungering for the word, we continued at work diligently in the House of the Lord." [*History of the Church*, 7:579.]
>
> And so the temple work continued until 1:30 A.M.
>
> The first two names that appear on the fourth company of the Nauvoo Temple register for that very day, February 3, 1846, are John and Jane Akerley, who received their endowments in the Nauvoo Temple that evening. They were humble, new converts to the Church, without wealth or position. Their temple work was their final concern as they were leaving their homes in Nauvoo to come west. It was fortunate that President Young granted the wish of the Saints to receive their temple blessings because John Akerley died at Winter Quarters, Nebraska. He, along with over 4,000 others, never made it to the valleys of the Rocky Mountains.[7]

Jane Akerley did make it to Utah, however, together with her daughter, Elsie Ann, who had been born in 1842, and her other children. The family settled in Fillmore, and it was there, as she stood by a well, that Elsie met a young man who had come from Heddesheim, Prussia (now Germany), and was passing through Utah on his way to the gold fields of California. Henry Jacob (H. J.) Faust was not of Elsie's faith, but he was quite taken with her, as was she with him. However, even as she shared with him her testimony of the gospel, Elsie let H. J. know that she would not marry outside her faith. H. J. did go on to California, where he spent just enough time to pan sufficient gold for a wedding band. Thereupon, he returned to Fillmore, joined the Church, and married Elsie. As they began their life together, he worked on the state capitol building in Fillmore and then on the transcontinental railroad. Later, he was called by Brigham Young to be the first bishop in Corinne, Utah.

His associations with Brigham Young continued; in fact, he later moved to Salt Lake City and built a livery stable on Second South, which included a United States courthouse on the second floor. Coincidentally, Brigham Young was tried in that courthouse after an arrest by U.S. marshals in October 1871. (President Young was acquitted of the charges.) H. J. was also active in state politics, and on July 13, 1872, during the Democratic ratification meeting held in Salt Lake City, he nominated Elder George Q. Cannon of the Quorum of the Twelve as a delegate to Congress.[8]

After moving to Faust Station, Utah, where H. J. was a Pony Express rider and oversaw the outpost, he and Elsie had a son they named James Akerley Faust. James later married Maud Wetzel, whose father, Edmund Wetzel, had joined the Church in Kentucky and then moved to Utah. James and Maud Faust had two sons, James, the eldest, and George, who would marry Amy Finlinson on October 3, 1917, in the Salt Lake City Temple.

George and Amy began married life in Delta, not long after the United States had declared war on Germany and entered into World War I. On May 27, 1918, George was drafted into the army and was sent to Fort Lewis for training. As President Faust tells of his father's entering the service, he says, "Father was not a big man, but he was quite spunky and determined. And he had decided that if he was in the Army, then he was supposed to fight, although the lieutenant who was filling up the 91st Division didn't think he was big enough. So Father, who was quite athletic and fast, despite his size, said to the lieutenant, 'Have you got any way to try out how good a man is?' Well, the lieutenant liked his spunk, and in three weeks he was on his way to France."

The day George set sail from New York to France, Amy gave birth to their first son, Augustus. As Amy waited for her husband's safe return, George served on the front lines of four of the major battles that were fought in France.

In a journal he kept while in France, George recorded the details of one battle in these words:

> There was heavy fog, and about this time the fog began to lift and the enemy had located our position and we were shelled unmercifully. Twenty-five percent of our platoon were casualties within 30 minutes, and we were ordered to return to the trenches. And we did, with the cries of agony and gruesome dead, which a short hour previous were stalwart men, leaving us with thoughts we cannot rid ourselves of. . . .
>
> The trenches were strewn with the dead and wounded, and first aid stations were established to care for those who could get to the trenches. However, those were only a few in comparison to the number who needed first aid. Some men were left for days and days to suffer a hundred deaths, and many died for lack of treatment.

On another occasion, he spent the night in a machine gun nest, protecting the sleeping soldiers:

> My head seemed to burst with aching, and I was allowed to lie down and not be responsible for the protection of anyone's life. I slept. No blankets, no nothing, but mother earth, in the same clothes I had been in for two weeks, without having even taken off my shoes to change socks and put them right on again.

Of one all-night march, he wrote:

> How I managed to make it that night without falling in my tracks is more than I can understand, unless it was that I did not use tobacco nor intoxicants of any kind and tried to live a most clean life, doing nothing to sap my vitality. But from that night until the day I write this, I have never had the pep I had before.

Despite all he had endured, George Faust's summary statement of the time spent in his country's service reflects something of what was at his core:

> I am not prepared at the present time to state whether or not
> this service to my country was a detriment or a help to myself.
> From a financial standpoint, I'm sure it was a hindrance.
> But if I had to do it over, I would do it the same way, because it
> was my duty.[9]

On April 27, 1919, George was discharged from the army.
Upon returning to Delta, he was finally able to see his son for
the first time, and he and Amy began to rebuild their life
together. Although most of his family was involved in farming,
George did not have a knack for it and started a tire repair business instead. In 1920 Jim was born, and in 1923 George and
Amy decided they would leave Delta and move with their two
sons to Salt Lake City, where George would enroll in law school
at the University of Utah as a thirty-three-year-old student.

NOTES

1. Unless otherwise noted, quotations from James E. Faust, as well as
family members, General Authorities, and other associates, are from tran-
scriptions of interviews in the possession of the author, or from the journals
of President Faust.

2. *History of The Church of Jesus Christ of Latter-day Saints*, 7 vols., 2d ed.
rev., ed. B. H. Roberts (Salt Lake City: The Church of Jesus Christ of Latter-
day Saints, 1932–51), 4:132.

3. "The Expanding Inheritance from Joseph Smith," *Ensign*, November
1981, p. 77.

4. *History of the Church*, 7:236–37.

5. Letter from George Finlinson to Anne Finlinson, 10 August 1868. Written
from Fillmore, Utah. Spelling and punctuation have been standardized.

6. Undated, unsigned letter to Susan Trimble.

7. "Eternity Lies Before Us," *Ensign*, May 1997, p. 18.

8. See B. H. Roberts, *A Comprehensive History of The Church of Jesus Christ of
Latter-day Saints, Century One*, 6 vols. (Salt Lake City: The Church of Jesus
Christ of Latter-day Saints, 1930), 5:464–66.

9. Excerpts taken from the unpublished journals and reminiscences of
George A. Faust, in the possession of James E. Faust.

2

THE SEEDS
OF TESTIMONY

GEORGE FAUST'S DECISION TO ENROLL at the University of Utah
Law School in 1923 did not create an easy set of circumstances
for his young family. When he and Amy, together with their
sons Gus and Jim, moved into a small house on Norris Court
(just west of the University of Utah campus), George had no
job, the family had no car, and the house was warmed by a pot-
belly stove and lighted by oil lamps. But George had been
encouraging other veterans of World War I to take advantage
of the benefits offered them, and he had concluded that he
should follow his own advice.

Gus remembers those years as a struggle, but he also
remembers them for the pattern they provided—as George let
it be known, by both word and deed, that getting an education
was not optional but essential for the Faust boys.

It was in the family's home on Norris Court that young Jim
became aware of the world around him. He and Gus were soon
joined by their next brother, Rex, who was brought into the
world by their aunt, Ada Faust—one of the first woman doctors
in Utah. (Before George completed law school, Amy had given
birth to the couple's fourth son, Dan. Their fifth son, Delano,
came later.)

As the boys grew, they were close and they were rambunctious. Rex recalls that they were typical boys with energy—and
in need of ways to release it. He recalls one time when the boys
turned a hose on in their neighbor's house, resulting in their
mother's having to mop up the mess; and Gus tells of a family

friend on Norris Court who predicted that the Faust boys would all end up in prison by the time they were eighteen.

Much of the family's entertainment came from their activity in the Salt Lake City Eleventh Ward, where Jim used to admire a stained-glass window depicting the First Vision. There was little money for any form of entertainment outside of ward functions, although the family was finally able to purchase a car.

"Those early cars were bad," Jim recalls. "In the winter you would snap curtains up to stay warm, and it had a glass windshield that was supposed to be clear but wasn't. It would fog up in the cold, so Mother would sew a little bag of table salt, which you had to rub on both sides of the windshield in order to get a little vision. And in those days you had to grind the valves on those cars regularly. I can remember father and his friend Preston Thatcher, who was also a law student, stripping down the motor and grinding those valves—and neither one was very mechanical."

The financial challenges were ever-present during George's time in law school, but one holiday season was particularly challenging. Young Jim's recollections of that year's Christmas are reflected in a fireside address he gave in December 1983:

> Grandfather and Grandmother Finlinson knew that we would have no Christmas if we did not come down to the farm in Millard County. So all of our family took the train from Salt Lake to Leamington, Utah. Where the money came from for the tickets, I will never know.
>
> Grandfather and Uncle Esdras met us at the railroad crossing in Leamington with a team of big horses to pull the open sleigh through the deep snow to Oak City. It was so cold that the huge horses had icy chin whiskers and you could see their breath. I remember how old Jack Frost nipped my nose and the extreme cold made it hard to breathe. Grandmother had heated some rocks and put them in the bottom of the sleigh to help keep us warm. We were wrapped and tucked into some heavy camp quilts with just our noses sticking out. Accompanied by the tinkle of bells on leather straps on the harnesses of the horses, we

musically traveled from Leamington over the ten miles to Oak City where our beloved grandfather and grandmother lived. So many dear ones were there that we could hardly wait to arrive. When we got there it was warm and wonderful and exciting.

In the corner of the living room was the Christmas tree—a cedar cut from the hillside pasture. It was already partially decorated by Mother Nature with little berries which helped give it a strong smell. Our decorations were popcorn strings made by threading popcorn through a needle and a thread which had to be handled carefully or they would break and strew popcorn all over the floor.

We also had paper chains to put on the tree, made by cutting up old Sears and Montgomery Ward catalogs with the paper links pasted together with flour paste. The sticky flour paste got all over our hands, faces, and clothes. I wonder why they didn't put sugar in it! With cream it could also have been served for mush.

I do not remember any presents under the tree. Under the tree were popcorn balls made with strong, home-made molasses. When we bit into the popcorn balls, it felt like they were biting back.

On Christmas Eve we all gathered around the wood stove, enjoying the warm comfort of the fire and the pleasant aroma of the burning cedar wood. One of the uncles gave the opening prayer. We sang carols and hymns. One of our aunts read of the birth of Jesus and of the "good tidings of great joy" (Luke 2:10). "For unto you is born this day in the City of David a Saviour, which is Christ the Lord" (Luke 2:11). Grandfather and Grandmother then told us how much they loved us.

The next day was Christmas, and we had a glorious dinner. But before we ate, we all got down on our knees for family prayer. I was so hungry. Grandfather prayed for the longest time. You see, he had much to pray for. He prayed for moisture because there was a drouth in the land, and the crops had been meager. The fall grain had been planted in the dusty ground. What harvest there was could not be sold for much because of the low price caused by the great depression. The taxes on the farm were delinquent because there was no money to pay them. He also prayed for our large family, his cattle and horses, pigs and chickens, turkeys—he prayed over everything.

During Grandfather's long prayer, my youngest uncle became

restless and gave me an irreverent pinch, hoping that I would shout to make things more exciting.

For dinner we had a huge tom turkey stuffed with delicious dressing. There was no celery in the dressing because we had only the ingredients that could be produced on the farm. But the dressing had plenty of bread, sage, sausage, and onions. There was an abundance of potatoes and gravy and pickles, beets, beans, and corn. Because Grandfather could trade wheat to the miller for flour, there was always fresh baked bread. To stretch the food, we were encouraged to take one bite of bread for every bite of other kinds of food. We had chokecherry jelly and groundcherry jam. For dessert we had pumpkin and gooseberry pie. It was all delicious.

As I look back on that special Christmas over a lifetime, the most memorable part was that we did not think about presents. There may have been some handmade mittens or a scarf given, but I do not recall any presents. Presents are wonderful, but I found that they are not essential to our happiness. I could not have been happier. There were no presents that could be held and fondled and played with, but there were many wonderful gifts that could not be seen, but could be felt.

There was the gift of boundless love. We knew God loved us. We all loved each other. We did not miss the presents because we had all these glorious gifts. It made me feel so wonderful and secure to belong and to be part of all that went on. We wanted nothing else. We did not miss the presents at all. I never remember a happier Christmas in my childhood.[1]

In 1927, George earned his degree from the University of Utah Law School and began practicing law in downtown Salt Lake. The family stayed in their home on Norris Court while he established his practice, and later George and Amy moved with their four sons to Cottonwood, some ten miles southeast of downtown Salt Lake.

"Cottonwood at that time was country," Jim says, "and we moved out there because Father wanted his boys to learn to work. So what to do? We built a chicken coop and got some chickens. We got some cows and then some sheep. We used to raise our own beef, and father would slaughter it in the fall as the weather was turning cold. Then he would cut the meat up and put it in canvas bags that he hung on nails on the north side of the porch so it wasn't in the sun."

Gus adds, "Father always found ways for us to learn to do chores. He didn't want us hanging around asking for things; he wanted us to learn that there was a relationship between work and money."

At about the same time the Fausts moved to Cottonwood, the United States was sliding into the Depression, which would last until the United States entered World War II in 1941. The Fausts were more fortunate than some, because in 1928 George had helped a young, single Catholic from Montana run for Salt Lake county attorney, and the man won. Knowing that he needed someone who knew the "territory" at his side and impressed with George's wisdom and judgment, John D. Rice made George Faust his chief deputy, which ensured a steady salary during the early years of the Depression. A few years later, George started a private practice with Judge Joseph Jeppson, with whom he continued a professional association for many years.

Jim's assessment of his father's beginning a practice during the midst of the Depression is simply, "I don't know how he ever made it."

Rex adds that his father was good-natured and friendly with all their neighbors, many of whom came to him with their problems. Knowing the tenuousness of their finances, he rarely charged them anything as he helped many save their homes— and often their marriages and families—as they tried to hold together lives devastated by the Depression.

"He'd always try to keep the families together. That was one of his great talents, and I know he saved many, many marriages in the Cottonwood area. And mercifully, he never went after fees. Many felt they should pay him in one way or another, though, and that led to a variety of barter situations.

"He got two old cows in payment once. He brought them home and we hated them, they were so hard to milk. Then he traded them to someone. He got a couple of old Buicks at one point. Years later he told me, 'If I had received all the money that was owed me through those years, I could retire.'"

Although George's sons would have learned the value of hard work anyway, the Depression certainly added to the demands placed upon them. On one occasion, the boys worked with a man who built a rock wall around their property as payment for legal services. And there were the never-ending routines and chores associated with running the small, one-acre farm.

"Every summer," Rex says, "Jim and I had to take turns spading the garden—and it was a big garden. It took us about a week to get it all ready. Our father could have gotten it plowed a lot easier, but he felt his boys ought to have something to do and saw that as a good project. And, oh, our backs would ache."

Many of the chores required the boys' attention seven days a week, such as milking the cows. As Jim remembers his years growing up, he says, "Farm life is a wonderful discipline in terms of having to meet the responsibilities of the eternal each and every day. Cows have to be milked on the Fourth of July and on Thanksgiving and Christmas. That's a tremendous discipline."

His brothers maintain that Jim at times found activities that kept him from taking his turn with milking, and his boyhood friend, Newell Stevenson, says that sometimes "those poor cows didn't get milked until 10 or 11 at night. George's boys had a tendency to forget about the cows, particularly if there was something more fun to do. And usually there was."

Even so, over the course of his childhood, Jim learned the importance of responsibility and hard work. One lesson that was particularly poignant involved a little lamb his father had found in the desert and entrusted to his care, a story he would share in the April 1995 general conference priesthood session:

> [After my father brought the lamb home and made me its shepherd], for several weeks I warmed cow's milk in a baby's bottle and fed the lamb. We became fast friends. I called him

Nigh—why I don't remember. It began to grow. My lamb and I would play on the lawn. Sometimes we would lie together on the grass and I would lay my head on its soft, woolly side and look up at the blue sky and the white billowing clouds. I did not lock my lamb up during the day. It would not run away. It soon learned to eat grass. I could call my lamb from anywhere in the yard by just imitating as best I could the bleating sound of a sheep: *Baa. Baa.*

One night there came a terrible storm. I forgot to put my lamb in the barn that night as I should have done. I went to bed. My little friend was frightened in the storm, and I could hear it bleating. I knew that I should help my pet, but I wanted to stay safe, warm, and dry in my bed. I didn't get up as I should have done. The next morning I went out to find my lamb dead. A dog had also heard its bleating cry and killed it. My heart was broken. I had not been a good shepherd or steward of that which my father had entrusted to me. My father said, "Son, couldn't I trust you to take care of just one lamb?" My father's remark hurt me more than losing my woolly friend. I resolved that day, as a little boy, that I would try never again to neglect my stewardship as a shepherd if I were ever placed in that position again.[2]

Jim's father was, without question, a strong disciplinarian, and he had a way of getting to the heart of a matter without wasting words. He had an unmistakable love for his boys and spent all the time with them he could. George loved to come home, change into his work clothes, and work in the yard. Or, more often, he would help Amy in the kitchen with dinner. "Father was a great cook," Jim says. "My wife, and everyone who knew him, will attest to that. She will also tell you that he dirtied every pan in the house. Mother was a good cook as well, but Father was always at her side."

George also loved to hunt and fish and took his sons, along with other family members and friends, on many memorable trips.

"I think the most miserable night of my life was courtesy of George Faust," says Newell Stevenson. "We went down to American Fork Canyon, and he showed us how to make a bed out of pine boughs. Well, I flunked pine boughs, and I spent the whole night finding a new pine bough under my back or my feet or somewhere."

Jim remembers a somewhat similar experience while on a fishing trip. "Father, my brothers, my Uncle Jim, and I went up to the Uintas to fish, and it rained every day we were there. It rained so much that all the canvas over us did was to break the raindrops into smaller drops. It wasn't a pleasant experience, and I don't know why in the world we didn't pack up and come home."

Jim says, "While I do not ever recall my father using the words, 'Son, I love you,' he showed his love in a thousand ways which were more eloquent than words."

He also set an example for the boys to follow, which they generally elected to do. "He tended to teach by his example, and he was very practical," Jim says. "For instance, he was in the bishopric while I was growing up, and when it would come time to go to sacrament meeting, which our ward held at 7:00 P.M., he would say, 'Boys, I'm leaving for sacrament meeting. If you want a ride, you'll have to come.' There wasn't any duress. That's just what we were to do. He wasn't always lecturing us and demanding obedience from us. It was just expected."

Not long after the Fausts moved to Cottonwood, George and Amy's fifth son, Delano, was born, and the five were as typical as boys could be. "We were pretty normal," Jim says, "in the sense that we were athletic and rambunctious and wrestled and tussled and so forth. My parents, though, were very under-standing. We'd wrestle on the front room furniture and tear the house up, but I don't remember either of them telling us to get off the furniture or anything like that."

Jim's mother was a very patient woman, owing in part, no doubt, to her deep spiritual strength and faith. She was an ardent student of the Book of Mormon, teaching classes in her home for women in the neighborhood and constantly quoting from it as she would teach and correct her sons. Jim recalls, "No one had to tell her that one can get closer to God by reading the Book of Mormon than by any other book. She was already there. She had read it, studied it, prayed over it, and taught from it. As a young man I held her book in my hands and tried to see, through her eyes, the great truths of the Book of Mormon to which she so readily testified and which she so greatly loved."[3]

On another occasion he said of his parents, "My father was a doer and an achiever, and I hope I inherited some of his ability to work hard and get things done. But I also think I inherited from my mother a portion of the spirituality, testimony, faith, commitment, and, I hope, the milk of human kindness with which she was so richly endowed. I don't know what would have happened to us boys if she hadn't been such a steadying influence in our home."

She also helped team up with George to hold the family together during the difficult years of the Depression. As Jim would later recall,

> [During the] Great Depression, . . . we had certain values burned into our souls. One of these values was gratitude for that which we had because we had so little. The Great Depression in the United States in the early Thirties was a terrible schoolmaster. We had to learn provident living in order to survive. Rather than create in us a spirit of envy or anger for what we did not have, it developed in many a spirit of gratitude for the meager, simple things with which we were blessed, like hot, homemade bread and oatmeal cereal and many other things.[4]

In addition to his parents, Jim enjoyed close relationships with extended family, both in Salt Lake and back in Oak City. His Uncle Jim, who had married and had a daughter, Marguerite, only to then have his wife die when Marguerite was three, had moved back to Salt Lake from California when George found him a job at the State Fingerprint Bureau of Identification. And in those days when the pace of life was slower, Uncle Jim, Marguerite, and Grandma Faust, who helped to raise Marguerite, would spend many of their evenings in George and Amy's home.

"To Grandmother Faust," Jim says, "her grandsons were

perfect, and it is a great thing in a young boy's life to have someone who thinks he's perfect."

Jim also heard his grandmother tell of listening as a young girl to Brigham Young preach in the Salt Lake Tabernacle during the prophet's later years. "She used to tell us about how he wore a red bandanna handkerchief around his head to protect him from the breezes. And then she would always share with us boys something she felt was tremendously important, which was that from her observations over an 87-year life she had observed that those who turned their backs on the leadership of the Church had not prospered spiritually or otherwise. Listening to Granny, who had known every prophet from Brigham Young through Heber J. Grant, we were taught the lesson that we should always be found sustaining the leadership of the Church."

Beyond time spent with family chores around the family's home and small farm, Jim found plenty of time for play. He quickly made friends when the family moved to Cottonwood, and there seemed to be no end to the fun they could concoct.

Because of the Depression, though, their entertainments required significant resourcefulness. Newell Stevenson remembers that while he and Jim and their friends spent a lot of time riding bikes, "we spent more time building and repairing them. We would get a frame somewhere and then wheels, a fork, and tires somewhere else, and we'd put all the parts together. But those kinds of bicycles were always breaking down.

"We were also great skiers. About a quarter of a mile from Jim's house was a rocky old hill, about 15 feet high. We'd pack the snow down, climb to the top, and then slide down. You couldn't say we skied down—we slid down. We started out with barrel staves, with a piece of shoe leather tacked on to serve as a binding. Then we'd just kick the snow off our farm boots, stick our feet into the loops, and off we'd go. One day we decided to build a ski jump that was maybe three feet high, and that was a disaster. On one of his attempts, Jim fell and broke his collarbone, and after that we just stuck with sliding down the hill."

Jim recalls Newell's great-uncle, Dr. H. S. Stevenson, coming to the house, where he and George set Jim's shoulder. "Sometime later," he adds, "I was with my father when somebody who knew about my accident started getting on me about being more careful and not causing my father the expense of paying for such foolish injuries. My father smiled and said to the man, 'Oh, if he didn't do some of those things, I wouldn't have him.'"

On another occasion—a camping trip George and his boys took with several other families—Jim and his friends were out in a meadow one afternoon hunting varmints so as to protect the tender grass that sheep in the area grazed on. Somehow, Jim was accidentally shot at close range just above his knee. His friends helped him back to camp, where his father bandaged Jim's leg to control the bleeding and then drove him to Coalville, Utah, where the nearest doctor lived.

> When we reached the doctor's office he laid me on an examining table. He looked at my bullet wound carefully, and then explained that it must be sterilized.
>
> When I understood how the wound was to be sterilized, I was afraid of the pain I might have and also that I would cry. I didn't want to cry. I wanted to show my father how brave I could be. In my heart, I said a silent prayer that Heavenly Father would help me so that no matter how bad it hurt I wouldn't cry.
>
> The doctor took a rod, about the size used to clean a gun barrel, and threaded a piece of sterilized gauze through a hole in one end like a giant needle. As my father held my hand, I gritted my teeth, shut my eyes, and tried to hold still while the doctor took the rod and pushed it through the hole in my leg. When it came out on the other side, he changed the gauze, put fresh antiseptic on it, and pulled it back through the hole. He pushed it back and forth three times.
>
> Heavenly Father heard my silent prayer, for the operation did not seem to hurt as much as I thought it would. I didn't cry! . . .
>
> As problems and difficulties have come into my life since, I have tried to face them by relying more on the help of our

Heavenly Father than on the comfort that comes from tears. I learned the valuable lesson that the pain of life's problems doesn't seem to be so great if I don't cry about them.[5]

There were other lessons the boys learned from George's love of hunting and fishing, as Jim recalls: "Although Father would take a break once in a while from work and take us with him, he would never countenance our getting out of school to go. Also, in those early days in Cottonwood, there were a lot of pheasants and other wildlife, and some folks in the neighborhood would poach. And poaching was another thing Father would not countenance. He was a man of tremendous integrity, and he was clear as to where the boundaries were."

Given the respect he had for his father, Jim was careful not to cross those lines; however, he was known to join in some of the mischievous pranks common among young boys. Newell remembers that the neighborhood kids often went to an old swimming hole on the property of Margaret O'Brien. "Sometimes the older kids would beat us over there, so we'd sneak up, tie their clothes in knots, and then let out a war whoop to make them think Maggy was coming. That led to a few quarrels with kids in the neighborhood."

One Halloween, as some of the kids in the neighborhood went about tipping over privies, Jim and Newell took some toilet paper and went over to Highland Drive, where they stretched the toilet paper across the street and held it up about three feet high as cars approached. "The idea," Jim says, "is that they would think there was some kind of barricade and slam on their brakes. The thing I remember about that is we seemed to have to wait about half an hour for a car to come by. Now, I'm sure it wasn't that long—we were impatient young boys— but it was amazing how little traffic there was back then."

He then adds, "In my own defense, I can't remember ever tipping over a privy."

Much of Jim's and his friends' lives also centered on activities and associations in the Cottonwood First Ward. In addition to the regular Sunday meetings and weekday Primary lessons and activities, Jim participated in many other activities and made close friends among both youth and adults alike.

"We had a very close-knit ward, and it was the center of our social life. It also provided us with much of our recreation. The men and the boys used to get together and play ball, which was a very nice thing. We called the married men the 'Stiffs,' and the single boys were the 'Limbers.'"

Jim found many examples of righteous living among the men and women he knew in his ward. He would tell, years later, of one such brother:

> One of the men who had the greatest dignity and commanded the greatest respect was an old Scandinavian brother who, after walking a couple of miles, traveled by streetcar to and from work at the Salt Lake City Cemetery. His work was to water and mow the grass, tend the flowers, and dig the graves. He said little because he did not speak English well, but he was always where he should be, doing what he should do in a most dignified, exemplary way. He had no problems with ego, or with faith, for while he dug graves for a living, his work was to serve God. He was a man of little status, but of great worth.[6]

Another neighbor with whom many of the young people became very close was Henry D. Moyle, who during Jim's youth served as his stake president (and lived in his ward) and who later was called to serve in the Quorum of the Twelve Apostles and then as a counselor to President David O. McKay.

President Moyle was a man of significant wealth but generous both with his means and his time. In particular, he was a great friend to the youth of the stake. Newell Stevenson recalls, "He had a lake on his property, which probably totaled nearly a hundred acres, that he used to let us swim in. That was our favorite place, although it was fed by springs and was just like ice. He also had some cute daughters we liked to hang around."

Jim also has said of President Moyle:

> President Moyle . . . was our leader. He was our example. We knew we could achieve anything because President Moyle was

guiding us. As we grew older, every time we applied for a job or
to enter a school, we would always put down, as a reference, the
name of our stake president. We knew of his personal interest in
us. We knew he would help us if he could.

I have tried to analyze why President Moyle had such a profound influence in our lives. I think it was because of his personal
interest in us. He was our friend. We knew that he was always
there when we needed him. It was said of him that when Henry
Moyle loved you, he loved you through and through.[7]

Jim also became acquainted with President Moyle's father,
James H. Moyle, who lived in Washington, D.C., but would
spend part of each summer with his son. Jim remembers that

as a young boy in the Cottonwood Ward, I was greatly impressed
when I listened to James H. Moyle tell in sacrament meeting of his
having heard both Martin Harris and David Whitmer, two of the
witnesses of the Book of Mormon, affirm their testimony concerning that book. . . .

When James H. Moyle visited David Whitmer, Whitmer was
an old man; he was out of the Church and was living in a log
cabin in Richmond, Missouri. Of this visit to David Whitmer,
James H. Moyle stated in [the Salt Lake Tabernacle] on March 22,
1908:

"I went to his humble home, . . . and I told him . . . as a young
man starting out in life I wanted to know from him . . . what he
knew about the Book of Mormon, and what about the testimony
he had published to the world concerning it. He told me in all the
solemnity of his advanced years, that the testimony he had given
to the world, and which was published in the Book of Mormon,
was true, every word of it, and that he had never deviated nor
departed in any particular from that testimony, and that nothing
in the world could separate him from the sacred message that was
delivered to him. I still wondered if it was not possible that he
could have been deceived, . . . so I induced him to relate to me,
under such cross-examination as I was able to interpose, every
detail of what took place. He described minutely the spot in the
woods, the large log that separated him from the angel, and that
he saw the plates from which the Book of Mormon was translated, that he handled them, and that he did hear the voice of God
declare that the plates were correctly translated. I asked him if
there was any possibility for him to have been deceived, and that

it was all a mistake, but he said, 'No.'" (Quoted in Gordon B. Hinckley, *James Henry Moyle*, Salt Lake City: Deseret Book Co., 1951, pp. 366–67.)[8]

In part from the testimonies of others—many of whom were so directly connected to early prophets, apostles, and other prominent figures in the Restoration—and in part because of his own convictions and spiritual witness, President Faust says of his convictions as a young boy, "I think I have inherited an element of believing blood, and I have to give credit to Edward Partridge and George Finlinson, together with their wives and so many others of my progenitors, for their devotion and commitment and tremendous example. Of course, I have always had a testimony and belief in the gospel. I think along the way there is always some ebbing and flowing and that faith comes in increments. But I think, like everyone else's, my testimony has benefited from one spiritual experience after another, until I have come to the point where I have a knowledge, not just a belief."

Part of that process for Jim included the usual steps of baptism, which was performed in the Salt Lake Tabernacle font, and preparing to receive the priesthood when he was twelve. He recalls:

> When I was 11 years old, I looked forward eagerly to my magical 12th birthday when I could become a deacon and a Scout. My mother helped me learn the Articles of Faith, the Scout Law and Motto, and other requirements so that I would have a good start when that special birthday arrived.
>
> Since I had no sisters, my brothers and I were given some of the inside chores as well as outside ones, such as milking and taking care of the animals. One day Mother left me to wash the dishes and clean the kitchen while she attended to a sick neighbor. I agreed to do these duties but put off doing the dishes. Time ran out and they didn't get done. In fact, they didn't even get started. When Mother came home and saw the kitchen, she put on her apron and went to the sink. She spoke only three words, which stung worse than the sting of a dozen hornets. They were the first three words of the Scout Law: "On my honor." That day I resolved that I would never give my mother cause to repeat those words to me again.[9]

Soon after he turned twelve, he also received his patriarchal blessing. "Several of us boys went together, including my friend Newell Stevenson. Having my patriarchal blessing at that young age was a stabilizing influence and a restraining influence as well. My mother would read mine to me once in a while, and as a result I've always recommended that people read theirs often. My blessing is only three-fourths of a page in length, but, as Heber J. Grant said of his, which was of similar length, I couldn't have asked for any greater blessing."

One of his early priesthood responsibilities was as a junior companion to a ward (now home) teacher, and the lesson he had learned from the loss of his lamb helped him keep a clear focus on his priesthood responsibilities:

> There were times when it was so cold or stormy and I wanted to stay home and be comfortable, but in my mind's ear I could hear my little lamb bleating, and I knew I needed to be a good shepherd and go with my senior companion. In all those many years, whenever I have had a desire to shirk my duties, there would come to me a remembrance of how sorry I was that night so many years ago when I had not been a good shepherd. I have not always done everything I should have, but I have tried.[10]

NOTES

1. "A Christmas with No Presents," *Friend*, December 1984, pp. 4–5.

2. "Responsibilities of Shepherds," *Ensign*, May 1995, p. 46.

3. "The Keystone of Our Religion," *Ensign*, November 1983, p. 9.

4. "Gratitude As a Saving Principle," *Ensign*, May 1990, p. 85.

5. "Friend to Friend," *Friend*, September 1974, pp. 12–13.

6. "Self-Esteem—A Great Human Need," Education Week devotional address delivered at Brigham Young University, Provo, Utah, 26 July 1983.

7. "The Stake President as a Spiritual Leader," satellite training presentation for new stake presidents, 22 August 1993. Unpublished manuscript.

8. "The Keystone of Our Religion," *Ensign*, November 1983, p. 9. James H. Moyle statement as quoted in Gordon B. Hinckley, *James Henry Moyle* (Salt Lake City: Deseret Book Co., 1951), pp. 366–67.

9. "We Seek After These Things," *Ensign*, May 1998, p. 44.

10. "Responsibilities of Shepherds," *Ensign*, May 1995, p. 46.

3

A GROWING
FAITH

As Jim grew into his teenage years, his interest in adventure also increased. On May 21, 1934, just before his fourteenth birthday, he and his cousin, Asael Lyman, left Jim's home in Cottonwood to ride their bikes to Oak City, where Asael's mother was staying—a distance of one hundred fifty miles.

It took some doing to get permission from Jim's parents to undertake the journey, which the boys planned to complete in a single day. When George and Amy finally agreed, Jim needed a new tire for his bike. He obtained the necessary funds by selling a calf to his father, which, after the cost of the tire, left Jim with $1.35 to finance the trip. (Asael had thirty-five cents for his share.)

After fixing Jim's bike, the two went to bed but couldn't sleep, so they got up, dressed, and headed south just before midnight. The route was up one hill and down another, until they got to the long uphill climb to Point of the Mountain, which separates Salt Lake and Utah counties. Through that long stretch, they had to push their bikes much of the way. They were plagued by dogs that came out to chase them but were armed with a blank pistol to scare the dogs off.

The eight or so miles from Point of the Mountain to American Fork were mostly downhill, which provided the boys with a bit of a break. As they rode through the town, they asked someone for the time and found it was 3:00 A.M. They then encountered a night watchman who was suspicious of them and wondered if they had stolen the bikes and run away. When Jim told the watchman he could call his father to straighten things out, the man let them go, but not before telling the boys they'd never make it to Oak City.

As they completed the long stretch to Provo, the morning sun began to break over Mount Timpanogos. They ate some wafers for breakfast as they contemplated the hundred miles they had left to go. Just out of Springville, they bought some soft drinks at a service station and then stopped in another store in Spanish Fork. The clerk there was amazed they had made it all the way from Salt Lake City. Because of an ordinance in Spanish Fork that prohibited bike riding on the highway through town, they had to take a detour to Payson.

By the time they reached Santaquin, they encountered a stiff head wind, which, when coupled with the heat of the day, made pedaling quite a struggle. When they reached Nephi, they were beginning to get exhausted and consumed prodigious quantities of soda pop and water. Between Nephi and Levan, they encountered quite a lengthy uphill stretch and again had to walk their bikes, although the downhill stretches were refreshing.

At Chicken Creek Reservoir, they turned off to head west over Fool Creek Pass. When they stopped at the first house to ask for a drink of water, they were told they could get all the water they wanted at the railroad station, where the trains got their water.

The ride up and over Fool Creek Pass was hard, and Jim and Asael had been on the road for about eighteen hours. When they finally reached the summit, evening was beginning to fall and they still had about twenty miles to go. The downhill stretch into Fool Creek was another welcome break, until Jim hit something in the road and toppled head over heels. Then Asael hit a rock and took a spill as well. At Fool Creek Flat, where they stopped for a drink, a family urged them to stay the night and complete their journey in the morning. But the cousins were determined to press on, convinced they would set some sort of record by reaching Oak City that day.

As they started out on the final ten miles, the sun was

beginning to set. In addition, the road was covered with heavy, loose gravel, making it easier to follow the cow trails that ran alongside the road. As darkness descended, the boys literally fell over in exhaustion on the side of the road, which woke them up enough that they could continue on their way.

At 10:00 P.M., almost twenty-four hours after they had left Jim's house in Cottonwood, the two cousins arrived at their grandparents' house in Oak City. Jim dropped his bike at the big gate, walked to the house, and collapsed on the lawn just as the family was getting ready for bed. The boys were filthy and their eyes were drawn, but their aunts got them some food and rubbed their black legs with alcohol to clean them up. Then Jim and Asael keeled over into bed.

News of the boys' feat spread quickly through the town, and an account of their ordeal appeared in the *Millard County Chronicle*, the local newspaper printed in neighboring Delta.

When Jim set out with Asael, he had no idea how hard the trek to Oak City was going to be, but he did know the way. Ever since his family had moved to Salt Lake in 1923, he and his brothers had returned each year to spend the summer with their grandparents, aunts, uncles, and cousins. ("I was related to about half the town," he says.) From his very first trip back to Oak City, his stays included two key components: healthy doses of hard work and heritage.

Spending summers in Oak City began in part because Jim's father attended summer school at the University of Utah and wasn't able to spend the time he wanted to with his sons, but they continued because of George's desire that his sons learn the meaning and value of hard work.

Grandfather Finlinson, Amy's father, owned considerable property in and around Oak City, and managing the crops, flocks, and herds was a family affair. So from an early age, Jim and his brothers joined in.

Jim's brother Gus describes their grandparents' house as "a colony," with many of their aunts, uncles, and cousins staying at the Finlinsons' home. The cousins would generally sleep out back together and would awake either to their grandfather singing, "Then wake up, and do something more / Than dream of your mansions above,"[1] or to their grandmother coming in from hoeing the garden. Grandmother Finlinson also prepared a huge spread for breakfast, which the boys needed as they faced the work ahead.

"Oh, did we work," Gus says. "Grandfather had us all assigned. Sometimes I got to ride the range with him, and sometimes Jim would go. We became very close working with him, as we did with all of our relatives. He was always kind and considerate of us, but there were also certain things he expected. He used to tell us that if he caught any of us swearing, he would fill our mouths with ashes. But he didn't tell us if they would be hot or cold, and we never found out."

In like manner, Jim remembers his grandfather's stand on the Sabbath:

> I confess that as a young boy, Sunday was not my favorite day. Grandfather shut down the action. We didn't have any transportation. We couldn't drive the car. He wouldn't even let us start the motor. We couldn't ride the horses, or the steers, or the sheep. It was the Sabbath, and by commandment, the animals also needed rest. We walked to Church and everywhere else we wanted to go. I can honestly say that we observed both the spirit and the letter of Sabbath worship.[2]

Even with his grandfather's farming operations, Jim could see the Depression's long arm reaching to Oak City. He remembers his grandmother making the soap they would use for Saturday baths and for washing their clothes. "Her recipe," he says, "included rendered animal fat, a small portion of lye as a cleansing agent, and wood ashes as an abrasive. The soap had a very pungent aroma and was almost as hard as a brick. There was no money to buy soft, sweet-smelling soap. . . . If you had to bathe with that homemade soap, you could become wonderfully clean, but you smelled worse after bathing than before."[3]

But there were other lessons Jim learned from the economic struggles his family faced:

As a boy I learned a great lesson of faith and sacrifice as I worked on my grandfather's farm during the terrible economic depression of the 1930s. The taxes on the farm were delinquent, and Grandfather, like so many, had no money. There was a drought in the land, and some cows and horses were dying for lack of grass and hay. One day when we were harvesting what little hay there was in the field, Grandfather told us to take the wagon to the corner of the field where the best stand of hay stood and fill the wagon as full as we could and take it to the tithing yard as payment of his tithing in kind.

I wondered how Grandfather could use the hay to pay tithing when some of the cows that we were depending upon to sustain us might starve. I even questioned if the Lord expected that much sacrifice from him. Ultimately, I marveled at his great faith that somehow the Lord would provide. The legacy of faith he passed on to his posterity was far greater than money, because he established in the minds of his children and grandchildren that above all he loved the Lord and His holy work over other earthly things. He never became wealthy, but he died at peace with the Lord and with himself.[4]

Grandpa Finlinson did give the boys some time off from work, although Gus says he grew up believing that everyone's workday started at five in the morning and ended at nine in the evening. Jim enjoyed the time he had to play with family and friends, but he also spent considerable time reading when there was a break. "When I was a boy, I was a reader," he says, "and down on the farm my aunts used to get after me. 'Why don't you go play with the boys,' they'd say. Well, I played with the boys. But I was also interested in reading and learning, so I did some of each."

Jim wasn't so serious that he couldn't get into a little trouble, though. On one Fourth of July, when he was about fourteen, he and an uncle and some friends cut a stick of dynamite in half and lit one half in the middle of the street. "We set it off just to make a little noise," he says, adding, "It was a foolish thing to do." The consequence, he found, was having to face the bishop: "In that little town, there was no sheriff or marshal or justice of the peace—the bishop was everything. He was the temporal and the ecclesiastical leader of the community. As I recall, he extracted a promise from us that we wouldn't do it again, and that was all there was to that." The other half of the stick, as a result, went unused.

At about that same time Jim's summers in Oak City came to an end, as his father felt it was time he find summer jobs and earn some money. But the summers Jim spent in this tiny Utah town were times he enjoyed, and times that taught him lessons he would carry with him through his life. It also provided a direct connection to his past, as he would listen to his Uncle Bill tell of walking across the plains as a boy, or to his mother and Aunt Angie tell the stories their great-grandmother had told them about living in the home of Joseph and Emma Smith and tending their children. And he could see the effects of the gospel on family and friends, as they tried to carry forth and live up to the heritage they had been given.

In reflecting on the "believing blood" that he descended from, Jim says, "I feel heavily the responsibility of living up to the heritage of the people who paid such a great price in leaving their homes and giving their very lives for the Church that had been restored. At the same time, I do not claim any preferences or consequences as a result of my heritage, as I'm mindful of the old saying that those who are always talking about their ancestors can be a little like the potato—the best part of them is underground."

Jim was a year younger than most of the students who started at Granite High School in the fall of 1934. While Jim was in the fifth grade, which met together with the sixth grade, the teacher found, as Gus tells the story, "that Jim and his friend Newell and a few others knew more than the sixth-graders. So the teacher moved them right in with them." Being a year younger as he began high school left Jim feeling a bit on the immature side, but he followed his brother Gus's lead (Jim says Gus was "something of a star" in high school) and joined the track and football teams. "Socially and in other ways it was hard being a year younger," Jim says, "and Gus's example of reaching out and being involved was something of a stimulus for me, for which I am very grateful."

Jim ran the quarter mile and mile relay on the track team. He notes that he never once beat his big brother in a race—and that their father could beat both of them for the first forty yards of a race. On the football team, he played guard and tackle, and as a pulling guard he had to "get out and lead the interference." He lettered in both sports, and learned many valuable lessons as well.

One was that with training and perseverance, he could compete, despite not having "any exceptional ability." Another was the benefit of keeping the Word of Wisdom, and yet another was that even given all the pain associated with training, "It felt good to be a competitor."[5]

During one scrimmage before a big game, Jim was having difficulty keeping the chin strap on his helmet fastened—and his helmet on. He recalls:

> On one important play I received a slight jar and my helmet went rolling away, but the play was still moving and I was in the middle of it. I didn't want to leave the action of the play and go find my helmet, so I continued to press hard to tackle the ball carrier on the other side. I put my head down to bore in and try to grab the ball carrier. One of the players who was running interference for the ball carrier hit me hard, and I went down and lost consciousness.[6]

In addition to living through an object lesson on the need to keep oneself protected, Jim also demonstrated his characteristic grit and determination as he jumped up after a moment and headed back into the lineup for the next play.

Through all of his activities—whether on the track or football field, or later as he became involved in debate and oration—Jim felt the constant support of his father. Newell says of George Faust, who at the time was a judge, "I don't think Gus or Jim ever played a game or ran a race that their father wasn't there. And I suspect that on a few occasions he must have reassigned the court schedule because he never missed. And that couldn't have been just by chance."

Jim quickly overcame the feelings of social inadequacy he felt upon entering Granite High and became, in the words of a young girl by the name of Ruth Wright, "a big man on campus." Although they would later marry, Jim and Ruth never dated in high school, but he knew her and was good friends with her brothers. Two years behind Jim, Ruth was likewise very active at their high school, serving as vice-president of her sophomore class, her junior class, and the student body her senior year.

"We would see each other on campus and sometimes at other functions," Jim recalls. "But Ruth didn't want for attention."

Nor did Jim, who dated frequently—often doubling with his brother Gus. "Father said we could each take the car one night for a date," Jim says, "and we quickly figured out that if we went together, we could go on two dates. What that generally meant was bringing a girl to sacrament meeting on Sunday, then bringing her over for dinner, and then going to another sacrament meeting."

Newell adds that the boys and their dates also "went to the high school dances and to Jerry Jones's Rainbow Rendezvous. In those days, we actually went and danced. We didn't go to stand in the middle of the floor."

Although George Faust's sons knew right where he stood on certain fundamentals, he also believed that his sons needed to learn to use their agency in making some of their own decisions. On one winter night, Jim learned that although his father would allow him to make many of his own decisions, he also knew what was best for his boys. As Jim tells the story:

> There was a blizzard, but I had a date I didn't want to cancel. Father counseled me gently not to go, but I was young and inexperienced—and thought I was a better driver than I was. As I headed north on Highland Drive to pick up my date, I could hardly see beyond the hood of the car, and in order to make sure

I didn't get hit by an oncoming car, I kept over to the right-hand side of what was then a two-lane road. As a result, I banged into a car parked off to the side.

Now, this was the family car—and we only had one. But when I got home and told my father what I had done, he just said, "Son, we're glad you weren't hurt." As I've looked back on that, I've thought he was extremely understanding because I had been extremely foolish.

To pay for his dates—and to save for a mission and college, which were two of George's absolutes—Jim worked each summer he was in high school. Given that the country was still in the thick of the Depression, he felt lucky to find whatever work he could. One job was at the Rocky Mountain Packing Corporation, where, after riding his bike the twelve miles to work, Jim caught hot cans coming off a conveyor belt for twenty-five cents an hour. He would later say, "Those of us who were favored with that job got to have the skin peel off our hands because of the heat and the moisture. I suppose you can start lower than that, but not much!"[7]

The Depression left an indelible impression on Jim, who would grow up knowing how quickly fortunes could be lost, and living accordingly. He would later say:

> Anybody who didn't go through that experience cannot possibly have a feeling or an understanding of the difficulty which this country, indeed the world, faced at that time. In our valley, 30 percent of the people were unemployed. People lost their homes. Our neighbors moved into a chicken coop because the mortgage on their home was foreclosed.[8]

He did, however, see the members of his neighborhood and ward step in to help those hit the hardest, and he was also aware of the Church's establishment in 1936 of the Church Security Plan (now the Church Welfare Services) under the direction of the president of the Pioneer Stake in Salt Lake City, Harold B. Lee.

Jim graduated from Granite High in 1937, having benefited from wonderful teachers, coaches, and seminary teachers. At about that time, at the age of seventeen, he was called to serve as a counselor in the ward Sunday School presidency, after having served as president of his deacons and teachers quorums, and as assistant to the bishop in the priests quorum.

He remembers well Bishop T. C. Stayner, who taught Jim as a priest, and who helped him understand the importance of honesty and integrity. "He didn't follow the handbook," Jim says, "and every lesson—every single one—was be honest, keep your word, have integrity. And then it would repeat. Be honest in all your dealings, be truthful. It got to the point where it was completely predictable, and a little bit tiresome, but the message stuck."

With a mission still two years away, he enrolled at the University of Utah, where he continued to run track, working part time to support himself and save for a mission. One summer he worked as a gardener for a lady in the neighborhood, who offered him thirty dollars a month for his services. Given that 10 percent of that would go to tithing, and tuition at the university was $110 per year, he told her he couldn't make it on that, so she raised her offer to thirty-five dollars, and he took the job.

Another year, he found, as school started, that he was a bit short on money and told his father he was going to have to move away from home and get a job to cover his shortfall. "Father said, 'You're doing all right,'" Jim recalls, "'and if you stay here, I'll help you a little.' So he gave me $25 to make up the shortfall."

About the time Jim was finishing his first year at the University of Utah, his brother Gus was called as a missionary to Brazil—the sixtieth missionary to go to a mission that had been opened in 1935.

A year later, Jim said to his friend, Newell Stevenson, "Newell, we've got to go talk to the bishop about our missions."

With the country just beginning to come out of the Depression, however, Jim did wonder if he would be able to go.

But when the bishop called George in to see if it was possible for him to support two missionaries, he said, "Bishop, I'll tell you the same thing I told you when Gus went out. I couldn't see then how I could feed my family for the next three months, and I'm in the same position now."

As his faith combined with his father's, Jim waited for his mission call to come, thinking it might be to Germany, given that he had studied the language in high school, he was of German ancestry, and his Uncle Jim had served in Germany. But when the letter from 47 East South Temple finally did come, Jim found that he would be joining his brother in Brazil.

NOTES

1. "Have I Done Any Good?" *Hymns of The Church of Jesus Christ of Latter-day Saints* (Salt Lake City: The Church of Jesus Christ of Latter-day Saints, 1985), no. 223.

2. "The Lord's Day," *Ensign*, November 1991, p. 33.

3. "Gratitude As a Saving Principle," *Ensign*, May 1990, p. 85.

4. "Opening the Windows of Heaven," *Ensign*, November 1998, p. 54.

5. "Keep Your Chin Strap Fastened," *New Era*, November 1981, p. 4.

6. Ibid.

7. "If You Are Starting at the Bottom, Then Reach for the Stars," Ricks College devotional address, Rexburg, Idaho, 17 April 1990.

8. *Church News*, 28 October 1995, p. 3.

4

MISSION, MILITARY,
AND MARRIAGE

To the newly called missionary from Cottonwood, Utah, Brazil seemed to be just south of the end of the earth, even though his older brother had been serving there for a year. Nevertheless, Elder Jim Faust was excited to be going, although with understandable apprehensions about the two-and-one-half years he would spend away from home. In October 1939, with no training in Portuguese but benefiting from being set apart by Elder Antoine R. Ivins, one of the seven presidents of the Seventy, Elder Faust entered the Salt Lake City Mission Home for a few days of instruction. One lesson that remained with him through the years came from Elder David O. McKay, who took a piece of chalk and wrote on the board, "It is a greater honor to be trusted than to be loved."

After finishing his stay at the mission home, Elder Faust boarded a train in Salt Lake bound for New Orleans. "When the train stopped in Soldier Summit, Utah," he recalls, "I must confess that the thought came into my mind, 'Maybe you'd better get off.' But I stayed on."

In New Orleans a group of missionaries, including Elder Faust, boarded a freighter headed for Santos, Brazil, a trip that would take twenty-one days. The accommodations were spartan, at best, and the missionaries spent much of their time studying and teaching each other the gospel. They also made friends with the crew, who one day challenged the missionaries to a boxing match, "for a little diversion," Jim says. "We paired off according to weight, and we had an elder in the heavyweight class and on down. I took on the ship's doctor, and afterwards he said, 'Jim, I think you cracked my rib.' It was all in fun, but when we got through with the matches, the crew had an increased respect for us."

The trip, Jim says, "was a pleasant experience and a transforming one—to leave the culture of Utah and be separated for a time and to then land down there in a country very different from the one I had come from."

In terms of size, Brazil is similar to but a bit smaller than the United States. But it was an underdeveloped country at the time—and foreign in every way. "When I got off the boat, people were talking in a strange tongue that sounded like a bunch of monkeys chattering. As a result of going with no language training, generations of missionaries were not very effective for the first six or eight months, as they had to learn the language while living in the country."[1]

In 1939, the Church in Brazil was almost nonexistent, with fewer than two hundred members, most of whom were Germans who had immigrated to Brazil after World War I. The first convert baptism took place in 1929, and the Brazilian Mission was established in 1935, with proselytizing being directed almost exclusively at the German-speaking population in southern Brazil. When Elder Faust arrived, the mission president was just beginning to make an effort to teach the gospel in Portuguese.

President J. Eldon Bowers met the new missionaries as they got off the freighter in Santos, and then, because the mission did not own a car, the group took a train to São Paulo. There President Bowers informed Elder Faust that he would be learning Portuguese. "I couldn't understand that," Jim recalls. "Here I had spent two years trying to get a little understanding of the German language, and I was being told I would learn Portuguese. Then he sent me down to Joinvile, a German colony where all I could hear was German, and where the signs and everything else were in German. But I was supposed to be learning Portuguese. It made absolutely no sense to me at all, until I wrote home and, I guess, expressed a little dismay at why I would be sent to learn Portuguese in a German-speaking village. Well, my Uncle Jim was the one who had the vision of what the mission president had in mind. He wrote back and said, 'Can't you see what he's doing? He's trying to make you a two-language missionary.'"

Elder Faust spent three and one-half months in Joinvile, learning more German and a bit of Portuguese—and learning the life and work of a missionary. The living conditions were not what the missionaries from the United States were used to, and the missionaries' diet consisted of "rice and beans—without any onions or bacon or flavoring of any kind," Jim says. "What saved us, though," he adds with characteristic optimism, "was the delicious fruit that is found in Brazil. Bananas were so cheap that you could buy a whole stalk for three and a half cents. Papayas grew wild, and we could pick them out of our own backyard. Then there were the pineapples and oranges. So we missionaries would get together about three times a week and mix up a Brazilian fruit salad, which consisted of all the fruit we could find, plus a little sugar, and which gave us a welcome break from the rice and beans."

The missionaries either rode bikes or used public transportation, paying a penny to ride the street cars (buses cost about half a cent more). Elder Faust's expenses amounted to under twenty-five dollars a month, and since his father sent twenty-five dollars, Elder Faust tried to save a little each month in case of medical problems or some other emergency. "When Gus returned home," Jim adds, "my father wrote me and said he could send me thirty dollars. But I still saved some each month and had enough to buy an old Model A Ford when I returned home."

Elder Faust's adjustment to the climate of Brazil was not immediate, and for some time he was affected adversely by the heat and humidity of the tropics. He developed a rash, which doctors suggested he treat by bathing in oatmeal, and he was constantly tired and dragging. Still, he did his best to keep going and to do the work he had been called to do.

One afternoon, however, he was particularly tired as he and his companion headed up the lane to their apartment. Just as they were going to turn off and take a quick side trip to the post office, Elder Faust heard what he describes as "a loud message. A voice in my head said, 'Go home. You're tired. You need to rest. You don't feel good. Let your companion go the post office, and you'll feel refreshed.'

"I didn't listen to that entreaty; I stayed with my companion. And later I learned why it was best that I had. But, more important, what I learned that day was that the voice of Satan can be reasonable and entreating. It wasn't harsh or discordant, and it certainly wasn't irrational. But had I responded to his encouragement, there could have been something of a cloud over my mission."

As Adolf Hitler invaded Poland in the fall of 1939, which brought about the beginning of World War II, the Brazilian government began to place restrictions on the activities and meetings of Germans living in the country, which had an effect on missionary work. Those restrictions accelerated President Bowers's plans to assign more missionaries to work among Portuguese-speaking Brazilians, and Elder Faust was transferred to Curitiba, to serve with a senior companion from Salt Lake City by the name of Elder William Grant Bangerter.

Elder Bangerter had formed a close association with Elder Faust's brother earlier in his mission and had stayed overnight with Elder Faust while he was serving in Joinvile. While there, Elder Bangerter says, "I saw a picture he had of a girlfriend, and I made the comment, 'She won't wait.' And that, of course, wasn't the one he married."

Elder Bangerter adds, "I knew a little of his family background, and when we were assigned, I was ready to be well impressed with him, which was not hard. He was a serious and devoted missionary, and eager to make a success of his calling. In fact, when we first came together in Curitiba, I had been working with a dynamic companion; and because of the way we worked, he and I were on the top of the list of the mission's comparative reports. Jim's first few months had been slower than he had wanted, and when we were assigned he said, 'How do you get your name on the top of the list so you can feel like you're accomplishing what we were called here to do?' I told him it was just a matter of going to work, and he said, 'I'd sure like to be up that way.'"

The task was a formidable one, however, as there were no members of the Church in Curitiba, the Book of Mormon was not available in Portuguese, there was no regular teaching plan, and, as Brother Faust would later say, "The Lord was not smiling on the Latin people at that time."

Jim Faust's grandson, Jason Coombs, who served in the Brazil Curitiba mission from 1997 to 1999, provides this perspective: "Imagine prospective converts asking my Grandfather and Elder Bangerter, 'So, how many people are of this Church?' and them having to respond, 'Well, in this city, you are going to be the first.'"

During one year of Elder Faust's mission, the seventy or so missionaries laboring in Brazil had a total of three convert baptisms among them.

"Unlike Samuel Smith," Jim adds, "we did not have the Book of Mormon in hand to leave with any who might be interested in our message, and the tracts we had were way over the people's heads. For instance, we had a tract about a God who speaks in modern times and one on eternal salvation, but I just had the feeling we weren't connecting. While these people were Christians, many of them were illiterate and they had no scriptural background. So, we prayed mightily that we could get the Book of Mormon published, and that did come in due course. Not surprisingly, it was only after the Book of Mormon was translated into Portuguese that the great harvest of converts came.

"What I also learned was that we were not effective proselyters, except for the personal testimonies that we bore. I think that was the only thing that saved us as missionaries—our individual witnesses and testimonies. You can give people all the doctrinal teachings in the world, but until they are touched by the Spirit, it doesn't connect."

The work was, without question, slow, but Elder Bangerter points out that "we served at a time when no one expected much success from their missions, and so no one thought the work to be difficult. I think we achieved more than we realized at the time, but converting vast numbers of people was not an uppermost thought in our minds."

Elder Bangerter and Elder Faust worked hard, however, and upon being assigned to serve together, they began going door to door, seeking opportunities to share their message with the citizens of Curitiba.

Their first day out was February 10, 1940, and as Elder Faust told the story:

> It was my first day tracting, and I could speak no Portuguese. We started up the street and Elder Bangerter, my senior, took all of the houses for a block or so. Then he turned to me and said, "This is your house." Fear struck in my heart. Since there were no doorbells, I clapped my hands together beyond the fence to get the attention of someone in the residence. Usually the maid responded. An older gray-haired lady leaned out of the window and asked in Portuguese, "What do you want?" I was in complete agony. I turned to my companion for help, but he kept his head down, marking in the tracting book. The passing seconds seemed like ages. In my heart, I prayed that I would be delivered. Just about then, she said, "Would you like to come in?" My feelings changed from agony to ecstasy.[2]

Other missionaries did most of the teaching of the Valeixo family, and the grandmother, mother, and children were baptized after Elders Bangerter and Faust had left Curitiba. But the family members, who were the first Mormons baptized in a city that in 1998 had ten stakes, would always remember the two young missionaries from Salt Lake City who introduced them to the restored gospel of Jesus Christ.

The two missionaries, together with the other missionaries assigned to Curitiba, continued their efforts, and they got to the point where they felt the need to arrange for a sacrament meeting that investigators could attend. So they rented a hall and built the benches for the investigators to sit on. On Saturday night, as they finished their preparations, they decided to varnish the benches, which didn't dry completely. The only two non-Mormons who came were the landlady of the hall and her sister, and when they stood up at the close of the meeting, there was varnish all over their dresses, which was quite upsetting to the women. They did, however, allow the missionaries to continue renting the facility.

After Elder Bangerter was transferred, Elder Faust had another companion, who one Sunday afternoon took off on a walk by himself. For some reason, as he was taking photographs of the governor's palace, he was arrested and thrown in jail. When the missionary didn't come home that night, Elder Faust and the other missionaries concluded that he must be in jail. When they went to the jail to inquire, the officials wouldn't tell them anything, so the group of missionaries stood outside and began singing, "We Thank Thee, O God, for a Prophet." Upon hearing the song, the incarcerated missionary stuck his head out the window, and the elders were finally able to arrange for his release.

Jim adds, "I should have stayed with him, but I don't recall that I was invited to go."

As is the case with all missionaries, Elder Faust looked forward to letters from home, which arrived three to four weeks after they were mailed. He notes that in addition to receiving regular letters from his mother, his father wrote him every single week during his mission and during his time in the military as well. Elder Faust also wrote faithfully and in one letter thanked his father for making the sacrifices needed to support him and his brother on their missions. His father wrote back, "Don't feel sorry for us. We've eaten too much, we bought a new car, and we're getting along just fine."

Despite the size of Brazil, the missionaries labored in relatively few cities, and Jim and Gus were able to see each other twice before Gus returned home. During their first meeting, in addition to the visiting one might expect of two brothers who were very close before their missions, Jim suggested that they run a race, for old times' sake. "I hadn't been out too long," Jim says, "and I decided that if I was ever going to beat him, it had to be then. But Gus declined the invitation." (Gus admits that he knew he would get beaten and that he was determined his record of never losing to his little brother would stand.)

It came as no surprise to those who knew him that Elder Faust was called to serve in various leadership positions during the course of his mission, including the call of district president in Belo Horizonte and then in São Paulo, which made him the presiding officer over all the missionaries and members in those cities.

The calls were not something he had expected, however: "My patriarchal blessing does indicate that I would 'preside among the people,' and when I received those callings on my mission, I felt that part of my blessing had been fulfilled. But I certainly did not expect any such callings, and my feeling then, as with the callings I have received since, was, 'Why me?' I was understandably concerned about being adequate and being able to lead and to motivate. What I learned in Brazil is that the essential ingredient in leadership is found in what the Savior said: 'Come, follow me.' You have to lead. And the leader has to know where he is going and then have the strength to take his people with him. Sometimes they go kicking and screaming, but I'm always glad when we get there."

Elder Faust served in those positions without the benefit of handbooks or manuals of any kind, which helped him learn two important lessons in leadership: "My ability to lead in the mission field—and in every calling I have had since—came from working with the scriptures and from remembering that there is a place where you can always get an answer—and that is when you get down on your knees and pray hard enough that an answer will come and bring a solution to the problems.

"Another important lesson I learned is that Church leaders have to have absolute integrity. The Saints, for instance, used to pay their tithing to me, and the mission president expected me to use the money to pay the rent for the halls. I had the tithes of the Saints in my possession, and I had to be a wise steward over those funds, accounting properly (at a time when there weren't the procedures and safeguards we have today) and making sure there was no defalcation or loss by theft. That was a worry to me because I didn't have a safe or safety deposit box. But I always made sure that I could account for every *cruzeiro* that was donated."

Elder Faust also benefited from his associations with what few members of the Church there were in Brazil—and in so doing, he gained a love for the Latin Americans that has never waned. He recounts this experience from his service in São Paulo:

> One day, my companion and I went out to visit a poor sister who was widowed. . . .
> " . . . we arrived at a humble home in a very isolated area. This home had a dirt floor and open windows without any glass. The wind and the flies could come right through. Never before in my life had I been in a home where people live with open windows and a dirt floor. Despite this, the house was clean and neat, curtains were hung, and the boards on the inside of the house were whitewashed. Despite being primitive, the home had a cozy feeling about it. We asked after this poor widow's health and well-being. She seemed quite happy and contented. We then began to have something of a gospel lesson. She participated freely. We thought that we were the teachers, but it soon became apparent that she knew more than we did. Her faith was deep, and her knowledge of the great eternal truths of where we came from, who we are, and where we are going was very profound. . . .
> This poor widow on the outskirts of São Paulo made the most of her straitened circumstances—circumstances that could not easily be changed. She realized that she should not make her life miserable by wishing it were otherwise. . . . This impoverished woman enjoyed her independence, and she owed no one any money. She was industrious and thrifty. She crocheted beautiful cloths which were sold in the city to satisfy her simple wants, but she was not poor in spirit. She was rich in the things that really matter.[3]

It was in the home of another member sister, on December 7, 1941, that Elder Faust heard over the radio that Pearl Harbor had been bombed and the United States would be entering World War II. "That was very ominous news," he says. "I knew I was going to be into it as soon as I returned home." The news also resulted in his staying an extra three months in Brazil. "Those were unsettling times," he adds, "but I got to have an extra long mission, which was a great blessing."

With German submarines plying the waters of South America, returning to the States by boat was not an option, and military personnel had priority on all airlines, which could only operate during daylight hours. When the time did come for Elder Faust to return home in June 1942, he had to fly standby the whole way. As a result, it took him five days to get to Miami, flying from Rio de Janeiro to Barreiros to Natal to Belém, Brazil, to Maracaibo, Venezuela, and finally to Miami, Florida. From Florida, Elder Faust took a train to Rock Springs, Wyoming, where his parents (knowing he would be drafted almost immediately) picked him up and spent some time together as they drove the rest of the way home.

"I was grateful to be home," he says, "and in part my gratitude was heightened by the fact that I knew what was ahead of me in terms of the military and World War II."

He was also profoundly grateful for the experiences he had had in Brazil and says that "the mission experience was one I was not sure I would have because of the economic circumstances of my family."

He is also quick to add that the blessings he received from having served and the work done by those early missionaries cannot be measured in terms of convert baptisms. "I baptized one man," he says, "and that was not a success story. My first companion, likewise, only baptized one person, and he thought his mission was a failure. But when I attended his funeral not long ago, a letter was read that he had received twenty years after his mission from the man he baptized, who indicated he had been true and faithful and had raised his family in the

Church. I have since learned that from that family there are two stake presidents serving in Brazil and a bishop serving in Provo, Utah. Likewise, how can I say my mission was not successful when Brother Bangerter and I found the first family to join the Church in Curitiba? We may not have taught and baptized them, but we found them."

Even before returning home to await induction into the military, Elder Faust and several other missionaries were made aware of opportunities with the U.S. government that would keep them from the draft. As Elder Faust recalls:

> We were told that Hitler planned to conquer the United States by coming up through South America. In an effort to stop what was called the Nazi Fifth Column activity, the United States Government, through the State Department, was recruiting Americans who knew the language, country, and culture. They would perform diplomatic work, including intelligence gathering.
>
> Some of us who were completing our missions were offered positions in the State Department, and some were named as vice-consuls of the United States. We were offered pay at a rate of about twenty times what our parents were sending us, and fifteen times what draftees in the armed forces of the United States were paid. Those who accepted this invitation could live out the war safely and comfortably without eating Spam or K-rations; they would not be shot at and would have plenty of money to spend.
>
> One of my companions who was offered such a position asked his parents about the advisability of accepting such employment. My companion's father went to see President J. Reuben Clark, Jr. The counsel received from the First Presidency was that we all should come home and be subject to the draft. We were encouraged not to put ourselves in a position of compromising our standards inconsistent with our callings and priesthood. We were too young, inexperienced, and immature to understand fully what President Clark already knew. . . .
>
> In my immature mind, I could rationalize that there was more than one way to fight a war. Was it not justifiable to do anything, literally anything to thwart the efforts of the hated Nazis? Were we not justified in doing anything and everything to defeat such an evil empire which was seeking world domination? I questioned which was more honorable: to be drafted into the armed

forces, where I may have to shoot someone and be shot at, or be in civilian life and fight the Nazis in a more subtle form of opposition. . . .

A great principle was involved, however: it is important always to follow the counsel of the prophets of the Lord. That requires some courage and faith.[4]

Upon returning home, Jim waited to receive his induction notice, which arrived within six weeks. In the meantime, he bought a Model A Ford with money saved during his mission and resumed what he knew would be a short-lived social life as a civilian. One of the first young women he asked out was Ruth Wright, with whom he had been acquainted at Granite High and who was working for Jim's uncle at the State Fingerprint Bureau. "Ruth," Jim recalls, "had my uncle's great respect and admiration, in part because she was working to help take care of herself, as well as to help her mother pay the mortgage on their home. Uncle Jim kept telling me I needed to come up to his office and see this Ruth Wright. When I did, she was so engaging that I was completely bewitched."

Ruth was from a family of four boys and four girls and says, "I had a special spot in the family, being the sixth of the eight children. Three older sisters spoiled me with hand-me-downs and love, then two older brothers and two younger brothers all teased, protected, and looked after me."[5]

When Ruth was a young girl, her father was called to serve a mission, which meant he would have to leave behind his wife, who was pregnant with their eighth child, and their seven children. Ruth shares something of the challenges her mother faced: "We had sixteen cows that had to be milked two times a day. There were fences to be mended, hay to be bought, and the household chores to be done. Mother baked bread daily and tended to the garden, from which we harvested our food. Then she sold eggs and milk to supplement our income." When asked if she ever heard her mother complain, Ruth responds, "I don't think she knew she could complain! She accepted these burdens—at least what I would call burdens—as a calling from the Lord. And when I saw my mother's faith, I just figured that's what I had to do."

Ruth was well-liked and active in high school and also had qualities that ran far deeper than the outward indications of her popularity. One year, she ran for queen of one of the high school dances but lost to another girl. Then the committee did a recount of the votes and found that Ruth had, in fact, won. When they told her, she asked that they keep the results quiet so the other girl's feelings wouldn't be hurt.

In addition to working after graduating from high school, Ruth attended the University of Utah for two years, eager to gain as much education as she could.

When Jim showed up at his uncle's office, Ruth was pleased to renew her acquaintance with him—and was also pleased to accept his invitation to come over for Sunday dinner a few days later. She took that to be a good indication that he valued and was proud of his family, and she enjoyed a lavish meal that George prepared for the young couple, as well as for Jim's brothers and other relatives.

The two began to date regularly after that Sunday dinner, although Jim's induction into the Army Air Corps came soon after that first date. "I knew what I had to do when I returned from my mission," Jim says, "and my notice came soon enough. My father did what he could to orient me, and he told me, 'Son, I'm going to give you different advice than I've ever given you before. When you're in the army, eat everything you can, sleep every chance you can, and don't volunteer for anything.' That proved to be good advice."

Fortunately for his and Ruth's budding relationship, Jim was sent to Fort Douglas in Salt Lake City for his indoctrination and then to nearby Camp Kearns for basic training. The close proximity of the two bases made it possible for them to go out, usually once a week.

In between dates with Jim, however, Ruth was busy dating several other young men, which created a bit of a dilemma when Jim proposed marriage. "I accepted his proposal without hesitation," Ruth says, "but at the same time he was asking, another young man was coming to pick me up for a date. When he arrived, I drove around the block with him to tell him I wouldn't be able to go out after all."

Jim knew there was competition and adds that he felt he held little interest for someone like Ruth, being a private in the army and earning only fifty dollars a month as such. Ruth remembers the sentiments he expressed to her mother in these words: "Sister Wright, I have nothing, I am nothing, but I love your daughter and want to ask for your blessing to marry her."

Jim adds, "I knew full well I had nothing to offer, and to make matters worse, during the war you never knew what was going to happen. Well, when I asked for Ruth's mother's blessing, she said, 'Jim, I think as much of you as I do of Will Erekson.' (Will was Ruth's brother-in-law and had become my stake president after President Moyle.) That just blew me away, to use today's vernacular. I didn't believe it then and I don't believe it now, but it was one of the finest encouragements I've ever received in my life. I was glad that I knew Will, though, as I don't think I would have made the grade except that in Ruth's mother I had a friend in court."

With Ruth having accepted his proposal, Jim sold his Ford for seventy-five dollars and put a little money with it to buy an engagement ring. Their courtship, interrupted as it was by Jim's military obligations, "was delightful in some ways but terrible in others," Ruth recalls, referring to the fact that soon after they became engaged Jim was transferred to the Chanute Field Army Base in Illinois for further training.

Because of his language experience, Jim was assigned to an intelligence division and enrolled in cryptographer's school. One night he was assigned to guard some barracks that had been fumigated, and as he stood in the cold winter's air, he noticed that there were no officers assigned to the duty—and he knew that they were all "in their beds, warm and comfortable":

As I walked around my post, I meditated and pondered the whole miserable, long night through. By morning I had come to some firm conclusions. I was engaged to be married and knew that I could not support my wife on a private's pay. In a day or two, I filed my application for Officer's Candidate School. Shortly thereafter, I was summoned before the board of inquiry. . . .

The questions asked of me at the officers' board of inquiry took a very surprising turn. Nearly all of them centered upon my beliefs. "Do you smoke?" "Do you drink?" "What do you think of others who smoke and drink?" I had no trouble answering these questions.

"Do you pray?" "Do you believe that an officer should pray?" The officer asking these last questions was a hard-bitten career soldier. He did not look like he had prayed very often. I pondered. Would I give him offense if I answered how I truly believed? I wanted to be an officer very much so that I would not have to do all-night guard duty and KP and clean latrines, but mostly so my sweetheart and I could afford to be married.

I decided not to equivocate. I admitted that I did pray and that I felt that officers might seek divine guidance as some truly great generals had done. I told them that I thought that officers should be prepared to lead their men in all appropriate activities, if the occasion requires, including prayer.

More interesting questions came. "In times of war, should not the moral code be relaxed? Does not the stress of battle justify men in doing things that they would not do when at home under normal situations?"

I recognized that here was a chance perhaps to make some points and look broad-minded. I suspected that the men who were asking me this question did not live by the standards that I had been taught. The thought flashed through my mind that perhaps I could say that I had my own beliefs, but I did not wish to impose them on others. But there seemed to flash before my mind the faces of the many people to whom I had taught the law of chastity as a missionary. In the end I simply said, "I do not believe there is a double standard of morality."

I left the hearing resigned to the fact that these hard-bitten officers would not like the answers I had given to their questions and would surely score me very low. A few days later when the scores were posted, to my astonishment I had passed.[6]

In December 1942, Jim was shipped off to Florida to attend

officer's school—and to await what he knew would be the orders to ship overseas. He and his fiancé discussed their plans through the mail and came to the conclusion that they wanted to be married before his next transfer. But there appeared to be no way for him to return to Salt Lake City to be married in the temple, so they concluded that Ruth would go through the temple in Salt Lake and then come to Florida, where they would be married by a Mormon bishop. Accepting that reality was hard for Ruth and for Jim, who had been promised in his patriarchal blessing that he would be married in the temple; but they could see no other alternative and made arrangements accordingly.

As Jim was nearing the completion of his training in Florida, he received orders to report to Harrisburg, Pennsylvania, where he would attend interrogating school. He was also told that in order for him to fit with the military's schedule, he would be given a ten-day furlough.

Ruth recalls, "I received a telegram two days before I was to leave for Florida, telling me to stay in Salt Lake, for we would be married in the temple after all. It was as if a miracle had happened, and I really believe that it did. Jim was one of the few officers at his school to be given a furlough."[7]

There still remained the challenge of getting home, and Jim quickly found that there were no airline reservations to be had and that the trains and buses were all booked as well. He hitch-hiked to Denver, where he was able to catch a bus to Salt Lake, and on April 21, 1943, he and Ruth were married for eternity in the Salt Lake Temple.

There was no reception—in fact, only Ruth's mother and grandmother and Jim's parents attended the ceremony—but the newlyweds were grateful just to be able to begin married life as they had always hoped and prayed to begin it.

After spending a day or two in Salt Lake City, the newlyweds traveled across the country to Pennsylvania, where they rented a single room in a home, sharing the bathroom down the hall with the other tenants.

In many ways, the two scarcely knew each other as they began life together; in fact, during their engagement Ruth expressed concern to her brother-in-law Will Erekson that she didn't know Jim very well. He simply responded, "Ruth, I've been married to your sister for thirteen years, and I don't know her very well either!"

Jim looks at their early days together and says, "It was good in many respects to be away from home and have to work together on the adjustments common to all marriages. We were alone and had to depend on each other. We couldn't even find a branch of the Church. And with the expense of traveling together back East, we went on thin rations for some time. There were weeks when we'd run out of money and live on milk and crackers until payday. It was just Ruth and me, and it brought us closer together."

The Fausts spent about two months in Pennsylvania, and then Jim received his orders to report to San Francisco, where he would board a Liberty ship headed for Suez, Egypt. Ruth accompanied him to California and then returned home to Utah, where she stayed with her mother and worked as a secretary for the army. (Jim notes that he and Ruth were broke when he finished his time in the military because they crossed the United States ten times in an old Ford that burned a quart of oil for every five gallons of gas.)

The trip to Suez ended up taking eighty-three days, during which time Jim and Ruth had no contact with each other. Jim had one friend on board, John Knasavich, whose wife stayed with Ruth while she was in San Francisco. There were four other officers on board—two German speaking and two Italian speaking—and there was one enlisted man who was Greek. The ship was operated by a British crew.

About 1,100 miles off the coast of New Zealand, the crew received orders to locate and rescue a tanker that had burned out and was just wallowing in the sea. "It was quite large," Jim recalls, "and the Liberty ship wasn't. We had orders to tow it in to Auckland, but when we would tie ropes to it, they would snap. We finally got two that held, but then we encountered terrible storms. We only averaged about three knots per hour, and it took us thirty days to pull the tanker into Auckland. Of course, that rescue mission added considerable time to our trip."

During his brief stay in Auckland, Jim went to visit Elder Matthew Cowley, who was the mission president of New Zealand. Elder Cowley mentioned to him that Jim's bishop back in Cottonwood had married Beatrice Going, who came from a well-known LDS family in New Zealand. "Brother Cowley said to me, 'You ought to go up and meet those folks—they might convert you,'" Jim recalls. "I thought I was converted but went up to see what he meant. They were wonderful people and were very kind to me. Percy Going had cleared this whole valley and was raising cows and sheep. I was fortunate enough to be there on a Sunday and spent the day with the family in church. They met in a little chapel they had built, and it was fast Sunday. The testimonies went all day, with a break for lunch, and everyone took a turn. I learned from Elder Cowley that this branch had 100 percent full-tithe payers, and it was, indeed, a wonderful, converting experience."

On his last night in Auckland, Jim met a Dr. Horn from Salt Lake City, who invited him to go with him to a movie. During the show, Dr. Horn heard Jim wheezing, and he told Jim to come see him in the morning so he could treat him for what was an obvious bronchial infection. But Jim had to ship out the next morning, and with no doctor on board the ship, his condition went untreated.

Not surprisingly, Jim was the only LDS soldier on board the ship, and he would often spend a portion of his Sundays at the bow of the ship, reading scriptures and singing hymns. Most days, he would spend a considerable amount of time reading; and every single day, he wrote a letter to Ruth. The letters were, of necessity, short, written on the one-page V-mail stationery supplied by the military, but each contained a bit of news and a lot of Jim's feelings for his new bride. (He would later say,

"I didn't have anything to think about on that boat for eighty-three days, and I got a little romantic.") A letter dated September 8, 1943, read:

> My Beloved Wife,
> The days go by quite rapidly, but I miss hearing from you so much it seems as though in a way I am not living.
> Anyway, I am thinking of you all of the time, and feel within myself that things will be alright. As long as both of us are healthy, I guess we shouldn't kick.
> I can't help worrying about you though, because not hearing from you makes it that way. How are Sherm and Rex? How is your stomach? How is your family?
> We have been teaching the Germans aircraft recognition, then I study awhile, and the time passes. I don't let things bother me, like the other three.
> Well, little lady, again today I want to remind you that I love you, and appreciate you, and pray for you. You are mine forever.
> Stay just the way you are, and smile in the mirror for me.
> With all my love,
Es*

One of the last letters he wrote was dated November 8, 1943:

> Dear Ruthy,
> Well, by the looks of things this will be about the last letter on board this ship. I can hardly realize that the trip is about over.
> All my hopes for the present are in expectation of mail, which I pray is there. We have had a safe passage and everything is alright.
> I'll cable you first thing, and will get these letters off as soon as possible.
> I love you my dear sweet wife, and hope you are alright. I worry about you, although I think you are able to take care of yourself. You are all I have, you know. Write me all of the news.
> I love you,
Es

---

* Within his family, Jim went by Es (short for his middle name, Esdras) in his younger years.

When Jim arrived in Egypt, he mailed all the letters he had written to Ruth, and several weeks later, her mother called her while she was at work to tell her she had received eighty-three letters from her husband. Ruth recalls, "By this point, I hadn't heard from Jim for over three months, and I was almost a basket case. When I told my boss that I had finally received mail from my husband, he let me take the afternoon off. So I went home and read every one of those eighty-three letters."

Upon arriving in Egypt, Jim was attached to the headquarters of the army in the Middle East. Not long after, he received orders signed by General Dwight D. Eisenhower to report to the Supreme Headquarters for the European area. But at about the same time, Jim developed an infection in one of his toes, and while he was having it examined, the doctor could tell he was having difficulty breathing and discovered that he was still suffering from the residual effects of pneumonia. Thereupon, the doctor told him he wasn't going anywhere and put him in the military hospital for treatment. Jim recounts an incident that occurred in the hospital:

> The hospital was staffed with native orderlies who were to keep the hospital clean, change the beds, and generally be of help to the patients. Because of the prevalence of malaria and its carrier, the mosquito, we slept under large mosquito nets which hung from the ceiling and covered the whole bed. One night as I went to bed I slipped my wallet under my pillow and drifted off to sleep.
>
> Some time later in the night I was awakened and startled to feel some hands slipping under my bedclothes. I suspected that a thief was after my wallet. I instinctively grabbed one of the hands and switched on the light. My wallet slipped out from under the pillow. To my surprise, I held the arm of the native boy who was the orderly assigned to clean my room. All he said in defense of his action was, "Don't worry. I am a disciple." He could tell from the look on my face that I did not understand. In further explanation, he said simply, "I am a disciple. I am a Christian. I do not want your purse. I was only tucking the mosquito netting around your bed to protect you from the mosquitoes while you slept." I came to know that this young man was not only a Christian, he was a disciple.[8]

Even with being placed on limited duty, Jim's assignments took him across Africa to Khartoum, Sudan, and then to Accra, Ghana. After spending about six months in the Middle East and traveling across much of the continent of Africa (a country he would later have responsibility for as president of the International Mission), Jim was reassigned stateside, which was welcome news to him and Ruth.

His first assignment upon returning to the States was in Orlando, Florida, where he received additional training in intelligence, and he was then transferred to Camp Ritchie in Maryland. "I was assigned to be an ordnance officer, in charge of maintaining machinery and equipment. My father was good with his hands and could fix anything, but I inherited none of his abilities that way and knew nothing about machinery. But I had some men who did, and I learned that you don't have to know everything yourself if you have good people around you who do."

One of the responsibilities of the group Jim oversaw was to analyze German equipment that had been captured and sent over to his base. "We'd work around the clock to try and figure out the impedimenta the Germans had developed. And sometimes we'd drive their vehicles around. I did struggle, though, with not knowing much about what I was doing, so one day I asked a friend who was the head of another section if he could get me transferred over. That request was turned down."

While Jim was based at Camp Ritchie, he and Ruth lived in Waynesboro, Pennsylvania, which had a small ward they attended. There they met the stake patriarch, William G. Stoops, about whom Jim would later say:

> Brother Stoops worked at a machine shop in the little town of Waynesboro, Pennsylvania. Everyone called him Pappy. He was a kindly, gentle, wonderful, exemplary member of the Church. All who met him honored and admired him. One time a nonmember with whom he worked said something like this: "I don't know much about the Mormon Church. I have never met with the missionaries, and I have never studied the doctrine. I have never been to one of their services, but I know Pappy Stoops, and if the

Church produces men like Pappy Stoops, it has to have much good in it." We never know the power of our own example for either good or bad.[9]

In August 1945, soon after the war ended in Europe, Jim was discharged with the rank of first lieutenant, and he and Ruth moved back to Utah. Having been married for more than two years and wanting to get on with his life, Jim had all but decided that he wouldn't return to school and would find another way to begin making a living. He recalls, "When I told my father that I didn't think I would return to school, he said, with his characteristic directness, 'What can you do?' That cut me to the bone, and it didn't take me long to get my application in to the University of Utah Law School."

NOTES

1. Devotional message delivered at the Provo, Utah, Missionary Training Center, 24 December 1992. Unpublished manuscript.

2. "The Law—A Key to Something Greater," remarks delivered at the J. Reuben Clark Law Society, Washington, D.C., 30 April 1990. Unpublished manuscript.

3. "The Message: Simply Happy," *New Era,* July 1985, p. 4.

4. "A Legacy of the New Testament," address given at CES Religious Educators' Symposium, Provo, Utah, 12 August 1988. Unpublished manuscript.

5. *Church News,* 22 January 1988, p. 4.

6. "Honesty—A Moral Compass," *Ensign,* November 1996, pp. 42–43.

7. *Church News,* 22 January 1977, p. 13.

8. "The Resurrection," *Ensign,* May 1985, p. 30.

9. "The Importance of Bearing Testimony," address given at Frankfurt Area Conference, Frankfurt, Germany, 28 May 1988. Unpublished manuscript.

5

LOCAL
LEADERSHIP

W\ HEN JIM ENROLLED IN THE University of Utah Law School in
the fall of 1945, he did so with his father's example firmly in
mind, as well as the examples of other lawyers he greatly
admired, such as James H. and Henry D. Moyle.

Jim had watched his father pursue a private practice that
focused on helping people out of their predicaments rather than
on amassing as many billable hours as possible. Jim had also
seen his father serve honorably as a judge for Utah's Third
District Court, a position his father later left because of the need
to stand for election at the end of each term and his determination to remain independent of the campaign contributions that
came, in large part, from the lawyers who argued their cases
before him.

Jim had also grown up aware of the absolute integrity of
President Henry D. Moyle. In addition, he had heard of a blessing James H. Moyle had received from President John Taylor
prior to his leaving for the East to study law. In that blessing
President Taylor had given this counsel:

> We say unto thee, this is a dangerous profession, one that leads
> many people down to destruction; yet, if [thou] wilt, with clean
> hands and a pure heart, fearing God and working righteousness,
> with a desire to maintain the truth and to defend the rights of the
> Church and Kingdom of God on earth; if thou wilt abstain from
> corruption and bribery and covetousness, and from arguing
> falsely and on false principles . . . and if [thou] wilt dedicate thy-
> self unto God every day and ask for His blessing and guidance,
> the Lord God will bless thee in this calling; and thou shalt
> be blessed with wisdom and intelligence, and with the light of

revelation; and thou shalt be an instrument in the hands of God to assist in protecting the rights and liberties and immunities of His people. . . .

We set thee apart on these conditions and under these circumstances to go forth, as [thou] hast desired, to study and become acquainted with all the principles of law and equity; and we say unto thee, if [thou] wilt abstain from chicanery and fraud and from covetousness, and if thou wilt cleave to the truth God will bless thee.[1]

Jim considered this inspired counsel a guideline in his own studies and later in his professional work.

Upon entering law school, Jim came under the tutelage of Dean William H. Leary, who had been dean of the school when George Faust had attended more than thirty years earlier. Dean Leary was known for his plain-spoken nature, and Jim recalls, "He used to tell my dad, 'You wouldn't have gotten in if you hadn't come in with a bunch of sheep.' I think I was in the same situation."

Dean Leary was also well known for his caustic responses to those who were unprepared or who asked what he determined to be a dumb question. On more than one occasion he'd say to a student, "That is such a stupid question, I'd tear my hair out if I had any left." But beyond such comments, which were aimed at the smarter and the poorer students alike, Jim remembers, "He taught us that a fundamental purpose of going to law school was learning to think straight. So that's what I tried to do."

One of Jim's friends in law school was Richard C. Howe, who, in 1998, was appointed chief justice of the Utah Supreme Court. The two would study together in the afternoons as Jim waited for Ruth to finish work, and then he would pick her up, go home for dinner, and continue his studies at their little apartment, often late into the night. Justice Howe recalls, "He was always well organized as a law student, and he was always prepared. He was also very interested in the subject and studied hard. It's my impression, though, that he never studied on Sunday."

Jim and Richard also worked together for the Salt Lake City roads department, fixing roads in the summer and running snow plows in the winter. In addition, Jim received military serviceman benefits, and with Ruth's income, they were able to pay their way.

As the Fausts' years in school passed by, there was one major concern and frustration in their life together. From the time of their marriage in April 1943, Ruth and Jim had wanted to have children but hadn't been able to do so.

In describing this period, Ruth says, "During those early years of our marriage, my greatest desire and dream was to be a mother, and that was what I prayed for most longingly. As the months turned into years and we still hadn't been able to have children, we would pray and pray, and then we would fast, and then we would pray some more. We went to doctors, we went to the temple, we kept praying, but still there were no children."

Jim says of that time, "The fact that we weren't able to have children was a great concern to both of us, but Ruth was particularly upset; she was so baby-hungry. We finally sought counsel from Will Erekson, who was Ruth's brother-in-law and had been my stake president. He indicated that Elder Charles A. Callis of the Quorum of the Twelve seemed to have a spiritual gift to bless couples to have children, so with the appropriate permission, we sought a blessing from the hands of Elder Callis. He first gave me a blessing, and then he and I gave Ruth a blessing, with him as voice.

"Things went from bad to worse over the next few months, with the doctor continuing to run tests and Ruth unable to get pregnant. Finally, we went out to Bingham to see Dr. Richards, and he said, 'Ruth, you're pregnant.' All she could say was, 'Really?'"

The Fausts' first son, James H. (who immediately was given the nickname of "Jimmy") was born May 30, 1947, the night before one of Jim's law school finals. "I only got a C on that test," he says, but he rejoiced with Ruth in the arrival of their first child.

At about that time, Jim and Ruth had concluded that for the forty-eight dollars they were paying in rent each month for their basement apartment, they could buy a house by obtaining a G.I. (serviceman's) loan. Jim arranged with Algot Johnson, who was the Sunday School president Jim had served as a counselor to, to build a small brick house for his family in his old Cottonwood neighborhood.

Justice Howe remembers well Jim's decision to build a house, which was contrary to the advice one of their law professors had given his class. "Willis Ritter, who later became a federal judge and was something of a notorious character, one day got off the subject and said, 'I want to warn you students about buying a house at these inflated prices. There's a danger that if the real estate market falls, you're going to be stuck with a heavy mortgage.' Of course, nothing could have proved to be more wrong than that prediction; in fact, Jim mentioned to me once that when he added on a couple of bedrooms about ten years later, he paid more for the addition than he had for the original structure."

Soon after moving back to his old ward, Jim was called to serve as a stake high councilor, and not long after, he was called by Elder Harold B. Lee to serve as a counselor in his ward's bishopric. "During that interview," Jim recalls, "Elder Lee asked me if Ruth and I had playing cards in our home. I said, 'Yes, we do,' and explained that my former missionary companions and I got together socially and played the game of Hearts. He didn't tell me to get rid of the cards. What he said was, 'From this day forward, you must not only avoid evil, you must avoid the very appearance of evil.' I don't know that I've always done that, but I've tried. And I do try. But I learned from that interview that it is incumbent upon all of us—as leaders and as members of the Church—to not do anything in our personal conduct that would give anybody else license to do something they have seen us do."

Those first years out of law school were an act of faith, Jim says. "My income was $110 a month, and $48 of that went to our house payment. Our car was paid for, but we had to take care of gas, oil, food, clothing, and medical insurance. In addition, Jimmy had to have a special formula because he couldn't tolerate milk. That cost a dollar a can, and it seemed like he drank a can a day. Finally, Ruth's brother was going on a mission, and we agreed to pay $10 a month, which we just did not have. But we paid our tithing, and somehow—somehow—we were able to do it. Sometimes we got to the point where we didn't have a dollar left; but through faith, it worked."

Not surprisingly, Jim was much more inclined to count on faith pulling them through than some of the other means that presented themselves. Once, during their early years of marriage, he and Ruth stopped in Las Vegas one night on their way to California with Ruth's brother. As they checked into the hotel, each was given a roll of nickels to get them started at the slot machines, and while Ruth and her brother contemplated giving their luck a try, Jim let them know he would have no part of it. In fact, he took them out to the street, where he tossed his nickels into the gutter. "I told them, 'That's what you'd be doing—just throwing money away.' We drove through Las Vegas a number of times after that, but nobody ever saw me put a nickel in a slot machine."

After going to school year-round, Jim graduated from law school in the spring of 1948, at the same time earning his bachelor's degree, the last two years of which he completed during that same three-year period. Not long after his graduation, two significant events occurred in Jim and Ruth's life.

The first took place as the ward in which Jim and Ruth lived grew to the size where it needed to be divided. As the new boundaries were drawn, the Fausts' home ended up in the new Cottonwood Second Ward, and Jim was sustained as its bishop on May 8, 1949. Most ward members had known him from the time he was a little boy ("warts and all," he says), and now he would preside over them as their bishop.

Jim tells of a ward member who, in good humor, made the comment that his call must have come from the Lord, because the members of the ward wouldn't have picked him; but Ruth tells of an elderly man, highly respected in the ward, who took Jim aside after the ward had sustained him to tell him in private that he would, without any hesitation, support him in every way that he could.

Likewise, Jim's brother Gus, who had just moved from the ward and knew its members, says that no one was surprised by the call of this twenty-eight-year-old and that the ward accepted him without equivocation.

If there had been any tendency on Jim's part to feel a bit of pride in the call that came at such a young age, his father set him straight that evening at Sunday dinner. As the family gathered, Jim recalls, "He let me know that just because I had been called as bishop I wasn't any better than anybody else, I wasn't to take myself too seriously or too piously, and I wouldn't be receiving any special preference among his sons."

(When an interviewer pointed out, years later, that from the day he left on his mission until the day he was called as bishop there had not been a moment's rest, President Faust quipped, "And there never has been since.")

Bishop Faust selected two fine men as counselors: Farron Cutler, who was several years older, and his boyhood friend Newell Stevenson, who had returned from a mission to Hawaii, served in the military, married, and moved back to Cottonwood. He also recognized immediately that he could fulfill his responsibilities as bishop appropriately only if he had the support of his wife, who had given birth to their second child, Janna, just before his call.

At about this same time, two of Jim's friends, Leo Glover and Elder Henry D. Moyle, suggested that he ought to consider running for a seat in the Utah State House of Representatives. "I took their advice and ran, and darned if I didn't get elected."

With all that he had to manage, Bishop Faust did what he could to help his wife with their children, but his legal, legislative, and Church responsibilities limited the time he was home. Being keenly aware that Ruth "had the principal burden of taking care of the family," he found somewhat unconventional ways to help, such as taking one of the children up on the stand to sit with him during sacrament meeting each week, so that Sister Faust would have a somewhat lighter load.

Although those who knew him felt that Jim was imminently qualified to serve as bishop, he felt inadequate and humbled by the call. He was, however, grateful for the experiences he had had as a district leader in Brazil, for the brief time he had spent as a high councilor and as a counselor in a bishopric, and for the training he received at the Friday night sessions of general conference, where President David O. McKay would sometimes draw from 1 Timothy 3 to instruct the bishops in their callings.

Newell Stevenson adds, "He knew what his source of strength was as a young bishop. We would often stop in the middle of a bishopric meeting, and we would kneel in prayer if there was something we couldn't decide upon or agree upon. He was very humble and prayerful, and he had very strong spiritual instincts that enabled him to do the right things and do them well."

Brother Stevenson also says of his leadership style, "He never rushed into anything. He wouldn't put matters off, either; in fact, there were some difficult matters he dealt with that had been unhandled issues in the ward for years. But he didn't hurry into things just because this or that was the way he thought it ought to be. More than once, I saw him change his mind completely as we would sit together in council and talk matters through. His other counselor and I would sometimes have different opinions, and he would never move ahead until we all agreed—and often it would be his opinion that had changed."

At the time Bishop Faust served in the Cottonwood Second Ward, bishops were responsible for raising ward budgets, building funds, and other assessments; and because the area where he lived was growing so rapidly, the financial demands were significant. "I think the greatest challenge I had was raising the funds," he says. "But I learned not to make assessments to people. I learned to call them in and visit with them and tell them the challenge we had. Then I would suggest a range of contributions we needed and leave it up to them. I found our ward members were more generous when approached that way than if I had made an assessment. The hardest part of that was convincing myself it could be done, but the faith of the people was great enough that if given the opportunity, they would come through. And I still believe that is true."

One of those who helped Bishop Faust learn to rely on the faith and devotion of those he served was Elder Moyle, who lived in his ward. "Elder Moyle used to come in for tithing settlement and write out his check to 'Bishop James E. Faust'— he took the scripture literally that tithing should be paid to one's bishop. As he would hand me his check, he would always say, 'Bishop, this is a full tithe and a little bit more, because that's the way we've been blessed.' Well, given my concern for budgets and so on, I decided I thought I'd see how he felt about the ward budget. So, I asked him—and I got straightened out. He said, 'Bishop, everything I have is yours, in the name of the Lord.' That was a very humbling thing for a young bishop to hear from one of the apostles, and that was Henry D. Moyle."

Bishop Faust was open to lessons from all quarters, one of which came as he sang in the ward choir:

> We had a good choir because our leader, Brother Alex Anderson, was a good leader. He, however, encouraged the bishop to sing in the choir. I felt that as a measure of support for Brother Anderson and the others . . . I would try to sing with the choir. Things went from bad to worse. Brother Anderson liked to invite the choir members to improve their talents by singing solos. One Sunday during choir practice he asked that the bishop sing a small solo. I found it very difficult to turn Brother Anderson down in front of the choir when the others who were not very good singers made a 100 percent effort. So during sacrament meeting they sang and I tried. I was literally so frightened and

upset that the paper trembled in my hands. I could hardly hold it. I felt embarrassed and I felt humiliated. All of my mask of dignity was gone. After the meeting as I walked down the aisle I was met with warm smiles and expressions of understanding and support. Someone said, "Bishop, it surely makes us feel good to see you scared." That day the bishop became more human.[2]

In reflecting on that day years later, he would add, "Instead of thinking you have to do everything perfectly as a leader, you do the best you can. And sometimes when you're doing the best you can, you find that you can't do everything as well as you'd like. But people are forgiving of our weaknesses and shortcomings, and they don't expect us to be perfect, especially when we're willing to laugh at ourselves and admit we're human."

There were many such lessons that Bishop Faust learned as he served, but there was also much that he contributed to the members of his ward, starting with those with whom he served in the ward leadership.

Brother Stevenson tells of a financial clerk Bishop Faust helped to mentor: "When this man was called, he had never had a checking account or written a check in his life. But Jim took time to teach him the fundamentals, and he turned out to be one of the most faithful, dedicated, and accurate clerks I've ever known.

"We had another member of the ward who was older and who had received assistance from the Church for years. Jim worked with him very patiently and made sure he did some work to go along with the help he was receiving. Well, this man became frustrated at one point that he didn't have some of the luxuries of life, so he wrote a letter of complaint to the president of the Church. Of course, the letter came back to Jim to handle, so Jim took me and we went to this man's house to talk with him. The man was mortally chagrined when we showed up, and although some bishops might have been perturbed with him, Jim didn't raise his voice or any such thing—he just very sweetly and quietly asked this man what he wanted that he wasn't receiving."

Part of Bishop Faust's ability to relate to and serve the members of his ward came from the fact that he got to know the members so well, but part came from his willingness to look past the obvious and see the potential in people. One example was a man Jim had known as a boy. Because of his family's circumstances, Jim's friend had not graduated from high school, and he began hauling gravel for contractors, a job that did little to improve his situation. He had also drifted some as a teenager but then married a good woman who helped to settle him down.

Bishop Faust called this man as the Aaronic Priesthood adviser, and he says, "He took his calling seriously. He literally wore out the handbook, studying it. He had a notebook filled with dates when all the young men in the ward would reach the age to be advanced in the Aaronic Priesthood. He kept good track of the young men."

After Bishop Faust was called into the stake presidency, he was involved in calling this man as a member of his ward's bishopric. "He needed a little nudging to become a full tithe payer, but he responded faithfully, as he had done before." Subsequently, President Faust recommended this man, in whom many might not have seen much potential years before, to be the bishop of their ward.[3]

"Jim would never leave something undone or put anything aside because it was hard—he just did it," Brother Stevenson says of his friend's time as bishop.

During his first two years as bishop, Jim also worked hard at building up his law practice and at serving as a state legislator. But when it came time for him to stand for reelection in the fall of 1950, he concluded that he wouldn't run. From the perspective of many who have known him over the years, Jim gained invaluable insight into politics and legislative processes during that two-year term, but he says, "That turned out to be something of a disaster. I had only been practicing for a very short time, and being in the legislature just about sank me because I wasn't able to take care of my practice. It was an engrossing experience—and an enlightening one—but I concluded that I just didn't have time to take care of my clients."

(For his participation in a sixty-day legislative session, which also took about a month of his time before and after, he received the sum of $300—which put his monthly income for what amounted to a four-month commitment at about $35 a month less than he had earned while in law school.)

Justice Howe also points out that Jim had taken on an assignment as an inheritance tax appraiser as part of his legal practice and felt that those responsibilities might conflict with his position as a legislator. "The Utah Constitution provides that a legislator shall not hold any other office of profit or trust," Justice Howe explains, "and I think Jim—in wanting to avoid any appearance of impropriety—felt there might be a problem in his doing both."

Even without the challenges associated with serving as a state legislator, Jim's family, professional, and Church obligations continued to place almost unlimited demands on his time as the responsibilities associated with each continued to grow. Then, after almost seven years as bishop, he was called as a counselor to President G. Carlos Smith in the Cottonwood Stake presidency.

Having served on the high council, President Faust had some perspective on the stake and its activities, but being a member of the stake presidency broadened his view considerably.

One important lesson he learned during his time as a counselor was the need to delegate. The stake had a large welfare farm, and when harvest time came, President Smith was in Europe and the other counselor, Heber Peterson, was likewise out of town. President Faust was new in his calling and wanted to fulfill his obligations, but he also had commitments at work that couldn't be postponed. He worried considerably about how he would arrange to get the crops in, but then, "all of a sudden one night," he says, "I decided that we had a wonderful, gifted high council and that the best thing for me to do was to not even show up at the stake farm. We had men of exceptional ability and talent, and so I gave them the assignment and asked them to give me a report every night on the progress. Even with the machinery breaking down and everything else that can go wrong with a harvest, we got the grain in."

He also became acquainted with many other Church members and leaders in the Salt Lake Valley, including a counselor in the Millcreek Stake presidency by the name of Gordon B. Hinckley.

During those early years of Church leadership, which took up virtually every night of the week, Jim worked hard during the day to build up his practice. Upon graduating from law school, he had been invited by his father's friend and former associate, John D. "Jack" Rice, to "hang his hat" in Jack's offices; and in exchange for free rent and access to the law library, Jim performed research and other duties for Jack as he began to take on clients of his own.

His approach to the law was careful, thoughtful, and conservative, owing in part to the advice his father had given him over the years and the example he had set as a lawyer. As one fundamental, Jim tried always to follow his father's counsel to begin a case by getting the complaint down right in the first place so that he wouldn't have to spend time amending it later. He learned another fundamental from Henry D. Moyle, who told him as he began practicing, "You take care of your office and your office will take care of you." It was also his nature to follow the counsel found in the Latin phrase *res ipsa loquitur* ("Let the matter speak for itself"), and he was never known for courtroom drama or theatrics, preferring instead to present a solid case and allowing the jury to then do its job. (He acknowledges that he once wished he could win all his cases but quickly learned that such would not be the case—and that accepting that fact kept him from lapses of judgment and ethics.)

Coupled with such underlying philosophies, he knew that, although it was his job to argue a particular position, "not

everything in life is black or white. There are other colors and
shades of black or white. It is important that we not judge. I
have learned in my many years in the arena of life that we don't
always have all the facts, and that being slow to judge will save
us from the effects of the principle enunciated by the Savior:
'Judge not, that ye be not judged.'"

His son, Robert, would later say of his father's approach to
the law, "He told me once that 'what's right and what's wrong
is different than what's legal, and I've tried to practice law at a
standard higher than what's legal. If it's wrong, you don't do it,
even if it's legal.'" And his friend, Justice Howe, who worked
with Jim on several cases, has said, "I know of occasions when
he turned down work because he didn't feel comfortable with
the case. He wanted to feel good about the person's cause, that
it was just."

Throughout his career, he would receive assignments from
the State Bar to perform *pro bono* work, and his first case
involved a young defendant who had stolen a motorcycle and
taken it across state lines. The case was assigned to Judge
Tillman D. Johnson, who was well into his nineties, and when
the case was called and Jim approached the bench with his
client, the venerable judge looked down and said, "Which one
of you is the accused?"

In another case he was involved with early in his career, Jim
watched as his associate, John Rice, took on a cause that few
lawyers would have pursued as aggressively. "He represented
a derelict woman in a divorce case, which he took all the way
to the Utah Supreme Court, and there he gave the most eloquent oral argument to the Court I ever heard. He said, 'My
client is a drunk. She has been abandoned by her husband, her
family, her church, and everyone except her lawyer. I took her
case to keep her from being taken advantage of.' Jack was a
deliverer, and he received a pittance for his work."[4]

He would say in ensuing years that although there are some
who joke that the "A" students in law school make the professors, the "B" students make the judges, and the "C" students

make the money, "President Marion G. Romney and I proved that adage wrong, because President Romney didn't become a professor and I didn't make a fortune. My primary interest in the practice of law was just to take care of my family and have time to fulfill my Church callings."

While President Faust was serving as a counselor in the Cottonwood Stake presidency, he watched his quiet little community grow by leaps and bounds, and the day inevitably came in 1955 when the stake needed to be divided. As the boundaries for the new stake were drawn, it occurred to him that President Smith and the other counselor resided in the old stake and he resided in the new. But he did not want to entertain the thought that he might be called. Nor did Sister Faust, who had her hands full with Jimmy and Janna, as well as with Marcus, who was born in February 1953, and with Lisa, who was born in November 1954.

She supported her husband in every way that she could, her children remembering that he would arrive home from work at about six, eat dinner with the family, and then change into a clean white shirt and head off to stake meetings—every night of the week.

Sister Faust's children, who were as rambunctious as could be in church, tell of her admitting in later years that there were weeks when she would wrestle them through the meetings and then say to herself, "I'm not going back to Church until the children learn to behave." Then, of course, she'd "repent" and be back the next week. They also say they never knew during those years the burden she carried; she would always greet her husband with a kiss, make sure he had a warm meal, and then send him off to his meetings with a smile and a kiss.

When Elder Henry D. Moyle came to divide the stake he had once presided over, he interviewed and asked for recommendations from the ward and stake leaders, and he then sought to know who the Lord would have serve as the new stake president. He felt inspired to call James E. Faust. Not surprisingly, that had been the answer Elder Moyle had received from virtually all the men he had interviewed. So, after calling President Faust to serve, Elder Moyle handed him the slips of paper on which other leaders had written their recommendations and quipped, "Well, Jim, even if we don't want you, your brethren do."

Overwhelmed with the new responsibility, President Faust took strength from knowing that the call had come from the Lord—and that he had the support of the members of the stake. Sister Faust, likewise, was overwhelmed; and, fearing the pressures this call would place on her young family, she initially shed tears. Then, she says, "I grew up that day."

As was customary, Jim, Ruth, and their children had Sunday dinner with his family later that day, and Rex Faust remembers his father giving Jim much the same advice he did when Jim was called as a bishop. This time, however, the counsel was directed toward Jim and Ruth's young children, as well. "There's one thing about it," George said. "You don't need to get the swelled head. It's just another calling, and none of you are any better than anyone else."

To Jim's sorrow, George Faust died not long after his son's call. George had sustained serious injuries in an automobile accident that he never quite recovered from, and he passed away some months after having a heart attack. His death created a significant void in Jim's life, as he had always been able to count on his father's sage advice and candor.

The challenges this thirty-five-year-old stake president faced were many, with one of the most significant being the need to build more buildings. President Faust first sought out property, ultimately acquiring ten sites that could be built upon. Then the stake began to build, following a program in which the Church would match financially the stake's labor. One of President Faust's high councilors, Leon Miller, was part owner of Standard Building Supply Company and proposed that with donated labor, the stake could complete a building for about $30,000 cash.

President Faust recalls, "We organized the labor, and we

had electricians, masons, carpenters, and laborers like myself. We would mobilize the whole stake and concentrate on a particular building. The Cottonwood Sixth Ward building was built in seven months, principally with donated labor. The bishop of that ward was a contractor, and he served as the contractor on that building. At one point, he came to me and said, 'President, I don't think we're going to make it,' and I said, 'Let's go back to work.' We got it done, even though the night before the dedication, there were people cleaning all night long.

"We were not a large stake, but we all worked together. We even had non-Mormons come over and help. One fellow who lived in the neighborhood came over on a Tuesday night, and then he came back Wednesday, Thursday, Friday, and Saturday. It wasn't long before he wanted to be baptized, and he ended up a bishop in the Church. We hadn't asked him to help; he just came and felt the spirit of fellowship."

During President Faust's almost thirteen years as stake president, the stake completed five chapels and a stake center.

Building chapels was not the only demand on the members' time; they also were involved in a cattle operation, as well as other welfare responsibilities. The brethren looked forward to two cattle drives each year, as they would move their herd from its summer grazing land in Park City to winter pastures sixty miles south. One spring, President Faust and his son Jimmy went up to Park City for the branding operation, and as President Faust held a big calf down, "it objected, raised its head, and hit me in the mouth." When Jimmy saw that his father had lost his four upper front teeth, he put on his overcoat to leave. "I said, 'What are you doing?'" President Faust recalls, "and he said, 'We're going home, aren't we?' I said, 'No, we're going to stay here and finish the job.'" (When the two returned home, Jim said to Ruth, "I'm just glad it wasn't one of the Adult Aaronics the calf kicked.")

Justice Howe, who lived in President Faust's stake during his years as stake president, remembers that his friend was "a very effective leader who was well organized but who didn't make a big noise." And while most of President Faust's nights were taken up with meetings, Justice Howe says his friend "hated long organizational meetings. He used to tell me that you could accomplish a lot in an hour—if you were well organized, didn't talk too much, and settled right down to business."

President Faust's son-in-law Scott Smith, whose father served as a bishop in the stake, adds that he could be firm when he needed to be and "ran a very tight ship. My father told me of one meeting at which the bishops and high councilors were called in to review and then sustain the stake budget. One bishop had a problem with the percentage of the budget his ward would have to raise and expressed his concern. President Faust listened and then gently reminded the bishop of the role of inspiration in making decisions for the stake. He then asked for a sustaining vote, and every hand went up."

During his years as stake president, Jim Faust became well acquainted with almost all of the General Authorities, many of whom came and visited his stake during the then-quarterly conferences.

Elder Harold B. Lee was one who had taken a special interest in Jim when he served in the legislature, and he visited the Cottonwood Stake several times during the time President Faust served as its president. After his first visit, Elder Lee recorded in his journal, "I . . . was delighted with the excellent spirit in evidence, with President James Faust presiding." After another visit, he wrote, "This is one of our better stakes under the direction of President Jim Faust. The leaders are younger and more responsive. The Seventies Quorums had given names of nonmember missionary prospects to Church members, who were requested to invite these members to the first session of the Conference where the center section of the chapel was reserved for them. They estimate that no less than 100 nonmembers were in attendance."[5]

Another visiting authority was Elder Thomas S. Monson, then a junior member of the Twelve, who recalls, "I found an administrator who had everything in order. I also like to have things orderly, so we got along very well right from the start. And his wife is a fabulous cook."

His visit occurred during the Vietnam War, and Elder Monson spoke to the priesthood leadership in the Saturday night session about the need for staying in touch with the servicemen from their wards. He told of how, as a young bishop, he had written to the fifteen young men from his ward who were serving in the Korean War, and how he heard back periodically from all but one.

He then shared that as he was dictating yet another letter to the soldier he had never heard from, the sister in the ward who was helping him said, "Bishop, don't you ever get discouraged? This is the fifteenth consecutive month you've written to Brother Bryson, and he's never replied." Elder Monson told the leaders his response was, "That's okay, we'll write him again." Then he told them of the response he received to that letter, which read as follows:

> Dear Bishop:
> I have received a letter from you. Quite a few, in fact. I'm slow in replying. I'm not much at writing letters, but I get the magazine. My group leader came by recently, and I've been ordained a priest.

After the meeting, as Elder Monson was shaking hands with some of those in attendance, up walked Brother Bryson, whom Elder Monson had not seen since he went into the military. When Elder Monson told President Faust of the chance meeting, he replied, "Oh, yes, he's one of our elders quorum presidents."

Another memorable visit was when Elder Hugh B. Brown visited President Faust's stake the week before Elder Brown was called as a member of the Twelve. As the two men walked to Elder Brown's car, President Faust asked if he had any personal advice, to which Elder Brown replied, "Yes. Stick with the Brethren." President Faust would later recall, "He did not choose to elaborate or explain, but he left that indelible message: Have the simple faith to follow the Brethren."[6]

Many others came to President Faust's stake, including Joseph Fielding Smith, Spencer W. Kimball, Stephen L Richards, N. Eldon Tanner, Howard W. Hunter, and Gordon B. Hinckley.

President Faust had formed a close association with Elder Hinckley, beginning when they both served as counselors in neighboring stake presidencies and then continuing as they served as presidents of their stakes. Coincidentally, President Faust was invited to give the invocation in the general conference session at which Elder Hinckley was sustained as an Assistant to the Twelve.

The Fausts also formed a special bond with President and Sister Tanner, who lived in the same ward, and the two families became close friends. President Faust says of President Tanner, "He was a man of few words, but when he spoke, you listened. He dedicated the chapel we built in seven months, and his one observation on what we had accomplished was, 'It's all leadership,' which was an impressive lesson."

On another occasion, President Tanner asked President Faust to handle a delicate, difficult situation. When President Faust told him he felt incapable of dealing with it and thought it ought to be handled by a General Authority, President Tanner just said, "Well, you can be fair, can't you?"

The lessons and examples the visiting General Authorities imparted stayed with President Faust as he moved into other leadership responsibilities, and of these experiences, he says, "It was a marvelous thing to have been instructed by the prophets of God. I've always felt I should have done better in my responsibilities, given the great men who taught me."

Having the association they did with visiting authorities was a unique experience for the Faust children, who numbered five when Robert was born in 1957; but they were typical children nonetheless, and Jim and Ruth faced very much the same challenges as the other parents they knew in Cottonwood.

Raising their children took time and work, but Sister Faust

expresses something of the basic premise she and her husband followed: "Each child who came into our home was a very special gift of God, in answer to prayer and the blessing we received early in our marriage. The very word *family* is sacred to us, as it represents our children and what they are—and what we love about each of them. They were a handful, which is normal; but for us as parents, family time was and is sacred."

Sister Faust tells of joining a social club when her children were young, which took her away from the home more than she had anticipated. She finally withdrew so that she could be at home more and says of her decision, "It's hard to ask the Lord to bless us if we're not doing our job."

Even with President Faust's demanding schedule, he tried to follow his father's example and took every opportunity to be with his children at special events. On Saturday, a day he often spent at his law office, he would wake the children up and assign them chores for the day before leaving, so that Ruth would have help—and wouldn't have to worry about getting the children organized. As with his stake, at home he also ran a tight ship, and the children knew that only when their chores were done could they play.

During the summer months, the children spent a good deal of time in the yard, which their father wanted to keep up as an example to the members of his stake. (Although the Fausts' home was on a lot nearly one acre in size, the children mowed the lawn with a push mower for several years and always had to move hoses to do the watering.) The family also had a large garden area, which sons and daughters alike helped care for. Robert recalls that he and Jimmy, in particular, hated working in the garden, and he once asked his father why he liked it so much. "He told me that in the practice of law you don't always see the tangible results of your efforts and hard work, but with a garden there is immediate satisfaction. I told him I didn't have that same need—but he still made me work in the garden."

There was also another area on the Fausts' property where Jim would sometimes go, when he had a little time, to dig or till. As Lisa recalls, it seemed to be a place where he could relax—and not worry so much about outcomes. "Sometimes we'd plant flowers there," she says, "but basically it was dirt. Even so, he would often change into his work clothes and just rototill the area."

As far as being handy around the house, Jim just wasn't. Sister Faust acknowledges the help of many kind neighbors who made repairs that Jim couldn't, and her children note that she baked a lot of pies in exchange.

As the children grew, it was understood that they would be active in the Church and obedient to the commandments. Robert tells of his father's placing great emphasis on the children's preserving their reputations and telling them, "If you ruin your reputation, you don't have anything." But, Robert says, he was much more concerned with the substance of a person's behavior than with outward form. "There were people in his ward when he served as bishop who didn't always come to church, but they paid their tithing. He felt that if they were paying their tithing, he knew where their heart really was. He was more concerned about those who came every week and professed their commitment to the Church but who didn't pay their tithing. That was a signpost for what he considered to be substantive indications of the true beliefs of their hearts.

"He saw to it that we went to church, but he wouldn't press things to the point where he was fanatical or where his approach would push us away from the Church."

As a recently returned missionary, the Fausts' oldest son, Jim, shared with his father the observation that sometimes it seemed to him that there are some who go to church each Sunday but who don't seem to implement in their lives the teachings they hear. Jim says his father thought for a moment and said, "You know, it's a little bit like the man who sits down at the piano and practices every day, but never learns the song."

Robert also recalls his father once saying, "The family does not exist for the Church; the Church exists for the family." And Janna tells of a time when she was receiving pressure to play on the ward softball team, which she didn't want to do. "Dad told me, 'You don't have to do that; you can be here to help your mother instead.'"

Marcus points out, however, that while his father could be flexible on some matters, he has always lived his life by certain absolutes—such as integrity, loyalty, honesty, and obedience to the commandments—and that he expected his children to do likewise. "My father has a very well defined and ingrained set of principles by which he lives and always has lived, from a very young age. He's very rigid in his adherence to these principles."

As an example of one of his father's absolutes—unfailing loyalty—Marcus tells of how Jim, from an early age, went with his father to have his hair cut by a fellow named Sam, one of George's old army friends. That tradition continued with Jim's own sons, although Marcus noticed that as the barber got older and his eyesight poorer, his father would first have Sam cut his hair, then schedule an appointment with another barber to have Sam's mistakes cleaned up.

Even with Jim and Ruth's best efforts, though, Jimmy, Janna, Marcus, Lisa, and Robert were still very much kids. On one hot summer day, Robert threw a brick through his window to get a little more air into the room. When it came time for their father to come home, Marcus helped Robert put a book in his pants, knowing he would be getting a spanking. Upon seeing the outline of the book, however, Dad began to laugh, and there never was a spanking.

Ruth tells of another occasion when the children wanted to plant a flower garden, so she took them to a nursery to pick out their flowers. "Marc planted his, but a couple of hours later, I noticed they were all gone. When I asked him what had happened, he said, 'Maybe they growed down,' and then added, 'but don't look over by the fence.'"

As Jim and Ruth reared their children, both remembered the lessons they had learned growing up during the Depression, and neither had desires for much beyond a comfortable home and moderate lifestyle. The children were well aware of their father's frugality, and Janna recalls that while her father "felt a tremendous responsibility to provide for our family and worked very hard, he was always careful financially and avoided debt like a plague. His profession was such that he only got paid when he worked—or when a settlement would come in. He could go a long time working on a case without receiving any payment, and then get a fee that would cover two or three years' worth of work. Mom and Dad couldn't allow themselves to live beyond their means or to have any debt because they didn't know if they could service it. As a result, when my mother had Robert, after fourteen years of marriage, we were still hanging our clothes out to dry in the winter."

Another insight into—and endorsement of—President Faust's provident lifestyle was shared by President Gordon B. Hinckley in the October 1998 general conference of the Church. President Hinckley said this of the Fausts' early years of marriage:

> He had a mortgage on his home drawing 4 percent interest. Many people would have told him he was foolish to pay off that mortgage when it carried so low a rate of interest. But the first opportunity he had to acquire some means, he and his wife determined they would pay off their mortgage. He has been free of debt since that day. That's why he wears a smile on his face, and that's why he whistles while he works.[7]

Jim did always drive a nice car, and his children remember that it was always spotlessly clean. Having a good vehicle was possible because Ruth's brother, Owen Wright, owned a car dealership and, in partial exchange for Jim's legal services, provided him with a new car every two years. One year, Owen brought a new Cadillac out to the Fausts' home and parked it in the garage for Jim to find when he returned home from work. Jim's response was not what Owen had expected, however: He wouldn't drive it. The car sat in the garage until Owen could pick it up and replace it with something more practical and, in Jim's view, less ostentatious.

Part of his decision stemmed from wondering how the members of his stake would feel seeing him driving around in a Cadillac. But part grew out of what he acknowledges as "a provident lifestyle, born of two things: a desire to follow the counsel of the Brethren, and fear. My fear came from living through a depression, and I am a strong believer that the people in this day and time have forgotten the story of the years of plenty followed by the years of famine."

President Faust's concern for the cleanliness of whatever car he drove did result in at least one vivid family memory. While on one of their regular family vacations, Jim noticed tar on the carpet of the car. So he lined everyone up and checked their shoes, all of which were clean. Finally, he checked his own shoes—and thereon found the source of the tar. "He didn't say a word," Lisa says. "He just got some solvent, cleaned the tar off his shoe, and we were on our way."

In addition to learning lessons in provident living, the Faust children learned repeatedly that they were not to expect any preferential treatment because their father was the stake president. Marcus tells of one stake conference at which the visiting authority decided to call some people out of the audience to bear their testimonies. As he instructed President Faust's counselor to call upon Marcus, who was then seminary president at Bonneville Junior High, President Faust overheard them, stopped the meeting, and, in a quiet exchange on the stand, vetoed the idea. "They called on someone else," Marcus explains, "because Dad did not want it to appear that he was using his position to promote his family."

President Faust's children do acknowledge some unique opportunities to associate with various General Authorities, however, and Lisa tells of going with her parents and her high school boyfriend (now her husband) to visit Hugh B. Brown, who by this time was becoming quite elderly. As they visited, President Faust commented on how beautiful an Oriental rug was, to which President Brown replied, "It is, isn't it. I think I'll take that with me to heaven." Then he chuckled and said,

"That's presumptuous, to think I'm going to heaven. I'll probably show up at the pearly gates with that rug under my arm, and St. Peter will look at me and look at the rug and tell me where to go."

President Faust shared in a good laugh and then said, "President Brown, if you're not getting in, there's no hope for the rest of us."

One thing President Faust shared with his two mentors, Presidents Tanner and Brown, was their philosophical orientation toward the Democratic party. Even after not seeking reelection in 1950, Jim continued to be very active in state and national politics. Among his various endeavors, he helped manage a campaign for Senator Frank Moss. He summarizes his political orientation by explaining, "I am a conservative on fiscal and property matters, and I am a liberal in terms of human values and human rights. I believe what is said in the Book of Mormon, that the Lord values all of his children equally—black and white, bond and free, male and female, Jew and Gentile—and that the Lord likewise has compassion for the heathen. As a result, I like to see all people enjoy every advantage, every blessing, every opportunity that comes to them by reason of citizenship. I also support what has been said by the Brethren—that it is in the interests of the Church to have a two-party system and not to have one party that is exclusively LDS and the other party exclusively non-LDS. Both locally and nationally, the interests of the Church and its members are served when we have two good men or women running on each ticket, and then no matter who is elected, we win."

President Faust served as president of the Utah State Bar Association from 1962 to 1963, maintaining that the only reason he won that election was because all the older lawyers thought they were voting for his father. He also served as a member of President John F. Kennedy's Civil Rights Commission in the early 1960s and attended a reception in the White House Rose Garden in that capacity. Jim recalls, "After he had given us our charge, President Kennedy came up to Scott Matheson (who later became governor of Utah) and me and asked if we would like to see his office. He pointed the way, and Scott and I walked into the Oval Office unattended; there was no one guarding it as there is today. As we looked around the room, Mrs. Lincoln, President Kennedy's secretary, came in, introduced herself, and asked if we'd like to see the rest of the executive offices, which we did. You certainly couldn't do that now!"

In 1968, after having served almost thirteen years as stake president, forty-eight-year-old James E. Faust was released—so that he could be called as one of the first regional representatives of the Church. President Harold B. Lee extended the call and assigned him to work with Neal A. Maxwell, also a regional representative, on the Church's new Leadership Committee under the direction of the junior member of the Twelve, Thomas S. Monson.

In some ways, the change of assignment increased Elder Faust's load, as he traveled many weekends to attend stake conferences, but Marcus recalls coming home one evening and seeing his father watching television in the den. "It was an odd feeling to see him in there, but after his release as stake president, we began to see him around the house in the evenings."

At about the same time, Elder Faust was asked to work with Elder Gordon B. Hinckley in coordinating the Church's opposition to an initiative to liberalize the state's liquor laws. (The initiative started out with widespread support but ended up being soundly defeated.)

During his four years as a regional representative, Elder Faust learned more and more about church governance and formed lasting friendships and associations. Then in October 1972, while attending a training seminar that he and his friend Neal Maxwell had helped organize, his life was unalterably changed.

88 3 333

NOTES

1. Remarks delivered by James E. Faust at the dedication of the Howard W. Hunter Law Library, Brigham Young University, Provo, Utah, 21 March 1997. Unpublished manuscript.

2. "An Even Balance," Brigham Young University devotional address, Provo, Utah, 17 March 1981.

3. "An Untroubled Faith," Brigham Young University devotional address, Provo, Utah, 28 September 1986.

4. "The Law—A Key to Something Greater," remarks to the J. Reuben Clark Law Society, Washington, D.C., 30 April 1990. Unpublished manuscript.

5. Unpublished journals of Harold B. Lee, 31 May 1959 and 9 December 1967.

6. "An Untroubled Faith."

7. "To the Boys and to the Men," *Ensign,* November 1998, p. 54.

6

WITH A HAND
TO THE PLOW

In late September 1972, as Jim Faust was driving home from his Salt Lake City law office, he approached the intersection at 4500 South and Highland Drive. Before he could turn right onto Highland Drive, the stoplight turned from green, to yellow, to red; and at that very instant, he says, "I received a very powerful message that at the next general conference I was going to be called as an Assistant to the Twelve. It was very clear to me what the call would be, and that it would not be to the Seventy or to the Twelve at that time. It was a very powerful message."

When he arrived home a few minutes later, he went into his bedroom and shut the door. Then, he adds, "Ruth, who is very sensitive, came in and asked if anything was wrong. I told her no, but that I needed to be alone for a little while. Then I made a few notes that I put in the pocket of my suit jacket."

Ten days later, on Thursday, October 5, Elder Faust was attending to his duties at a regional representatives' seminar that he had helped arrange with Elder Neal A. Maxwell (also a regional representative), under the direction of Elder Thomas S. Monson of the Twelve. The meeting was being held in the Seventeenth Ward Chapel in downtown Salt Lake, and the keynote speaker for the morning session was President Harold B. Lee, who would be sustained the next day as the eleventh president of The Church of Jesus Christ of Latter-day Saints. Elder Faust remembers that after his address, President Lee came down from the stand and greeted Elder Maxwell warmly, but that when he said hello to Elder Faust he seemed a little withdrawn. Then, as President Lee went to the back of the room, he motioned for Elder Faust to follow him. "So, I went with him to the back of the building," Elder Faust recalls, "and there I saw Henry Smith, who was the editor of the *Church News,* and Arthur Haycock, who was the secretary to President Lee. Both had rather serious demeanors. President Lee had me come into this little room, and he was so gracious and kind as he told me that he wanted to change my life. He then told me what a wonderful wife I have, and that the Lord had called me to serve as an Assistant to the Twelve. Among all the other emotions I felt at the time, I was grateful that the Lord had let me know ahead of time that this call was coming, because I could not have served one day without having the personal conviction that the call had come from the Lord."

Once his interview with President Lee concluded, Elder Faust went out to help Elder Maxwell make arrangements for the one o'clock session that was about to begin. Elder Maxwell recalls that upon seeing his friend, "I could tell he was shaken, and all I said, so that I didn't risk being inappropriate, was, 'Am I going to lose my companion, Jim?' He teared up, and we left it at that."

As President Lee met with Elder Faust, he told him that he could tell his wife of the calling, and no one else. At the same time the regional representatives were meeting, Sister Faust, who was then serving as a stake Relief Society president, was attending a meeting in the Salt Lake Tabernacle. When her meeting ended, Elder Faust found her and took her to a quiet spot behind the organ, where he told her what had happened that morning. "She asked me if I had known about this," Elder Faust says. "I reached in my pocket and pulled out the notes I had made several days earlier as I told her what had happened that night as I drove home. Then, as we both shed tears, she said, 'Why didn't you tell me?' and all I could say was, 'I couldn't even admit it to myself.'"

A few minutes later, Sister Faust encountered President Lee, who said to her, "The Lord has called your husband." Sister

Faust's response was simply, "He couldn't have gotten any better."

Between that Thursday afternoon and Friday morning, when his name would be presented for a sustaining vote, there was little Elder and Sister Faust could do but ponder their feelings and wait for the public announcement to come. Honoring President Lee's counsel to keep the matter confidential, he suggested to his mother that she be sure to watch the morning session of general conference, but beyond that he made no mention of this life-changing event to family or friends.

During the Saturday afternoon session of conference, Elder James E. Faust was able to make his first public statement since receiving the call.

His humility was immediately evident as he said,

> I have asked myself a hundred times, Why me?—because it is beyond my understanding that I should be asked to join these great brethren of the General Authorities. . . .
>
> . . . I have concluded that if there is one amongst all the General Authorities who is the weakest and the least qualified, then I can fill that position.

He then turned his attention to the gratitude he felt for family members and friends who had been instrumental in shaping his life:

> With all my heart I want to thank Ruth Wright Faust for letting me share her life and giving me the hope that we can share eternity together. She is more than a wife and a sweetheart because she has become part of my very being. With all my heart I want my children to know that I cannot succeed in this calling unless I also succeed as their father, and that they will always be paramount in my life.
>
> No man ever had a better father than did I, and I hope that I will always honor his good name. My widowed mother is among you in the television audience, and I am sure that she weeps. Many times in my childhood I have happened upon her on her knees, praying for her five sons, and I wish to tell her that this son continues to need her faith and prayers. . . .
>
> I wish President Lee to know that I sustain him, and He whom

President Lee represents, with all of my devotion and all of my
heart and all of my being. Under his hands I was ordained a
bishop, and by him called to the stake presidency, and he has
been for me all my adult life a great and beloved teacher and
exemplar for all that is noble and good. President Tanner has been
like a father to me, ever available, always helpful, kind, considerate, and he knows how much love and respect I have for him.

President Romney, as you know, has special qualities of inspiration and wisdom and has been a special friend and confidant,
and my respect and honor for him know no bounds. I would also
like to mention the profound influence that President Henry D.
Moyle and President Hugh B. Brown have also had on my life.
These are and have been truly great men of the earth.

I express appreciation to all the host of people who have
blessed my life, those from whom I have learned, my missionary
companions, those with whom I served in bishoprics, on high
councils, stake presidencies, and my beloved friends, the Regional
Representatives of the Twelve.

Elder Faust also allowed a bit of his wit to combine with his
expression of testimony and conviction as he concluded:

As long as I remember I have had a personal witness of the
divinity of Jesus Christ and of his church, and it has always been
easy for me to believe and to testify. . . .

I realize that life for me and mine can never and should never
be the same. For twenty-two years and until last Thursday morning I have been a lawyer, and since then I have been trying to
repent. Now I shall try to become one of the fishers and help these
brethren cast forth and draw in the nets of eternal life. And I
should like to say that if anyone has ever been offended by anything I have ever done in my church, professional, or political life,
I humbly ask their forgiveness. I mentioned to a friend of mine
who knew of this call that those who know me will say, "Surely
James Faust was called of the Lord because no one else would
have called him." . . .

Now as a humble follower of the divine Master, I bear witness to
the divinity of him as the Savior of the world, and of his church as
established in these days, now headed by President Harold B. Lee.[1]

After Elder Faust's brief comments, President Lee, who was
conducting, commented on his talk, as well as on the remarks

delivered by Elder O. Leslie Stone, who had also been called as an Assistant to the Twelve:

"As we listen to these men, great in business and public life, we remember what the great prophet of the Book of Mormon said, ' . . . to be learned is good if they hearken unto the counsels of God.' (2 Ne. 9:29)

"We can accept all the repentant lawyers and attorneys and businessmen there are in the world."[2]

Although the Fausts were stunned by the calling that had come, Gus Faust recalls that no one in the family was surprised by the news; and Grant Bangerter, with whom Elder Faust had remained close since their missionary days, points to comments he made at the next reunion of the Brazil missionaries as typifying those who knew Jim Faust well: "I spoke what I think all the others felt—that what we had seen happen was inevitable."

In accepting the call to serve as a General Authority, Elder Faust knew his and his family's lives would be changed in significant ways. And it was his family that was of utmost concern to him, prompting him and Sister Faust to call their children and their spouses together as soon as the call was made public to discuss what it meant to them as parents. The message was simple, and it would be repeated to the family with each of his subsequent callings: "I cannot succeed as a General Authority if I don't first succeed as a husband and as a father."

Elder Faust then set out to eliminate from his life anything that might distract him from his two responsibilities. Although President Lee had told him he could take what time he needed to close his legal practice, Elder Faust moved as quickly as possible to assign his clients and cases to others, including his son Jim, who was finishing his last year of law school at the time of his father's call. "I hadn't passed the bar yet," Jim recalls, "but during my final year I tried to save all the clients I could. I took care of what I could, and there was another lawyer with whom my father had been associated who handled all the court appearances."

Elder Faust recalls that "a few weeks after I was called,

I took a razor blade and went over and removed my name from the door of my law office. Someone else could have done that, but I felt I should be the one. I felt my name should be removed as soon as I was able to disengage from the law. I had to go to court only once after I was called as a General Authority, for which I was grateful. Once I had put my hand to the plow, I didn't look back. Being called as a General Authority was more than enough challenge for me."

As he took hold of the plow, Elder Faust had years of experience to draw upon in the arenas of Church leadership, the law, politics, social issues, and community service. At the same time, he felt the need for counsel and went to see his long-time friend, President Hugh B. Brown. "At the time," Elder Faust says, "President Brown was in his nineties and was not able to come to the office. So I went to his home and said, 'President Brown, what advice do you have for a new General Authority?' And he just said this: 'Stick with the Brethren.'"

Marcus Faust adds that his father mentioned in a private moment that he was going to attempt to pattern his ministry after that of President Brown's. "Dad loved President Brown because President Brown loved the people. He was a populist and had a common touch, which are traits I think my father shares with him."

Elder Faust adds, in acknowledging the influence President Brown had on him, that "people often thought that President Brown had a brilliant mind, which he certainly did. But his heart was bigger than his mind."

Elder Faust also recalls, with a chuckle, one other bit of advice he gleaned from President Brown: "He told me more than once, referring to the adulation that is received by the General Authorities, 'It's all right to hear those nice things that are said about you, so long as you don't inhale.'"

Almost immediately, Elder Faust began to receive assignments to preside at stake conferences—and to provide leadership training for various ward and stake leadership meetings. Here again, he drew on what he had learned from the many

General Authorities who had visited his stake over the years—and patterned his approach after those experiences:

"When President Lee first came to my stake, he called me and said, 'Jim, we're coming out to be with you. We want to get close to you, and we want to bless your people and testify to them.' What impressed me about President Lee, President Kimball, and so many of the other Brethren was that they made me feel like they were not coming to find things wrong; they were coming to help me. I knew what was wrong in my stake—I didn't need to have somebody come and tell me. What I needed was help, and the manner in which these brethren did their teaching was enveloped in a spirit of confidence and love which I very, very much appreciated at the time and have come to hold in sacred remembrance ever since. And that was true without exception of those great leaders. They had all been in my shoes. They all understood my situation.

"So, I tried to go out in the same spirit—in the spirit of helpfulness and humility, rather than trying to find things wrong. I would check some indicators of faith, but I had learned from Elder LeGrand Richards that statistics are not as important as the trends in the statistics—where a stake has been, where it is now, and where it's going. These good brethren are doing the best they know how. It's also important to remember that they didn't ask for these callings; they were called by the Lord. I think the role of visiting authorities is to build the Saints up and strengthen them, so I'm grateful to have learned from some of the great leaders of this dispensation, men who set an atmosphere in which you wanted to listen and wanted to learn, rather than creating an adversarial relationship."

Elder Faust's adjustment to the call, as viewed by his associates among the General Authorities, seemed almost effortless. Elder L. Tom Perry, who was sustained the same day as an Assistant to the Twelve, says, "There was no adjustment at all for him. He just moved into the calling like it was second nature. Our offices were just across from each other, and our secretaries sat side by side. I moved to Utah from the East at the time of my call, and I came out of a hard-pushing retail background. Elder Faust was—and is—the kindest, gentlest man I had ever been around, and he never seemed to get excited or riled. Perhaps because I'm not as much that way, once in a while he would caution me, 'We're dealing with Church people here, not business people.'"

Elder Faust's family, however, saw an increased softening as Jim moved from the legal profession to full-time Church service. Sister Faust observes that early in his legal career, her husband had a bit of the disposition of the redhead that he once was. "He and the Lord," Sister Faust observes, "decided that wasn't good for his profession or his Church work. The law can be adversarial, but then he would come home and go to his Church callings where a gentleness of the spirit is required. He knew he couldn't make the changes alone, so he put himself in the hands of the Lord."

Committing himself to the full-time service of the Lord brought about even greater sensitivity and gentleness, Elder Faust's children observe. Says Marcus, "He had been so involved in the Church, and his testimony had always been great and strong. But during his early years as a General Authority, our mother, in particular, could see the additional refinement of his spiritual development as he left the contentious arena of being a lawyer and an advocate and instead spent 100 percent of his time dealing with the affairs of the Church.

"In fact, my mother decided she needed to keep pace with him, so she started to attend Institute classes at the University of Utah."

As Elder Faust's son Jim took over his father's downtown legal practice, the two had frequent opportunities to visit over lunch and in other settings and to observe something of his adjustment to his calling. "Besides being a man of principle," Jim says, "my father is a man who doesn't chafe against the things he has to do. I went through Monticello once and learned that for some thirty years Thomas Jefferson took measurements of the weather at precisely 6:00 A.M, 12:00 noon, and 6:00 P.M. Then he recorded his findings in a journal. I remember thinking, 'That's Dad!' If the Lord gave him the assignment to do that, he would be right there at the designated times, whether he was sick or felt good or found the weather uninviting. And he'd do it for as long as he was told to, whereas most of us at some point would encounter an interruption where we'd say, 'What difference will it make if I don't do this? What's one day in thirty years?'

"In addition, he has a unique way of blending his ability to take on a task and get it done with his ability to not run people over with a tank as he does so. In my view, he learned many of the principles that have made him effective in his callings from his dad, while the caring and sensitivity he blends with his abilities came from the many great women he has been schooled by, particularly my mother and my paternal and maternal grandmothers."

Although he deems much of what he experienced in his first days as a General Authority too sacred to discuss publicly, Elder Faust does acknowledge, "Coming into the brotherhood of the General Authorities is a great, refining experience. I had come from a private law practice where, essentially, I was answerable only to myself and my own conscience. I learned a great and wonderful principle as I came into the body of the General Authorities and learned to work within the confines of section 107 of the Doctrine and Covenants, which says that the quorums of the Church have to function by the unanimous voice of their members. This requires total obedience and commitment to the president of the Church, as well as to the Quorum of the Twelve and the First Presidency. It's not like the Supreme Court, where you can have dissenting opinions. When the Brethren leave the Temple every Thursday, there is unity. That's a marvelous principle, and it takes some schooling to learn to operate within that revelation."

Elder Faust also gained greater appreciation for the abilities of those who preside over the Church—and for the source of their strength. Soon after he assumed his responsibilities as an Assistant to the Twelve, he had occasion to spend about an hour with President Lee discussing several weighty and challenging issues. After their meeting he recorded in his journal, "I was amazed at the President's grasp of difficult problems, and apologized for having to bring to him such matters of grave concern, confessing that they were problems too big for me. . . . His response was, 'They are too big for all of us without the help of the Lord.'"

Throughout his life, Elder Faust had come to know upon whose strength he must depend to serve effectively, but the assignments he received as a new General Authority caused him to seek an even stronger dependency on the Savior. He was immediately assigned to serve on the Church's Special Affairs Committee, which was chaired by Elder Gordon B. Hinckley and dealt with the wide range of political and social issues that affect the Church and its members. (The committee is now known as the Public Affairs Committee.) At the same time he was made chairman of the newly formed Foreign Affairs Committee and was appointed to the Board of Trustees of the Church-owned *Deseret News*, a daily newspaper based in Salt Lake City. Soon after, he was appointed to the board's executive committee, which included Elder Hinckley as chairman and Elder Monson as the third member.

He also received the assignment to serve as the director of the Melchizedek Priesthood MIA (MPMIA), which represented an organizational shift as President Lee formed it and the Aaronic Priesthood MIA to bring all Church auxiliaries under the priesthood umbrella and place added emphasis on the attention given to the Church's many single adults, ages eighteen and over. Two other General Authorities were assigned to serve with him—Elders Marion D. Hanks and L. Tom Perry. As the three looked for someone to assist them in their efforts, Elders Hanks and Perry suggested a young man who had just completed his doctorate at Yale University and had joined the LDS Institute faculty at the University of Utah.

Elder Hanks had been his mission president, and Elder Perry had known him when they both lived in the East. And although Elder Faust had never met the man his two associates recommended, he invited Jeffrey R. Holland in for an interview and then asked him to serve as executive secretary of the MPMIA.

Although the Church had sponsored programs for single adults over the years, President Lee was very committed to a much stronger effort that would provide greater support for those unmarried members who were over eighteen and who would fall under the direction of ward and stake priesthood leaders. President Lee had spent a part of his time in the Quorum of the Twelve as a single adult, having lost his first wife in 1962; and his second wife, Freda Joan Jensen, had lived her entire adult life as a single member of the Church before marrying Elder Lee in 1963. Elder Holland recalls that the MPMIA "was a very high priority in President Lee's administration. I don't know all the reasons for that, but I just have to think he was mindful of what his second wife, Joan, had experienced as a single adult. In addition, he was so knowledgeable in matters of Church government and so priesthood oriented that I think he wanted a way for the priesthood to pay attention to and put its arms around the whole issue of the single adults in the Church, whether they were the young adults or those who were older."

As Elder Faust and his associates, under the direction of Elder Monson of the Twelve, began to develop a concept of how they would structure and implement this new organization, Elder Faust was quite concerned that they proceed from an informed position. To that end, the group spent considerable time interviewing single adults from throughout the Church, as well as their local leaders.

Elder Holland tells of how carefully Elder Faust and the others would listen to women and men of all ages and from virtually every conceivable circumstance in which single members of the Church might find themselves. "He took this assignment very personally," Elder Holland recalls, "and he invested himself emotionally and spiritually in the lives of these people. As we tried to get a feeling for the dimension and breadth of the challenges they faced, we would all see the tears and hear the pain of these people who had been through divorce or the death of a spouse, or who had not had the opportunity to marry; and leading all of that was James E. Faust. He wanted to make sure that we took the time to know the dimensions of what we were dealing with and to learn how these good people were handling their own unique situations. And although these interviews and discussions took place over a number of months, Elder Faust was never inclined to shorten a conversation or assume that we ever knew as much as we ought to know. We were to keep listening and learning all the time."

Elder Perry adds that in those settings Elder Faust had a way of "making the individual feel warm and comfortable and relaxed. And when they would leave, through his influence, I think they viewed the world as a better place than when they came in. In fact, in our years of association from 1972 on, I've never seen him in a situation where he didn't have the individual he has been interviewing feeling comfortable in his presence and inspired after leaving. He possesses a most unique talent that very few men on this earth have."

In summarizing the work that was done to establish the MPMIA program, Elder Holland points to the strengths Elder Faust brought to his assignment. "There were at least three things," he recalls. "First is a quality he brings to everything, and that is a sensitivity and a largeness of heart and a depth of compassion that would be applied to single adults as it would be to anybody, anywhere, and in any circumstance.

"A second quality is his incredible judgment. He has a gift for counsel, and it is not insignificant or surprising to me that he now serves as a counselor to the president of the Church because he is gifted in counsel, in insight, in judgment, in discernment. When you need counsel, he is there, and the more you need it, the better he is. In fact, he is at his very best when the going is the toughest.

"Third, even though he had married Sister Faust soon after his mission, he had watched his sons and daughters, his extended family, and the members of his ward and stake worry about marriage and struggle, in some cases, with the challenges of being single. And as he had watched and cared for them, he had learned from them."

Although the two had never met before their association in the MPMIA, Elder Faust and Jeffrey Holland developed an immediate bond that grew into a lifelong friendship. "Those years in the MPMIA remain to this day one of the sweet experiences of my life because I was a nobody—and I'm still a nobody—just back from graduate school, a person whom he had never met. But he took me under his wing and treated me as courteously and as thoughtfully and as lovingly as he would have treated one of his own sons. He would take me to lunch and talk to me; we'd go for walks and he would talk to me. These were kind of 'ditch-bank' conversations as we would eat a bowl of soup or walk around the grounds, and they included endless teaching moments as he'd tell me of things he had learned as a high councilor or as a bishop or from President Moyle.

"I look back on that with great appreciation. I was spellbound. But it wasn't that he was trying to regale me with his experiences or entertain me; he was trying to teach a young man in whom I guess he saw some promise. And I say that knowing he treats everyone that way. I was no different from anyone else."

Elder Perry also formed a lasting friendship that began immediately after he and Elder Faust were sustained at general conference. The Fausts were quick to invite Elder Perry and his wife, Virginia, to their home for dinner, and, Elder Perry explains, "then I understood why he is such a good man—after I met Ruth. She is just a sweet woman who has compassion for everyone. She was a great help to Virginia when we moved out from the East as she took Virginia under her arm and helped her become acquainted with so many of the sisters."

Soon after the Fausts and the Perrys became acquainted, Elder and Sister Perry shared with the Fausts something few people knew—that Virginia was undergoing treatments for a form of cancer that ultimately would take her life in December 1974.

"Virginia was one who didn't want it to be known," Elder Perry recalls, "and Ruth was one of the few people who knew that she was having this difficulty. Our own children didn't really know how serious her cancer was, and her death was a real shock to them as a result. But Ruth became Virginia's confidant, encouraging her to keep her spirits up during that period."

Elder Faust provided similar support to Elder Perry, who adds, "He would always get after me if I wasn't paying enough attention to Virginia. He is a very thoughtful man that way."

The years between October 1972 and early 1975 were busy and demanding as Elder Faust fulfilled his committee assignments, and traveled throughout the Church to preside at stake conferences and tour missions. He also learned to adjust to the scrutiny that General Authorities are inevitably subjected to as their lives and teachings become increasingly more public. He tells of an article he wrote for the *Friend* magazine, in which he recounted the story of being shot as a young boy and not crying as the doctor dressed his wound. "I honestly believe that if you brace up and face the wind, it's better than hunkering down or caving in. But I got a letter from someone who said that if you don't let your emotions and your feelings out, then it can have an adverse effect on your emotional well-being. Now, there may be truth to that, but I learned early on that you can't prepare talks and messages with the idea that you're not going to get any criticism."

The preparation of his public messages was something to which Elder Faust gave considerable time. Literally, as soon as one general conference address was completed, he would begin on his address for the next, working on ideas, drafts, and revisions for months before each conference in April and October. Two of the first talks he gave after responding to his call in October 1972 focused in large part on single members of the Church, and he also addressed issues relative to fathers in the Church. In April 1975, in an address titled "The Sanctity of Life," he dealt with the increasingly prevalent practice of abortion. It was a talk into which he poured his "heart and soul," knowing that because of the legalization of abortion in the United States in 1973, the members of the Church and the world in general needed to be clear on the Church's position.

In reflecting on that talk, and others in which he or other General Authorities have dealt with controversial social issues, he says, "It is not our responsibility to tell the Saints and the people of the world what they want to hear. It is our responsibility to tell them what the Lord wants them to hear. Sometimes, if all of the messages and letters concerning a talk are positive, I wonder if I have failed somewhat in my duty."

The pressure Elder Faust has felt over the years to deliver messages that would instruct, challenge, and comfort the Saints was reflected in a comment he made to Elder William Grant Bangerter, his former missionary companion, who was called as an Assistant to the Twelve in April 1975. "When I became a General Authority and was assigned to speak for the first time, he told me, 'It never gets any easier,'" Elder Bangerter recalls. "And he was absolutely right."

In addition to his unending Church responsibilities, Elder Faust was careful to nurture his relationship with Sister Faust, their children and spouses, and the grandchildren that were beginning to bless his family's lives.

What little time he had away from Church assignments was spent with his family, and the evenings and available weekends were busy with visits, dinners, telephone calls, and other activities.

He would always find common ground for discussions with his family members, whether it was discussing the law with his sons (Jim by now had established his practice and Marcus was attending law school at Brigham Young University) or reading children's books and telling scripture stories to his grandchildren. His son-in-law Doug Coombs, who had married the Fausts' oldest daughter, Janna, just before Elder Faust's call as a General Authority, tells of a visit the Fausts made to San Diego, where Doug and Janna were living while Doug completed his medical internship.

"I was just a fledgling new doctor, and I took Dad to play golf one day. Because Janna and I had moved away from Utah soon after we were married, it was one of the first times I had been with him just one-on-one. And I'll never forget that as we were getting ready to tee off, he said, 'Doug, tell me about electrolytes.' I've since learned that's a character trait of his—he likes to meet you on your own turf and wants to talk to you on the grounds you're comfortable with. So, he asked me about electrolytes, even though I'm sure he couldn't have been all that interested in them."

In an effort to simplify their lives somewhat, Elder and Sister Faust decided to sell their home in Cottonwood, which sat on a large lot that required constant upkeep, and move to a condominium closer to the Church Administration Building (and the airport). Not long after that move in early 1975, while he and Sister Faust were in New Zealand touring a mission, Elder Faust received a telephone call from President N. Eldon Tanner asking him to move yet again—this time to São Paulo, Brazil, where he would serve as the area supervisor for all of South America.

Elder Faust's reply was immediate. "That's great," he told President Tanner. "When do we go?"

NOTES

1. "To Become One of the Fishers," *Ensign*, January 1973, p. 81.

2. Conference Report, October 1972, p. 91.

7

BACK
TO BRAZIL

THE ENTHUSIASM ELDER FAUST FELT over the call that had come
to return to Brazil stemmed not only from his willingness to do
whatever he was called to do but also from his love for the
people of Brazil—and all of Latin America. He had maintained
close contact with his missionary friends from Brazil, much of
his brother Gus's professional life had been connected to Brazil,
and he had watched with keen interest the progress of the
Church in Latin America. (The Church was still growing slowly,
but certainly faster than when Elder Faust had been there some
thirty-five years before.)

There was little time to arrange for the Fausts' move to
Brazil in July 1975, and there was much to be done. Sister Faust
was recovering from surgery she had undergone just prior to
President Tanner's call, the Fausts' son Robert was just graduating from high school, and their daughter Lisa was single
(although waiting for a missionary she would later marry) and
in her second year at the University of Utah. Furthermore,
Elder Faust was going as one of the first area supervisors to live
outside the United States and so had the additional responsibility of arranging for housing and setting up an office from
which to work.

Plans and decisions were made quickly. Because of his
father's situation, Robert was able to put in his missionary
papers early, and his call came to serve in the Brazil Porto
Alegre Mission. Lisa, much to her parents' delight, decided to
move with them to Brazil, where she would continue her education through correspondence courses and help her parents in

their responsibilities. (Elder Faust has since said, "Lisa served her own mission during her eighteen months in Brazil, and she and Ruth provided the only secretarial support I had, in addition to everything else they did.") And Elder Faust traveled to Brazil almost immediately to find housing for his family and begin making arrangements to preside over a vast and varied continent.

As he looked for a home in São Paulo, he was amazed by how expensive real estate was in that city; and the real estate agent showing him around kept taking him to large and expansive houses, complete with marble entryways and staircases. As Elder Faust struggled to select something that would be comfortable for his family and a prudent use of the Church's resources, he asked the agent for advice.

"The agent," Elder Faust recalls, "recommended several homes that had two stories and staircases made of marble (which is a cheap commodity in Brazil), but as I looked at them I said to myself, 'No, that little man from Arizona, Spencer W. Kimball, is going to come down here and visit us, and he is not at all pretentious.' So I picked out a single-story house that was the cheapest of all the ones we looked at and was proximate to where the temple was to be built in São Paulo."

It didn't take long before the Fausts were ready to move; in fact, Lisa remembers that her father "was very anxious—driven, really—to get down there and get at his responsibility." As it happened, Robert's visa came through just two weeks after he had entered the Language Training Mission, and so arrangements were made for him to meet with his parents and sister at the Los Angeles International Airport where the family would head south together. (Robert recalls that he learned Portuguese in much the same way his father did: "They put me with native Brazilians in the middle of nowhere, and I just learned it.")

Although they left Salt Lake City as the summer was heating up, they arrived in Brazil in the middle of winter. Their house had no furniture—or furnace—when they arrived, and

Elder Faust tells of how they just threw mattresses on the floor and endured the cold. After a few days, a Church physical facilities representative brought them a portable heater they could use during the day, but it presented enough of a fire hazard that they couldn't use it at night.

Sister Faust and Lisa set out to buy furnishings for the house, and in short order they had made a very comfortable home out of very little. Elder Faust, in the meantime, tried to establish an office to work out of, but tried unsuccessfully for three weeks to get a telephone line installed. He met with the head of the telephone company in São Paulo to no avail, and inasmuch as he kept receiving telegrams from President Ezra Taft Benson (then president of the Quorum of the Twelve) asking for his telephone number, he finally made arrangements to travel to Brasilia and meet with the minister of communications for all of Brazil.

"He was not a lawyer or a politician," Elder Faust recalls. "He was an engineer. I told him that the Church had invested a great deal of money in South America and that we wanted to build a temple in São Paulo. I then explained that I had responsibility over all of South America, but that without the ability to communicate I might just as well go home. This man didn't make any specific promises, but he did tell me during our visit that when he was in the service during World War II, his bunkmate was a member of the Church—and a very good friend. When I got back to São Paulo later that day, the telephone company had strung a line and I finally had a phone."

Elder Faust notes that Lisa seemed to learn the language by osmosis; conversely, Sister Faust acknowledges that "although I prayed for the gift of tongues, I didn't receive it." What she was blessed with, though, was an immediate love and appreciation for the people and cultures of South America. "When Lisa and I would get lost," she says, "people wouldn't just give us directions, they would have us get in our car and then lead us to where we needed to go. I also learned the importance of a touch, as I experienced the custom of kissing the person you're greeting on each cheek. I will admit that at first I didn't know if I enjoyed that custom, but I learned to love it—and to see it as a sincere form of greeting. And I learned in many different ways that you don't have to have the latest fashions or other things we sometimes work so hard for in the United States. Many of the people in those countries make do with so little, and yet they are so giving and warm and happy."

One of the immediate—and consuming—responsibilities Elder Faust faced was finding support among the Saints of South America to build the temple in São Paulo that President Kimball had announced at an area conference in that city the previous March. Elder Faust had accompanied Presidents Kimball and Tanner on that trip and remembers the concern, even before the announcement was made, over whether the Saints would be willing and able to raise their portion of the temple's costs (this being before the Church began paying the entire cost of temples and other buildings out of general funds). "As we met with the local leaders before the announcement was made publicly and explained that they would need to raise one-third of its cost, it was evident that nobody had the vision of what it meant to sacrifice for a temple. One of the stake presidents said, 'We can raise $5,000 in our stake,' and one of the Americans in the group said, 'President, *I'm* going to give that much.' Thus, President Kimball was a little bit uncertain as to whether to proceed with the announcement. He turned to President Tanner and asked, 'Should we go forward?' and President Tanner answered, 'Yes.'"

With that, the announcement was made, and Elder Faust set out to oversee construction and work with the local leaders to raise their share of the estimated $4 million that the first temple in Central or South America would cost.

At the time, inflation was rampant throughout South America, with Brazil experiencing rates of 100 percent annually and Argentina hitting 500 percent. At the outset, the fund raising did not go well, and when President Kimball asked Elder Faust at the October 1975 general conference how the

Saints were responding, Elder Faust had to tell him they hadn't made as much progress as he had hoped. Elder Faust recalls President Kimball's saying, "You tell those folks that if they don't want a temple, we'll build it somewhere else." So Elder Faust went back and told the Saints, in a spirit of firmness coupled with faith, "'If you think someone is going to give you a temple, you're mistaken. Now, we've got to make up our minds whether or not we want a temple.' And bless their hearts, they did."

Given that so many had so little, seeing the Saints sacrifice so much during the two years they were there had a profound effect on Elder and Sister Faust.

The examples are endless as people worked two jobs to be able to contribute, as missionaries had their parents sell cars in order to help, as families skipped vacations and instead provided manual labor for the construction. Primary children saved their precious pennies to contribute, and adults displayed the attitude of one member who said, "I'll sell my car and my television set before I stop contributing to the temple."[1]

Stake and ward leaders throughout all of South America called upon their members to contribute, and the missionaries served as emissaries as well. Because of inflation, the money donated quickly decreased in value, and so the Saints responded by donating wedding rings, precious stones, and other jewelry that had greater value. Elder Faust tells of how the Saints "took literally the call of the Lord in the Doctrine and Covenants wherein he said, 'Come . . . with all your gold, and your silver, and your precious stones . . . and build a house to my name' (D&C 124:26–27)."[2]

On one such occasion, two missionaries were explaining to a man in Argentina that if he had anything to give, it would be a great help in building the temple. The man brought forth his gold dental bridge to give to the missionaries, who told him they certainly couldn't take his teeth. He responded by saying, "You can't deny me the blessings I will receive by giving this to the Lord for his temple."

Upon receiving the man's bridge and hearing the story, Elder Faust paid generously for the gold and from that day on has kept the man's contribution as a reminder of countless sacrifices the Saints made. (In President Faust's current office, it is one of three items he displays on the credenza behind his desk, the others being photographs of his wife and President Hinckley.) He also purchased two of the wedding rings that were donated, which he and Sister Faust still wear, and he has said, "Ruth and I decided, as a part of our contribution to the temple, to buy this gold bridge and the two wedding rings for many times their intrinsic value. We appreciate and highly value these objects as a remembrance of the offerings of the faithful, humble people of the Church to one of our temples."[3]

In both the planning and construction of the temple, Elder Faust knew that if the dream of a temple in São Paulo was to become a reality, all that was done had to be done in the Lord's way. Early on in the process, Elder Faust called a meeting of the local leaders to discuss what would be involved in obtaining the construction permits needed to begin the work. Emil Fetzer, who served as the Church architect at the time, tells of the meeting in which this issue was discussed: "After considerable discussion on the challenges associated with obtaining these permits, Elder Faust suggested that we go around the room and allow each of those in the meeting to express their view. As we did so, the local leaders pointed out that the permits could be obtained much more quickly if we would follow the custom of paying the local officials to move our applications through the bureaucracies—a procedure they all agreed we should follow. But when it was Elder Faust's turn to speak he said, 'Brethren, we cannot, we will not, do anything that is illegal or is not right. We absolutely won't do it.' There were some protests—some of the men pointed out that that's just how business is done in South America—but we followed Elder Faust's direction. All of the permits were obtained in a timely manner."

When the actual work commenced in March 1976, Elder Faust and others continued to feel the Lord's influence in its construction. Ross Jensen came from Salt Lake City to supervise the construction, and he and Elder Faust quickly determined that although marble was inexpensive, plentiful, and beautiful, the pollution in São Paulo would be so corrosive that the building ought to have a facade of cast stone instead. As a result, Jim Magleby was sent to Brazil from Buehner Stone in Salt Lake City to cast the stone for the temple, which, he explained in an interview, "is like a giant puzzle. We must make 3,000 panels of 400 different sizes and shapes which, after they are finished, must fit perfectly on specific places over the exterior temple walls. Our tolerance on the size of each panel is four hundredths of an inch."[4]

Brother Magleby had cast the stone for the Los Angeles and Washington, D.C., temples, but found the work in Brazil to be particularly primitive and challenging. He was sustained, however, by a dream he had years earlier in which he found himself working on a very important building where the workmen under him could not understand him and he couldn't understand them. Believing his current assignment to be a fulfillment of that dream, he set up shop in a little shack on the temple grounds and taught Brazilian laborers how to cast stone.

As the work progressed toward the spire of the temple, Brother Magleby was having difficulty figuring out how to reverse a pattern to be used on the tower. In frustration, he tried to convince himself that a minor defect where no one could see it would not make any real difference, but one night he received the inspiration he needed to correct the flaw, as well as a strong witness that this was to be the House of the Lord and that even minor flaws were unacceptable.

"Then, of course, there were cost overruns," Elder Faust adds, "and so we had to reassess the Saints. We decided that because the Saints in São Paulo were proximate to the temple, we had to increase each of the stakes' assessments from $55,000 to $78,000. When we called the four stake presidents in and explained the need, there was no complaint. As we were leaving, I said to President Benjamin Puerta, who had a small stake of about 2,200 members—half of which were Primary children—that I had been in his shoes and knew what this meant. He said, 'Don't you worry, Elder Faust. If you need $100,000, we'll raise it.' He was the first to have his money in, and he ended up serving as the second president of the São Paulo Temple."

Even before construction began on the temple, Elder Faust knew what the Saints' sacrifices would bring them. At the October 1975 general conference, some five months before the ground-breaking would occur, he spoke of walking early one morning across the temple grounds, noting the pegs in the ground that marked the dimensions and layout of the temple, and pondering both the sacrifices that were being made and the blessings that would come.

He spoke of the growth of the Church in South America, which then numbered over 152,000 members and had grown by some 8,000 converts in 1974, and compared that to his missionary days when "we held our meetings in rooms that were small and unfit for the lofty message we were trying to teach." He spoke of recalling that morning, "with eyes wet with tears, . . . being told by one of our great South American stake presidents that when he comes to general conference in Salt Lake, he and his wife will have to decide which two of their five children they will bring to be sealed to them in the Salt Lake Temple. . . . Now their plans have changed. They are planning to take all five children to the first temple in South America."

Then, in conclusion, he bore his testimony by stating, "The Spirit of God has been distilled and has rested mightily upon the countries in South America since the time of my youth when missionary work there was so difficult. How does the work of God go there now? Problems—there are many; challenges—they are great, but the progress is almost unbelievable. What I have said about South America can be said of many other parts of the whole world. This is a great worldwide Church, and so far we have only seen the beginning. Having seen what I have seen in South America, I cannot deny that this is the work of God."[5]

Although his work on the temple consumed much of his time, Elder Faust had significant responsibilities as the presiding authority over all of South America. (In the summer of 1976, his load was reduced somewhat as President A. Theodore Tuttle assumed responsibility for the western half of South America.) He traveled frequently and extensively, organizing stakes, providing leadership training, and overseeing many other aspects of the Church in South America.

The growth of the Church in Latin America was at once a blessing, as individuals and families benefited from the gospel's influence and teachings, and a challenge, as wards and stakes were formed in areas where the majority of members were recent converts and the ranks from which to draw leaders were thin. With characteristic optimism, Elder Faust proceeded from two premises, the first being that "the gospel doesn't convert strong leaders, it makes them," and the second being that the Church in South America would benefit greatly from the returned missionaries. "President Kimball asked me once how we were going to provide the leadership for all the people who were coming into the Church and I said, 'President, I couldn't sleep one night if it weren't for the returned missionaries.'"

In both cases, extensive training was called for, and Elder Faust was appreciative, yet again, of the great men he had learned from while serving as a stake president. On one occasion, he and an associate visited with a stake president who was struggling, and whose stake was struggling as well. As the two concluded their meetings and began driving back to São Paulo, Elder Faust's associate commented that he found it interesting that Elder Faust had not done more to correct the situation. Elder Faust listened to his observation and then said, simply, "I've been on the other side of that table."

In reflecting on that experience, he observes, "I just knew as I was working with this brother that I had to get him to a point where he was receptive to what I was trying to teach him, rather than getting on him about how low sacrament meeting attendance was, and so on. Of course, what I was trying to teach him was that he needed to raise the spirituality of the people in his stake, and that if he would do that, the other things would fall into place. That was something of a unique experience in that I don't ever remember when I took so long to get to the point where I felt like I was ready to deliver the message. We just listened for a good long time.

"This man was doing the best he could, he was just struggling. He had a stake full of people who were new in the Church, and he hadn't been too long in the Church himself. But he was doing his best, as was the case with all of these humble, great men in Latin America. In many cases they were unlettered and unlearned, but they had great spirits and faith. I remember calling a stake president and telling him that he would be expected to come to general conference, assuming he understood that the Church would pay his way, which was the practice at the time. Not knowing that, he thought for a moment and said, 'That's all right. I can sell my house.'"

Elder Bangerter, who took Elder Faust's place as area supervisor in 1977, tells of how providing leadership training and helping local leaders understand the nuts and bolts of organizing everything from a high council to a Relief Society "was just in his nature. These were things he knew and had done. But there is something about Elder Faust—both during his time in Brazil and since—that is most unusual. Wherever he goes, he can draw people to him in a very warm and personal way. He just has an unusual talent to get to know people, and in the short time he was in Brazil, he got to know so many of the members so personally. He could call them by their name—and by their nickname. He has a warmth and camaraderie with people that I find unusual; in fact, I'm not sure it compares with anyone else."

During their time in Brazil, the Fausts maintained close ties with their friends and associates in Salt Lake City, and hosted a number of General Authorities who came to Brazil on assignment.

Lisa remembers well sitting next to Elder Bruce R. McConkie, a more senior member of the Twelve, at a dinner for mission presidents and watching in amazement as he would look around the room and then use his spoon to flip olive pits out of the open window behind him. And Elder Faust enjoys telling of taking Elder McConkie to have his shoes shined in São Paulo and watching the look on the shoeshine boy's face as Elder McConkie put his size 15 shoes up to be polished. (Elder Faust paid the boy double for his efforts.)

Elder Perry, by then a member of the Twelve, tells of traveling to Brazil on his first assignment after marrying his second wife, Barbara Dayton Perry. "This was our honeymoon, even though we were out on assignment, and Jim and Ruth both did so many little things to help Barbara feel welcome and to get oriented to this new life. Then they did a great thing. Jim had arranged to fly us to Iguaçú Falls so that we could have a few days alone. He hadn't told us; he just handed us the tickets and told us he was taking us to the airport for a three-day honeymoon. That is characteristic of him, to do little things that you wouldn't expect people to even think of doing."

Frequently, Elder Faust heard from his friend, Elder Hinckley, who would write with news of political affairs in Utah and other events. Inevitably, Elder Hinckley would include in his letters the statement, "I miss you. I wish you were here," as he would detail troublesome issues he was having to deal with. In subsequent years, President Hinckley would say, "When Brother Faust went to Brazil, I felt a great loss in his not being here. He's a man of wisdom, a man of judgment. He knows the political environment well. He had been in the legislature and knew his way around politics. That had been very helpful to us all, and I missed him."

As Elder and Sister Faust traveled home for the October 1976 general conference, Elder Faust was informed of a major change in Church administration, as the calling of Assistant to the Twelve was being discontinued and the First Quorum of the Seventy was established in its place. In addition, Elder Faust was called to serve as a member of the Presidency of the First Quorum of Seventy, although he was not informed as to when he would return from Brazil. However, his comments seemed to suggest that his time in Brazil would soon come to an end, and the sum of his experiences over the previous fifteen months provided the framework for his remarks on the need for a personal relationship with the Savior.

In introducing his topic, Elder Faust observed:

> It has been interesting to return to this country from South America and see the billboards and signs memorializing a revolution in this country which happened two hundred years ago. In the world I think we need fewer revolutions and more revelations. In my opinion, the greatest change in South America is a spiritual revolution which is coming about as a result of the influence of this Church and of the temple now under construction in São Paulo—and that influence is all within the counsel of Paul to the Ephesians: "the perfecting of the saints, . . . the unity of the faith, and . . . the knowledge of the Son of God." (Eph. 4:12 , 13.)
>
> There is a great humility and timidity in my soul as I presume to speak about coming to a personal knowledge of Jesus Christ, the Redeemer of the world and the Son of God.
>
> Recently in South America, a seasoned group of outstanding missionaries was asked, "What is the greatest need in the world?" One wisely responded: "Is not the greatest need in all of the world for every person to have a personal, ongoing, daily, continuing relationship with the Savior?" Having such a relationship can unchain the divinity within us, and nothing can make a greater difference in our lives as we come to know and understand our divine relationship with God.[6]

He then outlined "five beginning, essential measures which will greatly clear the channel for a daily flow of 'living water' from the very source of the spring, even the Redeemer Himself: . . . a daily communion involving prayer . . . , a daily selfless service to another . . . , a daily striving for an increased obedience and perfection in our lives . . . , a daily acknowledgment of His divinity . . . , [and] a daily study of the scriptures."[7]

In conclusion, Elder Faust spoke of his own testimony of the Savior in these words:

During the years of my life, and often in my present calling, and especially during a recent Gethsemane, I have gone to my knees with a humble spirit to the only place I could for help. I often went in agony of spirit, earnestly pleading with God to sustain me in the work I have come to appreciate more than life itself. I have, on occasion, felt the terrible aloneness of the wounds of the heart, of the sweet agony, the buffetings of Satan, and the encircling warm comfort of the Spirit of the Master.

I have also felt the crushing burden, the self-doubts of inadequacy and unworthiness, the fleeting feeling of being forsaken, then of being reinforced an hundredfold. I have climbed a spiritual Mount Sinai dozens of times seeking to communicate and to receive instructions. It has been as though I have struggled up an almost real Mount of Transfiguration and upon occasion felt great strength and power in the presence of the Divine. A special sacred feeling has been a sustaining influence and often a close companion. . . .

As I come to a new calling, I recognize that I am a very ordinary man. Yet I gratefully acknowledge one special gift. I have a certain knowledge that Jesus of Nazareth is our Divine Savior. I know that He lives. From my earliest recollection I have had a sure perception of this. As long as I have lived, I have had a simple faith that has never doubted. I have not always understood, yet still I have known through a knowledge that is so sacred to me that I cannot give utterance to it.[8]

The following March, Presidents Kimball and Romney traveled to São Paulo to participate in the laying of the cornerstone for the temple. While there, President Kimball surveyed the home Elder Faust had purchased and said, "This is just right," and President Romney told him, "Jim, we need you back home."

In June 1977, his return home became official as Elder Faust received a letter from the First Presidency informing him that he was being called to serve as president of the International Mission. In this assignment, he would replace Elder William Grant Bangerter, who would in turn take Elder Faust's place as area supervisor for the eastern half of South America. The letter informed him that the change would "take effect as soon as the duties of this office can be turned over to you," and that "in this capacity, you will serve under the direction of the Missionary Executive Committee of which Elder Thomas S. Monson is chairman."

There was much that Elder and Sister Faust had given to the people of South America as they provided leadership training; as they worked to build the temple, both as manual laborers and as motivators; as they served as home and visiting teachers, in addition to the more public responsibilities they held; as they witnessed and participated in miracles that included healings and the saving of lives and souls. But as they returned to their home in Salt Lake City, they knew that, on balance, they were by far the greater beneficiaries of their stay in São Paulo. For they had learned, as had the pioneers who settled the valley they were returning to, that "faith is more important than life itself," Elder Faust explains. "And through those lessons, I found myself purged of worldly interests and concerns as I came to understand more fully the words of the Savior, 'Peace I leave with you, my peace I give unto you'" (John 14:27).

NOTES

1. *Church News,* 15 January 1977, p. 3.

2. Ibid.

3. "The Covenant People of the Lord," address given at regional representatives seminar, Salt Lake City, Utah, 3 April 1987. Unpublished manuscript.

4. *Church News,* 15 January 1977, p. 10.

5. "The Keys of the Kingdom," *Ensign,* November 1975, p. 57.

6. "A Personal Relationship with the Savior," *Ensign,* November 1976, p. 58.

7. Ibid.

8. Ibid., p. 59.

8

AN INTERNATIONAL MISSION

The International Mission, over which Elder Faust presided as he served in the First Council of the Seventy, was established in 1972 and included those parts of the world where there were no organized stakes or missions. Almost all of the African continent was included, together with the vast countries of Egypt, India, the Soviet Union, and China. In addition, there were many smaller, scattered countries, such as Israel and Greece. Branches of the Church existed in a few of these countries; in most of the areas, however, there was no formal Church organization. For the few members there were, often their only contact with the Church was through Elder Faust and his two counselors, Edwin Q. Cannon and Keith Garner.

"Our responsibility," Elder Faust says of the duties he assumed in the summer of 1977, "was to tend to these members' needs. We were the focal point of the correspondence that would come from members and nonmembers in these countries, and they would also pay their tithing through us. I never heard much from many of these people, but every single month I would get a tithing check from them. It was very humbling to see the devotion and faith of these Saints spread all over the world."

Elder and Sister Faust traveled frequently and extensively, often enduring primitive conditions in developing countries in order to meet with individual members or small groups of Saints. "Sister Faust was a trooper," Elder Faust recalls. "We would have to stay up all night in airports to catch planes, and often the airline schedules were totally irregular."

Among the many trips they made together, Sister Faust remembers well the trips she made with Elder Faust into Eastern Europe and East Berlin, where they were struck by undersupplied markets that stocked only withered apples, cola drinks, and liquor. "It was amazing to me," she says, "how the Saints in these countries hung together. These were people who lived in constant fear, who were under suspicion, who lived in cities where it appeared as if the people just didn't care. Yet when we would hold a meeting with the Saints, the sisters would put a white tablecloth and a picture of wildflowers on the table to make the room look nice. These were often drab buildings, but when the opening prayer was offered, the Spirit would fill the rooms in abundance."

Elder Faust held the first conferences of the Church in several of these countries, and he called several couples who sacrificed to serve as special representatives in such countries as Hungary, Greece, and Poland. One couple he called to go to Warsaw, Poland, was Brother and Sister Teofilo Rebiki, whom he knew from Curitiba, Brazil, a region with a strong European influence. When the Fausts visited Brother and Sister Rebiki during the beginning of a cold Polish winter, Elder Faust found that Brother Rebiki, who had sold his home to raise the money needed to serve in Poland, did not have an overcoat or other clothes that would keep him warm during the winter. His attempt to give Brother Rebiki his own coat failed, and so upon returning to Salt Lake, Elder Faust had the Rebikis transferred to warm Portugal for the winter.

The Fausts also traveled to Egypt, Israel, and Africa, areas with which Elder Faust was acquainted from his time in the military more than thirty years earlier. In Israel, Elder Faust became acquainted with a number of members of the Church living in the Holy Land, including David Galbraith, president of the Jerusalem District of the Church and director of Brigham Young University's study abroad program in Jerusalem.

BYU had first started sending groups to the Holy Land in 1968; and in 1972, thirty-eight students, accompanied by two faculty members, spent six months studying in Iraq, Egypt, Lebanon, Jordan, and then Jerusalem. Their arrival in Jerusalem required a shift from housing small groups in local homes to renting space in the City Hotel. As the groups came regularly and as they grew in size, Brother Galbraith (who became the full-time director of the Jerusalem Center in 1973) and his associates regularly had to find larger facilities to house the groups that came, moving from homes to hotels to larger kibbutzes in the process.[1]

Brother Galbraith recalls that "our group in Jerusalem was one of those little pockets of Saints that Elder Faust blessed. There were several such pockets in the Middle East, and although we were few in number, that's what the International Mission was geared to work with—just handfuls of people, whether they were in Africa or wherever."

He also adds that when Elder Faust visited this small branch in September 1977, its leaders, who also headed up BYU's study abroad center, were in the early stages of discussing with the university the possibility of building a permanent center that would be able to house the students and faculty who were studying in the Holy Land—a project with which Elder Faust would soon become intimately involved.

As Elder Faust approached his assignment to watch over a few scattered Saints in Africa, he was faced with a challenging situation created by the fact that the Church, at the time, did not ordain men of African descent to the priesthood. As a result, the Church's only official presence was in South Africa, where a mission had been established in the mid-1850s. Even there, the work had been slow (there were no missionaries in South Africa from 1865 until 1903 and again from 1915 to 1921), although by 1970 there were over 6,000 members of the Church in South Africa, and on March 22, 1970, the first stake had been organized.[2]

The rest of this vast continent's roughly 600 million inhabitants were under Elder Faust's stewardship, although only a handful knew anything of the Church. Those who did, however, had a rather unique relationship with the Church.

In 1958, a Nigerian named Honesty John Ekong wrote to Church headquarters asking for information on the Church's beliefs. His request was answered by LaMar S. Williams of the Church's Missionary Department, who corresponded for a time with Mr. Ekong and then with other individuals in Nigeria who had an interest in the Church. The result was that when Elder N. Eldon Tanner visited Nigeria in 1962, he found four groups who identified themselves with The Church of Jesus Christ of Latter-day Saints, although none had been baptized. Elder Tanner later said:

> I found they were holding services under our name and seemed to be sincere and knowledgeable about the teachings of the Church.
>
> When speaking with the leader of the largest group, he said he had about 4,000 members in his congregation. He said they were baptized members. I explained that the priesthood was necessary in order to baptize. He said he understood that, but he wanted his people to know they were members of a church.
>
> The leader realized black African men couldn't hold the priesthood until [a prophet] said they could. He said he knew someday, however, they would be allowed to hold the priesthood, and they were trying to live worthy of that privilege.[3]

In a somewhat similar manner, the Church had unofficially taken root in Ghana, where a chapel bore the name of the Church and 456 individuals had been baptized into this group by 1978.[4]

In addition to traveling through parts of Africa, Elder Faust made and maintained contact with Church members who had dealings in Africa. He learned all that he could from these associates, hoping the day would come when the Church could move into these countries. He also received frequent letters from individuals and groups in Africa, pleading that missionaries be sent and that authority be given to enable those who had already been converted to the gospel to become members of the Church.

In the early months of 1978, Elder Faust and his two

counselors in the International Mission presidency were scheduled to meet with the First Presidency and discuss the Church's involvement in Africa. Elder Faust took a stack of letters he had received from Nigeria and Ghana, and on the top of the stack he put a letter from a young boy who had written that his greatest hope was to one day sit in the Salt Lake Tabernacle and there hear the Lord's prophets speak. "I explained to President Kimball and Presidents Tanner and Romney that these were the letters we had received just that month," Elder Faust recalls, "and President Kimball said he would like me to read one. I picked the one from this little boy, and as I read it, I saw a tear trickle down President Romney's cheek. I knew then that we probably could look forward to going into Africa with authority."

In addition to the issues affecting the Church's entrance into Africa, Elder Faust knew that as the São Paulo Temple neared completion, the Church faced similar issues in Brazil, where persons of African descent and intermarriage were prevalent.

During his time in Brazil as area supervisor, Elder Faust had often had to deal with worthy Church members who desired both priesthood and temple blessings but who were not able to receive them. On one occasion, a young man of African descent came to Elder Faust and told him of his desire to serve a mission. After careful thought Elder Faust concluded to call this young man to serve as a temple construction missionary. The young man gratefully accepted the calling, despite knowing he might never be able to enter the temple after its dedication, and Elder Faust remembers well his faithful response: "He told me during our interview that those who had Negro blood could do things more fully and completely than others. When I asked him what he meant by that, he said, 'We can pay more tithing. We can pay a more generous fast offering. We can be totally faithful in attending sacrament meetings and Sunday School. It is our privilege to do that.' And there were many others who had like faith and who worked on the temple with great love and affection, even though it appeared to them that they would not be able to receive the blessings of the temple themselves."

As President Kimball, together with his associates, "witnessed the expansion of the work of the Lord over the earth" (D&C Official Declaration—2) and sought to fulfill the divine injunction to take the gospel to "all nations, kindreds, tongues and people" (D&C 42:58), he wrestled at length with the doctrine restricting those of African descent from receiving the priesthood. By his own account, he spent many hours in the Salt Lake Temple pleading with the Lord on this issue, and he also consulted with his counselors and the Quorum of the Twelve.[5] In addition, he sought for Elder Faust's thoughts on more than one occasion. Finally, in early June 1978, a revelation was given granting the priesthood to "all worthy male members of the Church . . . without regard for race or color" (D&C Official Declaration—2).

Elder Faust recalls that meeting on June 8:

> All of the General Authorities were summoned to the upper room of the temple for a special meeting. . . . On the way over to the meeting, I was walking with one of my fellow presidents of the First Quorum of the Seventy, because at that time I was not a member of the Twelve. My beloved associate asked me if I thought the meeting pertained to a particular current problem, and I indicated that I thought not, without making any further explanation. In my heart, however, I had the hope that such a revelation as did come might be announced. No one had indicated that such might be forthcoming; my feelings came only from the broodings of the Spirit.[6]

The announcement made possible the opening of missionary work in Africa, but Elder Faust, together with the First Presidency and the Twelve, knew that in the opportunity there would also be challenges. His experiences in Brazil, first as a young missionary when the Church's rate of growth was almost imperceptible and then as a General Authority when the pace of the work was accelerating rapidly, provided Elder Faust with much-needed perspective as he and others contemplated how to introduce missionary work into Africa. He knew that it would be possible to baptize whole villages and tribes, if the Church had a mind to do so. But he had also seen the challenges associated with rapid growth in South America and felt it best to bring converts into the Church one by one—and at a pace the Church could manage—so that the enthusiastic new converts could make the transition to becoming committed, active members.

With characteristic caution and careful thought, he supported a course of action that would first send two seasoned Church leaders—Edwin Q. Cannon and Merrill J. Bateman (the latter of whom had lived and worked in Africa as a student and as a businessman)—on an exploratory visit to Ghana and Nigeria, where they were to learn what they could about the unofficial "branches" that sought an association with the Church, members scattered throughout the two countries, and the political and social climates missionaries would encounter.

On Wednesday, September 27, 1978, Elder Faust placed a telephone call to a longtime friend and legal associate, Rendell N. Mabey, asking that Ren and his wife, Rachel, meet with him that afternoon.

When the Mabeys arrived for their 3:30 appointment, they found that the meeting also included Brother Cannon and David M. Kennedy, special ambassador for the First Presidency. After some brief small talk about the growth of the Church, Elder Faust informed the Mabeys that the Brethren had concluded that the first missionaries to enter Africa should be seasoned couples with leadership experience in foreign countries and that he would like the Mabeys to consider the possibility of serving as unofficial missionaries in West Africa for a one-year period.

Although the Mabeys were ready to accept the assignment on the spot, Elder Faust asked that they take time to talk and pray together about this proposition and to then let him know of their decision.[7]

As Elder Faust concluded the last meeting of the day, he no

doubt knew the import of helping make the arrangements that would send the first Latter-day Saint missionaries to countries populated by more than half a billion inhabitants—many of whom had been praying for years that the fulness of the gospel would be sent to them. What he did not know was that extending this calling would bring to a close his service as a member of the Presidency of the First Quorum of Seventy.

NOTES

1. See Steven W. Baldridge, *Grafting In: A History of the Latter-day Saints in the Holy Land* (Jerusalem: Jerusalem Branch, 1989), pp. 14–15.

2. James R. Moss, R. Lanier Britsch, et al., "The International Church," Brigham Young University, Provo, Utah, 1982, pp. 236–39. Unpublished manuscript.

3. Ibid., pp. 243–44.

4. Ibid., pp. 244–45.

5. Edward L. Kimball, ed., *The Teachings of Spencer W. Kimball* (Salt Lake City: Bookcraft, 1982), pp. 450–51.

6. Remarks delivered at the Sidney B. Sperry Symposium on the Scriptures, Brigham Young University, Provo, Utah, 28 January 1984. Unpublished manuscript.

7. See Rendell N. Mabey and Gordon T. Allred, *Brother to Brother* (Salt Lake City: Bookcraft, 1984), pp. 8–13.

9

THE HOLY
APOSTLESHIP

WHEN ELDER DELBERT L. STAPLEY died August 19, 1978, at the age of 81, Elder Faust lost a friend with whom he had shared "a close affinity and relationship." The two men, in addition to their frequent associations as General Authorities, had occasionally played golf together, along with President Tanner and Elder Franklin D. Richards. Elder Faust adds, "I loved him and appreciated him, and have nothing but the closest feeling for him."

The ensuing days between mid-August and the October general conference brought some "strange forebodings" to Elder Faust's mind, but he of course kept those private, even as several close associates indicated their sense that he might be called to fill the vacancy in the Twelve.

Then just before three o'clock on Thursday, September 28, after having spent the morning and early afternoon attending meetings of the General Authorities in the Salt Lake Temple, he received a telephone call from D. Arthur Haycock, personal secretary to President Kimball. "Jim," Brother Haycock said in a joking tone, "I want you to come down and tell me how to vote" (a reference to the upcoming state and national elections).

Elder Faust recorded the events that followed in his journal:

> I immediately went down and was ushered into the office of President Kimball. The President and I were alone, and I reported a matter in the International Mission. Then he advised me that I was being called to become an Apostle and a member of the Quorum of the Twelve, and that the Brethren of the First Presidency and the Quorum of the Twelve had just approved it.

He indicated his great love and affections for my beloved Ruth, and said that she would make a welcome addition to the society of the First Presidency and the Twelve and their wives, and advised me that I could tell her and no one else.

President Kimball also indicated that he understood how I felt, for I was of course moved to tears as I indicated I would be pleased to accept, but asked how I could ever fill such a calling. He showed great compassion and love, and indicated that I could come back down and see him, if I wished. He embraced me and kissed me on the cheek, and we parted.

Elder Faust had but a moment to ponder the weight and significance of the calling he had just received; he then quickly returned to his office, where he was scheduled to conduct a meeting of the executive committee of the *Deseret News* board. Elder Thomas S. Monson was the first to arrive for the meeting at 3:30, and as he came in he asked his longtime friend if he had seen President Kimball. "I indicated I had," Elder Faust records. "Elder Monson then embraced me and told me how much he loved me and appreciated me, and how happy he was for me to come into the Quorum. We delayed the start of the meeting as he, in all of the love and kindness of a brother, counseled me to just be myself and for Ruth to just be herself."

As that meeting continued, Elder Faust excused himself and called another close friend, Elder Gordon B. Hinckley, to let him know he would have to miss a meeting of the Special Affairs Committee which Elder Hinckley chaired. "Brother Hinckley expressed his love and appreciation, and was most kind and gracious," Elder Faust writes.

As he concluded that call, Elder Faust received a call from President Kimball who, among other things, asked if Elder Faust had called his wife. When Elder Faust told him he had not yet had a minute to do so, President Kimball said, "I think you better call her now." Elder Faust records:

I went into Elder A. Theodore Tuttle's office because the *Deseret News* meeting was being held in my office, and I called Ruth. She asked if it were I who had just called, and I said no, that I thought it was the President of the Church. She had just awakened from a short nap. I advised her that I knew who the wife of the new Apostle was. She understood perfectly well and indicated her support and love and confidence, which I so desperately need.

Soon after, Elder Faust was able to conclude his business for the day and return home to be with his wife and attempt to gather his thoughts. That evening Elder Howard W. Hunter called and informed his friend that none had held his hand higher to sustain the new member of the Twelve than had he.

Elder Faust concluded his recorded thoughts for Thursday, September 27, by writing: "It is impossible to adequately express the feelings of unworthiness and inadequacy that such a call brings. I could not serve, but for the absolute conviction which I have concerning the Savior and His work upon the earth."

When Friday morning finally came after a long and largely sleepless night, Elder Faust went about his assigned duties and attended a meeting for the regional representatives. As he sat in the congregation and looked up at the members of the Twelve seated on the stand, he received several knowing looks and smiles of encouragement. After that meeting, he met briefly with President Ezra Taft Benson, president of the Twelve, and "advised him that I would continue to sustain him and would continue to accept every assignment that he gave me. He expressed his appreciation and love, for which I was grateful."

During the afternoon, he received visits from Elder Bruce R. McConkie and from Elder L. Tom Perry, who had been assigned as Elder Faust's teacher and mentor as he came into the Twelve. His last visitor of the day was Elder Boyd K. Packer, who "recalled the sweet agony of the day that he was called." He also reminded Elder Faust of a conversation they had had five years earlier as they returned home on the same airplane from conferences in California. At the time, Elder Packer had shared his impression that Elder Faust would, at some point, serve in the Twelve.

As Elder Faust walked out to his car to return home for the

evening, he encountered Presidents Kimball and Romney. "President Kimball was very warm and affectionate," Elder Faust recalls, "and asked how Ruth was receiving the news. I advised him that she felt weak and quite overcome. Then I asked him if it would become easier after I was sustained, and he said yes. I asked him if that were a promise, and he said yes."

That evening the Faust home was filled with children, in-laws, and grandchildren—some of whom suspected what was transpiring and others who did not seem to be aware—and Elder Faust did his best to enjoy the evening. Then he went for a swim in their condominium's pool and sat in the whirlpool to relax, after which he went to bed and endured yet another sleepless night.

The next morning at ten o'clock, the 148th Semiannual General Conference of The Church of Jesus Christ of Latter-day Saints was convened. As Elder Faust walked into the Tabernacle and took his seat with the seven presidents of the Quorum of the Seventy, it appeared to some who knew him that he looked "absolutely ashen." One associate later commented, "I could see that you had wrestled long and agonizingly about something," and another close friend quipped, "I wondered if we were going to need to give you artificial respiration."

Gratefully, President Kimball, in opening the conference, immediately put forth the name of James Esdras Faust to fill the vacancy in the Twelve. President Kimball then proposed the name of William Grant Bangerter to take Elder Faust's place as a president of the Quorum of the Seventy, along with Elders F. Burton Howard, Teddy E. Brewerton, and Jack H Goaslind Jr. to serve in the First Quorum of the Seventy. When the vote was unanimous in the affirmative, Elder Faust did find a measure of relief, as President Kimball had promised.

After having lunch with Sister Faust, three of their children and their spouses, and the Fausts' longtime friends, Newell and Fran Stevenson, Elder Faust returned for the Saturday afternoon session of conference, where he was scheduled to speak. The business of the conference was conducted, including the sustaining of Doctrine and Covenants—Declaration 2, the revelation on the priesthood, after which Elder Gordon B. Hinckley was the first speaker. Elder Faust followed, responding to his call in these few words:

> No one has ever come to this calling with a greater sense of inadequacy than I do at this time. In the sweet agony of the pondering, in the long hours of the days and nights since last Thursday, I have had the feeling of being completely unworthy and unprepared.
>
> I understand that a chief requirement for the holy apostleship is to be a personal witness of Jesus as the Christ and the Divine Redeemer. Perhaps on that basis alone, I can qualify. This truth has been made known to me by the unspeakable peace and power of the Spirit of God.
>
> I acknowledge the soothing and sustaining love of my beloved Ruth, who is as much a part of me as my heart and soul. I wish to express my deep love and affection for each member of our family.
>
> I first learned the names of the ancient and modern apostles in Primary. My mother was one of my teachers. I am certain that never in her wildest dreams did she ever think that any of those whom she taught would one day sit in the council of the special witnesses of the Lord Jesus Christ.
>
> I was born with partial color-blindness. I have learned to love all of the people in the countries where I have been as a missionary, soldier, or General Authority, regardless of the color of their skins. I hope to be a disciple after the manner and example of President Kimball and the others in their love for all, and especially for the humble, the downtrodden, the poor, the afflicted, the needy, and the poor in spirit. I am mindful that if we forget these, we can in no way be his disciples.

He expressed his gratitude for the First Presidency, his new associates in the Twelve, those with whom he had served in the Seventy, Elder Stapley, and the other General Authorities; and he then concluded his brief remarks by pledging "to God and his prophet, President Kimball, my life and whatever energy and little ability I may have, fully and completely and without reservation, for I know that Jesus is the Christ, the Son of God."[1]

Even with the public announcement of his call and the sustaining vote he had received, Elder Faust continued to carry deeply personal thoughts and understandable feelings of inadequacy that would continue for days, weeks, and even months. As he walked out of the Tabernacle that day, he confided to his friend, David M. Kennedy, something of what was in his heart as he said, "David, there must be ten thousand men in this Church more able and qualified to serve in the Council of the Twelve than I am." Brother Kennedy's response brought a smile to Elder Faust's somber face as he declared, "No—fifteen thousand."[2]

After the Saturday afternoon session of conference, Elder Faust arranged for his family to meet together in an upper room of the Salt Lake Temple, where he shared something of his feelings and testimony and the family had an opportunity to discuss this monumental change in Elder and Sister Faust's lives. During their time together, Elder Faust shared with his family what he had said when he was called as a General Authority six years earlier, that he could only succeed as a member of the Twelve if he first succeeded as a husband and a father. Then he committed to his family that he would do everything in his power to honor the responsibilities he had so gladly accepted.

The activities of General Conference continued on Sunday, and at the conclusion of the afternoon session, Elder and Sister Faust were taken to the temple, where he was instructed in his duties, ordained an apostle, and set apart as a member of the Council of the Twelve. At the conclusion of the meeting, he was told by members of the Twelve that this was the first time that the wife of a member of the Twelve had been present for her husband's ordination. Knowing his dependence on his sweetheart of over three decades, Elder Faust uttered a silent prayer of gratitude for her presence.

The First Presidency and the Twelve then went across the

street to the Relief Society Building, where they posed for photographs of the two presiding quorums of the Church. After a time, the First Presidency excused themselves, while the members of the Twelve continued to be photographed as a quorum. "There was a special friendship and camaraderie," Elder Faust recalls, "as well as some friendly kidding and joking, particularly toward me. I was not in the right place at one point, and Brother Packer said, 'Jim has just been a member of the Quorum a very short time and he is already out of line.'" He then adds, "The great kindness and solicitude of all of the members of the Council of the Twelve toward me has been a very great teaching lesson. They were most solicitous, and most thoughtful, and most kind. It was a most significant day in my life."

Elder Faust acknowledges that it would be nice if those called to the apostleship had time "to go out into the desert, as it were," but when Monday morning came he was awake at 5:00 and in his office at 6:45. Noticing that Elder Marvin J. Ashton's light was on, he stopped by for a brief visit and then began a very full day that included countless telephone calls from friends, interviews with the media, and meetings. Toward the end of the morning, he was honored to be called into Elder McConkie's office, where he heard a report from Saul Mesias de Oliveria, who had recently returned from serving as president of the Brazil São Paulo Mission, and who was to be set apart as a regional representative. When Elder McConkie invited Elder Faust to set Brother de Oliveria apart in Portuguese, he was pleased to do so.

Elder Faust spent the early afternoon meeting with Elder Perry, who counseled him regarding meetings, routines, and procedures of the First Presidency and the Twelve. Then he turned his attention to the responsibilities he still carried as president of the International Mission, calling Edwin Q. and Janath Cannon to serve as a missionary couple in Nigeria and Ghana. As a fitting conclusion to his first full day as a member of the Twelve, Elder and Sister Faust met with their family for family home evening.

The next morning, Elder Faust joined with the First Presidency as they called Rendell N. and Rachel Mabey to serve a mission to Africa and as they instructed the Mabeys and the Cannons concerning the work they would be performing. Joining in the calling of the Mabeys culminated a historic occasion Elder Faust had set in motion just prior to his own call. In the process, he reflected on the privilege it had been to see the beginnings of the Lord's work on two vast continents, and he has since said, referring to the time he spent as president of the International Mission (a calling he would hold until the following January), "The blessing for me was having my own faith built and strengthened by the humble, faithful Saints all over the world who were trying to live the gospel, keep the commandments, pay their tithing, and be an example."

The first days of Elder Faust's ministry as a member of the Quorum of the Twelve had at once the effect of expanding his view of the work in which he was engaged and of reinforcing an already refined sense of spirituality and humility. Comparing his call to the Twelve with the many other presiding offices he had held, Elder Faust says, "The differences, in part, are a matter of scope. When you become a member of the Twelve, you're no longer an area supervisor for South America, as I had been as a Seventy. Members of the Twelve are, of course, Apostles to the entire world, and so there is an enlargement of your vision as you move from one quorum to another."

Of the refining effect of the calling, he explained to a reporter the day after his call, "From a personal standpoint, it's a very devastating experience. Yet at the same time, there's a sublime, comforting feeling, a healing feeling that comes." He also noted, "I don't think my feelings can be explained. I don't think anybody who has not experienced it can really have an understanding."[3] (In the ensuing years, he has continued to be circumspect about the private and deeply spiritual nature of his experience, explaining simply, "There are just some things that are too sacred to share.")

Even as an acknowledged physical and spiritual pain continued for days and even weeks after his call, Elder Faust began adjusting to a new calling and responsibilities that he likens to "walking into a much larger room."

He immediately began receiving hundreds of telephone calls and letters from all over the world, as family, friends, and well-wishers extended their greetings and congratulations. Some came from close associates, including Elder Neal A. Maxwell (who would follow Elder Faust into the Twelve three years later), who wrote, "I felt [as we served as regional representatives] that I was in the presence of someone special. Time has only confirmed that for me. You will fly with a different flock now, but as you take wing know that you go with my full love, support, and, most important, my witness and trust as to your divine placement in the Twelve now at this point in history."

Others came from individuals not as well acquainted with Elder Faust, but who had been touched by his special blend of kindness and familiarity. A Church operator wrote, recalling times they had visited, "I remember you always called me 'Deona' instead of 'Sister Black' as everyone else did, which pleased me."

A letter he particularly treasured came from his beloved aunt, Angie Finlinson Lyman, who had been an integral part of his youth, and who, he says, stepped in when his mother died and continued to mother him. In part, she wrote, "I feel it is a great honor to our family and have wondered who is the most pleased, the relatives on this side or our loved ones on the other side. I'm sure your mother and father and Faust grandparents are very happy about it, and I am sure Grandmother and Grandfather Finlinson are very happy about it. I don't know if any of them have buttons to burst off. Maybe they just use zippers." Then she adds, "I feel very humble and feel the best way to support you is to live the best I know how, and I'm going to suggest that the other members of the family do so."

As he took on the increased demands placed on those called to the Twelve, Elder Faust continued an effort he began when called as a General Authority to eliminate anything from his life that was not central to one or the other of his two priorities—his divine trust as a member of the Twelve and his sacred responsibility as patriarch of his family, which by now included, in addition to his five children, four "children-in-love" (as the Fausts have always called their sons- and daughters-in-law) and eight grandchildren. He also immediately found himself faced with an unrelenting calendar filled with meetings, appointments, and travel, all of which he approached with genuine humility and unflagging devotion as he set out to fulfill each assignment he was given and each challenge he faced.

His first meeting with the full Quorum of the Twelve came the Thursday after his ordination, as he joined in the weekly meeting held in the Salt Lake Temple. He continued to be overwhelmed by the kindness and courtesies afforded him by each member of the First Presidency and the Twelve, noting Elder Hunter's thoughtfulness at inviting him to walk over together and President Benson's graciousness in welcoming him and encouraging him to participate fully. Elder Faust was invited by the First Presidency to respond to his call, which he did by alluding to a theme that would help define his approach through the ensuing years as he joined with his Brethren in administering the Lord's work upon the earth. "I recalled the statement of Solomon who, when he was called as Israel's king, said, 'I am but a little child: I know not how to go out or come in' (1 Kings 3:7). I indicated that I had a like dependency upon the Lord and that I requested and hoped for the blessing of Solomon—a wise and an understanding heart."

The next morning, Elder Faust met with the First Presidency, as well as David M. Kennedy and Wilford W. Kirton (the Church's legal counsel), "regarding the challenge of bringing new resources of the Church together for the full correlation of international efforts. It is intended that the Church concentrate its resources for increased recognition and fulfilling the scriptural assignments to go into all of the world." During this meeting, President Kimball informed Elder Faust that the First Presidency was forming the Foreign Affairs Committee, upon which two members of the Twelve would serve (along with others)—Gordon B. Hinckley and James E. Faust. "Over my protestations," he recorded in his journal, "I was advised that I would become the chairman of this committee."

After having lunch with Sister Faust and several other family members, Elder Faust headed for the airport, where he learned that one leg of his flight to Cleveland (where he was to reorganize a stake presidency) had been canceled, that he was being rerouted through Chicago, but that he would be on standby for the flight from Chicago to Cleveland. He noted later, with his usual optimistic outlook, "I had no difficulty, however, and arrived in Cleveland shortly before 1:00 in the morning."

The next day, after deciding upon the new stake president and inviting him and his wife to come at 5:30 P.M. for an interview, Elder Faust was able to travel to Kirtland, Ohio, where his forbear, Bishop Edward Partridge, had lived and served with the Prophet Joseph. While there, Elder Faust and his hosts visited the Whitney store, where Joseph Smith and his family had lived for a time and where the School of the Prophets had been held, and also the Kirtland Temple.

After returning from his conference assignment in Cleveland, Elder Faust received a letter characteristic of the many he would receive over the years, as his testimony touched the souls of Saints the world over. A young convert of six years wrote, "I personally began to understand a little more the specialness of [the apostolic calling] as you bore your testimony of Jesus Christ, the Son of God. I'm sure I've heard others speak words similar to the ones you spoke, but for some reason they struck my very soul with a clarity I never before had felt. The gospel has become much clearer to me since that day because of your special witness of our Lord. . . . Why it has taken me six years to reach an understanding that seems [so] simple I'll never know. But your witness as an Apostle of the Lord Jesus Christ prompted an understanding of the Son of God I've never had before, and I thank you most sincerely for it."

Although humbled by such an expression, Elder Faust was more comfortable receiving such a compliment than the public and media attention that followed his call. The Monday after his conference in Cleveland, Elder and Sister Faust responded to yet another request for a newspaper interview. He noted afterwards, "Ruth and I are embarrassed with the publicity and wish it weren't required." But because it was, he responded graciously and cooperated in every way that he could.

The next Sunday found Elder Faust, accompanied by his wife, presiding at a stake conference in Payson, Utah, after which the Fausts drove back to Salt Lake City and attended a sacrament meeting and missionary homecoming for one of President Tanner's grandsons. Then it was off to yet another homecoming, and then an evening with family members. Such was the typical pattern for those Sundays when Elder Faust either did not have an assignment or could get home in time to be with family and friends.

With his call to the Twelve also came increased requests for Elder Faust to meet with individuals and provide counsel and blessings. There were, of course, more requests than he could possibly fulfill, and in those instances when he did agree to help, he made sure that the requests came through proper channels. His compassion was evident when, just days after his call, he met with the paraplegic son of a former associate and "felt that the Lord had a special blessing for such a valiant young man."

His wisdom, likewise, was evident that same day as he met with a family whose parents had filed for divorce. After counseling with the husband and wife, together and individually, he called the children in and "told them that their parents were having a difficult time, that both parents loved them and that they should love both parents." He also indicated to the children "that neither parent was totally at fault, neither one was totally free from blame, that the children should try to be part of the solution and not part of the problem, and not undertake to judge either one of their parents, but simply to love them both."

In the midst of all the demands placed upon him in those early weeks, Elder Faust moved into the office formerly occupied by Elder Stapley (and next to that of David M. Kennedy) and directed those who were redecorating to make sure their work was appropriate. "I have been telling them," he recorded, "that I want it pleasant and warm, but simple in taste—and to have the feeling that here is where a humble disciple works."

As his first month as a member of the Quorum of the Twelve drew to a close, Elder Faust was honored to accompany President Kimball and other General Authorities to the first of many temple dedications he would attend during his years in the Twelve. Although each would be important in its own right, this one had a particular significance that he contemplated as he and Sister Faust boarded an airplane in Salt Lake City and flew back to their former home—São Paulo, Brazil.

As the group of General Authorities and their wives attempted to make the various airline connections that would get them to São Paulo just hours before the dedicatory services were to begin, they encountered a delay in Porto Alegre, Brazil, that took some time to resolve. While the group waited with anticipation and concern, Elder Faust watched as President Kimball patiently took time to visit with a young man who had approached him, rather than allowing himself to be distracted by the disruption in the group's travel plans. As Elder Faust translated for President Kimball, he learned that this young man, who was employed at the airport, was a less active Church member who had married a woman of another faith.

Upon hearing of his circumstances, "President Kimball spent a full ten minutes with him, encouraging him, loving him, and counseling him. In the process of that ten minutes, President Kimball embraced him three or four times and kissed him to let him know of his love. The young man was touched."

In like manner, when Elder Faust and the others arrived in São Paulo, with little time to spare before the first temple dedicatory session, Elder Faust was importuned by a local stake president to first come with him to a local hospital where a fifteen-year-old boy was unconscious and suffering from a serious accident. Although concerned about the time, Elder Faust sensed the need to administer to this boy, who, when they arrived at the hospital, was being hooked up to life support equipment. After a blessing was given, Elder Faust proceeded to the temple.

The dedicatory services for the São Paulo Temple took place over four days—October 30 through November 2. On the morning of the fourth day, as Elder and Sister Faust were enjoying breakfast with President and Sister Kimball and some of the Fausts' old Brazilian friends, President Kimball received a telephone call from Elder Boyd K. Packer, who was also in São Paulo for the dedication (along with Elder Hinckley). "After breakfast," Elder Faust recalls, "President Kimball invited me into his bedroom and advised me that he wanted me to conduct the dedicatory session that afternoon, and advised that I should contact Arthur Haycock for the program. He said that Elder Packer had called and indicated that since President Kimball might wish to conduct the last session, there would be only one left for one of the Twelve to conduct, and that I should conduct it because these were my people. I thought it was a very generous act."

Elder Faust spent the lunch hour "trying to familiarize myself with the way a dedicatory session should be conducted. Both Ruth and I were thrilled and excited. She reminded me that with my conducting a session, my involvement in the temple had come full circle, because I had conducted the ground-breaking ceremony, as well as the cornerstone-laying ceremony."

It was an emotional experience for both Elder and Sister Faust, as they watched the eyes of all present fill with tears as the congregation sang "The Spirit of God" and as they listened to President Kimball once again offer the dedicatory prayer.

In his modesty, Elder Faust acknowledged afterwards the "mistake" he made of recognizing that President Kimball was seated on the stand but not indicating that he was presiding at the session. Then he pointed to the abilities of Elder Packer, "who has done a heroic work in the fact that in all of his talks he has spoken in Spanish. Considering the fact that he has never lived in one of these countries, he does remarkably well!"

In addition to the dedicatory sessions, President Kimball presided at a meeting for some 1,200 missionaries, 70 percent of whom were Brazilian. Then on Saturday and Sunday, a regional conference was held at the Iberapuera Stadium, a huge complex owned by the State of São Paulo that seats 20,000 people. The regional conference in São Paulo was the last of five that President Kimball presided over on what was for him a 24,000-mile trip that took him from Salt Lake to Washington, D.C., England, South Africa, Uruguay, Argentina, and finally Brazil. Elder and Sister Faust accompanied President Kimball and those traveling with him to each of the regional conferences in South America.

Two general sessions of the conference were held during the day on Saturday, with a meeting for all women and a priesthood meeting scheduled for the evening. When the women's meeting ended at 7:00 P.M., it was raining so hard that President Kimball couldn't bear the thought of sending the women out into the deluge to wait for their husbands and fathers, so he invited them to stay for the 7:30 priesthood meeting as well.

Showing a similar sensitivity, as Elder Faust listened to the first several speakers in the Sunday morning session, he noticed that each was taking less than his allotted time. He also considered that his former mission companion and the newly called president of the São Paulo Temple, Finn Paulson, had not had an opportunity to speak during the six sessions of the regional conference. "It occurred to me that it would be well if we had time to hear from him," Elder Faust recalls, so he passed the suggestion to Brother Haycock, who cleared the idea with President Kimball and let the other General Authorities know. Elder Faust then turned around and held up five fingers to alert President Paulson, and moments later, Elder Packer did the same. President Paulson finally realized that he was going to be called upon, and when the time came, Elder Faust notes, "He did exceptionally well, and it was something of a special talk."

In the afternoon session, the agenda called for Elder Faust to speak just prior to President Kimball, who would be the concluding speaker. As the time approached for Elder Faust's remarks, he leaned over and told President Kimball that he would leave plenty of time for him, to which President Kimball replied that he only wanted ten minutes. "I told him that I would be sure he had more," Elder Faust recalls, "and his response was, 'If you don't take enough time, I'll call on you again.'"

Using the Portuguese he had learned as a missionary and polished as an area authority, Elder Faust spoke extemporaneously, rather than from the text he had prepared. He told the thousands of Saints, many of whom had also participated in the temple dedication, that he and they must never be the same after the week they were concluding. He reminded them that the temple was not the temple of the Brazilians but that it was "the house of the Lord" and that it was for all those worthy Saints who came from any part of the world.

He then spoke of the suffering he had endured during the four weeks since his call as an apostle and shared that he continued to feel "inadequate, unworthy, incapable, weak, and poorly prepared." Even with such feelings, his love for the Savior was evident, as was the great love he felt for the Brazilians who were gathered, many of whom shed tears of joy as they listened to the testimony of one they counted as their own.

As Elder Faust took his seat and looked out over the vast audience, the hand of the Lord was evident as he considered the growth of the Church since he had left Salt Lake City for São Paulo thirty-nine years before. And when the conference concluded a few minutes later, with the Saints having heard the prophet's closing remarks, Elder Faust observed, "Thus came the conclusion of one of the most moving and greatest weeks of my life, during which we had meeting after meeting filled with the powerful spirit."

NOTES

1. "Response to the Call," *Ensign,* November 1978, p. 20.

2. "An Untroubled Faith," BYU devotional address, Provo, Utah, 28 September 1986.

3. *Daily Universe,* 3 October 1978, p. 1.

10

A WITNESS
TO THE WORLD

As ELDER FAUST RETURNED HOME to Salt Lake City, he knew that even as the people of Brazil and South America would always hold a unique place in his heart, he was, by scriptural injunction, called to be one of a unique group of "special witnesses of the name of Christ in all the world," and to "officiate in the name of the Lord, . . . to build up the church, and regulate all the affairs of the same in all nations." He also pondered the Savior's charge that "the decisions of [the presiding quorums of the Church] . . . are to be made in all righteousness, in holiness, and lowliness of heart, meekness and long suffering, and in faith, and virtue, and knowledge, temperance, patience, godliness, brotherly kindness and charity" (D&C 107:23, 30, 33).

Elder Faust continued to wrestle with the weight of such a charge, and in addition to his own personal petitions of the Lord, at one point he asked his three sons, Jim, Marcus, and Robert, to administer to him so that he might find relief from the spiritual and physical agony he was enduring. He took strength and comfort from that blessing, as well as from Sister Faust, of whom he says, "No one could have a more supportive, understanding, and loving companion through all the circumstances of my life, both professionally and ecclesiastically. That's just the woof and warp of that wonderful woman."

He also was strengthened by the unique brotherhood enjoyed by members of the Twelve, a group comprising twelve different and unique individuals who adhere to the scriptural charge that "every decision made by [the First Presidency, the Twelve, and the Seventy] must be by the unanimous voice of the same" (D&C 107:27). Elder Faust adds, "These are men of experience, accomplishment, ability, and intelligence, and matters are discussed openly and candidly. Often, I have held an opinion which, after a discussion in reason and inspiration, I have completely reversed. It is a marvelous thing, after a discussion is had and everybody has expressed his thoughts and feelings, to have the president say, 'Brethren, I think this is what we should do,' and to then have the confirmation that the decision is the mind and will of the Lord."

Early in his tenure in the Twelve, Elder Faust recorded his thoughts after one of the many meetings in which he saw this process unfold. "A sweet spirit of mutual respect and admiration prevailed amongst the Brethren, although they expressed themselves with divergent views. Elder Bruce R. McConkie indicated that he thought the Lord deliberately chose men of diverse backgrounds for the Council of the Twelve Apostles, citing Matthew the Publican, who was an agent of Rome, and on the other hand Simon the Zealot, who belonged to the group of zealots whose function was to overthrow the yoke of Rome."

On another occasion he added, "It is marvelous to see how the Lord chooses those who serve him. They are not all out of the same mold. They have different backgrounds, different training, different experience; yet it all comes together after an issue is discussed and prayed about, pondered and evaluated, to where there is a burning feeling in the bosom of all that it is the mind and will of the Lord."

Elder Faust found that in their many meetings it was not uncommon for one or more of the First Presidency and Twelve to miss because of travel or illness (although a quorum must be present for binding decisions to be made), but he also notes that there is always a void when one is gone. At the beginning of one meeting, Elder Faust recalls, President Romney walked by him and asked who was missing. "I said, 'Howard [W. Hunter],' and he replied, 'Well, he's the main one.' And so the absent members seem to be the main ones."

Of Elder Faust's early contributions to the Quorum, Elder

Perry states, "I have never seen a member of the Twelve come in who was more prepared to be part of the Twelve than Elder Faust. It seemed there was no adjustment at all. When I was the twelfth man, I wouldn't dare speak. I thought that was part of the learning process—you sat there and absorbed. But he started making a contribution immediately upon coming in. Everyone recognized his stature and his keen mind, and they were very anxious to have him respond.

"In their years in the Twelve," Elder Perry continues, "there were two whom the rest of us always paid close attention to whenever they would speak: Howard W. Hunter and James E. Faust. President Hunter probably said less in the Twelve than any other member. But when he spoke, you knew you should listen. Elder Faust was the same way. He seemed to weigh an issue carefully, and then when he would come forth with his view, you could almost write it down as the course we should follow. It was that perfect."

(Elder Faust, in his modesty, would often respond to such comments by quoting President N. Eldon Tanner's father, who taught his son, "The less you say, the less you have to answer for.")

Elder Maxwell adds, "There is a tendency among some at Church headquarters to be so obedient that people don't speak up. But Elder Faust has always been willing to be candid with the Brethren. He not only has a contribution to make, he also has the courage to speak up. I valued that combination during our years of association in the Twelve, as I do to this day."

As he adjusted to being one of the Twelve, Elder Faust also gained an increased appreciation for the warmth and collegiality of the Brethren, whether in formal settings or in more personal moments.

He quickly learned that, contrary to long-standing jokes about LDS meetings running on "Mormon Standard Time," the Brethren of the Quorum were so anxious to meet together in their Thursday morning meetings in the Salt Lake Temple that they generally began fifteen minutes early. He enjoyed the opportunity to travel with his brethren and found that, as they did so, the bond they shared stood out to others. On one occasion, as he boarded a flight at the Salt Lake City International Airport with Presidents Kimball and Romney, along with Elders Hunter and O. Leslie Stone, one of the flight attendants saw the five men and remarked, "Here comes the basketball team."

Elder Faust was always quick to take note of the thoughtfulness of his associates and recorded countless small acts of kindness he observed among the Brethren. On one occasion, he received an impromptu call to come down and discuss a matter with President Kimball, who then, on the spur of the moment, asked that his counselors join them in the discussion. At the end of the meeting, President Kimball apologized to Presidents Tanner and Romney, saying, "I'm sorry to have interrupted you brethren. I know I interfered with some important work."

For his part, Elder Faust was diligent in trying not to cause offense to another, and he was quick to make amends if he felt he had done so. He once went to Elder LeGrand Richards and apologized for what he considered to be a "less than gracious comment" made in reference to the outcome of a political race. "He had not thought anything of my remark," Elder Faust records, "but I still apologized and asked for his forgiveness because I hold him in such great love and esteem."

With the same thoughtfulness he always extended to his immediate associates, Elder Faust then returned to his office and telephoned a man he had called as stake president the weekend before and apologized for a comment he felt might have been misconstrued and for not having had time to visit with the man's wife relative to the call before it was extended.

At the time of his call to the Twelve, the average age of the First Presidency and Quorum of the Twelve was almost seventy years old, and while Elder Faust certainly saw the blessings of strength in the General Authorities' lives, he could also see that none was immune from the vicissitudes that often accompany advancing years.

One of the early challenges he witnessed was when Elder Howard W. Hunter suffered a heart attack in 1980. Elder Faust recalls that as the two men visited, "Elder Hunter said that when he gets over this he will probably have a nervous breakdown because he doesn't have anything to do."

As the early 1980s passed, he saw more and more the problems that President Kimball and his two counselors were having, although he marveled at their ability to continue to play an active role in the leadership of the Church, despite their advancing years. Those who were ailing often coped in part by maintaining their humor, and Elder Faust recalls that in one meeting, President Hinckley (who in 1981 was called as a third counselor to the First Presidency to help carry the load) observed that President Tanner had forgotten his glasses. Upon hearing this, President Romney retorted, "That's all right—he can borrow mine. They don't do me any good!"

Other moments were more moving, such as a meeting of the First Presidency and the Twelve at which President Hinckley asked President Kimball if he had anything he wanted to say to the Brethren. "I'd like to be released," was his simple but poignant response. At the conclusion of another meeting not long after, Elder Faust recorded, "These great warriors of the First Presidency have been great exemplars to the whole Church. There are problems, though, and Brother Howard Hunter said in the Temple on Thursday, 'We don't know what to pray for. The only thing we can pray for is that the Lord's will be done.'"

Not all the challenges Elder Faust observed were associated with advancing years. One Monday morning, he checked in with Elder McConkie who, the previous Saturday, had fallen off the roof of his house as he was cleaning rain gutters. "I urged him to see a doctor," Elder Faust says, "but he felt that wasn't necessary. Instead, he told me that 'when a McConkie lands on his head, it doesn't hurt a thing.'"

Even at the relatively young age of sixty-two, Elder Faust faced his own set of challenges, as tests conducted in November

1982 indicated that under stress some of his heart vessels were impeded. The advice given him by his doctors, including Dr. Russell M. Nelson, a renowned heart surgeon who had operated on President Kimball several years before and who would join Elder Faust in the Twelve in April 1984, was that the condition could be treated by medication but that bypass surgery was an option that should be carefully considered.

"After some soul-searching, some prayer, and some fasting," Elder Faust wrote, "I concluded that it might be well for me to consider a bypass operation before I have had any heart damage and while I am in good health. My reason for so thinking is that even though the possibility of heart attacks might not be life-threatening, it would be difficult to manage if it happened when I am in a distant, emerging country." With that decided, he called Dr. Nelson's secretary and scheduled the surgery for Friday, November 19, in part to use the coming holiday season to recover, thereby attempting to reduce the amount of time he would be unable to carry out his Church responsibilities.

On Wednesday, November 17, Elder Faust attended various meetings during the day, then checked into the LDS Hospital in the afternoon, where he was run through various tests. ("The day was not pleasant," he wrote in his journal that day—a rare admission for a man who could almost always find a positive note upon which to end each day.)

The next morning, he left the hospital and attended the Thursday temple meeting of the First Presidency and the Twelve, returning that afternoon for the preoperative work. Then on Friday morning, Dr. Nelson spent six and one-half hours performing eight bypasses, which was more than he had anticipated but which he later told Elder Faust would ensure a healthy heart for years to come.

Elder Faust spent the next several days in the hospital, including Thanksgiving Day. He noted, in anticipation of the event, that "it has been organized for the family to go to Janna and Doug's, but I will have my turkey here at the hospital." He also observed that a friend who had come in on the same day for heart surgery had already gone home, but that "he only had four bypasses."

On Friday, President Tanner was admitted to the hospital, and in Elder Faust's view he was "doing very poorly, although he sent word up that he would see me at the office next week." Then on Saturday, Elder Faust received a telephone call, telling him of President Tanner's death. "The head nurse was visiting with me at the time," he wrote. "She is not a member of the Church, but upon hearing of his death, she broke down and cried." Although Elder Faust was released from the hospital the next day, he was unable to attend the funeral of his longtime friend and mentor—and the first member of the Church's two highest presiding quorums to die since Elder Faust had been sustained as an apostle four years earlier. He was, however, able to watch the proceedings on television, and he recorded something of his sentiments after the funeral: "There has passed from us one of the greatest men of our lifetime. To take away from each of us the influence of President Tanner would be to take away from each of us something very profound and significant in our lives."

Through the course of events surrounding President Tanner's passing—and then the death of Elder LeGrand Richards just a few weeks later—Elder Faust "felt a sense of gratefulness to belong to a group of men who have such care and solicitude for their associates."

He drew comfort and strength from his brethren—as well as his family and friends—as he endured a slower and more painful recovery than he had anticipated. Although there were days of discouragement, he still maintained his positive outlook, noting before Christmas, "I would feel normal if I had all my strength back and there was no chest pain." And he was greatly encouraged as Dr. Nelson examined him six weeks after the surgery and told him that "my life would be lengthened and be stronger and fuller, and that there would be no limitations on my activities."

The recovery process continued for many more weeks, although Elder Faust began returning to the office for the better part of each day beginning in early January. His drive to get going again was evident, as he recorded in late January that "I am anxious to have an overseas trip so that my Brethren will reclassify me and not think of me as a cripple." (From the first days following his surgery, his determination to return to normal was noted by his associates, prompting Elder Monson to send his friend a customized cartoon showing a businessman sitting up in a hospital bed, fully dressed with suit, tie, and hat. A nurse is walking into the room, saying, "Well, Mr. Faust, are we ready to go home?" This mischievous touch of humor prompted President Faust to later acknowledge, "I'm bad—but Brother Monson is worse!")

Even as Elder Faust tried to speed up the process of recovery, his brethren were sensitive to his continuing pain, which resulted in his having to follow their counsel to not go on a scheduled trip to Chile in early March. In late March, he did travel fifty miles south to preside at a stake conference in Springville, Utah, but during the April general conference two weeks later, he recalls that as he stood at the pulpit to deliver his address he thought, "Oh, I've got heart pain."

Of the periods of frustration he encountered during the months of his recovery, Elder Faust adds, "These callings rest upon us, and we just seem to be driven to fulfill our responsibilities and do the work we've been called to do." Gratefully, the week after general conference, he was able to endure a short trip to Pocatello, Idaho, for a stake conference, and the next week he traveled all the way to Eugene, Oregon. Before the month ended, however, his desire for an overseas trip was fulfilled as he flew to Hawaii for two very full days of meetings. After his return flight arrived in Salt Lake on Monday morning, he went straight to the office (as was his practice) and spent the afternoon in meetings. By the time he returned home to have dinner with Sister Faust, he recorded, "I kept falling asleep, so we couldn't have family home evening. Finally, I quit fighting it and went to bed."

Even with the fatigue and frequent pains that accompanied his recovery, Elder Faust's trip to Hawaii marked his return to the unrelenting travel schedule the Twelve keep as they administer the Lord's affairs and minister to His children throughout the world. During his nearly seventeen years in the Quorum, he circled the globe countless times, with most weeks seeing him—and, as assigned, Sister Faust—heading off to destinations ranging from St. Louis to Sri Lanka.

He faced his fair share of late arrivals and departures, canceled flights, and lost luggage. More than once, his plane sat on airport tarmacs waiting for mechanical failures to be fixed, and on one of many trips to the South Pacific, he and the other passengers had to wait for a pig to move off the runway before they could take off. He took such inconveniences in stride, however, never complaining but always noting when something went right—such as the time his and Sister Faust's plane arrived late in Chicago, causing him concern over making their connection to Frankfurt; but then he happily discovered that the plane they were to leave on was parked at the very next gate. "That would never happen again in a million years," he would note.

Upon returning from one of several extended tours of South America, he summarized his view of airplanes with this observation: "It is always tiring to ride in airplanes, but they are marvelous and make it possible for the Church to expand and do its work in the world."

One of his early international assignments as a member of the Twelve came in the summer of 1979, as he was assigned to accompany a Brigham Young University performing group on a groundbreaking tour of mainland China.

Although the university took the lead in making the arrangements for the trip, Elder Faust was involved in a number of delicate negotiations and difficult decisions. About a week before the twenty-six-member group was to leave, the university received a telegram from the Chinese authorities asking that the Young Ambassadors limit themselves to a few handheld instruments and minimal sound and lighting equipment. Bruce Olsen, who was then an assistant to President Dallin H. Oaks in charge of university relations and who oversaw the tour's arrangements, explains that the group was used to—and planning on—traveling with thousands of pounds of instruments, equipment, and costumes. Not knowing how to respond to this last-minute request, those responsible for the tour met with Elder Faust to discuss their options. "We decided that we'd just go on faith—and with all of our equipment—and that the Lord would open the way," Brother Olsen recalls.

The group got as far as Shanghai, at which point the airport officials wanted what Brother Olsen describes as "a large amount of money for us to continue on to Beijing (Peking). We worried that we would have to pay the overage for every flight we had scheduled. We decided to pay the money in Shanghai and see what happened, and it turned out that we only had to pay it once." (During the rest of the tour, the group met with no problems over its equipment and put on performances that resulted in BYU's becoming the best-known western university in China for years to come.)

Elder and Sister Faust became well acquainted with each of the student performers, providing them with spiritual uplift, encouragement, and any help that was needed with homesickness. When the heat in some cities was beyond unbearable, Elder Faust would remind the students that "when conditions become intolerable, they generally change," and Sister Faust would buy a fan for each of the young ladies. When the group headed out of a hotel on what was Father's Day in the States, Elder Faust had the sensitivity to call upon a young woman to pray who would help put the day in its proper context as she petitioned, "Heavenly Father, today is Father's Day, and we're not with our fathers. But we pray that thou wilt bless them and help them know we love them. And we thank thee for being our Eternal Father." As he listened to that prayer, Brother Olsen reflected, "I felt that Elder Faust could elicit that kind of sincerity and insight from the group because he set the tone that made the students feel comfortable expressing their deepest feelings in prayer."

Brother Olsen learned much from Elder Faust during the trip, as the two would "sit on spotlight boxes behind the scenes" and discuss all sorts of subjects. He also learned something of Elder Faust's leadership style as the group faced a quandary partway through the trip. In addition to performing, the group had planned various educational and cultural activities, including a visit to the Great Wall and the Ming Tombs. But given how the Chinese authorities had scheduled the various events and excursions, the group was faced with the prospect of having to perform on a Sunday if the students were going to see these great landmarks. "When we found out about this conflict after arriving in China," Brother Olsen recalls, "Elder Faust looked at me and said, 'Well, Bruce, what are you going to do?' And I thought, 'You're the member of the Twelve; what do you mean, what am I going to do?' But I could see that he expected me to make the decision and that he wasn't going to provide much guidance—or interference. Finally I said to him that if we were in Israel, we would observe the Sabbath on Saturday, which would be Sunday at home; so I proposed that we perform on Sunday and honor the Sabbath on Monday, which would likewise be Sunday back home. He listened and said, 'That's a good decision.' But it was one he had me make myself."

In addition to his responsibilities with the Young Ambassadors, Elder Faust also made arrangements, with prior approval from President Kimball, to rededicate the land of China for missionary work, Elder David O. McKay having dedicated the country during his visit fifty-eight years earlier. His prayer reflected that of Elder McKay's, both in content and in the fact that both prayers were offered in the Forbidden City and expressed the hope "that thou wilt honor and recognize each of the great promises which [Elder McKay] spoke for the future benefit of this people and this great land."

After the group's performances in Peking, Elder Faust noted in his journal a sentiment that summarizes the entire experience: "For us to have had the four performances in Peking, two of which were major performances in the Red Mill Theater and in the Forbidden City, is beyond our wildest hopes and imaginations. It is amazing that the Vice Minister of China National Travel again came this evening, as did the Director of the North American Activities. He has been very loyal, very friendly, and we have gotten along very well. . . . We have seen many wonderful, interesting things, and it has been quite a singular experience. I am grateful that Ruth is with me and that she takes such an interest and a delight in the things and the people that we meet."

It was a trip that would continue to open doors for both BYU and the Church for years to come, but as Elder Faust returned home his thoughts were with the students, all of whom had become close friends during their weeks together. In addition to getting to know them, he had also gathered each of their home telephone numbers, and on his first morning back in Salt Lake City, he called each of the parents to share with them something of the group's experiences, as well as his gratitude for their sons and daughters.

There were months when Elder Faust ate more meals on airplanes than he did in his home, although he was not inclined to complain. He did, however, note once the difference between the meals he was served at stake conferences and those he ate on airplanes: "The wives of the stake presidency brought a meal for us, together with lovely china. It tasted just delicious, and it caused me to wonder why a person can never get a meal like that in the hotels or on airplanes. I concluded that maybe it's because they have male chefs. I asked my wife why this was, and she said that these women prepare the food they serve with love, which I think is a substantial answer." Then he added an observation that is indicative of his appreciation for the many meals he has been served by faithful Saints the world over: "One dish that was truly outstanding was an apple strudel. It was just tremendous."

A trip that Elder and Sister Faust took in the company of Elder and Sister L. Tom Perry suggests something of the demanding schedules Elder Faust kept—as well as the experiences he had and the joy he felt in associating with the Saints.

More often than not, his departure times were scheduled at the end of busy days, which was the case on Wednesday, May 8, 1985, as Elder and Sister Faust started the day by attending the funeral for A. J. McKay, whom the Fausts had known in the Cottonwood area of Salt Lake City. In his account, Elder Faust summarizes the qualities of a man who "was not distinguished in letters or scholarship, but who was a most personable, smiling, happy, Christlike man—and one of the best family patriarchs we had in the Church." He then made brief mention of the honor he felt in being asked to speak and elaborated instead on the tribute paid by Brother McKay's daughter, Marilyn Mismash, who said: "I know how much our Father in Heaven loves us because I had a father who loved me that way."

From there, Elder Faust attended to a full day of meetings, finished packing, and visited a grandson who had just undergone surgery. Only then did he and Sister Faust head to the airport, where they and the Perrys boarded a flight to Los Angeles. In the process, they met a missionary who, like them, was traveling to Tahiti, so the Fausts and the Perrys welcomed him into their traveling party. Upon boarding their connecting flight in Los Angeles, the Fausts immediately went to sleep for the duration of the eight-hour flight, which arrived in Papeete, Tahiti, at 2:00 A.M. There, they cleared customs, visited with the local leaders who were on hand to greet them, checked into their hotel, and got what little rest they could before beginning a full day of touring the temple complex, chapel sites, and other buildings under construction.

The next day, the Fausts and Perrys were joined by Elder Robert L. Simpson and his wife, who had flown in from

Australia, where Elder Simpson was serving as area president. The group attended a temple session, held a mission meeting for two hours, and then concluded the day by attending a feast and program that the local leaders had planned to precede the area conference.

On Saturday, Elder Faust and his associates met with the mission president to review the challenges associated with a far-flung mission. Afterwards, Elder Faust asked to go back and once again see the temple, which he described as "a jewel." The group then participated in a lengthy leadership meeting, which was scheduled late in the afternoon to avoid the heat of the day. At the same time, Sisters Perry, Faust, and Simpson met with a large group of sisters. Elder Faust recorded, "We had a great meeting. Elder Simpson conducted and did very well. Elder Perry has a special enthusiasm, and a way of telling stories and projecting himself. But it was hard to have two translators side by side—one in French and the other in Tahitian. Tomorrow we will have two sessions, one for each language."

Upon completing two sessions of the area conference on Sunday, the Fausts and Perrys left Monday morning for Tonga, by way of New Zealand. On the flight to Tonga, which took them across the International Date Line and resulted in their losing a day, they were seated next to a young returned missionary with whom they visited during the flight. They were greeted in Nuku'alofa, Tonga, by a group of Church leaders— together with a brass band—with whom they met before checking into their hotel.

After a fitful night's sleep, caused by sweltering heat and their room's air conditioner not working, the Fausts got themselves up and ready to catch a 7:00 A.M flight that would take them to Vava'u, Tonga. When they arrived at the airport, they learned that their flight was delayed for about an hour because the pilots had decided to sleep in. When they finally did take off from the grass runway, Elder Faust records that "the trip was the most beautiful trip I have ever seen in my life. The sun was just coming up over the water, and we were low enough to see the configuration of the ocean and the islands and the sky. We then found that arrangements had been made to fly us over two volcanoes. To our surprise (this being a small plane), the pilot came down low and pulled right into the cone of the volcano and circled around and tipped it so we could look down to see the hot lava. The mission president wanted to get another picture, so we went around again! It was so thrilling that we were not unduly concerned. The pilot had great skill."

After the plane had set down on a dirt landing strip carved out of a coconut grove, the group was greeted by a large group that had spread out mats and brought numerous leis. There was also another brass band—something Elder Faust had never experienced before this trip. Before going to a four-hour priesthood leadership meeting, Elder Faust's group was treated to a large lunch, and after the meeting, they were guests at a feast of "endless kinds of foods—turkey, chicken, pork, shrimp, lobster, and a fruit boat that was out of this world. They went through a formal ceremony in which they symbolically killed the pig for Elder Perry and then recited some of the early history of the Church in Tonga. It was quite a special occasion."

During their time in Vava'u, Elder Faust learned that the local members could find all manner of reasons for two feasts each day. He concluded that the food was healthful when, at one meeting, the closing prayer was offered by a 101-year-old woman, who pushed away the arm of a local leader who attempted to help her up to the stand. He was also reminded of the fact that, in Polynesia, "If you look at anything, it's yours," and took note of the reverence of the children, who, he said, "sat peacefully with their arms folded, not wiggling or fussing. I get the feeling that the Tongans keep a firm hand on the young people."

On the last night of their two-week tour, the Fausts witnessed firsthand the great faith of the Tongan people—a faith so prevalent throughout the Islands that Elder Faust once instructed Sister Faust, "If I'm ever sick, please call upon the Polynesians to pray for me." During the course of the day, as the members put up ten thousand chairs in the outdoors and prepared for their concluding meeting with the two visiting apostles and their wives, rain fell off and on, even as the clouds on the horizon grew darker. As Elder Faust commented during the day about what appeared to be continuing bad weather, the local leaders told him not to worry about rain. "I didn't know whether to interpret this as their having greater faith than we have, or that they wouldn't be bothered that much by the rain," Elder Faust says; but that afternoon, as the four o'clock meeting began, there not only was no rain, but the skies were clear and blue.

The next morning, as the Fausts and Perrys were getting ready to board their flight, they learned that it would be too late to make their connection in Auckland, New Zealand. As they began to explore other alternatives, they received word back that they would, in fact, be able to make their connection because the connecting flight had gotten a late start out of Sydney, Australia. However, their flight from Hawaii to Los Angeles was late arriving, which resulted in their missing the last flight to Salt Lake City that evening. When the airline offered to put the two couples up in a hotel that night—at the airline's expense—Elder Faust refused, pointing out that they were attempting to make too close of a connection (an "illegal" connection, in airline parlance) and that for the airline to pay for their rooms "wouldn't be quite right."

After the two couples boarded their flight the next morning, "we taxied out, waited, taxied some more, and waited some more," Elder Faust recalls. When the flight finally arrived in Salt Lake at 11:15 A.M., Elder Faust went straight to the office, where he took care of correspondence requiring his immediate attention and then spent the afternoon in meetings. When he arrived home shortly after 5:00, he and Sister Faust (who was just finishing up the laundry from the trip) headed out to have dinner with their son Jim and his family, and then they stopped by to visit their daughter Lisa and her family. Upon arriving home, they watched the news, Elder Faust reviewed the

minutes of the meetings he had missed while abroad, and then
the two finally went to bed, thus bringing to a close one of a
countless number of trips the Fausts would take during his
years in the Twelve.

Whether he was being treated to a Polynesian feast, a traditional American dinner of roast beef and potatoes, or the deli-
cacies unique to countless other countries he traveled to, Elder
Faust was always appreciative of the hospitality of the Saints.
He especially welcomed the opportunity to stay with Church
members in their homes, and he did all that he could to ensure
that his host families felt comfortable having him there. On one
occasion, a stake president and his wife had insisted that Elder
Faust take their bedroom, and in the middle of the night, their
small son came and got into bed with him. Not wanting to
alarm the boy, Elder Faust simply let the boy go right to sleep
next to him.

In reflecting on his many experiences with Saints throughout the world, Elder Faust has said, "It has been a nice experience to stay in the homes of our members. There are sometimes
interesting circumstances, such as the stake president who had
seven daughters and one bathroom, but those things work out.
I am full of appreciation and gratitude for the goodness and
kindness of the Saints, particularly as extended to this humble
servant. For those of us who have to deal with the day-to-day,
hour-to-hour challenges of the worldwide Church, it is a spiritual and healing experience to be with the Saints in their
homes."

Those to whom he ministered as he traveled throughout the
Church likewise felt it a blessing to have an association with
Elder Faust, whether for a few minutes or over a number of
years. As he visited the missions and stakes of Zion, much of
his time was spent calling and training local leaders, particularly stake presidents and patriarchs, and he was mindful of his
need to make those calls under the guidance of the Spirit—and
with the love and encouragement that he had felt from both

President Lee and President Kimball as he had been called to the offices he had held as a General Authority.

Providing some insight into the process, he notes that, for him, the experience of calling stake presidents is somewhat different from that of calling patriarchs. "In calling a stake president," he says, "the visiting authorities counsel together and with the local brethren to get their feelings and to learn something of the strengths and abilities of those in the stake. Then we take the matter to the Lord and seek for His inspiration. Interestingly, so many of the times the brethren—and sometimes their wives—have already known by the Spirit that they were going to be called, which brings to mind something Elder McConkie used to say—that the Lord isn't very good at keeping secrets."

Elder Faust was continually touched by the faith of the good men who would accept these calls, and by the faith and support of their wives. He knew from his own experience what these calls would mean to these couples—both in terms of workloads and blessings—and drew strength as he witnessed their willingness to serve and their faith in the Lord's ability to sustain them in callings they could not fulfill on their own.

On one occasion, he called a man to serve as stake president and then suggested that he take some time to consider who he might call as counselors. The man immediately recommended two men—one a bishop in the stake and one a high councilor—but Elder Faust suggested that he and his wife might wish to take a little more time to consider the decision. The two went into a room to be alone, and after about ten minutes Elder Faust looked in to see how they were coming. "I found them upon their knees in an embrace," he recounts, "with this brother speaking in a modulated, soft voice to the Lord. I don't know that they were aware of my presence, but when they finished, still on their knees, they embraced each other and kissed, and I saw a unity and love that, if it were practiced by all married couples once in a while, would result in happier families and fewer divorces."

In the case of calling patriarchs, Elder Faust explains, "When the right man was presented, the inspiration was there. It was a sudden confirmation that here is the man who should be patriarch. Just why there is that difference, I don't know that I know." He did find, as with stake presidents, that often the man knew the call was coming. He tells of interviewing a man in Idaho "who had received a witness that he was to be called some three weeks before, although from a logical standpoint that shouldn't have been because of the two patriarchs already serving in the stake."

In ordaining and setting apart patriarchs, Elder Faust also knew the source of inspiration that would enable these brethren to function in their sacred callings, and he helped each man he called learn this principle. In one instance, Elder Faust interviewed a man to determine his worthiness to serve as patriarch. When the man protested that he was incapable of serving in such a capacity, given that he had only an eighth-grade education, Elder Faust reassured him of the inspiration evident in the calling. Elder Faust recorded, "I told him to come back with his wife at 7:00 [to be set apart]."

In all that he did as he administered the affairs of the Church in the wards, stakes, and missions of Zion, Elder Faust always attempted to take the time needed to deal appropriately with whatever situation he was handling and to teach and train the Saints and their leaders with "gentleness and meekness, and by love unfeigned" (D&C 121:41). A myriad of letters attest to his thoughtfulness, including one written by a wife whose husband was called as a patriarch: "You didn't hurry through and you took the time to explain things to him in his important calling as stake patriarch."

Another woman wrote, after encountering Elder Faust several times at a stake conference:

> I am writing of the experience I had as I watched an Apostle of the Lord bending down and shaking a very small boy's hand and telling him how glad he was to meet him, of insisting on going through an open door to a waiting group last, of having a strong

arm around weak shoulders and being hugged for a long period of time, of being so personal and patient to each individual. Then after sitting down from speaking to the combined congregation for a few brief moments and being concerned that I had said the right things, to have that Apostle lean over—across our stake president and an aisle—and whisper to me, "That was marvelous, such powerful words. I'm so glad I was able to come up here and get to meet you" (and in my usual, eloquent manner, I responded by crying).

At home and as he traveled, Elder Faust also sought to perpetuate a practice he had learned from President Kimball—giving dollars to young men to help them begin their missionary funds. Once, as he was having a snack with some of his family, a young boy came up to him and asked, "Are you really James E. Faust?" Elder Faust said that he was and then asked the boy what his name was and what he was going to do when he turned nineteen. When the boy said he didn't know, Elder Faust gave him a brief lesson in the importance of missionary service—and a dollar to start his missionary fund.

Another time, as he and Sister Faust were having dinner at the home of Bruce and Christine Olsen, Brother Olsen, who was then serving as a bishop, told Elder Faust of a young boy in his ward who had recently been diagnosed with a serious, degenerative disease and asked if he might be willing to visit with the boy and give him a blessing. Elder Faust said he would be happy to, so the two men walked over to the boy's house. Brother Olsen recalls, "He went into the home and first administered love, as he always does, and then administered a priesthood blessing to this boy. When we were through, he gave the boy a dollar for his missionary fund. Now at this point, no one would have dreamed he would live long enough to go on a mission, let alone have the ability to serve, but when the boy turned nineteen he was called to serve a two-year mission at the Provo Temple and the adjacent Missionary Training Center. His parents took him every day, and although he is now in an electric wheelchair, the promise was fulfilled that Elder Faust had given him."

He would often receive reports from young men as their funds grew, with one boy writing, "Last time I wrote I told you I had approximately $200 in my missionary fund. I am happy to announce I have almost $800 now." Elder Faust's son-in-law, Scott Smith, tells of having a group of priests from Idaho stay in his and Lisa's home, and taking the group to meet Elder Faust during their visit. As Scott recalls, "One of the priests told him that ten years before he had given this boy a dollar while at a stake conference. When Dad asked him how many dollars the boy had now, he thought for a moment and said, 'About $4,000,' and you could just see tears well up in Dad's eyes."

Another contribution that Elder Faust has made to the lives of many members of the Church is blessing them that they might have children, just as Elder Charles A. Callis blessed Sister Faust and him early in their marriage. "The Lord does give particular gifts to people, it seems to me," Elder Faust says. "Brother Callis had it, and we were blessed with our son, Jim. Now, these gifts come from the Lord, and those who hold the priesthood are only the vessels. But being able to bless these couples—which I have done only if it has been approved by their bishops and stake presidents—has been a humbling but satisfying part of my ministry. A woman in the Northwest had been married for eighteen years, and the stake president impor- tuned me to give a blessing to her and her husband. She con- ceived and carried and delivered a beautiful little girl, and that dear sister came clear down from the Northwest just to show me that baby. I have never seen a woman look so adoringly and lovingly upon a child as that woman. But again, that's not me; that is a gift from the Lord."

Elder Faust is quick to teach, however, that those who hold the priesthood have the same priesthood he does, and tells of traveling with Elder Hugh B. Brown once to dedicate a stake center. "Elder Brown was known to have the gift of healing, and the priesthood leaders brought a number of people to him seeking blessings. For some reason, he told them, 'You have the same priesthood I do,' and he didn't give any blessings. Why he didn't on that occasion, I don't know." But Elder Faust believes the local leaders learned an important lesson.

During his years in the Quorum of the Twelve, Elder Faust also had to deal with many difficult challenges as he traveled throughout the Church, and in those circumstances he could mete out the firmness and forthrightness that was called for.

As he traveled to one stake conference, he knew he would have to deal with a group of women that was spreading erroneous teachings among the members of the stake. "We proceeded to meet with some of the sisters," he recounts, "together with their bishops and husbands, who were involved in false doctrines. I came down quite hard on them, and then we interviewed the sisters individually, with their own bishops and their own husbands." The next morning, he met with the bishops in the stake to instruct them in the matter, "although we made it clear we wanted no witch hunts." On the trip home he recorded, "This was one of the most challenging stake conferences I have had since I was called either as a Regional Representative or a General Authority." Yet he responded aptly to the challenge that was placed before him.

At another conference he conducted an interview with a man who had been excommunicated, including his wife in the interview as well. As the two petitioned Elder Faust relative to the man's reinstatement, he had to tell them that the few months that had passed were insufficient for the repentance process to be complete. The wife pleaded with Elder Faust to view her husband's situation otherwise, and while he acknowledged that "her plea touched my heart, I did them a kindness by telling them what they did not want to hear."

There were many others, however, who did want to hear the advice Elder Faust had to offer, and who were then willing to follow his counsel, even when it ran counter to prevailing and popular notions. In March 1989, as Elder Faust accompanied President Hunter to California for a regional conference, he was introduced to a college freshman who had happened to come to the Saturday afternoon leadership meeting with his bishop and elders quorum president—and who was faced with a difficult decision.

Jason Johnson was a starting basketball player for a local junior college, and his team was about to play its last game of the season, a game that would determine whether it would move into state playoffs. His coach, who knew Jason was a Mormon, asked him several days before the last game if he would be willing to come to a special practice the Sunday before the Monday game. As the coach explained the situation, the team was very much in need of the extra practice, and he had scheduled it late in the day so that Jason could attend his church meetings first.

Jason explains that he was typical of many young Latter-day Saints who, on the one hand, are working to solidify their testimonies but who, on the other hand, are somewhat torn by interests such as basketball. "I told the coach that I wouldn't come to the practice, and he became quite upset and told me that if I didn't, I would not only not play in the game but that he would see to it that I never played basketball again for any school. When he said that, I began to question my decision, and the next day I asked my bishop about a meeting I had heard of where two General Authorities were going to speak, hoping that by listening to them I might get some help in making this decision."

After the first two hours of a four-hour meeting, Jason went with his bishop and elders quorum president into the cultural hall for a refreshment break, and the three began discussing, once again, Jason's options. As they did so, the elders quorum president suggested that Jason ask Elder Faust his opinion, and as Jason was responding that he certainly did not want to bother an Apostle, he suddenly found himself being introduced to Elder Faust.

"As we began to talk," Jason recalls, "he immediately disarmed me with his kindness. I was an athlete who was a bit full of himself, but I could tell that, somehow, he understood me and my situation. And as soon as I sensed that, I was ready to listen to whatever he had to say. He took my hand and walked me over to the far corner of the gym, holding onto my hand and arm as we walked. I can't remember everything he said, but I do remember very clearly knowing that he knew exactly how I felt.

"After I had explained the situation to him, he put his head down and thought for a minute. Then he looked at me and said, 'When you have a moral decision like this that the scriptures don't give you an exact answer to, it's difficult.' Then there was another long pause, after which he put his hand on my shoulder and said, 'Well, Brother Johnson, if you have enough faith, you won't go to practice tomorrow.' Then he walked away."

Jason chose to follow Elder Faust's advice, and the next day at church, as he partook of the sacrament, he knew he was in the right place, doing the right thing. The next day, he suited up and was ready to play, even though the coach had told him he would not use him. True to his word, the coach didn't start Jason—for the first time that season—but within a couple of minutes he changed his mind and put Jason in. "I scored 17 points and played the best game I had played all year," Jason recalls, "although our team lost by one point. Whether we won or lost, though, is not the point; in fact, I'm not sure our Heavenly Father cares much about who wins or loses basketball games. What I learned from my few minutes with Elder Faust was that an Apostle can understand an eighteen-year-old kid and that by putting my Heavenly Father first, I would be happy."

Whether he was counseling a young athlete, a newly called patriarch, or a seasoned stake president, Elder Faust taught a consistent and essential lesson as he traveled throughout the Church and ministered among the Saints—that when faith is coupled with obedience, the Lord will strengthen and bless His children in all they are called upon to do.

11

UNASSUMING
SERVICE

As ONE OF THE PRESIDING OFFICERS of a worldwide church, Elder Faust did his part to deal with countless challenges and assignments during his years in the Quorum of the Twelve. The volume and complexity of the issues he and his brethren face would be simply overwhelming were it not for that singular source of strength with which Elder Faust has become intimately acquainted since his earliest days of service in the Church.

At the conclusion of one meeting of the Twelve during his early years in that quorum, he recorded something of the challenges the Brethren face, as well as a simple, straightforward sentiment that has been at the heart of how he has handled every assignment he has ever been given: "These are interesting times. In a worldwide Church, we have challenges and problems. The Brethren in their wisdom could not run this Church for one hour. Inspiration is so desperately needed." With that as his guide, he has sought to combine what he considers to be his "meager abilities" with the divine guidance he knows is needed to do the work of the Lord.

Those who have served with him know well the contributions Elder Faust has made to the kingdom, but he, in his humility, has opted to stand to the side when credit is given.

Says his associate Elder Neal A. Maxwell, "Elder Faust deserves the dignity of causality, but he doesn't claim it. He has facilitated many things in the Church that he wouldn't want people to feel call for any special credit directed toward him. One of his mentors, of course, was N. Eldon Tanner, who had developed that ability to a high, high degree, and I think Elder Faust is not only instinctively that way, but I think he watched President Tanner and has wanted to follow that example."

Elder Maxwell tells the story—"at my own expense"—of the two men being asked by the First Presidency to handle "a delicate political assignment. As the assignment was being given, President Tanner, who was always good to build people up, said to President Kimball and President Romney, 'I can't think of two better men for this assignment,' and I, in false modesty, said, 'Oh, I'm sure you can get two better men than us.' As quick as a flash, President Kimball said, 'Well, while we're looking, would you mind going ahead with the assignment?'

"That is indicative of the confidence and trust the Brethren have in Elder Faust," Elder Maxwell continues, "and of the fact that he has been at the crossroads many times, but doesn't feel he needs to put up a signpost that says, 'Faust was here!'"

Even when asked, Elder Faust has never been one to make an issue of who he is or where he has been, as was once the case during his early (and less recognizable) years in the Twelve when a woman encountered him on one of the Church Office Building elevators and asked him who he was. "Oh, one of the janitors," he replied jokingly.

On another occasion, Elder Faust had gone out for an early Saturday morning walk near his neighborhood and came upon a woman in a Church parking lot taking stacks of boxes into the building. When he offered to help, he learned that she was a ward Young Women president and that she and the young women were going to assemble and sell one hundred pizzas that day. The woman, on the other hand, became suspicious that he didn't know where the kitchen was and began wondering if he might be planning to mug her. It was only when he ordered two pizzas and gave the woman his name and address that she realized he was anything but a threat to her well-being.

Even as he worked not to take himself too seriously, Elder Faust worked hard to fulfill the responsibilities he was given.

Elder Perry, in commenting on the qualities that underlie Elder Faust's contributions to the Church, points to at least four:

> First, he understands people. Whenever we're discussing personalities, he can analyze people better than anyone I've ever been around. He just seems to have an intuitive judgment about their particular capabilities and qualifications. Second, he's a deeply spiritual man. He's close to the Lord, and any time something comes up that we can't quite agree upon, he will suggest that maybe we need a little more thoughtful, prayerful study before we can move forward. Third, he can organize thoughts in a concise, logical way, and his contributions to our discussions are always in the fewest possible words expressed in the clearest, most understandable way. Fourth, he is a very powerful speaker when he is behind the pulpit. His sermons are down to earth, they are on subjects that are meaningful and useful, and they have an uplifting, spiritual tone to them.

One of the many issues to which Elder Faust brought his talents and spiritual insight within days of being called to the Twelve was dealing with the rapidly increasing membership of the Church, particularly in areas of explosive growth such as Latin America and Africa.

In late 1980 he recorded, referring to the Church's budget for the coming year, "We have the kind of problems we have been praying for, which are growing pains. The wise administration of the Church, however, keeps us in a good position." In a subsequent interview he would offer something of the basic principles he has encouraged Church leaders to follow as they deal with a burgeoning membership: "Growth is one of our biggest blessings, as well as one of our greatest challenges. When new members are brought into the Church in great numbers, we have to make sure that the missionaries are teaching all the lessons and that those who are baptized understand and are ready to comply fully with the requirements given in Mosiah 3:19. We certainly need to make hay while the sun shines in areas of rapid growth, but that does not mean we shouldn't have some kind of reasonable assurance that every person who is baptized is sincere and has a beginning knowledge of what is required in terms of commitment, service, the Word of Wisdom, tithing, and so forth. We welcome new converts and we're grateful for them; we just hope and pray that the Spirit of the Lord touches them so they will enter on a path of faithfulness and devotion whereby the windows of Heaven can open up to them so they can receive all the blessings the Lord has for them."

Coupled with the challenge of helping to manage the growth of the Church was Elder Faust's assignment to serve on the Church's Missionary Committee, in which capacity he helped supervise the Church's entire missionary effort—and to call the ever-growing number of new missionaries. Often he would find himself assigning anywhere from three hundred to five hundred new missionaries "in a single sitting," and he readily acknowledges the inspiration that guides that process: "The calling of missionaries is a very interesting process, in that the inspiration which comes is really very confirming and almost instantaneous. Sometimes there is no logical reason for the assignment, as with those who, for example, have studied Spanish for four years and get assigned to Bulgaria. When I received my call, I fully expected to go to Germany, given my ancestry and the fact that I had studied the language, but when I opened the letter and it said I was going to Brazil, I was disappointed for about fifteen seconds, after which I didn't want to go anywhere else. Having now served as one of the prophets, seers, and revelators who is responsible for making those calls, I would say that you just can't deny the inspiration or the revelation."

In 1985, Elder Faust's assignment was shifted from the Missionary Committee to the Genealogy Committee, and there he worked, along with Elders Boyd K. Packer and Dallin H. Oaks of the Twelve, to recommend and oversee the implementation of changes made in the Church's genealogy program. "Our desire was simply to demystify genealogy. The name of the work, as a result, was changed to 'Family History,' and we sought to make the process more user-friendly so that it wasn't so technical and forbidding to the average person. I don't want to take any credit for the changes that were made, but I think it's marvelous to see a simpler process and people who are now able to do much of the work from home. Our being able to supply sufficient names to keep our many temples busy is the fruit of that effort, although I would hasten to add that with all the temples being built, it is going to take many more names to keep up."

Elder Faust's longest-standing committee assignment began even before he was called as a General Authority, as he was asked to serve with Elder Hinckley on the Special Affairs Committee (the name of which was later changed to Public Affairs, a committee which now reports to the First Presidency through him). This committee's primary charge is summarized by some close to Elder Faust as bringing the Lord's work "out of obscurity and darkness" as it presents the Church, through public relations efforts, to audiences on local, national, and international levels, as it takes advantage of ongoing advances in communications technology to present the Church's message, and as it oversees the Church's involvement with political issues that have moral implications.

A public relations practitioner who has worked with Elder Faust since the early 1980s—first as a Church employee based in New York City and then as a consultant on various projects and issues—is Steve Coltrin, whose father served with Elder Faust as a missionary in Brazil. "Before there was an Elder Faust who was known to the Church, and certainly before I had ever met him," Brother Coltrin recalls, "I can remember my father telling my mother, on more than one occasion, that his former companion was someone who was absolutely real and genuine—and someone who was very comfortable with himself.

"As I came to know him through our public relations efforts, I found that these personal qualities guided all that he did in taking the message and image of the Church out to the world. Early in my professional association with the Church, I was asked to serve on an advisory group that discussed a number of issues relative to the Church's image. At one meeting, the group had a lengthy discussion about how the Church is referred to—by members and nonmembers alike—and after the meeting I made the comment to Elder Faust that perhaps it would be well for members to not refer to themselves as 'Mormons' because that could take away from the respect we should have for the Savior. He listened and then said, 'Well, that's interesting, Steve, but we sort of are who we are.' His comment wasn't really an endorsement or a rejection of what I (and others in the group) had said, but it was very typical of his basic philosophy—that we should be honest about who we are, no more and no less. Now, the Church has worked over the ensuing years to put more emphasis on the actual name of the Church, but I learned a great lesson from that brief exchange— that in public relations efforts of any kind, you should proceed from the truth of what you are. That isn't always the approach public relations practitioners take, but in my experience, anything else will invite disaster."

One of the many public relations issues Elder Faust helped to guide during his years in the Twelve had to do with "historical" documents brought forward by Mark Hofmann, who became well known in the early 1980s for "finding" documents relating to early Church history and who later confessed to forging the documents and to murdering two individuals in an attempt to cover up his forgeries.

After participating in a meeting of the Twelve at which the Brethren discussed a document purporting to be a blessing from Joseph Smith to his son, Elder Faust noted the comments of Elder LeGrand Richards, who told of his grandmother's experience of witnessing the Prophet's mantle falling upon Brigham Young after Joseph and Hyrum Smith's martyrdom. "Elder Richards related that nobody had any question about who should succeed the Prophet," Elder Faust wrote, "and then he added that this personal testimony was worth more than any written documentation."

Coupled with his testimony of the power of the Spirit was Elder Faust's determination, both before and after the documents were determined to be forgeries, that the Church be completely aboveboard in how it dealt with what were viewed by some as troublesome issues for the Church. One of the countless examples that shed light on his philosophy that "we are who we are" occurred as the Hofmann case was winding to a close. In a journal entry of April 10, 1986, Elder Faust writes of his involvement in preparing a press release that would detail what the Church paid for the documents it acquired from Mr. Hofmann and then adds, "We will take some criticism, but because we are being absolutely straightforward and truthful, it will, in the long run, redound to the credibility of the Church."

In matters of politics, Elder Faust explains that the Church's position is to take no position—except in those instances where a moral issue is involved. "We don't tell public officials how to do their duty," he says. "We tell them they have to answer to their own conscience. But when it comes to moral issues—such as abortion, alcohol, or gambling—then we have the right and the duty to speak out. Now, when it comes to commenting on the particulars of legislation, we are careful, remembering the adage that the legislative process is a lot like making sausage and hearkening back to Joseph Smith's statement that people need to be taught correct principles and then be allowed to govern themselves. So, we very carefully avoid expressing personal opinions and ideas to the legislature, and the Public Affairs Committee is set up so that if there is a rumor that the Church has taken a certain position, anyone can call and find out whether or not that is the case. We just do not do things in a corner. We are open and aboveboard in the positions we take on moral issues."

Beyond his own involvement as a state legislator and with other political activities, Elder Faust's involvement with the Church's institutional position on political issues came as he was asked to work, in 1968, with Elder Gordon B. Hinckley on the issue of selling liquor by the drink in the state of Utah. He continued to be involved with that and many other political issues during his years in the Twelve, and he often worked with Bonner Ritchie, a professor of organizational behavior at BYU who served for many years on the State Liquor Commission.

Brother Ritchie recalls, "As we would meet to discuss the Church's position on liquor issues, Elder Faust was as good as anyone I've ever seen at prioritizing, delineating, and defining the constructs, principles, and issues that were important to the Church. There was no ambiguity—you never wondered what he thought or what he felt was important—but he also made it plain that the Church would only get involved with issues that have an obvious moral component, and that its position would then be on the principle, not on the details."

Brother Ritchie, in part because of his professional interests, also paid close attention to Elder Faust's leadership style during their years of association. "He is a man of few words," Brother Ritchie says, "and is not given to much small talk. He states the principle, makes sure you get the message, and then moves on. He's never, ever rude, but he's very focused. He is also very careful in his use of power. I have never seen him pull rank, although he could have. I have never seen him use his power to dictate a position. Instead, he will approach an issue from the position of teaching a philosophy, a set of clear principles."

One of Brother Ritchie's most memorable insights into Elder Faust's leadership style came one night as he returned home and found a note from his son saying, "Dad, call Jimmy," with a number following. "I didn't know anyone named 'Jimmy,' but I dialed the number and it was Elder Faust. I asked him later about asking my son to have me call 'Jimmy,' and he said he hadn't wanted to worry my children or appear to be pretentious. Those who study leadership are always interested in men and women who have power but don't use it, and my experience with Elder Faust is that he practices the condescension spoken of in the scriptures—not in the sense of lowering oneself, but in relating to people at their level, rather than in a superior-subordinate relationship."

Bruce Olsen, who first met Elder Faust on their trip to China in 1979, is another who has seen his work from a unique vantage point. After serving in the early 1980s as a mission president, teaching at BYU, and then running the corporate communications office for a large Utah company, Brother Olsen was invited to become managing director of the Church's Public Affairs Department, in which capacity he worked closely with Elder Faust and the other members of the Public Affairs Committee. Brother Olsen observes, "Together with President Hinckley, Elder Faust has been something of a watchdog over those moral affairs that affect the Church. He was involved with and carefully guided the Church's role in defeating horse race gambling in Utah. In that campaign, the Church tried very carefully to stay back a step and give support when it was needed. It requires a delicate balance for the Church to work with people on an issue but to not be too heavy-handed—to put the finger on the scale when and where it will make a difference—and Elder Faust is one who helps the Brethren to know just how to reach that balance.

"Both within Utah and nationally," Brother Olsen adds, "Elder Faust has been a voice to keep the Church out of social issues where other churches and organizations have ended up on the rocks. There are many good people with causes who come to the Church in the hope that the Church will come down on their side and support their cause. Generally, the Church's response is that it chooses not to get involved, and Elder Faust has been one of those voices on the Public Affairs Committee that has carefully guided those decisions."

Representative of the Church's involvement in those issues it decides to weigh in on, Elder Faust once recorded, referring to the Church's efforts to not allow pari-mutuel betting in Utah, "This is a moral issue. The Church has a right and a duty to speak out. Even some of our own people speak of 'free agency,' yet the phrase 'free agency' does not appear in the scriptures.

What does is 'moral agency,' and we have determined to support the First Presidency and the Quorum of the Twelve in their effort to not permit gambling to come into the state."

Several weeks later, when a local newspaper accused Elder Faust of "chastising" the state legislature for its position on the issue in a large public meeting, Elder Faust noted, "Fortunately, I have a tape of my remarks, and I said no such thing. But what to do about it is a question."

The conclusion he came to was characteristic of Elder Faust's quiet ways, as he privately informed the publisher of the newspaper that an error had been made, opting not to make the issue any more public than it already was. When the publisher called to apologize, Elder Faust indicated that he was not interested in a printed retraction; and when the publisher then asked if he could obtain a copy of the tape, Elder Faust indicated that he might be willing to send it, "on the condition that he not be too hard on the reporter."

During his more than three decades of involvement with the Public Affairs Committee, Elder Faust has been at the center of countless issues and decisions, but Brother Olsen points to two particular decisions that Elder Faust has helped to shepherd along.

The first was the decision, in the early 1990s, to retain the services of the Edelman Agency, a worldwide public relations firm enlisted to help the Church in its efforts to takes its message to broader audiences and, in the words of its head, Dan Edelman, "to correct the myths and falsehoods about the Church." Brother Olsen explains, "Working with the Edelman Agency has given the Church a breadth that we used to lack. It has given us contacts in the world that we didn't have before. The idea of building bridges through getting the Brethren out to meet with prominent people in their own settings, including the editorial boards of large media organizations, has come about as a result of Edelman's involvement. Much of what the Church has seen President Hinckley do in dealing with the media has been the result of the efforts of the Edelman group, and then-Elder Faust was a key, behind-the-scenes sponsor of that initiative."

The second initiative Brother Olsen points to is the logo of the Church that was introduced in the late 1990s and places a very clear visual emphasis on the focal point of the Church, Jesus Christ. "Elder Faust was very much in favor of that effort," Brother Olsen recalls. "From the first time he saw the treatment that is now used, he liked it—and then gently sponsored it as it moved through the channels of approval."

Elder Faust is also known for the bridges he has built with the members and leaders of other faiths—both in and outside of Utah. Within Utah, where members of the Church comprise the majority of the population, he has been especially concerned that Church leaders and members maintain constructive relationships, whether in their own neighborhoods or within the circles of influential ecclesiastical or political leaders. During one community event Elder and Sister Faust attended, a leader of one of the Protestant churches in the state made some very derogatory remarks about the LDS church. Sister Faust recalls, "I became steamier and steamier as he went on, but Jim just listened patiently. Afterwards, he went up to this man and said, 'Now, Reverend, if you feel that way, we must be doing something wrong. I'd like for us to have lunch together so that you can let me know what your concerns are.' They did, and the two have been good friends ever since."

In matters of partisan politics, with which he was once involved, Elder Faust maintained an active personal interest after being called as a General Authority but also made sure to have absolutely no involvement, except as assigned by the Church. As he would watch local and national elections, he was always concerned about candidates and their supporters conducting themselves appropriately. During one particularly heated election season he noted, "The political pot is boiling, with both sides claiming excesses on the other side. It is a disappointment when the campaigns degenerate, and I have been disappointed in the way some of our people have acted. At one of our Church schools, students were rude to a senate candidate, and at another, they were very impolite to the governor's wife. They injure the cause they are trying to promote when they go to excess."

Regarding his own party affiliation subsequent to being called as a General Authority, he once recorded, "I'm glad I am past being involved in politics on either side. I can honestly say now that I am neither a Democrat nor a Republican; I am an Apostle."

Elder Faust did, however, maintain a more active involvement with the legal community, both in and outside of Utah, particularly as the Apostle would deliver talks to legal groups in which he emphasized the need for dignity, integrity, and decency on the part of all who practice at the bar.

He didn't mind joking about his profession, as was the case when he quoted Benjamin Franklin as saying, "God works wonders now and then; behold, a lawyer, an honest man." But he would hasten to enjoin his listeners to adhere to the highest of ethical standards as he would note, "The State and the nation can survive with an occasional lapse of moral integrity from the executive and legislative branches, but it cannot survive with a corrupt judiciary."[1]

In speaking to a group of BYU law students, Elder Faust dealt with an issue he knew they would one day face:

> I alert you that if you practice law you must be prepared to answer people who ask how you can be a good member of the Church and a lawyer. This question stems not only from misunderstanding but also from the fact that the law and lawyers are generally controversial, and many of our court and administrative proceedings are adversarial in nature. The Prince of Peace did not advocate controversy, but he was involved in it. The adversary system, imperfect as it is, has evolved as the best means of extracting the truth out of controversy. Is not truth to be sought above other virtues?
>
> Lay people will ask how you reconcile your religious convictions with being an advocate for a "criminal" or a "crook." Many forget the fundamental principle that people are presumed

innocent until convicted. I sincerely believe that no committed
member of the Church who is trying to keep the laws of God
needs to compromise his or her religious and moral convictions
in the practice of law. The canons of ethics, with which I hope you
will become fully acquainted, support and are in harmony with
the moral teachings of the Church. These ethical standards fully
encourage many of the moral principles of our Church, specifically those high standards of honesty, integrity, loyalty, truthfulness, and sincerity.

In my opinion there need be no conflict between what the
Savior has taught through the Church and what you do as a professional lawyer. Indeed, if you are careful about observing the
high moral standards the Church represents, you will stand out
in your profession. Sir Thomas More did. Although he was
beheaded, he fitted well the description of Job, "a perfect and an
upright man, one that feareth God, and escheweth evil . . . and . . .
holdeth fast his integrity" (Job 2:3).[2]

Even as the years passed, Elder Faust remembered well certain principles he learned from the practice of law, and he could
be quite specific in advising his audiences on fundamental principles they should follow. A list he presented to a group of graduating law students contained not only sound advice for these
future lawyers, but also an interesting insight into the man
making the suggestions:

> First, honesty isn't the best policy, it is the only policy.
> Second, never commingle the client's money with your own.
> My years with the Bar Association taught me that more lawyers
> are disciplined for violation of this rule than any other kind of
> professional wrongdoing.
> Third, always take the high ground. Another way to say this is,
> keep your own soul. It is important to move to the higher ground,
> particularly when economic pressure might force a compromise
> in your moral position. My law school dean, Dean William H.
> Leary, a devout Catholic, explained it this way: "When it is three
> weeks before Christmas and you have no money for Christmas
> presents for the children, rather than yield to the temptation to do
> something cheap or shoddy to get a fee in, you get down on your
> knees and ask for divine help."
> Fourth, don't make an enemy of your opponent. Emotion runs

high, especially in litigation. Civility and respect for an opposing opinion will get justice for your client more readily than unreasonable belligerency.

Fifth, don't overstate your case. Don't understate it either, but if you overstate it, you may have to eat your own words. This could give you a terrible stomachache, and—worse yet—destroy your credibility.

Sixth, give some of your time to your client. Do not charge him for all of the time you spend learning your trade. Careful preparation more than brilliance is the key to success in the law.

Seventh, don't let your client or his cause compromise your integrity. If you lie to a judge or a fellow attorney even once, you are irreparably injured. Integrity is the portion of truly great lawyers.

Eighth, pray for wisdom.[3]

Certainly, the most public part of Elder Faust's ministry while a member of the Twelve has come twice each year—April and October—as he participates in and speaks at the general conferences of the Church. No matter how many times he has addressed an ever-enlarging international audience, he has remained convinced of the advice he gave to Elder W. Grant Bangerter in 1975: "It never gets any easier."

Elder Faust's preparations for the addresses he would deliver each conference would inevitably begin almost as soon as one conference would end, with ideas being developed and drafts being written and rewritten over the course of four or five months. As an Apostle, rarely was Elder Faust assigned a topic, and, he says, "The hardest part is to come up with an appropriate subject, which comes only through the still, small voice of inspiration." After completing work on the final draft for one talk just days before conference, Elder Faust recorded, "I don't know why it is so hard for me to bring it all together, but I am sure it is to bring home to me over and over again how dependent I am upon the Lord for His help."

Even with months of advance preparation, which included rehearsing each talk to ensure that it fit exactly the time he was allotted, Elder Faust experienced his share of unexpected situations that required him to make last-minute adjustments. After the April 1985 conference, he recorded, "I spoke next to last; and as I looked down at the clock when I was just getting into the talk, I noticed that I only had four minutes left." Not wanting to cut into Elder Packer's time, Elder Faust made drastic cuts as he went along, noting, "Fortunately, it came along satisfactorily, although I felt I left out an important part. But on balance it was a good experience because I felt a little more confident in being able to handle an emergency situation up there." (Although he delivered a condensed version, the talk, which dealt with the Resurrection, was published in its entirety.)

During the April 1990 general priesthood session of conference, as Elder Faust listened to President Thomas S. Monson's talk on being our brother's keeper, he discovered that Elder Monson was using a story about the Martin Handcart Company that was central to the talk Elder Faust had planned to give Sunday afternoon. "I had to shift gears and substitute the story of Emma Batchelor," he recorded, "so I got up early and worked on it. Margaret Bury [his secretary] was good enough to come down and get it ready for the teleprompter and translators."

Underlying the many talks he has delivered have been at least two guiding philosophies. The first is an intrinsic part of Elder Faust's character and was stated in these simple words delivered at the April 1987 general conference of the Church: "I come prayerfully to this pulpit—not to judge, but to teach and to caution." He is never reluctant to teach the doctrines he feels the world needs to hear—hard though they may be to some, at times—but it has never been his intent to judge or condemn; rather, he has sought to lift and inspire.

The second is found in a moment shared by his son, Marcus, who, in preparing an address he was to deliver to a group of legal scholars, faxed a draft to his father, asking for his reaction. "When I got the manuscript back," Marcus recalls, "he had written at the end, 'So what?' Initially, I was crushed, but when I asked him about his comment, he apologized for not explaining what he had meant and then told me, 'Whenever I write something or prepare a talk, I ask myself that question when I'm done. I use it to force myself to consider, what does this really mean? Is this just a nice gathering of thoughts and stories, or is there something here that is going to help and guide people?' By that standard, Dad will make sure that every sermon he gives provides an answer to the question, 'So what?'"

At the conclusion of each general conference, Elder Faust would feel enormous relief, both from the weight of having to address a worldwide gathering and from the crush of meetings and responsibilities that accompany conference. He would often note in his journals his thoughts on his talks in words such as, "I was grateful I didn't embarrass the Church." In addition, he and Sister Faust established a tradition when he was first called as a General Authority of spending Sunday evening with as many family members as could come. His children tell of him almost always lying on the floor in front of a fire as the younger grandchildren would climb on him and as those who wished to would reflect on the messages they had heard in general conference.

The time he spent with his family on those Sunday evenings provided a much needed respite from the work that preceded and followed each general conference. Perhaps more important, though, the time he spent in those Sunday evening settings captured the individual reality of the vast work with which he was involved, as he, with his family—along with so many other faithful families throughout the Church—gathered together to share their testimonies and to encourage each other in their efforts to live lives more closely aligned with the teachings of the Savior and His prophets and apostles.

N O T E S

1. Unpublished remarks delivered at the Pro Bono Recognition Dinner, Salt Lake City, Utah, 10 September 1996.

2. Unpublished address delivered to BYU law students, Brigham Young University, Provo, Utah, 22 November 1987.

3. Unpublished remarks delivered at the J. Reuben Clark Law School Convocation, Brigham Young University, Provo, Utah, 19 April 1985.

12

A CONSCIENTIOUS STEWARD

As HARD AS HE HAS WORKED to fulfill his responsibilities as a General Authority, Elder Faust likewise has given his all to his family. His demanding schedule aside, he and Sister Faust have spent almost every evening they are in town with family members, and if there isn't a personal visit, there is inevitably a telephone call. His daughter Janna tells of how, over the years, people who know of her father's position would often ask if she ever saw her father. "I see him all the time," she explains, "and if I don't talk to him every day, I risk hurting his feelings. It seems to me that he and Mom need us to be their friends as much as they need us to be their family."

Upon learning that he and Sister Faust were going to be grandparents once again, Elder Faust recorded in his journal how happy that made him, and then declared, "Children are very welcome in our family." And his grandchildren attest to how welcome they feel—from Grandma buying "the right kinds of cereals" for when grandchildren would sleep over, to back and neck rubs, to always having something on hand to keep the grandkids happy as they would stay with Grandma and Grandpa Faust.

One grandson, Jason Coombs, remembers a hot summer Saturday when he and his friends, who were about ten at the time, didn't have anything to do and couldn't find a parent to take them swimming. "Grandpa was a member of the Twelve, but I didn't realize the busy life that he had," Jason recalls, "so I called and asked if he could come get us and take us swimming and maybe play some basketball with us. And he did!

Then he took us around the tunnels underneath the Church office buildings and Temple Square complex, which my friends didn't even know were there. He spent all afternoon with us, even though, in looking back, I'm sure he had many other things he could have been doing."

On another occasion, when Jim's daughter, Brittney, stopped by with her boyfriend late one evening to visit her grandparents, Elder Faust reluctantly explained that he and Sister Faust were in their pajamas and about to get into bed. To make up for their inability to visit at the moment, however, he arranged for the two couples to go on a double date and eat barbecued ribs together. All of this was in keeping with a sentiment he expressed once, when he had to rearrange his schedule to attend a grandfather-granddaughter outing with two of his granddaughters: "I decided that if I am willing to give my life for each of these girls, I should be willing to alter a meeting schedule."

In a number of family settings, Elder Faust used an object lesson to demonstrate the need for his family members to be close to one another. He would pull out a small stick and ask a grandchild to try and break it, which they always were able to do. Then he would bring forth a bundle of sticks and ask the same grandchild to break it. They almost always failed, and he then would point out the strength that comes when family members remain close and pull together in facing the challenges of life.

At every opportunity, Elder Faust would encourage and organize family activities, including Sunday dinners, golf and ski outings, vacations, and the like.

One particularly memorable getaway among many was a hiking trip that Elder Faust took with his children, in-laws, and grandchildren to Escalante, Utah. John Faust, a grandson, recalls a long hike through the sandy terrain and then coming to a sheer cliff they needed to rappel down to reach the river below. "I remember Grandpa starting down that cliff and calling out,

'Why can't we call a helicopter to take us down?' But he made it, with my uncles' help."

That evening, the family participated in a short devotional together, and as they looked into the starlit night, Elder Faust read to them from Moses, telling of the creation of worlds, which are unnumbered to man but numbered unto the Lord (see Moses 1:33, 35). During the rest of the trip, he would share with his family a lesson here and there, and John remembers, at one point, his grandfather telling him about the threefold mission of the Church as they walked along a trail together.

After spending two more days hiking, the time came for Elder Faust to climb up another cliff and out of the canyon, which he did, again, with the help of his sons and sons-in-law. Then he watched as the grandchildren "went up the cliff like monkeys."

In addition to taking time to get away with his family, Elder Faust also included them, as appropriate, in some of his Church assignments.

One such opportunity came on Christmas Eve, 1992, when he and Sister Faust invited their children and their families to join in presenting a devotional service for the missionaries serving at the Provo, Utah, Missionary Training Center. After eating dinner in the cafeteria with the missionaries, the Fausts went into the main assembly room and began the meeting. At the outset, Elder Faust recorded, Lisa and Scott's baby, Amanda, "stole the show. Then we introduced our family and told the missionaries that today we wanted them to be part of our family, that we didn't want any of them to be lonesome or homesick, and that tonight we would be their loving grandfather and grandmother. There were some tears in the group."

After scripture readings, musical numbers, and concluding talks by Elder and Sister Faust, "Ruth and I stood and shook hands with as many missionaries as came up. Some of the kids needed hugs."

One of the missionaries in the congregation that evening was the Fausts' grandson, Jamie Coombs, who was preparing to leave for Brazil on his mission. It wasn't until that evening that most of the missionaries in his district found out who his grandfather was; in fact, after he had offered the invocation and remained seated with the Faust family, some of the missionaries in his district (including his future wife, who was preparing to serve in Portugal) debated whether to pass a note to him, indicating that he probably ought to follow the usual practice of taking his seat with the rest of the congregation.

During all his years as a General Authority, Elder Faust has tried the best he could to provide as normal an existence as possible for his family, given the very public nature of his calling. Inevitably, when they went to a restaurant or other public place, people would come up to visit, which was something Elder Faust enjoyed but which, at the same time, drew undue attention to him and his family. "I can't be unresponsive and ignore people who come up," Elder Faust says, and his family adds that whenever he is out and about, he goes out of his way to greet people and get to know something about them.

He does, however, downplay the position he holds, and Marcus tells of himself and his wife, Susan, going with Elder and Sister Faust to attend a session at the Washington D.C. Temple. "Dad presented his recommend, which is a special one issued to the General Authorities and looks somewhat different. The gentleman who was checking recommends did not know what it was and told my father he wouldn't be able to enter the temple. Rather than embarrassing the man by telling him who he was, Dad politely excused himself and we all left."

Even his grandson, Jamie Coombs, says it was not until later in his life that he understood the importance of his grandfather's call. "He's always been Grandpa," Jamie says, "and he's always made it a very high priority to be close to us. Other than general conference, I really didn't have any experience with what he did when I was younger. In fact, sometimes I would be a little disgruntled when, as young kids, we had to dress a little nicer when we went with him to places like amusement parks."

Jamie's sister, Melissa Coombs Jones, adds, "I asked him once how he feels when we go places and people recognize him and come over to visit with him—whether it bothers him or embarrasses him. He patted my hand and said, 'It's just the calling.'"

Elder Faust also has worked to ensure that the family receive no special preferences as a result of his calling. His children tell of how people will often ask questions of them, expecting that they will have "inside" information on various issues affecting the Church, but Marcus notes, "In terms of knowing what's going on in the Church, the *least* amount of information we get comes from him." Robert adds, "When he comes to our house, he comes to get away from the pressures of his Church calling. His focus is on what we and the kids are doing, rather than the Church being the agenda item for our get-togethers."

At the same time, Elder Faust has never attempted to downplay his responsibilities as the patriarch of his family and has sought to serve his children, in-laws, and grandchildren in every way that he can. His daughter, Janna, says, "He's the epitome of a patriarch in a family, which all men can be, with the priesthood enriching that role even more. He promotes certain traditions in the family, and whenever we're together, he tries to encourage some kind of cohesive conversation or teaching moment. Our visits, although certainly not formally structured in any way, also aren't just loose-ended. He likes to hear what people are thinking, and, if it's possible, he likes to have a family prayer."

Janna's husband, Doug, adds, "He's made the suggestion that we have personal priesthood interviews with our children, and he's set the example by having PPIs with each of his children and their spouses. I was probably a little intimidated by that at first, but what he does, really, is indicate his support for us. Everything he says is couched in terms of, 'What can we do to help you?' Those are moments that just draw you to him all the more because you know that he really has one interest—and that is to help us."

The Fausts' daughter, Lisa Smith, tells of the support her parents have given to her family, particularly during the years her husband, Scott, served as bishop of their ward. "He gave Scott just a few words of advice when he was called: 'Delegate or die.' Then he would keep track of concerns or issues and offer a word of encouragement when it was appropriate. I remember mentioning to him once that Scott had a funeral to conduct in the ward, and later he called and asked Scott how things had gone. That was one of those many times that I've thought how phenomenal it is that this man, who has so much going on, has time to remember little things about our family; that even as he is helping to run a worldwide church, he can remove himself from all of that and plug right into our every-day lives."

Scott points to the wisdom his father-in-law would always show in his role as patriarch and tells of dealing with a situation in his ward that resulted in a man's being deeply offended by something Scott had done and making a point of telling him so. "As Dad listened to the situation, he told me he felt I had handled it correctly. Then, after thinking for a moment, he said, 'As for the man and your relationship with him, kill him with kindness.'"

The family also saw many situations where Elder Faust would sense that someone needed help and seek that person out. Melissa tells of how, when she was sixteen, she and her family were in San Diego, California, at the time of the San Diego Temple dedication. "I was caught up in my teenaged woes and my little crises, and one night Grandpa visited with me and asked if he could give me a blessing. I went to my mom and dad and asked if I had done something wrong, and they explained that he just felt I might need a little extra help in my life (he had asked my father first if it would be okay if he offered to give me a blessing). When he gave me the blessing, he said that I would know who I was and that I would be able to recognize my own character and make good, sound decisions. That had a big impact on me—both his words and the fact that he had the energy, during a very busy time, to think about me."

One grandson, who, like his grandfather, served a mission to Brazil, tells of how, during his high school years, he struggled some with his identity and with being as obedient as he knew he should be. "As Grandpa would come over on Sunday and have dinner with us," he says, "I was worried that he would judge me, but he would always give me a hug and show me the love he felt for me. I knew he could tell I wasn't doing all the right things, but he never said anything about it to make me feel like he didn't love me. Instead, he tried to teach me in a subtle way—by coming to my soccer games, by calling me and asking me how I was doing. At the time, I didn't attach much value to it, but the day came when my relationship with him became important to me once again—and when I knew I needed to make some changes in my life. I remember one day sitting down with him and saying, 'Grandpa, I want to be your friend again and get to know you again.' We had a good talk and then he said, 'What can I do to be a better grandfather and a better friend?' There was no lecturing, no telling me what I needed to do to straighten up; instead, in his humility, he wanted to know what *he* could do to strengthen our relationship."

In acknowledging that the members of his family are not immune from life's challenges, Elder Faust observes, "Children and grandchildren have to come to their own light and testimony, and they can't borrow it from me. Coming to the point where they get their own light is part of growing up, part of maturing, and challenges are just a part of that process. I remember my father telling me of a fellow who was eighty when he lost his sixty-year-old son. This old fellow's comment was, 'I knew I'd never raise that boy.' In like manner, the work of family relationships is never done. You can never say, 'I've got my children raised.' You can never say, 'My grandkids are over Fool's Hill.' It's an ongoing process for all of us."

Elder Maxwell adds this observation: "Years ago, as we

were driving home one night, I listened as my friend told me, through some tears, of one of those family challenges we all seem to face in one form or another. He's always been so grateful for all that has gone well in his family, but he's honest as a father and a grandfather that you should never assume that parenting is an unbroken chain of successes. Those experiences have given him added empathy in his ministry, and they are also evident in his very genuine inquiries about other people's families."

Always there to provide support, whether in his capacity as a father, grandfather, or leader in the Church, has been the woman Elder Faust refers to, with love, as "Ruthy." Of her mother's unique role in Elder Faust's life, Lisa says, "His greatness is because of her. I have no doubt about that." Of his grandmother, Jamie Coombs states, "My grandmother is a saint. She does not have any flaws." Then he adds, "My grandmother knows more about sports than any grandmother I know. She reads the sports section everyday. I asked her once why she does that, and she said that she wants to be able to relate to her grandchildren."

(Though modest about her own abilities, Sister Faust did acknowledge once in an interview, "The right to communicate heart-to-heart with each child and grandchild must be earned."[1])

A talk Elder Faust was assigned to deliver to a training session for General Authorities soon after his call to the Twelve is indicative of the depth of his appreciation for and devotion to the girl who, in 1943, took a chance on a young man she felt she hardly knew:

> When Elder Packer gave me this assignment, he asked a very penetrating question, "What would you have been without Ruth?" I could have answered immediately, "Not much," but he already knew that. I took him seriously. I spent the next twenty-four hours thinking about what I would have been without the loving, sweet support and the discipline of Ruth Wright in my life. It shocked me a little to even think about what life would be

and would have been without her. I would have to answer honestly that without my wife, I would have been pretty much a failure. I do not claim to be an expert in marriage. I have only been
married once, but thanks to my good wife, it took. . . .

I am not going to bother you with all of the experiences in marriage that have caused me to appreciate my wife so much because
you have all had the same experiences. But I cannot help remembering during the twenty years that I was bishop and stake president, coming home tired and weary, and Ruth would say, 'Have
you called . . . so and so?' I would say, 'No,' and I would be without strength to look up the telephone number and dial it. So she
would silently take the phone, dial the number, and hand it to me.
I remember leaving her in the hospital immediately after a serious operation to go to South America to find a home for the Area
Supervisors. I also remember [leaving our home in São Paulo to
deal with a very difficult situation] and she did not say, 'Do you
have to go?' Or, 'When will you be back?' She did as she has done
all these years, and sent me out with a kiss and her blessing, and
with a silent encouragement to not come home until my work
was done.

Then he added this encouragement, to himself as well as to
the others assembled:

Perhaps in these times of great stress we can become what we
ought to be in terms of our relationship with our wives, but perhaps the eternal everyday causes some of us to be more casual
than we ought to be. . . . I feel that Ruth deserves a better me.
Under the direction of the First Presidency, we have the responsibility to be instruments to impart righteousness to the world.
Unless we impart a full measure of righteousness to our wives
and families, we will be blunted instruments to the rest of the
world. . . . I know that the Gospel is true, and I know that a substantial part of that Gospel is how I treat Ruth on an hour-by-
hour, day-by-day, ongoing basis.[2]

In addition to the countless public expressions of his
love for Sister Faust is one of many more private moments
recorded in his journals: "I walked over to the Temple with
Elder Mark E. Petersen for our Thursday morning meeting, and
bumped into my sweetheart, Ruth. My heart skipped to see her

unexpectedly. What a delight she is in my life! What a magnificent blessing!'"

From his years of association with the Fausts, Elder Holland observes:

> This is an unusual relationship and romance—and I have to say "romance," because that's what it is. He is so considerate and gentle and attentive. If they are walking together, he will make sure he walks at her pace, as he takes her arm. If they are in a public setting, he is always looking around to see where she is and make sure she's okay.
>
> She, on the other hand, is absolutely, flat-out adoring of this man. He is twenty-eight feet tall in her eyes. If you ask her how he did with a talk, she lights up like a Christmas tree. If his name is even mentioned, she looks like 220 volts just got plugged in.
>
> I'm sure he's only been able to do what he has done because of the unqualified, uncompromised, unlimited adoration and support and love and loyalty of his wife; and she has had exactly the same kind of support from him. I can't imagine that this was just handed to them from on high; I think that kind of relationship and romance has to be worked at and earned.

Although as Elder and Sister Faust travel throughout the Church much of the attention is given to him, there are also those who recognize the unique spirit of Sister Faust—and the strength of the relationship these two share. After the two had attended a stake conference in Japan, a seventeen-year-old high school student wrote:

> It was a moving experience for me to be able to shake the hand of a General Authority. . . . Sister Faust was wonderful too. When I saw you and Sister Faust, I could see the love that existed between the two of you. When I met Sister Faust, my first impression proved to be true. She is truly a beautiful mother, easygoing in her ways, and full of grace and elegance. Indeed, I must say she is a wonderful example of motherhood and some day I'd like to be just like her, full of love and kindness.

The Fausts' children are likewise very much aware of the depth of Elder and Sister Faust's relationship, prompting Lisa, when asked in an interview, "What makes your father the happiest?" to respond simply, "My mother." When the interviewer asked if there was more she would like to add, she said, "No, just my mother, that's all I need to say."[3]

A favorite moment in the family came during the Christmas season of 1994, as Elder and Sister Faust opened their presents from each other. At the urging of her children, Sister Faust had agreed to have a portrait taken, which they thought Elder Faust could keep on his desk. The Fausts' granddaughter Nicole recalls the moment he opened his present: "As he unwrapped the gift and saw what it was, he pumped his fist in the air as he let out a Portuguese expression meaning 'Wonderful!' The family members became absolutely silent as he continued to look at the picture, and then he began to shake as tears rolled down his cheeks. He was so touched, he couldn't speak. After he composed himself, he went over and gave Grandma a hug and a kiss, and then he was unusually quiet the rest of the evening."

In addition to the time he spends with his wife and family, Elder Faust also makes certain he maintains his friendships, both with those he has known for years and those of more recent acquaintance. Of his father's many friendships, Elder Faust's son Jim says, "In all of his walks of life, he has met so many people with whom he has established a bond and a connection. In addition, he has an amazing memory for people and their lives, which my mother has as well, and they both have an ability to convey their love and concern in a way that is genuine. Now, most of us would think that you can only have so many special relationships in your life, but in Dad's case, that's not true. From Howard W. Hunter to his former missionary companions to the man who cares for the plants in his office, he will always find something they share in common, and he will use that connection as a means of giving them his attention. Interestingly, he is not flamboyant, but he has an amazing ability to connect with people."

In addition to trying, whenever possible, to attend gatherings of old friends and missionary companions, wedding receptions (often after having performed the sealing), and the like,

Elder Faust has maintained many remarkably close associations with friends, both old and new.

Elder Albert Choules Jr., who first met Elder Faust while serving as a regional representative in Arizona (and who subsequently served as a member of the First and Second Quorums of Seventy), tells of getting to know Elder Faust as the two were assigned to divide a stake in the Phoenix area. "I was single at the time, my first wife having died about two years earlier, and for some reason Elder Faust chose to stay with me, rather than the stake president (where I'm sure he would have been fed better). He took an interest in my situation, and after we got the new stake presidency called, he suggested we go for a walk across the street through a cotton field. As we did, he asked me about a woman I was dating, how I was doing, what my feelings were, and so forth. His interest didn't end there, however, and when he returned home, he took the time to write Marilyn (whom I did eventually marry) and shared some thoughts with her that she was thrilled to receive."

On another occasion, while visiting with Sister Faust's brother, Owen Wright, and his wife in Idaho, Elder Faust went out for a walk one morning and struck up a conversation with a man who was laying sod in his front yard. The two talked for some time, and during the course of their conversation, Elder Faust learned that although the man was a member of the Church, he had not been active for many years. From the interest Elder Faust showed that morning, the man began the process of returning to full activity and eventually asked his newfound friend if he would perform the sealing for the man, his wife, and their children.

Elder Faust's secretary of many years, Margaret Bury, tells of his friendship, thoughtfulness, and wisdom over the years, particularly during a time of great loss in her life. "This person, though not a family member, was very near and dear to me," Sister Bury recalls. "When I learned of the person's death, I called Elder Faust to tell him of the news and to say that I would be late coming in. We talked for a minute, and then, as

I found myself not wanting to be alone, I went next door to visit with a neighbor. About an hour later, I returned to my home to get ready for work, and as I walked in the telephone was ringing. It was Elder Faust, who said, 'Thank goodness I've reached you. After we hung up, I realized who this person was to you and knew you shouldn't be alone. And I've been worried because I couldn't get through."

Later that day, she adds, "Something set me off and I started weeping. He came out and saw me, and through my tears I told him I was sorry to lose control. Then he draped himself over a huge printer we used to have and said, 'Margaret, it's really tough to lose a parent. I haven't gotten over it yet.' He didn't use a cliche; rather, he thought the situation through in his sensitive mind and said what was appropriate from his heart."

Another associate tells of going through a rather public and misunderstood divorce—and of finding that Elder Faust was one person who did not rush to judgment and dismiss this man for what some might have perceived as his shortcomings. Instead, Elder Faust kept track of his friend and, after his second marriage, met with him and his new wife. "As we discussed certain challenges that were still ahead of us, he listened and then said to my wife, 'Sister, I think a little patience here is all that's needed.' I'm not sure she would have accepted that advice from anyone else, but she knew he had listened and understood, and when I asked her later how she felt, she said, 'Elder Faust told me to be patient, and I'm going to be patient.' And as time went on, we saw just how true his words had been."

Elder Faust also maintained an active involvement with the Church on a very local level, as he attended church in his home ward or with family, served as a home teacher, attended tithing settlement, and served in other ways that some might not expect of an apostle. He was often called upon to speak wherever he found himself attending church, and his family tells of his concern over not causing meetings to run long. Robert shares that at the conclusion of one meeting, which had already gone over when Elder Faust stood to give the closing remarks, his father simply said, "Remember who you are, and act accordingly"—and then sat down. (Elder Faust more than once quipped that church meetings—whether administrative or otherwise—"don't have to be endless to be eternal.")

His directness and humor were also often evident, as when he was asked to say a few words at the conclusion of a sacrament meeting during which a ward leader had been released and had borne a particularly tearful testimony to the ward. "Sister Jones," he observed, "you've been released today—and you're still alive. When I'm released, I'll be dead."

Although Elder Faust often wished that his presence at meetings did not attract as much attention as it did, he also counted it a great privilege and blessing to him to attend a regular block of meetings whenever he was in town. Once, after attending fast and testimony meeting in his own ward, he recorded, "It was very comforting to hear the humble saints bear powerful testimonies to the great absolutes of the Church, which we do not change nor alter, and of the mission of Jesus Christ as the Lord, Savior, and Redeemer, of the mission of Joseph Smith, the restoration of the gospel, the truthfulness of the Book of Mormon, the restoration of the priesthood, and so forth."

In addition to being able to attend his own ward on occasion, there were also times when, by being at home, he was able to have involvement in the very issues he dealt with as a General Authority. During the 1983 floods that turned several Salt Lake City streets into rivers, Elder Faust attended church one Sunday and there, with the rest of his ward, heard the call for all able-bodied members to help sandbag a section of the stake that was threatened by rising waters. He recorded, "Since I had been in on the planning as part of the Executive Committee of Welfare Services, I wanted to see how the process worked," and so he joined with his fellow ward members in the effort.

When the Relief Society and priesthood quorums in the

Fausts' home ward were asked to make sandwiches for the Salvation Army soup kitchen, Elder Faust left the office early to go home and make the twenty he had signed up to help with, adding those to the twenty Sister Faust made. He then went with the ward to the soup kitchen and there helped to serve those who came for a meal and to clean up the tables and chairs after. His thought at the conclusion of the day was, "I was a little ashamed that I live in such comfort and pleasant circumstances."

Even with his favorable circumstances, Elder Faust has worked to follow the teachings he learned as a boy growing up during the Depression—namely, simplicity, frugality, and self-sufficiency. He and Sister Faust have always taken care of their own housekeeping, with Elder Faust helping out with vacuuming, replacing furnace filters, gardening, and shopping— "which I would usually foul up," he notes, with Sister Faust adding that he also attracts many who are willing to help as he navigates the grocery store aisles. He practices moderation in what he buys for himself, and once, when Sister Faust insisted that his overcoat had long since gone out of style and was showing signs of wear, he reluctantly agreed to buy a new one—but then had the old one "remodeled" so that he could continue to wear it as well. On another occasion, he rather reluctantly parted with a twenty-five-year-old television set when he found that it was finally beyond repair.

In an effort to simplify their lives further and cut back on Elder Faust's time commuting, the Fausts decided in 1986 to sell their condominium and move to a recently renovated apartment complex near the Church Administration Building. When the process followed a pattern typical of the frustrations that generally accompany the buying and selling of a home, Elder Faust concluded one challenging day with the observation, "So, we worry, and say our prayers." After weeks of delays and setbacks, the deal on both properties finally closed, only to then have one of the checks paid to him not clear the bank (a matter that was quickly resolved). Through it all, Elder Faust kept a

philosophical outlook, no doubt knowing that neither his calling nor the demands of his office could spare him from the frustrations of life common to all.

Through all of his associations—with family, friends, his
Brethren of the General Authorities, staff members, and sometimes even strangers—those close to Elder Faust during his
years as a member of the Quorum of the Twelve have experienced much of his wisdom, kindness, counsel, humor, encouragement, and concern. Interestingly, many of those same people
knew little of the significant contributions he made, both to the
Church and beyond. Even within the close family circles, Elder
Faust was never one to attach his name to any of the Church's
advances, and his children generally had to learn from other
sources all that their father had contributed to the work of the
kingdom.

Such was certainly the case with the planning and construction of the BYU Jerusalem Center, for although his children
knew of the frequent trips he took to Israel and of their father's
association with the center, it was not until they went as a family to Jerusalem that they came close to fully realizing how integral he had been to this facility and to its purposes.

The idea for the trip came from Elder and Sister Faust, and
Janna tells of the 1987 family dinner at which it was discussed.
"The adults had gathered at my parents' home, and after dinner my father said, 'Your mother and I have a proposal. We
would like to spend your inheritance and take you and your
spouses to Israel. This has always been a dream of your
mother's, to have each of you with us in the Holy Land, and we
would like to take you next Christmas.' Then, in keeping with
his strong sense of organization and his belief in helping those
who help themselves, he added, 'We will pay for half of the
trip, and if you will save $167 a month from now until next
December, we will all be able to go.' Then he told us he knew
we could each do it, and we all agreed we would find a way."

A year later, on December 26th, Elder and Sister Faust,
accompanied by their five children and five "children-in-love,"

flew to Israel, and there the children let out a collective gasp as they rounded a corner and saw the magnificent structure their father had been involved with—and then learned something of the extent of that involvement.

Jim explains that much of that insight came one evening as the family had dinner with David Reznik, a Brazilian-born Jew who had served as the architect for the center. "David told us something of his history, and how he and his wife had emigrated to Israel in 1948. Jerusalem, at the time, was war-torn, as well as being old and in general disrepair, and the Jews were setting out to build up the State of Israel. During this time, David received a postcard from a friend showing the New York City skyline with its many skyscrapers, and on the back this friend had written, referring to all the work needing to be done in Israel, 'Where are the architects to build up Israel?'

"David never forgot that, and he told us that several years later, after he had traveled through Europe and seen so many cathedrals and other architectural wonders, he sent this same friend a postcard from Europe asking, 'Where are the Dukes?'—meaning that an architect is of no use unless he has a commission. Then David turned to my father and said, 'I am the architect; he is the Duke!'"

Of course, the process of building the Jerusalem Center involved many, many people—some in Salt Lake City and others who lived in Jerusalem and dealt with the challenges on a day-to-day basis. But those involved with the center point to Elder Faust, together with his beloved friend, President Howard W. Hunter, as the men who had a vision of what the center could and should be, and who then worked to turn their vision into a reality.

In reflecting on his years in the Twelve, Elder Faust acknowledged, "One of the most meaningful experiences I had in the Twelve was working with President Hunter, Elder Jeffrey R. Holland (who, through much of the process, was president of BYU), and so many others in acquiring the land for and building the Jerusalem Center. That was a highlight of my service—not only because I had the association of these wonderful men, but also because the witness of the guidance of the hand of the Lord in bringing it all about was confirming to my testimony."

The hope that BYU and the Church might build a center for study-abroad students in Jerusalem predated Elder Faust's call to the Twelve. In fact, he was aware of the issue from his service as president of the International Mission. Soon after his call to the Twelve, Elder Faust received the assignment to work with Elder Hunter in beginning the process of establishing such a center.

Elder Holland recalls that in 1979, "Elder Hunter was asked by the First Presidency to take the assignment for this project because of his involvement with Elder LeGrand Richards in acquiring the funding for and overseeing the construction of the Orson Hyde Memorial Gardens in Jerusalem. Because the Brethren generally don't have solo assignments—given the benefit of two minds and two witnesses—early on, the First Presidency assigned Elder Faust to serve with Elder Hunter in fulfilling this assignment."

From the outset, writes David Galbraith,

> the development of the Jerusalem Center was a First Presidency project that included Brigham Young University. The logic of the joint building effort was obvious: first, it satisfied the requirements of the BYU-sponsored educational programs operating in the Holy Land, which were becoming increasingly attractive to Latter-day Saint students and tourists alike; and, second, it met the ecclesiastical imperatives of the Church, which included a physical presence in the Holy Land after an absence of nearly two thousand years.[4]

The first step in the process that Elders Hunter and Faust faced was acquiring an appropriate parcel of land upon which a center could be built. A number of possibilities had been explored over a several-year period, but after President Spencer W. Kimball returned in 1979 from dedicating the Orson Hyde Memorial Garden, which is located on the Mount of Olives and overlooks Jerusalem, it was evident to all concerned that the ideal site was a parcel of land located at the northern end of the Mount of Olives, in an area known as Mount Scopus.

Obtaining permission to lease that land—and at the same time working with David Reznik and his associates to develop plans for the building—was a five-year ordeal that saw Elders Hunter and Faust making numerous trips to Israel. As they traveled together, and especially as they walked the streets of Jerusalem and visited other sites where the Savior had ministered, the two men developed a closeness that went far beyond the friendship they had already enjoyed for many years. Often, after long days of meeting with government officials and attorneys (both Israeli and Palestinian, since the land was claimed by both sides), as well as with the faculty and students who had come to Jerusalem from BYU, the two apostles, together with then-President Holland, were able to go to the Garden Tomb where they would read from the scriptures, seek for the renewal of their souls, and ponder the import of their undertaking.

Finally, in early 1984, after some of the most arduous and delicate negotiations in the lives of these two former lawyers, Elder Faust was summoned to a meeting in President Hinckley's office, along with Elder Hunter, President Holland, and several others involved in the project. Elder Faust recalls that after much discussion relative to rezoning issues, building permits, construction costs, and architectural plans, "President Hinckley expressed his opinion that we ought to get the contracts signed as soon as possible and asked Brother Hunter to go over. Brother Hunter said he would appreciate some assistance, so President Hinckley said, 'All right, Jim, you go with him.'"

Two days later, Elder Hunter, Elder Faust, and President Holland left Salt Lake City to complete the assignment given them by the First Presidency. On Saturday, the three men observed the Sabbath with BYU study abroad groups from

Jerusalem, Vienna, and London as they held a sacrament meeting in the Orson Hyde Park.

On Sunday, as the three men prepared to sign the lease on the property, they received word that there was yet another hurdle that had been placed in their way, but after receiving the assistance of Mayor Teddy Kollek, whom Elder Faust describes as "one of the wisest, most durable politicians in the world," they were assured the signing would take place on Monday.

The next morning, the group was able to meet with the director of Lands Authority and sign the necessary agreements, but only after coming within three blocks of a terrorist attack on their way to the meeting. After the signing, the Jewish attorney retained by the Church and BYU observed, "Speaking for my family, who have been in Jerusalem for fifteen generations, you have a priceless piece of property." And at the end of the day, Elder Faust recorded, "It has been an historic day. A little hectic, but otherwise, quite wonderful."

Having overcome what at times seemed to be insurmountable obstacles during the planning stages of the Jerusalem Center, Elder Faust and his associates were entitled to the hope that with the commencement of construction, the worst of their challenges were behind them. Such was not to be the case, however, as the sight of cranes going up on the side of Mount Scopus increased the ire of certain extreme elements in Jerusalem who feared that, when the center was completed, Israel would be overrun by Mormon missionaries seeking to convert the Jews.

This was an issue that had been dealt with during the preliminary work, but with construction underway, the cries from small factions of the Orthodox Jewish community reached their crescendos. Elder Faust continued making frequent trips to Jerusalem, together with Elder Hunter and President Holland, as the three would meet with government officials and religious leaders to assure them that the center would be used to support the academic programs of BYU, function as a meeting place for LDS groups, and be open to all from the community who wished to come. No matter what the three men said, however, the opponents of the center continued to press their demand that the construction be halted and that the Mormons go back to Salt Lake City.

At one point, David Galbraith informed Elders Hunter and Faust that a group of Orthodox Jews had informed him that they had found a wealthy man who was willing to purchase the half-finished center from the Church. Elder Faust's response was, "They may have found a buyer, but they haven't found a seller." Brother Galbraith adds,

> Those of us who were on the front lines in Jerusalem—who were having our phones tapped, our utilities shut off, our families threatened—needed someone who could lift us up and help us realize that this was the Lord's work and we would not fail. Elder Faust would explain to us that inasmuch as this was a First Presidency project, the adversary no doubt felt threatened and would do all he could to stop it. In the face of all this opposition, Elder Faust's was the voice that encouraged us to see our way through.

Beyond buoying up those whose lives were so intertwined with the construction of the center, Elder Faust also did much to orchestrate the university's and the Church's response to the opposition. He oversaw the efforts of an Israeli public relations firm that advised the Church on relevant issues, and he arranged for 154 United States Congressmen to write a letter of support to their counterparts in the Israeli Knesset. He also, more than once, joined with Elder Hunter and President Holland in meeting face-to-face with those who opposed the center in an attempt to reassure them that it would not be used as a means of proselytizing among the Jews.

A critical juncture occurred in July 1985, as opponents to the center called once again for the government to halt construction and staged demonstrations at the Wailing Wall in Jerusalem as a show of opposition. Once again, Elders Hunter and Faust and President Holland traveled to Jerusalem in yet another attempt to find a resolution to the conflict. During that trip, the three men met with the leading rabbis who opposed the center, during which Elder Faust was part of the following exchange:

> Jerusalem Chief Rabbi, Mashash: You are honorable and intelligent people and so you will understand. The opposition does not stem from a single religious group—the Jews are united—we can't be silent, we will not. . . .
>
> We know about your missionary achievements and so we can say your efforts to obtain land for a missionary center was a misunderstanding. Because of that we feel we can ask you to stop construction! Otherwise we will have to fight. If we do not succeed in this meeting it will be a very serious fight. We pray that it will not come to that.
>
> Elder Faust: We appreciate your statement and we know of your sincerity, but please examine your hearts and see if there is not a way we can exist together in this land.
>
> You speak of a fight; we are not here to fight. We look upon you as a covenant people. We do not want a worldwide fight—it can only hurt each of us, including the State of Israel. . . .
>
> Rabbi Porush: Our relations with the Christian community since 1967 have been excellent, but there is a big difference between the Christian churches that have been built here and the huge Center you are building. We have no objection to a church, but your place will be a missionary center. If your youth are really devoted, and we know they are, then they must missionize; otherwise, they would not be Mormons.
>
> You have chosen to build on such a sacred place—Mt. Scopus is the heart and soul of the Jewish people and we simply cannot tolerate your center on this sacred ground overlooking the Temple Mount. No law passed by the Knesset of Israel can obligate me if it contradicts the Torah.
>
> If a people has no alternative, then their resolve becomes greater than an atomic bomb! Did you see? Our people were crying at the Western Wall. Place your Center in Egypt or Greece, anywhere, but not in Israel.
>
> Elder Faust: It gives us sorrow to feel our presence is not welcome. We have good relations with Jews all over the world. In Salt Lake City we are very close to the Jewish community. Mormons elected a Jewish mayor and a Jewish governor. . . .
>
> We have lived together with the Jewish community for many, many years with mutual respect and tolerance for each other. We

feel we have done nothing wrong in establishing our Center here, nor do we intend to do anything wrong in the future. We appreciate this opportunity to meet you and to discuss these matters directly.

In reflecting on that meeting and others, Brother Galbraith observes, "Elder Faust was truly a man of peace, always looking for ways to calm our often agitated Jewish friends who sought an end to our presence in Jerusalem, or to calm the troubled waters among the Latter-day Saints in Jerusalem who were sometimes offended by the opposition."

In time, the opposition did subside, and by the time the center was completed in 1988, fully eighty percent of the citizens of Israel held a favorable view toward the Jerusalem Center.

Through those years, those involved with the center saw much more than a building being built; they also witnessed the love and friendship that existed between President Hunter and Elder Faust—two men with like legal minds, unshakable faith, and the wisdom needed to work their way through ten years of one entanglement after another.

The full depth and meaning of that friendship is known only to the two, although those who were with them saw enough that they would conclude, in the words of Elder Holland, "that these two men forged a bond and friendship that is one of the sweet stories to come out of this entire effort." (Elder Faust acknowledges, with a chuckle, that when Elder Hunter married his second wife, Inis Bernice Egan, in 1990, he and Sister Faust accompanied the newlyweds on their honeymoon—to Jerusalem.)

Brother Galbraith adds, "One of the things that always impressed me about Elder Faust was how loyal he was to Elder Hunter. Elder Hunter, with his age and the demands of his office, sometimes showed the strains of these trips more so than his younger colleague, but Elder Faust was always there to help him. He protected Elder Hunter in many ways—spiritually, mentally, and physically—and he made sure we didn't place too many demands on him. While they were in Jerusalem, they could, at times, relax and enjoy each other's company in a way that I suspect was not possible in Salt Lake City. Theirs was more than a brotherly love; they enjoyed a beautiful relationship that would not be common among many men."

Elder Holland adds that each showed a great regard for the other's opinion as issues were discussed and decisions made, with Elder Faust always finding a way to defer to his senior companion. He also tells of one setting where that deference became rather difficult. "We arrived at the point of needing to choose the stone for the exterior of the center, and the contractors brought forth four or five slabs with various shades of red running through. Elder Faust, true to his nature, suggested that this was something Elder Hunter should decide, and Elder Hunter said, no, that Elder Faust had better judgment in such matters. They went back and forth for about twenty minutes in this courteous manner, and what neither one of them was willing to admit is that they were both color blind and could not see the distinctions in any of the stones placed before them."

When the project finally came to a completion in 1988, the two men, again with President Holland accompanying them, traveled with their wives back to Jerusalem to sign the final lease. Elder Faust noted in his journal, the day before the anticipated signing, "We are hoping to be able to sign the lease tomorrow, but being in Israel, we are not certain that it will come about. If things go as usual, we will have to push it." The next day, as the group was about to get in their cars to go to the signing, they received word that "it was all off." As Elder Faust worked to sort out what the complications were—and to solicit support from key allies—"All of a sudden, right out of the blue, here was another call from our attorney, Joe Kokia, saying, 'Come on down and sign.'"

Even with that, Sister Faust recalls that the group got stuck in an elevator as they were leaving for the signing, and that a group of men had arrived with axes to open the doors just as they finally opened on their own. Through it all, even as Elder Faust wondered when the elevator doors would open, he maintained the attitude he had expressed at the height of the opposition, after a thorough discussion of the matter with the First Presidency and the Twelve: "We concluded that we should rely upon the Lord to lead us through, that it was through His service and providence that we are where we are, and that if it came to the worst case scenario that we had to leave the center, it would not be the end of the work, although tragic. In the past, we have walked away from temples, as well as homes and cities, and this could happen again."

After the lease was signed later that day, Elder Faust says, "President Hunter said to the Hollands and to Ruth and me, 'Let's go to the Garden Tomb, for old times' sake.'"

That the Church and BYU were never forced to walk away from the project has been a blessing beyond what few could have imagined at the outset. Physically, the Jerusalem Center provides some two hundred students, faculty, and staff with living quarters, classrooms, a library, and two large auditoriums. It is carved almost unobtrusively into the side of Mount Scopus, even as it affords those who live and visit there panoramic views of Jerusalem. It provides a place for community events and concerts and hosts tens of thousands of visitors each year. The gardens that surround the center provide, through ancient grinding mills and grape and olive presses, a reminder of life in ancient Israel, as well as a place to meditate upon the significance of the sacred ground on which the center stands.

At another level, the Jerusalem Center has proven to be a bridge between cultures—Jews, Moslems, and Christians; Israelis, Palestinians, and Arabs. "Early on," Elder Faust recalls, "Mayor Kollek said to us, 'This building can be a bridge to peace.' When it was completed, many years later, he visited us at the center and said that as the mayor of Jerusalem he had fought many battles, but that the most significant battle he had been part of was over the Jerusalem Center. He added, as he had told us many times over the years, that this really hadn't been a battle over the building, but it was a battle against prejudice and ignorance and bigotry. To him, the Jerusalem Center became a symbol of Jerusalem as an open city."

In 1993, Elder Faust returned to the Jerusalem Center yet again, this time with the Mormon Tabernacle Choir, which performed a series of concerts throughout the Middle East, culminating in performances at the center. At the conclusion of one of the group's final concerts there, Elder Faust recorded, "The news media has been very, very generous, and newspapers which opposed us before have been very loud in their praise. One of them called the group 'a choir of angels.' As we visited with people after the concert, somebody in the group said, 'The Mormon Tabernacle Choir has been able to do in thirty minutes what the community has not been able to do in twenty years in terms of uniting the community.'"

Even with such praise, the Church has been true to its word (and to the undertakings that President Ezra Taft Benson signed for the Church and President Holland signed for BYU) that it not allow proselytizing—until such time as it is permitted by the Israeli government. Students who attend the center are instructed that they are not to hand out tracts of any sort (including the Book of Mormon) or to engage in conversations with the citizens of Israel that could, in any way, be construed as an attempt to convert.

Yet Elder Faust would always note, as he visited the center after its completion, the effect living in the Holy Land had upon the students. To a group of BYU faculty and staff, he stated in 1994:

> I have had a close relationship with only one of the functions of the University at the Jerusalem Center for Near Eastern Studies. You are well aware of the long struggle that it took to establish that presence in the holy city. You may not be aware of the miracles which took place to bring it into being. Yet the greatest miracles of the Jerusalem Center experience occur in the lives of the young men and women who are able to attend there. The monument there is not the magnificent building in the prime location of Jerusalem, nor in the world-class architecture, but in the lives of those who are able to go there.[5]

Just over two weeks after Howard W. Hunter, Elder Faust's friend and companion, was ordained and set apart as president of the Church on June 5, 1994, President Hunter called Elder Jeffrey R. Holland to serve as a member of the Quorum of the Twelve. Not surprisingly, he also asked that Elder Holland join with Elder Faust in overseeing the center.

Then in early 1995, President Hunter assigned himself, along with Elders Faust and Holland, to return to the Jerusalem Center, as well as to conduct a regional conference in Birmingham, England. Before the three men could leave, however, President Hunter's health took a turn for the worse, and so Elder Faust and Elder Holland set out on the trip without their beloved friend.

The morning after their arrival in England, Elder Faust recorded, "I was awakened by Elder Holland, advising me that President Hunter had passed away. We were in shock because we had hoped and prayed that we could fill this last assignment that he had given to us. . . . We were so saddened that we did nothing but count the great blessings we had had of associating so closely with such a great man."

Upon the advice of President Hinckley, Elder Faust and Elder Holland stayed to conduct the sessions of conference scheduled for Saturday and Sunday, although they had to move the Sunday morning session up one hour in order to catch their return flight to Salt Lake City. ("The great host of 11,000 Saints were notified by their home teachers," Elder Faust recorded, "and it was wonderful to see the Church work.")

As the two men then traveled the long distance home, Elder Faust says simply, "We did so with heavy hearts."

Elder Holland shared deeply in that same sentiment and later added, "As we sat side by side on those two flights, I had the distinct impression that I was flying home with the next counselor in the new First Presidency that was about to be formed. I kept that impression to myself but took great delight, even in the midst of overwhelming sorrow, in the anticipation of a First Presidency that would include President Gordon B.

Hinckley, President Thomas S. Monson, and President James E. Faust."

NOTES

1. *Women of Devotion* (Salt Lake City: Bookcraft, 1990), p. 16.

2. "Husbands, Love Your Wives," unpublished address to General Authorities, Salt Lake City, Utah, 4 April 1979.

3. Jolene Meredith, "Friend to Friend," *The Friend*, October 1975, p. 6.

4. David B. Galbraith, D. Kelly Ogden, and Andrew C. Skinner, *Jerusalem: The Eternal City* (Salt Lake City: Deseret Book, 1996), pp. 455–56. For a more thorough treatment of the background and history of the Jerusalem Center, see pp. 450–73.

5. Address given at Brigham Young University conference, Provo, Utah, 23 August 1994.

13

A SPIRITUAL
STATESMAN

Upon arriving home late Sunday evening, "tired and sad," Elder Faust was faced not only with his own personal grief, but with a number of responsibilities relative to President Hunter's funeral on Wednesday, March 8, 1995, and what was scheduled to be the selection of a new president of the Church the next Sunday. Some of those responsibilities stemmed from his overseeing the Church's public and media relations functions, and as the week progressed, he noted his appreciation for the "magnificent" work of the Public Affairs staff. A responsibility that weighed more heavily upon him was responding to the request that he speak at his beloved friend's funeral.

On Tuesday, March 7, 1995, a viewing was held in the Church Administration Building, where some 22,000 people filed by President Hunter's open casket. Elder Faust noted in his journal, "It was very touching to see the sweet faces of the humble Saints and the children who came. In the evening, when the viewing was to stop, there was still a long, long line. But the Brethren decided that they would let the people continue as long as anybody wished to come. What a great tribute to a great man."

The next day, Elder Faust paid his own public tribute to President Hunter. After reviewing the significant accomplishments of a relatively brief administration, Elder Faust suggested:

> Perhaps the most remarkable occurrence during his short time as President of the Church has been that the members of the Church all over the world have become bonded to him in a

special way as their prophet, seer, and revelator. They have seen in him the personification of the attributes of the Savior himself. They have responded in a remarkable way to his prophetic messages of making our lives more Christlike and of making our temples the center of our worship. He invited any who found themselves outside the circle of the Church to return and to have their tears dried in the process. He knew what it was like to be without a companion. He knew what it was like to have physical limitations. He was in so many ways the personification of the counsel of Alma:

"And now I would that ye should be humble, and be submissive and gentle; easy to be entreated; full of patience and long-suffering; being temperate in all things; being diligent in keeping the commandments of God at all times; asking for whatsoever things ye stand in need, both spiritual and temporal; always returning thanks unto God for whatsoever things ye do receive" (Alma 7:23).

No doubt the membership of the Church came to respect and love him so much because he possessed so abundantly these Christlike qualities. Surely his intense sorrow and suffering over a period of many years also contributed to their affinity for him.[1]

Elder Faust told of President Hunter's love for the Holy Land, noting that "his desire to be where the Savior walked and talked seemed insatiable." He then provided a more personal perspective of an unassuming man whose callings had made him very public:

Although outgoing in so many ways, yet he was also a private man. He had no inner conflicts and tensions. He had no ego needs. With all his wisdom, he could sit among his brethren and say very little. He was at complete peace with himself. As Shakespeare said, "In peace there's nothing so becomes a man / As modest stillness and humility" (*The Life of King Henry V,* act 3, sc. 1, lines 3–4).

His delightful sense of humor was ever present. His beloved sister, Dorothy, also possessed this same charm. At one time we were together in Venice with a couple of hours to spare before going on to Jerusalem. I asked my wife, Ruth, "What have you always wanted to do in Venice?" And she replied, "I've always wanted to take a gondola ride and have you sing 'O Solo Mio.'"

President Hunter then responded, "If Jim's going to sing, I'm not going to go!" We went for the gondola ride, but I did not sing! . . .

President Hunter's spiritual depth was so profound as to be unfathomable. Having been under the guiding influence of the Lord Jesus Christ as his special witness for so many years, President Hunter's spirituality was honed in a remarkable way. It was the wellspring of his whole being. He was quiet about sacred things, humble about sacred things, careful when he spoke about sacred things.[2]

Following the funeral, Elder and Sister Faust accompanied the cortege to President Hunter's burial site, a place the two men had gone to almost twelve years earlier when Elder Faust helped then-Elder Hunter select a burial site for his first wife, Clara Jeffs Hunter.

Thursday and Friday, Elder Faust noted, were likewise "busy days getting ready for the monumental events which will transpire this coming weekend and for the press conference on Monday."

Of the events that occurred on Sunday, he recorded:

> This morning at nine o'clock the Quorum of the Twelve, including President Hinckley and President Monson, were to assemble. At 8:10 I received a call from President Gordon B. Hinckley telling me there was a cart going over and would I wish to go with him. I told him, "Of course." I met him about 8:15, and we arrived at five minutes to. I was embarrassed because my seat was the only empty one. I think everybody wondered if I was going to be the new second counselor in the Presidency, but President Hinckley hadn't said one word! . . .
>
> [After the selection of Gordon B. Hinckley as the president of the Church,] he nominated Thomas S. Monson and James E. Faust to be his counselors. This announcement came as a surprise and a relief. It was a relief because I had been denying feelings and also because several of my brethren had expressed their feelings that I was going to go into the Presidency. . . . It was, of course, one of the most overwhelming experiences of my life.

At the conclusion of the meeting, President Faust was presented with several legal documents he needed to sign as a member of the new First Presidency, and he added, "I was so rattled that I couldn't sign my name straight."

He then returned home to tell his wife what had just transpired. She would acknowledge later, "I had a feeling that he was going to be called, but when I would tell him I hoped he'd let me know if he had any inclinations, he'd just say, 'No, no.'"

That evening, President and Sister Faust visited with two of their children and their families but said nothing of what had taken place earlier in the day. The next morning, at 9:00, President Faust followed President Hinckley and President Monson into the Joseph Smith Memorial Building, where a press conference was held to announce the reorganization of the First Presidency. As he helped field the questions that came from the media, President Faust also stated something of the feelings he held for the two men with whom he would serve. He reiterated those sentiments two weeks later in general conference, saying,

> I have had the great privilege of associating in various Church assignments with President Gordon B. Hinckley for forty years. I know his heart. I know his soul. I know of his faith. I know of his dedication. I know of his great capacity. I know of his love of the Lord and God's holy work. I have a great personal affection and regard for him. I also know that he has been foreordained and marvelously prepared to be the President of this church in our day and time.
>
> My association with President Thomas S. Monson has also been long and blessed. We have worked closely together for decades in several capacities. His mind and memory are unique; his faith simple and absolute. President Monson is a big man, but the biggest part of him is his great heart. He has tremendous talent. I feel very humbled to serve with President Hinckley and President Monson.[3]

As the world heard the news, so did President Faust's children and grandchildren, who were not surprised by the announcement, but who were shocked nonetheless. One of the grandchildren living in Utah got an immediate taste of how this calling would affect the family as he was all but mobbed after the announcement and peppered with questions and well-meaning (but not always sensitive) counsel. A thoughtful school principal soon suggested he might want to go home for the remainder of the day, which he did. Lisa and Scott's five-year-old son, Jacob, began to cry as he watched the announcement with his mother and father. When Scott, concerned over Jacob's reaction, asked what the tears were for, the young boy said, "Because I'm going to be late for school!"

That evening, President and Sister Faust called their family together so that, in President Faust's words,

> I could explain to them that my first responsibility was as a husband, father, and grandfather. I reviewed how all of us would have to conduct ourselves better and be more representative of what we ought to be. I also told them that I was not any better than any other elder in the Church, and that we as a family would only be better if we acted better, and that we should treat everyone with respect and courtesy and kindness. Much that we had to say to them was an expression of love, which Ruth did beautifully.

As the family visited, President Faust recorded, "Little Ashley (Jim's daughter) came over and hugged me. Then she cried and said, 'You're the most wonderful grandfather in the world. I don't want to lose you as my grandfather.' I told her, 'Ashley, I'm still going to be your grandfather.'"

Several days later, President and Sister Faust took his brothers and their wives to dinner, continuing their long-standing tradition of regular get-togethers. Afterwards, his brothers asked to see his new office, and while they were there visiting, he recorded, "I read the words of Gideon to my brothers: 'My father is poor in Manasseh, and I am the least in my father's house' (Judges 6:15). I told them that was the way I felt about the matter because I do not consider myself better in any way than they are. I also bore my testimony to them that any honor that is paid to me comes only because of the offices that I have held and do hold now."

If anyone in the family had any doubts about the extent to

which their father and grandfather would have time for his family, those concerns were dispensed with almost immediately, as he and Sister Faust continued to call, visit, and welcome their ever-growing family into their home. President Faust's secretary, Margaret Bury, notes that upon leaving the office each day, his attention would visibly shift to "What can I do now for Ruth?" Then he and Ruth would turn their focus toward their family.

Whereas the family felt no sense of loss, President Faust's brethren of the Twelve did. At their first quorum meeting after Elder Faust's call to the First Presidency, President Boyd K. Packer, who had just been called again as acting president of the Twelve, said, in beginning the meeting, "Today we've lost two men. We've lost James, and we've lost Esdras."

Elder Joseph B. Wirthlin adds, "It was a definite loss to the Twelve because he was one who never hesitated in voicing his opinion. He was fearless of speaking up as to what he thought was right. For Brother Faust, right was right and wrong was wrong, regardless of who he was speaking to or what the situation was. We lost his forthrightness, his honesty, and his willingness to point something out that was certainly of no benefit to himself."

Elder Perry shares something of his feelings as he watched his friend move into the First Presidency in recalling, "When he was called, I sent him a letter and told him that at last I could feel comfortable—that I never felt comfortable about him being junior to me in the Twelve. I had always looked up to him and admired him so much. He got after me for sending him that letter, although I think he appreciated it."

Having had a close association with President Faust since their days together as regional representatives, Elder Maxwell observes, "It has been wonderful to see him grow. He started off so very able and distinguished, and yet his growth is so illustrative of what the gospel can do. As good as the James Esdras Faust was that I began to know in the 1960s—and he was good—he has grown to become so presidential and a spiritual statesman. He is 'Exhibit A' in terms of what the gospel can do. And I'm not sure that, in his meekness, he realizes how much he has grown."

As Elder Holland watched Elder Faust deal with the many difficulties that arose during the construction of the Jerusalem Center (an experience he summarizes with the quip, "We may not have crossed the Plains, but we helped to build the Jerusalem Center"), he saw his friend's abilities tested in some of the hottest fires of adversity. In commenting on the contributions President Faust immediately made as a counselor to the President of the Church, Elder Holland says, "When things are calm, you might not have occasion to know he is in the room. But when the pressure comes, that is when President Faust is at his best. My experience with him over many years has shown me that the grimmer the situation is, the more difficult the challenge is, the better James E. Faust is going to be. In those situations, he is the one you want whispering in your ear what you need to hear; and in that sense, he was born to be a counselor."

In describing something of the work and responsibilities of the First Presidency, President Monson states:

> This is a hierarchical church, and the presiding high priest is the president. With his two counselors, you have the Quorum of the First Presidency, which is the highest governing organization in the Church. The workload and detail involved in presiding over every aspect of a worldwide church is enormous. In addition, there are many, many issues that ultimately must be dealt with by the First Presidency, from questions of doctrine and exceptions to policy to the cancellation of sealings and restoration of blessings. I remember after President Kimball went into the First Presidency, he came back and met with the Twelve one day. During that meeting he said, "I was in the Twelve for many years, and I never dreamed of the detail the First Presidency has to deal with. It has been like night and day." And he was a detail man who could outwork anyone. When you come into the Presidency, you're required to take a broader view. It's a different type of calling.

From the perspective of one who had spent fourteen years as a counselor in the First Presidency, President Hinckley felt the man he called as his second counselor was particularly well suited to such work:

> As a member of the Twelve, Brother Faust was a man of strong opinions and had the courage to state them. I never found a time when he wasn't right on track, and that's why I asked him to serve as my second counselor—because I appreciated that among his many other virtues. He has an excellent mind and is a very thoughtful man. He thinks before he speaks. He doesn't just shoot from the hip. He thinks things through, or he asks questions to get the facts so the facts don't get him. He's absolutely reliable in every respect. You don't have to worry about Brother Faust.
>
> He is a man of balance. He doesn't ride hobby horses. He gets the big picture and sees the whole church. He has good experience and background. He comes through a line of ancestry in the Church who have been true blue through the years. He honors and respects his progenitors and lives up to what they might expect of him. He is a man of conviviality. He's nice to be around. He has a strong sense of humor that is never out of place. He is quiet and reserved for the most part, but very able. I don't find anything lacking that I could wish for in Brother Faust. He has been a wonderful counselor and one whom I very greatly appreciate.

After attending his first meeting of the First Presidency on Tuesday, March 14, President Faust recorded, "It's like putting on glasses and being able to see things I've never seen before, much of which I couldn't comprehend."

In addition to the broader perspective he had to adjust to, President Faust found that the day-to-day demands of the office were quite different from what he had known in the Quorum of the Twelve. For one thing, he spent considerably more time in meetings and noted during his first week, "I get challenges to be sure I'm in the right meeting." On one of those early days, he was sitting in his office attending to some work when his private line rang. As he answered, he heard the voice of President Hinckley, who said jovially, "Jim, were you going to join us for our meeting?"

As the three men began to work together in earnest, President Faust became all the more aware of the burden

President Hinckley carried—and of the strength and stamina with which he had been blessed. He was just shy of eighty-five years old when he became president of the Church, yet he embarked on a never-ending series of national and international trips that brought him in contact with Saints who had not had personal contact with a prophet for the better part of twenty years. President Hinckley's desire to be out among the Saints meant that Presidents Monson and Faust often remained in Salt Lake "to hold down the fort." When the two were in town together, President Faust was more than happy to be able to defer decisions to President Monson, but he remembers well, a few months after he began serving in the First Presidency, when Presidents Hinckley and Monson were both out of town, which left him in charge.

"I was frightened," he acknowledges. "President Hinckley and President Monson were both on long flights, and I knew I couldn't get in touch with either of them. The concerns and the burdens were so great that I felt physically ill, and I thought to myself, 'What am I going to do with this great responsibility and authority?' But the Lord came through and whispered in my ear, 'Nothing, if you're smart.'" On another occasion, as Presidents Hinckley and Monson left together to preside at a temple dedication, President Faust asked President Hinckley what he should do while the two men were gone. "Do what you want," the prophet responded. Then he added, "But you're accountable!"

"For the first year and a half of his calling," President Faust's daughter Janna observes, "you could tell he didn't feel comfortable wearing that mantle. I think he has since become more peaceful about it, in part because he has realized that, even with the unrelenting weight, all he can do is the best he can do. He did not, however, wear his discomfort for the world—or even the family—to see because he knew that it would only distance himself from others. It is a fine art to wear the responsibility but not have it wear you, and that is something he learned to do over the years of his service in the Church."

When the pressures of the office would allow, President Faust would try to get a break, if only for a few hours. His son Robert tells of a day, early in his father's time in the First Presidency, when the two men drove out to the west desert of Utah. "Dad has an appreciation for the outdoors, and he especially loves the desert, with its sagebrush, sunsets, and simplicity of life. He was craving the crisp, clean views and the isolation you can find in the desert, so we got in the car and took off."

He also found infrequent occasions to play golf with family members, and after playing his first round while in the First Presidency—five months after his call—he noted, "playing nine holes of golf with Doug and Janna saved my life, and gave me a chance to breathe." His son-in-law Scott Smith points out that it wasn't always easy for President Faust to leave the pressures of his office behind, relating, "One day as we were walking onto the green to putt, I said, 'Dad, are you going to putt with your seven iron?' He chuckled and said, 'Oh, I was thinking about the budget appropriations committee meeting.'"

Such breaks were good for his soul, but as President Faust faced the challenges of helping to administer the affairs of the kingdom each day, he also knew well where the strength had to come from as he and his brethren worked their way through the myriad issues and challenges they faced each day.

During a particularly difficult time, which occurred in March 1998 when two missionaries were kidnapped in Russia, Elder Holland saw yet again the absolute faith that President Faust would carry into whatever situation he faced. "As we were battling through that situation for several very long days and nights, I was reporting to the First Presidency frequently," Elder Holland says. "As we would discuss the different approaches that could be taken to gain the missionaries' release, President Faust kept saying, with an unmistakable depth of feeling, 'The help has to come from heaven. We'll use what we can from our government, we'll use what we can from the Russian government, but we have to pray down a blessing, as Enos did, praying the whole day and the whole night long if we have to.' Several times during our discussions, he was right up on the edge of the table about that point." (The missionaries were released, unharmed, after being held for three days.)

In a very different setting, President Faust's friend Newell Stevenson had the same lesson reiterated as he complimented President Faust on his April 1999 conference talk, which dealt with the making and keeping of covenants. "I was joking with him a bit after the conference," Brother Stevenson recalls, "and I said, 'Where does all that wisdom come from? It certainly doesn't come out of the Jim Faust I knew in high school.' He just smiled and said, 'It has to come from the Lord.'"

Such reliance upon and closeness to the Spirit is also the source of a unity within the First Presidency that, likewise, has made their work possible and for which President Faust has frequently expressed his gratitude. In an April 1999 training session for the General Authorities, he observed,

> President J. Reuben Clark used to plead with us in General Priesthood Meeting: "Brethren, let us be united." I reaffirm that plea. It is a tribute to the genius and leadership of President Hinckley to say that he encourages his counselors to forthrightly speak their honest convictions and feelings on any subject. President Monson and I hope we are helpful to the President in fulfilling our responsibilities in the quorum to which we belong. However, after a full, frank, and open discussion, our individual opinions yield so that we become in full accord with the decisions of the President. I have learned much in this regard from President Monson. It is part of his greatness, after an open discussion and then receiving counsel from President Hinckley, to hear him say—and quite frequently—"Your desires are my desires and your feelings my feelings."

To those who know these three men, the love and unity they share is unmistakable, and Sister Faust summarizes something of the feelings that exist in the First Presidency when she says, "Jim will often come home and say, 'I am working with a genius.' Then Marjorie Hinckley will tell me that her husband comes home and says, 'I am working with a very wise man.'"

In addition to his daily associations with the Brethren of the General Authorities, President Faust works closely with his two secretaries, Margaret Bury and Sheila Kartchner, who have gained a unique perspective on the man they work with from day to day. (Sister Bury began working for him in 1983, and Sister Kartchner joined the office soon after he was called as a counselor to President Hinckley, although she had worked with him in various capacities since the late 1960s.)

Of that which lies at the core of his fundamental character, Sister Bury observes, "I see him as a very contented man. He is not grasping for something, like you see with so many men in the world. Rather, he is comfortable with himself, which enables him to be comfortable around others. Part of his contentment grows out of a deep well of spirituality, and another part, as I've observed him, stems from a very happy marriage. He and Sister Faust have a true partnership. As an example, he won't release a talk until, as he puts it, 'The master editor has had a look at it.' He values her opinion and treats her with such respect and kindness."

In his working relationship with others, Sister Kartchner tells of a General Authority who had been called to chair a committee that reported to the First Presidency through President Faust. "As the two men met, this brother outlined some issues and the research he had done on them, and then asked President Faust what he thought. President Faust responded by asking this man what he thought, which may not have been the answer he was looking for, but is typical of President Faust wanting and allowing people to fully function in the calling they have. He may lead you along, but he is not inclined to dictate a position."

Sister Bury adds, "He can do that, in part, because of a complete lack of ego. If he has an ego, we've never seen it; instead, he would rather see other people develop. Interestingly, the strength with which he will voice certain views comes about because as he deals with an issue, he takes himself right out of it. Then, once he has taken himself out of the issue emotionally, he can speak to the issue itself."

In terms of how his office runs, both women point to a strong sense of organization, an efficient use of time, and the ability to delegate. They also add an intangible not taught in law school or business management courses—his desire to have a happy office. Sister Kartchner notes, "He's a cheerful person, and he is never moody. You know that when he walks in the door each morning, you're going to be dealing with the same person who left the night before. When we read in the scriptures about the qualities of love unfeigned, long-suffering, kindness, and tenderness, those are principles that he practices each and every day."

Sister Bury adds that it is very important to him how he treats other people, and that "he is 100 percent a gentleman at all times. The one time in our years of association that I have ever seen him come close to being upset was when someone had treated the prophet rudely and with contempt. And after he had dealt with the issues affecting this man, President Faust immediately extended a hand of love and support to this man's family, who he knew were suffering."

She also shares a view that is held by many: "I remember telling Sheila, when she first came to work in the office, 'You're going to find that it won't take any time at all before President Faust has wound himself right into your heart.' And that's exactly what he does. It's not something that is calculated, or even conscious—it just happens."

NOTES

1. "Howard W. Hunter: Man of God," *Ensign*, April 1995, pp. 26–27.
2. Ibid., pp. 27–28.
3. "Responsibilities of Shepherds," *Ensign*, May 1995, p. 45.

14

CONTINUING
WORLDWIDE SERVICE

BEYOND THE WORK THAT GOES ON inside the Church Administration Building, President Faust takes a very active and very public role in countless ways. From community functions to meetings with government and religious leaders to presiding at functions ranging from ground breakings to area conferences, he maintains an extremely active pace as a member of the First Presidency. Although he travels less than during his years in the Twelve, nonetheless, his service throughout the worldwide church continues to be significant.

Some trips have occurred with little public notice but with great significance to the Church, as was the case in April 1997 when President and Sister Faust traveled, in the company of Elder and Sister Russell M. Nelson, to China, Hong Kong, and Taiwan. Among their other meetings and responsibilities, the two Church leaders joined with Elder John H. Groberg in meeting with Mr. Tung Chee-Hwa, who became the chief executive of Hong Kong when it reverted to the control of mainland China in 1998. During their meeting, the Church leaders advised Mr. Tung of the Church's current activities in Hong Kong, including missionary work, the recent dedication of the Hong Kong Temple, and three chapels that were under construction. President Faust recorded, after their meeting, "He is very wealthy, and he is quite self-assured, gracious, charming, and a delightful personality. He gave us assurances that freedom of religion would obtain and continue under the one-country, two-policy program. We advised him that we had recently purchased a piece of ground with a building on it next to the temple and indicated that it was going to be something of a cultural center for people to learn English, take care of humanitarian work, and serve as an employment center. He seemed quite pleased with this. We asked him if he had any suggestions for us and he said, 'Just keep on doing what you're doing.'"

One year later, President and Sister Faust traveled with Elder and Sister Joseph B. Wirthlin on a much more widely publicized trip to Brazil. During their ten-day tour of the country, President Faust presided at the ground-breaking ceremonies for temples in Campinas and Porto Alegre and held several regional conferences and meetings for the missionaries. In addition, he was honored at a red-carpet ceremony in São Paulo, where he received the "Paulistano Award," which made him an honorary citizen of São Paulo and which had been awarded to only two other men—Pope John Paul II and the Dalai Lama. In responding to the award, President Faust noted that he had always considered himself a "Paulista," but that to become a citizen of a city he loved so much was "very humbling." With all the publicity that accompanied the award, he continually downplayed his part as its recipient, noting on one occasion, "I'm not very smart, but I know full well that this honor and recognition came to the Church and to the office that I hold, rather than to me personally." His brethren in the First Presidency acknowledge that, given his humility, it took some arm-twisting to convince President Faust to accept the award, but that he was finally willing to do so on the basis that it might do something further to help bring the Church out of obscurity.

In order to do just that, President Faust, in accepting the award, asked his grandson, Joshua Smith (who was serving in the São Paulo Mission at the time), to stand up. He then talked about his ties to Brazil, about his time there as a missionary and his time as area supervisor. Then he noted that, given his service, his son Robert's mission, and, at that point, the missionary service of five grandsons who had served in Brazil, his family's involvement in that great country spanned three generations. As the formal ceremonies were being concluded, a reporter approached Elder Smith and mentioned that it was nice he had been able to travel the long distance to Brazil to see his grandfather receive this award. Elder Smith clarified the misperception by stating, "I'm happy for my grandfather, but I didn't come here for that reason. I came because I was called by a prophet of God to preach the gospel of Jesus Christ, and I'm here to fulfill that call."

Another grandson, Elder Jason Coombs, likewise had the opportunity to visit with his grandparents as they traveled to Curitiba, Brazil, for meetings with the missionaries and a fireside for the 7,500 members who attended. Elder Coombs was asked to conduct the missionary meeting, in his role as an assistant to the president, and President Faust noted in his journal that his grandson "did very well." But Elder Coombs also had the privilege of watching as his grandfather ministered to a recent convert to the Church, who was one of hundreds lining the walkway as President and Sister Faust made their way to the chapel for the meeting.

This man says of the moment he shared with President Faust:

> As a recent convert my wife and I had little knowledge about the General Authorities of the Church. When we heard that we would have a special opportunity to listen to a member of the First Presidency, we did not understand exactly what that meant. Before the meeting began, I was chosen to work outside of the chapel to help with the crowds, and as President Faust and his group arrived, I was worried about keeping the people organized and, at the same time, trying to at least get a glance of the president. When he came down the walk, I found myself next to him and being introduced to him by Elder Coombs. As I shook his hand, he stopped and put his hand on my shoulder and began to tell me that adversity is necessary so that our knowledge can grow and we can become closer to the Lord. Then he said that if my wife and I would serve in our callings, follow in righteousness, and be firm in the gospel, we would be leaders in the Church of Jesus Christ.
>
> As he said these words, he did not let go of my hand, and I had

the feeling that his hand had embraced my whole being, providing me with enormous protection and peace. In addition to this feeling of peace, I felt the strength of the Holy Ghost, not only because of President Faust's presence but also because during those very days I was passing through some grand difficulties in various aspects of my life. I knew then that the Lord would not give us a burden without helping us be able to carry it.

In addition to the witness this new member received, as Elder Coombs listened to his grandfather speak with a man he knew nothing about, he likewise could see that this new convert had just been ministered to by a prophet of God.

As Elder Wirthlin watched the Fausts endure the rigors of a very demanding schedule on that trip, he noticed at least three things. The first was the love President Faust showed for Sister Faust. "He is a model for us all," Elder Wirthlin says, "with his gracious kindness and respect for Sister Faust. He honors her as few men honor their wives. He would always have her go ahead of him and never took a step ahead of her. He paid tribute to her in so many ways during the trip, and I witnessed that theirs is an absolute model of a beautiful marriage."

As the two men walked through areas where President Faust had served as a missionary, Elder Wirthlin also noticed that "he never said anything indicating that he endured any difficulties during his mission. He doesn't talk of hardships or challenging conditions; instead, everything he relates is on the positive side."

Finally, Elder Wirthlin says, "He is very easy to travel with, and he is appreciative of anything anyone does for him. If there were mistakes that others made on the trip, in arrangements or any other aspect, you would never have known it from him. He never appeared to be flustered, and he was never critical. It was a smooth, wonderful—almost heavenly—trip."

Closer to home, President Faust is constantly involved in hosting visiting dignitaries, speaking at civic functions, and presiding at Church conferences many of the weekends he is in town.

One of the many groups with which he met was the leadership of the Southern Baptist Convention, who were in Salt Lake City in June 1998 for their national convention and to encourage their members in a missionary effort among the Latter-day Saints living in Utah. Of that meeting President Faust recorded,

> At the beginning, I felt it might be useful to have a word of prayer, so I asked the Baptists if they would be offended. They indicated they would not, and Elder Maxwell gave a very Christ-centered prayer. I then shared that we consider them to be God-fearing people and indicated my experience in the service with the Baptists, particularly that when I was treading water waiting to go to officers' school, the Baptist chaplain, Dr. Perego, invited me to be his assistant.
>
> I then indicated we were going to agree on all matters, and that the first thing we were going to agree on was to disagree about doctrine. Having said that, we continued to talk about the social problems on which we agree such as pornography, drugs, teenage marriage, Sunday worship, the family, and so forth. We had a very cordial meeting, and when it was over they called upon one of their group to offer a prayer. There was a fine spirit.

Later that year, on October 20, President Faust was honored to be asked to address a luncheon of the International Association of Chiefs of Police during their annual conference, which was held in Salt Lake City. He paid tribute to the work of policemen throughout the world and then stated, in part:

> Our nations will not be stronger than our families. This is because a strong family is the basic unit of our society. It is in the family and the churches of our society that the values of honesty, decency, morality, and respect for the law are taught. Your work will never become easier until violence decreases. These family values are not generally taught in the schools, and the only place where they will be taught effectively will be in the homes and in our churches. Over the centuries, the churches have been the conservators of moral values such as faith, goodness, sexual fidelity, and respect for others. With these values strongly in place among the citizenry, there would be less crime and violence.[1]

At the conclusion of his remarks, those attending the luncheon gave President Faust a long, standing ovation, a point he failed to mention to his secretaries when they asked him how his speech had been received. When they later heard of the chiefs' response and mentioned his omission to him, President Faust, with a tinge of embarrassment, said, "Oh, they had been sitting for a very long time."

One of the assignments he enjoys the most is presiding and speaking at area and regional conferences, many of which he can attend without traveling far from Salt Lake City. Before attending one in Provo, Utah, he observed, "It's nice to be among the Saints in a less formal setting than we sometimes are—and to just relax and be ourselves."

In beginning the four-hour priesthood training session held Saturday afternoon in the Provo Tabernacle, President Faust's companion, Elder Neil L. Andersen of the First Quorum of Seventy, told of meeting with President Faust to review the status of the stakes involved and to make plans for the conference. Elder Andersen then said to those gathered, "He listened and then said, 'Neil, we're going to have to work very hard at this conference.' I agreed, although I wasn't certain what he meant; and then after a pause he added, 'We're going to have to work very hard to make sure we don't do any damage.'"

In his remarks to the priesthood leaders, President Faust alluded to the strong statistics of the stakes represented, but then noted, "Institutionally, you are doing a great work, but how are you doing personally? I would importune you to bless your families as their patriarch." He then stressed the importance of fathers being worthy and willing to give priesthood blessings to the members of their family and added, "I could ask for a blessing from President Hinckley any day of the week, and I'm sure he would give it to me. But the blessing I really desire is a blessing from the hands of my father, who has long been dead."

He offered some practical advice on living within one's means and not falling victim to speculative investing, noting, "Some of you people think the stock market can only go up, that real estate can only go up. But they can come down." He then closed his formal remarks by admonishing the brethren, "We must watch our very thoughts, as well as our actions. We must keep the Church clean. If we do not keep the Church clean, it will not be the Church of Jesus Christ."

In opening up the session for questions and answers, he quipped, "Now, what are your questions? What are we doing wrong in the Church? Don't be shy. Everyone else tells us."

Many of the questions centered on current social issues. When asked about the possibility of widespread problems as computer clocks switched from 1999 to 2000, he said, making a point that went well beyond the question, "I don't believe there will be any great, catastrophic happenings. I think the greater danger is that our own moral compasses will go awry. I've lived most of my life without computers and have gotten along just fine."

When asked about the presidential impeachment hearings that were taking place in Washington, D.C., at the time, particularly what he thought the biblical significance of those hearings might be, he said, simply, "There is a phrase in the law, *Res ipsa loquitur*—'Let the matter speak for itself.'"

As he concluded the Saturday session of the regional conference, President Faust did so first, by bearing his testimony, which he always does, and second, by pronouncing an apostolic blessing upon those in attendance, a responsibility he feels is incumbent upon him by virtue of his calling.

In the Sunday morning session, which nearly filled the 23,000-seat Marriott Center on the BYU campus, President Faust made certain that those in attendance had an opportunity to hear from Sister Faust, who, with her gracious sense of humor, stated, "I wish he would testify more—and me less."

President Faust then centered his remarks on a story of President David O. McKay's horse that didn't like restraints and ended up dying after eating from a bag of poisoned oats. (He likewise told the story in the priesthood session of the April 1999 general conference.) After gaining the attention of both the youth and adults, he shared a wide range of thoughts on the fundamental principle of benefiting from the restraints the Lord has placed upon us and then concluded with the encouragement, "We want you to keep doing what you're doing—only do it a little bit better. You're not perfect yet, and that is the Savior's commandment to us."

The proceedings of the Provo regional conference are a sampling of the work he does as he counsels, teaches, and bears witness throughout the world in similar meetings.

President Faust's increased public presence has resulted in the unavoidable loss of what little anonymity he had enjoyed during his years as an Apostle. He quickly found, after moving into the First Presidency, that virtually everyone he met—LDS and non-LDS alike—seemed to know who he was. He was accepting of the change, though, and with his characteristic graciousness, he would make those he met as comfortable as he could and visit with people whenever it was feasible. One evening, as he and Sister Faust went with some of their family to a local restaurant, they ran into a neighbor who was hosting an out-of-town guest. As their friend began to search for the appropriate title to use in introducing his non-Mormon associate to a member of the First Presidency, President Faust quickly eased his friend's discomfort by extending his hand and saying simply, "Hi, I'm Jim Faust."

One Monday morning, as he came out of his office to greet his next appointment, he saw a grandmother, daughter, and granddaughter leaving the lobby area of the Church Administration Building. When he asked who they were and was told they had come in with the hope of being able to see President Hinckley's office (which wasn't possible), he hurried out of the building after them and visited with them on the front steps. Upon being told of the moment, his daughter-in-law Susan Faust observed, "In a situation like that, he would feel it was a privilege for him to meet them, not for them to meet him."

As he has traveled among the Saints, concerns over time, security, and the sheer crush of people wanting to greet him have made it impossible for him to shake hands with as many members as he did in the past. But when a young boy indicated to his father that he had felt slighted by President Faust—and word of the unintended offense got back to him—he had his secretaries track down the boy's name and address and then wrote a personal letter of apology.

He also has found that as a member of the First Presidency he comes under more scrutiny from all quarters, particularly as people wonder—and sometimes even speculate—about his age and physical well-being. One misperception he continues to deal with is the idea that he is afflicted with Parkinson's Disease; well-meaning individuals have often called his office to offer solace, advice, remedies, and the like. Although he knows well the seriousness of the illness, he laughs when asked about the notion so many hold, saying, "That's a rumor that's abroad in the land." Then, with his characteristic ability to extract a principle from virtually any point of discussion, he adds, "What I have are familial tremors, which come to me from a long line of faithful, wonderful relatives. They have no effect on my well-being, and the fact that I have them doesn't bother me a bit because of everything else I inherited as a consequence of my heritage. My grandmother had them, and my uncle had them, and if I could be as good as my grandmother, with all her tremors and shakes, I'd be very grateful."

Although he agrees with Sister Faust's observation that "growing old is not for sissies," President Faust appreciates the significant measure of good health with which he has been blessed. He was particularly pleased when, after having some concern over a pain in his knees, he was told by his doctor that he had not come close to wearing out his cartilage—and that, in fact, he had the knees of a twenty-year-old.

Even with demands from his calling that could consume every waking minute, President Faust has worked to ensure that at least some of his evenings each week are set aside for family. Sometimes children, grandchildren, and great-grandchildren come to visit; other times, President and Sister

Faust call on their family. But always they are concerned with their family's needs. Janna observes, "He tries so hard to be sensitive to what we're involved with, and he also reinforces those things that are important—the things we should be concerned about. He is always there, either by phone or in person, to do whatever he can to help us help ourselves."

The Fausts' grandson John Faust adds that his grandparents always want to know what they can do for the family—and that they are then there to actually do what they've offered to do. Over the years, that help has been in the form of everything from baby-sitting to counseling grandchildren who were about to go to the temple for the first time (and then going with them) to spending time with family members who were making life-changing decisions. One of many moments John shared with his grandfather occurred just before he began law school at BYU—the first of the Faust grandchildren to follow their grandfather and his three sons into the law. "We had dinner together," John says, "and he gave me some encouragement, saying, 'There is no other education like the law. It's going to teach you to think.' He also talked with me about the need to keep my focus on helping clients—not on making money. He told me, 'When I first started practicing law, I could have charged people a lot of money, but I didn't. I wanted to help them.'"

John's sister, Nicole Faust Hunt, tells of traveling two thousand miles from home to attend BYU as a freshman—and of the blessing of having her grandparents nearby. "They were my surrogate parents," she says, "and although I wouldn't bother them with all the details of my life, I asked them lots of questions about dating, boys, and so on. He would tell me, 'Now, Nicole, all you need to worry about is finding a man who loves you and who loves the Lord.' His advice is really very simple—that if you focus on the things that really matter, the rest is going to work itself out."

As Nicole and her husband began their family, President and Sister Faust were as proud as two great-grandparents could be, and he also gave her some simple counsel to remember as her children began to grow. "He'd say, 'If you don't discipline him, society will,'" Nicole says. "He is concerned that we teach our children self-discipline and self-control—and that we, as parents, be the schoolmasters."

She adds that his advice is always welcome, solicited or not, for two reasons: "The first is the manner in which he offers it. Some people would sit you down and be pushy about what they're telling you, but he isn't. It's a very relaxed, gentle form of counsel that doesn't feel like it's being pushed on you. The second reason is that he doesn't tell you specifically the things you should do; in fact, there are times when you'll go to him and ask for his advice, and you leave, thinking, 'He didn't answer my question.' Many times he'll say things in such a way that there are many meanings and many levels of understanding, and if you were to take what he said at face value, you might feel there wasn't much to what he told you. But if you sit and listen and really think about what he says—and then let the Spirit talk to your heart—every answer you could ever need would be right there."

Jim Faust adds that as a father, he welcomes the active participation of his parents in his children's lives—and that Grandma and Grandpa Faust have done much to help the parents in their family inculcate correct ideals in their children. He also points out that his children will sometimes listen to their grandfather when they won't listen to their father. "Sometimes my kids will tell me they have an opportunity to do such and such, and it's something I'd prefer they not do. They'll say, 'Oh, Dad, it won't hurt,' and I'll tell them, 'Okay, you call Grandpa, and if he says yes, you can do it.' They've never called."

In addition to a number of trips the Fausts have taken as a family, President Faust arranged in 1997 for his two daughters to travel with him and Sister Faust while he fulfilled a series of assignments in England. (They, of course, did not travel at the Church's expense.) In addition to his official responsibilities, President Faust arranged for the four family members to visit the town where Sister Faust's great-grandfather, Joseph Wright, lived before coming to the United States and the town of Thursby, where George Finlinson and the Trimble family joined the Church.

During a day of sightseeing and shopping, as President Faust waited while Sister Faust and their daughters went through several ceramics shops, he had a little fun with a stake president who was accompanying the group. "I'm going to prove to you I'm a prophet," he said, rather uncharacteristically. When the stake president said he didn't need any proof, President Faust continued, "No, I'm going to prove it. When my wife and daughters come out of this shop [it being the third they had been to that day looking for a set of china], they'll tell us we need to return to the first shop." And, just as he predicted, such was the case.

The next summer, President Faust and his three sons spent six days in France (and two days in transit), using President Faust's father's journals to guide them to the various places he had fought in World War I. Those eight days were the first time in President Faust's years as a General Authority that he had taken that much time off—and it was the first trip he had taken overseas (or almost anywhere, for that matter) that did not involve a Church assignment.

The four men made their way through France, with the sons taking turns driving and navigating, and Jim tells of how fortunate they were to arrive at museums five minutes before an English tour was scheduled or pull up to a cathedral just as a car was pulling out of an overflowing parking lot. "It quickly turned into a joke that we really liked traveling with Dad," Jim says.

Even without any assignments, and in a country with a relatively small Latter-day Saint population, President Faust still came upon those who recognized him. One day at noon, as he and his sons were eating hot dogs they had purchased from a vendor in a park, a group of students from Bountiful, Utah, saw him and came over to visit. Embarrassed that he was eating and they weren't, President Faust bought hot dogs for the entire group.

Another day, President Faust says, as he and his sons walked along the beaches of Normandy, "An LDS woman, accompanied by a non-Mormon friend, came up and said, right out of the blue, 'Hello, President Faust.' I didn't have on a suit or a white shirt, but she recognized me. Then she said to her friend, 'This is one of our prophets,' and she began to cry. Meeting her that way made me feel very, very humble."

As the four men traveled, they also reflected on the life of their father and grandfather, and especially on the qualities of loyalty, devotion, and integrity that were so evident as he served his country and then throughout the rest of his life. President Faust valued the time together with his sons and says, "I had a perfect trip with our daughters in England, and I had a perfect trip with our sons in France. I had the chance to spend two nights in a room with each of my boys, and we had a chance to talk about them and their families. It was choice."

Marcus adds, "As my father gets older, I've noticed that more and more his heart is turning to his father and mother and grandparents and aunts and uncles. I think he has a greater perspective of the past and the future, and I think he is trying to pass some of those stories and our heritage on to us." Marcus also notes that the one difficulty in planning the trip was convincing his father to leave Sister Faust for such a long time. "I don't think he would have done that for any other reason," Marcus says, adding, "he hates to go even twenty-four hours without her."

Susan tells of how she and Marcus went to a department store to buy a lamp for Sister Faust and of calling to explain the choices to her in-laws. "I described two lamps, one of which was twice as expensive as the other, and, of course, Mother wanted to be conservative and get the less expensive of the two. But Dad said, 'Now, Susan, we don't buy many lamps, and the price doesn't matter.' If we had been buying something for him, price certainly would have mattered; but because the lamp was for his Ruthy, it didn't."

President Faust's secretaries often see the tenderness and love he shows for Sister Faust, and Sister Bury tells of a day when the four of them had lunch together and Sister Faust was commenting on a new pair of glasses she had, which she didn't feel comfortable in. "President Faust listened and then said, 'Oh, I like what's behind them.'"

In commenting on the priority President Faust places on his relationship with each member of his family, Janna says, "I think he has worked hard to implement in his family those things he has learned in his Church positions. Our family is a microcosm of the ten-million-member church that he helps to preside over. Even as he speaks in general conference, I have noticed that those talks are for his family every bit as much as they're for the Church as a whole."

In his October 1997 address to the priesthood session of general conference, President Faust indicated his own need to be reminded of and remain committed to the gospel principles he has taught throughout the world for some sixty years:

> President J. Reuben Clark, Jr., a counselor in the First Presidency, used to say from this pulpit, "Brethren, I hope I can remain faithful to the end." At that time, President Clark was in his 80s.
>
> As a young man, I could not understand how this wise, learned, experienced, righteous Apostle of the Lord Jesus Christ could have any concern for his own spiritual well-being. As I approach his age, I now understand. I have the same concern for myself, for my family, and for all of my brethren of the priesthood. Over my lifetime, I have seen some of the most choice, capable, and righteous of men stumble and fall. They have been true and faithful for many years and then get caught in a web of stupidity and foolishness which has brought great shame to themselves and betrayed the trust of their innocent families, leaving their loved ones a legacy of sorrow and hurt.
>
> My dear brethren, all of us, young and old, must constantly guard against the enticements of Satan.[2]

Elder Neal A. Maxwell once observed, "President Faust has not pitched his tent on the hillside and said, 'This is as far as I can make it.' Rather, he continues to climb each day in terms of his intellectual perceptivity and his spirituality. His teachings reflect that. His life reflects that."

What motivates him in that constant climb to serve more effectively was expressed in a moment he shared at the conclusion of his grandson Jason Coombs's missionary farewell in 1997. He began his brief remarks by quoting the words of the Apostle Peter, who said, "For we have not followed cunningly devised fables, when we made known unto you the power and coming of our Lord Jesus Christ, but were eyewitnesses of his majesty" (2 Peter 1:16).

Then, alluding to the family he and Elder W. Grant Bangerter had tracted out in 1940 that subsequently joined the Church, he continued,

> Jason has been called to serve in Curitiba, Parana. In 1940, there were no members of the Church in Curitiba, nor in the whole state of Parana, so far as we knew. There are now seven stakes in the vicinity of Curitiba.
>
> The rest of that story is that Sister Faust and I were privileged to go back forty-seven years later to Curitiba, Parana. The Valeixo family, which we had found, came to the airport. These children, these grandchildren, had now grown old and had gray hair. As we walked out from the airplane, it seemed as if the whole family descended upon us, and in the loving style of the Latins, there were many *abraços,* or hugs. But one of the women, now a gray-haired grandmother, took my two hands. She wept in an expression of appreciation and gratitude, and the tears from her eyes dropped on the backs of my hands. She then took her other hand and rubbed the tears into the backs of my hands as if they were salve.
>
> Now, I repeat, I was not the one who taught her. I was not the one who baptized her. But I was the humble messenger who, with my companion, brought the words of truth and salvation to this family. And I think that in all my life, I don't remember a greater expression of gratitude for anything I have done than that woman who wiped her tears from the backs of my hands. This is the work of God.

From his service as a missionary through every subsequent calling he has accepted, James Esdras Faust has served as an unassuming yet stalwart emissary of the Savior. In so doing, he, like Peter, has been an eyewitness of the Savior's majesty as he has watched the work grow throughout the world. He has traveled to every corner of the kingdom. He has ministered to the Saints in countless and varied ways. In the view of those who have seen him serve, he has made significant contributions to the growth of the Church. In his estimation, he has been the humblest, even the weakest, of those whom the Lord has called as His "especial witnesses" to the world, with his efforts having value only as he has served in the strength of the Lord.

NOTES

1. Address to International Association of Chiefs of Police, Salt Lake City, Utah, 20 October 1998. Unpublished manuscript.

2. "Pioneers of the Future: Be Not Afraid, Only Believe," *Ensign,* November 1997, p. 45.

*George Augustus Faust
(about age 45)*

Amy Finlinson Faust

*George Augustus Faust
(World War I)*

*Amy Finlinson Faust (left)
and a friend*

Left to right: *Jim, Rex, and Gus Faust*

Jim Faust caring for a young lamb entrusted to him by his father

Young Jim Faust and some of his family in about 1933
Back row, left to right: *Jim's parents, George and Amy Faust; unknown;*
Jim's paternal grandmother, Maud Faust; Uncle James Ackerly Faust;
and Jim's brother Gus. Front row: *Rex, Jim, and*
(on the far right) *cousin Marguerite*

Jim, Rex, and Gus Faust (on the far right),
with their cousin, Marguerite

Elder Jim Faust, taken prior to his leaving for Brazil in 1939

Elders (and brothers)
Jim Faust (left) and Gus Faust
in Brazil (1939)

Elder Faust poses with a group
of Brazilian children

A group of missionaries gathers in front of the
mission home in Curitiba, Brazil

*World War I veteran George Faust with his three sons who served in World War II
Left to right: Gus, Rex, and Jim, and their younger brother, Delano*

Jim Faust and his father, during Jim's service in World War II

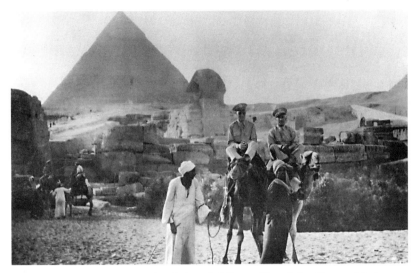

Lieutenant Jim Faust (right) *and fellow officer John Knezevich in Cairo, Egypt, fall of 1943*

Father and sons in 1947
Left to right: *Delano, George, Dan, Rex, Jim, and Gus*

An engagement portrait of Ruth Wright

Ruth Wright

Ruth's mother,
Elizabeth Hamilton Wright

Ruth Wright (far left) *and a group of high school friends*

The bride and groom on their wedding day, April 21, 1943

The telegram that kept Ruth Wright in Salt Lake City

Ruth Wright Faust with her handsome soldier, Jim

*The newlyweds on the
Susquehanna River near
Harrisburg, Pennsylvania*

*A proud father holds his
four-week-old son, Jimmy*

*On his graduation day from the University of Utah Law School, Jim is
joined by his mother (left) and his grandmother, Maud Wetzel Faust*

In the spring of 1953, Jim plays with Janna (left), Jimmy (right), and the Faust's newest arrival, Marcus

The Faust family in the late 1950s (clockwise, from upper right): Jimmy, Jim, Marcus, Robert, Ruth, Janna, and Lisa

The Faust family in the early 1990s
Front row, left to right: *Janna, Sister Faust, Lisa;*
back row, left to right: *Robert, Jim, Elder Faust, and Marcus*

Elder Faust takes time for a horseback ride with two of his grandsons, Jason Coombs (front) and Jamie Coombs (back)

President Faust joins with grandchildren, friends, and daughter Lisa in a birthday celebration

Elder Faust and grandson Matthew Smith feed the ducks at Old Farm in Salt Lake City

President Faust and grand-daughter Sara Faust stand on the corner of the foundation of the Nauvoo Temple in August 1997

President Faust holds the first of his great-grandchildren, Marcus Faust, in July 1996

As a member of the Cottonwood Stake presidency, President Faust (right)
poses with the stake president, G. Carlos Smith (center),
and the first counselor, Heber G. Peterson

Jim Faust (far right) *helps to show off the fish caught by his son,*
Marcus. Also seen are *Elder Hugh B. Brown* (second from left),
and Jim's brother-in-law, Owen Wright.

Elder James E. Faust during his years as an Assistant to the Twelve

Facing page, top: *Elder Faust, then junior member of the Quorum of the Twelve, listens as President Spencer W. Kimball addresses a session of general conference*

Facing page, bottom: *Elder and Sister Faust greet conference visitors outside the Salt Lake Tabernacle*

Elder Faust joins in singing a congregational hymn during the 1978 area conference in São Paulo, Brazil

Elder Faust visits with a group of children during his 1979 trip to mainland China

Elder and Sister Faust pause at the border of Nazareth

Left: Elder Howard W. Hunter and Elder Faust visit the Garden Tomb during one of their many trips to Jerusalem

Elder Faust greets Egyptian President Anwar Sadat during a 1979 trip to Egypt

Elder Faust at a meeting of the Abah Branch, in the state of Imo, Nigeria, in February 1979

Elder Faust baptizes a new member of the Church in the Ekeonumiri River, near Imo, Nigeria

Elder Faust, together with President Philip T. Sonntag, visits with a group of Polynesian Saints

Elder and Sister Faust enjoy a moment together during a trip to the South Seas in 1986

Left to right: *BYU President Jeffrey R. Holland, President Howard W. Hunter, Sister Patricia T. Holland, and Elder and Sister Faust gather in Jerusalem in 1986*

Elder Faust visits with two Israeli children

Elder and Sister Faust stand inside the Jerusalem Center during its construction

Left: *Elder Charles Didier of the First Quorum of the Seventy* (back row, left) *and Elder Faust pose with members of the Otovalo Ecuador stake presidency*

Elder and Sister Faust (left) *pose with members in Accra, Ghana, in April 1991*

President Gordon B. Hinckley addresses the media and introduces his two counselors, Presidents Thomas S. Monson and James E. Faust, at a March 13, 1995, press conference

*President Faust wipes away
a tear after addressing the
Sunday morning session
of the April 1995 general
conference*

*President Faust joins in sustaining Gordon B. Hinckley as the fifteenth
president of the Church on April 1, 1995*

President Faust joins with Presidents Hinckley and Monson in welcoming Mrs. Margaret Thatcher, former prime minister of Great Britain, to Salt Lake City in 1996

President Faust visits with Rex E. Lee (left), then president of Brigham Young University, and Teddy Kollek, who served for twenty-eight years as mayor of Jerusalem, during the August 1995 commencement exercises at which Mayor Kollek was awarded an honorary doctorate from BYU

President Faust shares a thought with Presidents Hinckley and Monson during the October 1996 general conference

Presidents Hinckley and Faust invite a young girl to participate in the July 24, 1997, ground-breaking of the Church's new Conference Center

After serving as the grand marshal of the Salt Lake City Days of '47 Parade in 1997, President Faust greets spectators at the end of the parade route

Elder M. Russell Ballard gives a kiss to Amy Faust as she and her grandfather join in the Sesquicentennial Spectacular held in Provo, Utah, on July 24, 1997

President Faust reflects on the faithfulness of the Martin and Willie Handcart Companies during the filming of a 1997 documentary at Rocky Ridge, Wyoming

President and Sister Faust serve as grand marshals of the Oak City, Utah, homecoming parade, August 15, 1997. Oak City is the town where Jim Faust was born and where he spent many summers as a boy.

President Faust receives the "Paulistano Award" from the city of São Paulo in 1998

A portrait of Ruth Wright Faust presented to her adoring husband for Christmas of 1994

President Faust is awarded an honorary doctorate degree during BYU's August 1997 commencement exercises

President Monson hugs his beloved associate after President Faust is awarded an honorary doctorate degree from BYU in August 1997

Friends and associates for almost fifty years, President Gordon B. Hinckley and President James E. Faust share a lighter moment during the October 1998 general conference

PART 2

THE TEACHINGS OF JAMES E. FAUST

ABORTION

IN TIMES PAST we have looked upon a person who saves another human life as a great hero; yet now we have come to a time when the taking of an unborn human life for nonmedical reasons has become tolerated, made legal, and accepted in many countries of the world. But making it legal to destroy newly conceived life will never make it right. It is consummately wrong. ("The Sanctity of Life," *Ensign,* May 1975, 28.)

MOTHER TERESA DELIVERED a message that cut to the very heart and soul of the social ills afflicting America, which traditionally has given generously to the peoples of the earth, but now has become selfish. She stated that the greatest proof of that selfishness is abortion. . . . "If we accept that a mother can kill even her own child, how can we tell other people not to kill each other? . . . any country that accepts abortion is not teaching its people to love, but to use any violence to get what they want." ("Mother Teresa Has Anti-Abortion Answer," *Salt Lake Tribune,* 15 Feb. 1994.)

Then she alluded to the concern that has been shown for orphan children in India and elsewhere in the world, for which she expressed gratitude. But she continued, "These concerns are very good. But often these same people are not concerned with the millions who are being killed by the deliberate decision of their own mothers. And this is what is the greatest destroyer of peace today—abortion, which brings people to such blindness." (Ibid.) . . .

In conclusion Mother Teresa pled for pregnant women who don't want their children to give them to her. She said, "I am willing to accept any child who would be aborted and to give that child to a married couple who will love the child, and be loved by the child." (Ibid.) What consummate spiritual courage this remarkable old woman demonstrated. How the devil must have been offended! Her remarkable declaration, however, was not generally picked up by the press or the editorial writers.

Perhaps they felt more comfortable being politically or socially correct. After all, they can justify their stance by asserting that everyone does it, or it is legal. Fortunately the scriptures and the message of the prophets cannot be so revised. ("Trying to Serve the Lord without Offending the Devil," *BYU Speeches*, 15 Nov. 1994, 60–61.)

ONE OF THE most evil myths of our day is that a woman who has joined hands with God in creation can destroy that creation because she claims the right to control her own body. Since the life within her is not her own, how can she justify its termination and deflect that life from an earth which it may never inherit?

The great medical profession, for which I have such great respect [and] that for centuries has been committed to the preservation of life under the cardinal principles of treatment—"do no harm" and "protect life"—now finds itself destroying almost a million unborn children a year in the United States alone. Each of these, because of tiny chromosomal differences, would have been different from any other person born in the world. How many with special gifts like unto Moses, Leonardo da Vinci, and Abraham Lincoln might have been among them? ("The Sanctity of Life," *Ensign*, May 1975, 28–29.)

ACCEPTANCE

I WAS BORN with partial color-blindness. I have learned to love all of the people in the countries where I have been as a missionary, soldier, or General Authority, regardless of the color of their skins. I hope to be a disciple after the manner and example of President Kimball and the others in their love for all, and especially for the humble, the downtrodden, the poor, the afflicted, the needy, and the poor in spirit. I am mindful that if we forget these, we can in no way be his disciples. ("Response to the Call," *Ensign*, Nov. 1978, 20.)

ACCOUNTABILITY

FROM [VARIOUS] EXPERIENCES [I had as a young lawyer], I learned that some individuals did not think they were responsible or guilty in any way even though they had violated the law. They felt they were not to be blamed. They had abdicated their consciences. They may have committed the wrongful act, but they felt it was really their parents' fault because they were not properly taught, or it was society's fault because they were never given a chance in life. So often they had some reason or excuse for blaming their actions on someone or something else rather than accepting the responsibility for their own actions. They did not act for themselves but were acted upon.

Mickey Mantle, American baseball star of many years ago, recently admitted to years of various forms of substance abuse. Upon receiving a liver transplant in an effort to save his life, he made an amazing statement. He said, "Don't use me for a role model." He also said that he was committing the rest of his life to being a better example. Mickey Mantle finally accepted the responsibility for his mistakes. Unfortunately, he died shortly thereafter. In World War II, many of us went through officers' training. We were taught that the only appropriate answer when we made a life-threatening mistake was, "No excuse, sir." ("Acting for Ourselves and Not Being Acted Upon," *Ensign,* Nov. 1995, 46.)

ACTIVATION

MANY OF US have sat in ward councils, priesthood executive councils, and other meetings on the ward levels. We took the time to identify the names of those who had lost their way. But our efforts to reach them could have been more effective. At times we were too judgmental. Sometimes we lost track of the individual in our focus on the program. I do not criticize the programs and activities. I am grateful for them. They are necessary. They are inspired and great. I only ask for greater concern for the individual and the family, which, after all, is the purpose of God's holy work. "This is my work and my glory— to bring to pass the immortality and eternal life of man." (Moses 1:39.) . . .

There is what might be called "selective neglect" of some of our members. For example, occasionally we hear of divorced members being treated differently than those who are widowed. Be sensitive to the needs of all, regardless of the reason for their singleness.

Be aware of the needs of the less active. Unfortunately, leaders too often respond to more visible needs and overlook more critical concerns. Regular attendance at church cannot become a standard measure of need. Do not let the phrase "out of sight, out of mind" reflect your ministry. ("The Responsibility of Church Leaders to Members of the Church Who Are Single," Church Satellite Broadcast, 23 Feb. 1992.)

ADVERSITY

IN THE MANY trials of life, when we feel abandoned and when sorrow, sin, disappointment, failure, and weakness make us less than we should ever be, there can come the healing salve of the unreserved love in the grace of God. It is a love that forgives and forgets, a love that lifts and blesses. It is a love that sustains a new beginning on a higher level and thereby continues "from grace to grace." (D&C 93:13.) ("A Personal Relationship with the Savior," *Ensign*, Nov. 1976, 59.)

SOME OF THE blessings available in overcoming economic adversity are:

First, and perhaps most important, our faith and testimony can be strengthened. . . . We learn to recognize the Lord's hand in helping us. In hard times we have a chance to reevaluate and reorder our priorities in life. We learn what is most important to us. . . .

Second, we may learn the need for humility. Our dependence upon the Lord becomes a means of developing teach-ableness, an important aspect of humility.

Third, family members learn cooperation and love for each other by being forced to draw closer together to survive.

Fourth, personal dignity and self-respect may be achieved. Someone said, "Be glad there are big hurdles in life, and rejoice, too, that they are higher than most people care to surmount. Be happy they are numerous." (Anonymous.)

Fifth, we can become stronger and more resilient. Edmund Burke said: "Difficulty is a severe instructor, set over us by the supreme ordinance of a parental Guardian and Legislator, who knows us better than we know ourselves, and he loves us better too. . . . He that wrestles with us strengthens our nerves, and sharpens our skill. Our antagonist is our helper." ("Reflections on the Revolution in France," in *Edmund Burke,* Harvard Classics, 50 vols., New York: P. F. Collier and Son Co., 1909, 24:299–300.)

Sixth, we learn patience. . . . He who learns to bear his adversities while working to overcome them increases in patience, and thus he is not overcome by his circumstances. . . .

Seventh, we rise to heights previously unobtainable by the use of talents and skills which might not have been developed otherwise. . . .

Eighth, we can learn to trust the Lord and thus overcome fear. "If ye are prepared ye shall not fear" (D&C 38:30). ("The Blessings We Receive As We Meet the Challenges of Economic Stress," *Ensign,* Nov. 1982, 88–89.)

IN THE PAIN, the agony, and the heroic endeavors of life, we pass through a refiner's fire, and the insignificant and the unimportant in our lives can melt away like dross and make our faith bright, intact, and strong. In this way the divine image can be mirrored from the soul. It is part of the purging toll exacted of some to become acquainted with God. In the agonies of life, we seem to listen better to the faint, godly whisperings of the Divine Shepherd. ("The Refiner's Fire," *Ensign,* May 1979, 53.)

IN LIFE WE all have our Gethsemanes. A Gethsemane is a necessary experience, a growth experience. A Gethsemane is a time to draw near to God, a time of deep anguish and suffering. The Gethsemane of the Savior was without question the greatest suffering that has ever come to mankind, yet out of it came the greatest good in the promise of eternal life. ("The Blessings of Adversity," *BYU Speeches*, 21 Feb. 1978, 29.)

INTO EVERY LIFE there come the painful, despairing days of adversity and buffeting. There seems to be a full measure of anguish, sorrow, and often heartbreak for everyone, including those who earnestly seek to do right and be faithful. The thorns that prick, that stick in the flesh, that hurt, often change lives which seem robbed of significance and hope. This change comes about through a refining process which often seems cruel and hard. In this way the soul can become like soft clay in the hands of the Master in building lives of faith, usefulness, beauty, and strength. For some, the refiner's fire causes a loss of belief and faith in God, but those with eternal perspective understand that such refining is part of the perfection process. ("The Refiner's Fire," *Ensign*, May 1979, 53.)

DO NOT PRESUME, because the way is at times difficult and challenging, that our Heavenly Father is not mindful of you. He is rubbing off the rough edges and sensitizing you for your great responsibilities ahead. ("The Blessings of Adversity," *BYU Speeches*, 21 Feb. 1978, 32.)

THE DIVINE SHEPHERD has a message of hope, strength, and deliverance for all. If there were no night, we would not appreciate the day, nor could we see the stars and the vastness of the heavens. We must partake of the bitter with the sweet. There is a divine purpose in the adversities we encounter every day. They prepare, they purge, they purify, and thus they bless.

When we pluck the roses, we find we often cannot avoid the thorns which spring from the same stem.

Out of the refiner's fire can come a glorious deliverance. It can be a noble and lasting rebirth. The price to become acquainted with God will have been paid. There can come a sacred peace. There will be a reawakening of dormant, inner resources. A comfortable cloak of righteousness will be drawn around us to protect us and to keep us warm spiritually. Self-pity will vanish as our blessings are counted. ("The Refiner's Fire," *Ensign*, May 1979, 59.)

RECENTLY I MET with a family who had lost a precious son through an unfortunate automobile accident. They wondered when the comforting spirit of the Holy Ghost would envelop them to sustain them. My counsel was that when they were prepared to say to the Lord, "Thy will be done," then would come the sweet peace which the Savior promised. This willing submission to the Father is what the Savior exemplified in the Garden of Gethsemane. ("The Grand Keys of the Relief Society," *Ensign*, Nov. 1996, 96.)

ADVERSITY IS THE refiner's fire that bends iron but tempers steel. ("The Blessings of Adversity," *BYU Speeches*, 21 Feb. 1978, 28.)

JEFF AND JOYCE Underwood of Pocatello, Idaho . . . are parents of Jeralee and their other five children. . . . One day last July, their daughter Jeralee, age eleven, was going door to door collecting money for her newspaper route. Jeralee never returned home. . . .

Two thousand people from the area had gone out day after day to search for her. Other churches sent support and food for the searchers. It was learned that Jeralee had been abducted and brutally murdered by an evil man. When her body was found, the whole city was horrified and shocked. All segments of the community reached out to Joyce and Jeff in love and sympathy. Some became angry and wanted to take vengeance. After Jeralee's body was found, Jeff and Joyce appeared with great composure before the television cameras and other media to publicly express their profound thanks to all who had helped in the search and who had extended sympathy and love. Joyce said, "I know our Heavenly Father has heard and answered our prayers, and he has brought our daughter back to us." Jeff said, "We no longer have doubt about where she is." Joyce continued, "I have learned a lot about love this week, and I also know there is a lot of hate. I have looked at the love and want to feel that love, and not the hate. We can forgive."

Elder Joe J. Christensen and I, representing the General Authorities, were among the thousands privileged to attend Jeralee's funeral service. The Holy Spirit blessed that gathering in a remarkable way and spoke peace to the souls of those who attended. Later, President Kert W. Howard, Jeralee's stake president, wrote, "The Underwoods have received letters from people both in and out of the Church stating that they prayed for Jeralee, and they hadn't prayed in years, and because of this, they had a renewed desire to return to the Church." President Howard continued, "We will never know the extent of activation and rededication this single event has caused. Who knows the far-reaching effects Jeralee's life will have for generations untold." Many have come into the Church because they wanted to know what kind of a religion could give the Underwoods their spiritual strength.

I mention the good coming from this tragic event with Jeralee's parents' full approval and encouragement. Their sweet daughter was like the lad who had only five barley loaves and two small fishes to give to the cause of the Savior, but by the power of God, countless thousands have been spiritually fed. ("Five Loaves and Two Fishes," *Ensign*, May 1994, 6–7.)

A P O S T A S Y

AMONG THE ACTIVITIES considered apostate to the Church include when members "(1) repeatedly act in clear, open, and deliberate public opposition to the Church or its leaders; (2) persist in teaching as Church doctrine information that is not Church doctrine after being corrected by their bishops or higher authority; or (3) continue to follow the teachings of apostate cults (such as those that advocate plural marriage) after being corrected by their bishops or higher authority" (General Handbook of Instructions [1989], p. 10–3).

Those men and women who persist in publicly challenging basic doctrines, practices, and establishment of the Church sever themselves from the Spirit of the Lord and forfeit their right to place and influence in the Church. Members are encouraged to study the principles and the doctrines of the Church so that they understand them. Then, if questions arise and there are honest differences of opinion, members are encouraged to discuss these matters privately with priesthood leaders. ("Keeping Covenants and Honoring the Priesthood," *Ensign*, Nov. 1993, 38.)

THE DISPENSATION OF divine truth in which we now live, in distinction from previous dispensations, will not be destroyed by apostasy. This is in fulfillment of Daniel's prophecy that "the God of heaven [would] set up a kingdom which shall never be destroyed" nor "left to other people." (Daniel 2:44; D&C 138:44.) President John Taylor affirmed this also when he said, "There is one thing very certain . . . and that is, whatever men may think, and however they may plot and contrive, that this Kingdom will never be given into the hands of another people. It will grow and spread and increase, and no man living can stop its progress." (*Journal of Discourses,* 25:348; also 14:367.) ("The Prophetic Voice," *Ensign*, May 1996, 5.)

OVER THE YEARS many offshoots and splinter groups have not stayed with the Brethren. This is not a new phenomenon. After the Crucifixion of the Savior, Peter and the Apostles were preaching to a hostile audience. Gamaliel, a man learned in the law, defended their right to preach. After recalling the ill fate of two different groups that had risen up and drawn people away, he presented this sure test of truth. Said he: "If this counsel or this work be of men, it will come to nought:

"But if it be of God, ye cannot overthrow it; lest haply ye be found even to fight against God." (Acts 5:38–39.)

In the great Sermon on the Mount, the Savior posed a poignant question: "Do men gather grapes of thorns, or figs of thistles?" He goes on to say: "A good tree cannot bring forth evil fruit, neither can a corrupt tree bring forth good fruit. . . . Wherefore by their fruits ye shall know them." (Matt. 7:16–20.) The sweet fruits of this work are now known over much of the earth. ("The Prophetic Voice," *Ensign,* May 1996, 6.)

THOMAS B. MARSH was [a] favored associate of the Prophet Joseph. Over this pulpit in the April 1984 general conference, President Hinckley reminded us that Brother Marsh was serving as the President of the Quorum of the Twelve when he chose to disregard the decisions of the First Presidency and other Church leaders in a dispute between his wife and another woman over some milk strippings. (Gordon B. Hinckley, "Small Acts Lead to Great Consequences," *Ensign* 14 [May 1984]: 83.)

When, as did the prodigal son, he finally "came to himself" (Luke 15:17), he wrote to Heber C. Kimball, who had been his associate in the Quorum of the Twelve, stating:

"Having lost my wife three years since, I began to awake to a sense of my situation; . . . I know that I have sinned against Heaven and in thy sight and have rendered myself unworthy of your confidence; or of a place in the family of Heaven. . . . I deserve no place among you in the church even as the lowest member; but I cannot live long so without a reconciliation with the 12 and the Church whom I have injured." He then recited the typical lesson his years of rebellion had taught him: "The Lord could get along very well without me and He has lost nothing by my falling out of the ranks; But O what have I lost?! Riches, greater riches than all this world or many planets like this could afford." He pleaded with his brethren for comfort and peace and their smiles upon him. (Thomas B. Marsh to Heber C. Kimball, 5 May 1857, Brigham Young Collection, Church Historical Department.)

After being rebaptized, Thomas came to Salt Lake City, where he asked Brigham Young, the President of the Church, for forgiveness. He was invited by President Young to speak at a Sunday service where Thomas offered this advice to his listeners: "If there are any among this people who should ever apostatize and do as I have done, prepare your backs for a good whipping, if you are such as the Lord loves. But if you will take my advice, you will stand by the authorities." (*Journal of Discourses* 5:207.) ("The Prophetic Voice," *Ensign,* May 1996, 7.)

I BELIEVE THOSE who find fault would be surprised at how often the leadership of the Church prays for them. . . .

We do not wish any who have questions [about the Church] to prove that they are sincere in their feelings by leaving the Church. That is not what we want. We hope that their sincerity would be manifested rather by building upon those feelings that have kept them in the Church. Their faith can be strengthened by following their intuitive judgment and the purest and noblest feelings of their own souls. By looking to a source higher than themselves, they can receive answers to their questions from the divine source. If there have been some mistakes, there is a way back. The doors are wide open; welcoming arms are outstretched. There is a place for all; there is a contribution for each to make.

In the spirit of Wilford Woodruff's letter to Lyman Wight, an Apostle who became separated from the leadership of the Church, we say to all: "Come home to Zion, mingle in our midst, confess and forsake your sins, and do right, as . . . all men have to do, in order to enjoy the favor of God, and the gift of the Holy Ghost, and have fellowship with the Saints. . . . We all feel interested in your welfare; you have no enemies here; the longer you stay away from us, the more alienated your feelings become" (quoted in Ronald G. Watt, "A Dialogue between Wilford Woodruff and Lyman Wight," *Brigham Young University Studies,* Autumn 1976, p. 113).

The leadership of the Church will continue to pray for its

critics, its enemies, and those who seek to do it harm. ("The Abundant Life," *Ensign*, Nov. 1985, 7, 9.)

ATONEMENT OF JESUS CHRIST

MANY WHO THINK that life is unfair do not see things within the larger vision of what the Savior did for us through the Atonement and the Resurrection. Each of us has times of agony, heartbreak, and despair when we must, like Job, reach deep down inside to the bedrock of our own faith. The depth of our belief in the Resurrection and the Atonement of the Savior will, I believe, determine the measure of courage and purpose with which we meet life's challenges.

The first words of the risen Lord to His disciples were, "Peace be unto you." (John 20:19.) He has also promised, "Peace in this world, and eternal life in the world to come." (D&C 59:23.) The Atonement and the Resurrection have taken place. Our Lord and Savior suffered that appalling agony in Gethsemane. He performed the ultimate sacrifice in dying on the cross and then breaking the bonds of death.

All of us benefit from the transcendent blessings of the Atonement and the Resurrection, through which the divine healing process can work in our lives. The hurt can be replaced by the joy the Savior promised. To the doubting Thomas, Jesus said, "Be not faithless, but believing." (John 20:27.) Through faith and righteousness all of the inequities, injuries, and pains of this life can be fully compensated for and made right. Blessings denied in this life will be fully recompensed in the eternities. Through complete repentance of our sins we can be forgiven and we can enjoy eternal life. Thus our suffering in this life can be as the refining fire, purifying us for a higher purpose. Heartaches can be healed, and we can come to know a soul-satisfying joy and happiness beyond our dreams and expectations. ("Woman, Why Weepest Thou?" *Ensign*, Nov. 1996, 52.)

IT HAS BEEN almost two thousand years since the wondrous occasion when death was conquered. We still do not know how the Savior was able to take upon Himself and bear our transgressions, our foolishness, our grief, our sorrows, and our burdens. It was indefinable and unfathomable. It was almost unbearable. The indescribable agony was so great in Gethsemane that "his sweat was as it were great drops of blood falling down to the ground" (Luke 22:44). The haunting cry on the cross, in a loud voice in His native Aramaic, "Eloi, Eloi, lama sabachthani?" which is, being interpreted, "My God, my God, why hast thou forsaken me?" (Mark 15:34) gives but a mere glimpse of His suffering and humiliation. One cannot help wondering how many of those drops of precious blood each of us may be responsible for.

Even though, as a man or a woman, we are born, live a brief moment, and then die, through the atonement of Jesus Christ we will all live after death. Through the divinity which is within us as a gift of the great Creator, we can come to complete fruition as heirs of God with eternal powers, dominions, and progression without end. Paul said this gift is a free gift (see Romans 5:15). Through the Mediation and Atonement we will be resurrected ourselves without going through any part of the atoning agony that the Son of God went through. ("The Supernal Gift of the Atonement," *Ensign*, Nov. 1988, 12–13.)

WE CHALLENGE THE powers of darkness when we speak of the perfect life of the Savior and of his sublime work for all mankind through the Atonement. This supernal gift permits us, through repentance, to break away from Satan's grasping tentacles. ("Serving the Lord and Resisting the Devil," *Ensign*, Sept. 1995, 6.)

THROUGH THE ATONEMENT and those singular events surrounding it, all of the terrible individual and collective sins of mankind were taken upon the Lord's shoulders. The marvelous result of this great suffering was that he was able to redeem

from physical death the believers and the obedient as well as
the unbelieving and disobedient. (D&C 46:13–14; Acts 24:15; 1
Corinthians 15:22.) Every person ever born or yet to be born is
the beneficiary of both the mediation and the atonement of the
Savior. (Alma 11:42.) ("The Supernal Gift of the Atonement,"
Ensign, Nov. 1988, 12.)

IT IS NOT necessary for anyone to depend continually upon the
testimony of another person regarding the mediation, atonement, and resurrection of Christ as our Redeemer and Savior.
Each can savor the sweetness of the truths of the gospel by obedience to the principles, ordinances, and covenants. One can
still go to the Garden of Gethsemane, but the Lord Jesus cannot
be found there, nor is he in the Garden Tomb. He is not on the
road to Emmaus, nor in Galilee, nor at Nazareth or Bethlehem.
He must be found in one's heart. But he left us the great
Comforter (John 14:16) and the everlasting power of the priesthood. ("The Supernal Gift of the Atonement," *Ensign,* Nov.
1988, 14.)

BEAUTY

MEMBERS OF THE Church are to seek after loveliness. We do not
seek a veneer painted on by a worldly brush but the pure,
innate beauty that God has planted in our souls. We should
seek after those things that endow higher thoughts and finer
impulses. ("We Seek After These Things," *Ensign,* May 1998,
45.)

BIRTH CONTROL

I [WISH TO] speak . . . of the present-day challenge to the words
of the Lord recorded in Genesis: "Be fruitful, and multiply, and
replenish the earth." (Genesis 1:28.) All my life I have heard the
argument that the earth is overpopulated. Much controversy
surrounded a recently concluded United Nations International
Conference on Population and Development held in Cairo,

Egypt. No doubt the conference accomplished much that was worthwhile. But at the very center of the debate was the socially acceptable phrase "sustainable growth." This concept is becoming increasingly popular. How cleverly Satan masked his evil designs with that phrase.

Few voices in the developed nations cry out in the wilderness against this coined phrase "sustainable growth." In *Forbes Magazine* of September of this year, a thoughtful editorial asserts that people are an asset not a liability. It forthrightly declares as preposterous the broadly accepted premise that curbing population growth is essential for economic development. The editorial then states convincingly that "free people don't exhaust resources, they create them." (*Forbes Magazine*, September 12, 1994, p. 25.)

An article in the *U.S. News and World Report* entitled "Ten Billion for Dinner, Please," states that the earth is capable of producing food for a population of at least eighty billion, eight times the ten billion expected to inhabit the earth by the year 2050. One study estimates that with improved scientific methods the earth could feed as many as one thousand billion people. ("Ten Billion for Dinner, Please," *U.S. News and World Report,* September 12, 1994, pp. 57–60.) Those who argue for sustainable growth lack vision and faith. The Lord said, "For the earth is full, and there is enough and to spare." (D&C 104:17.) That settles the issue for me. It should settle the issue for all of us. The Lord has spoken. ("Trying to Serve the Lord without Offending the Devil," *BYU Speeches,* 1994–1995, 61–62.)

BOOK OF MORMON

SOME TIME AGO I held in my hand my mother's copy of her favorite book. It was a timeworn copy of the Book of Mormon. Almost every page was marked; in spite of tender handling, some of the leaves were dogeared, and the cover was worn thin. No one had to tell her that one can get closer to God by reading the Book of Mormon than by any other book. She was already there. She had read it, studied it, prayed over it, and taught from it. As a young man I held her book in my hands and tried to see, through her eyes, the great truths of the Book of Mormon to which she so readily testified and which she so greatly loved.

As a young boy in the Cottonwood Ward, I was greatly impressed when I listened to James H. Moyle tell in sacrament meeting of his having heard both Martin Harris and David Whitmer, two of the witnesses of the Book of Mormon, affirm their testimony concerning that book. They, along with Oliver Cowdery, had testified in connection with the original publication of the Book of Mormon "that an angel of God came down from heaven, and he brought and laid before our eyes, that we beheld and saw the plates, and the engravings thereon; and we . . . bear record that these things are true" ("The Testimony of Three Witnesses," Book of Mormon). . . .

However, the Book of Mormon did not yield its profound message to me as an unearned legacy. I question whether one can acquire an understanding of this great book except through singleness of mind and strong purpose of heart. We must ask not only if it is true, but also do it in the name of Jesus Christ. Said Moroni, "Ask God, the Eternal Father, in the name of Christ, if these things are not true; and if ye shall ask with a sincere heart, with real intent, having faith in Christ, he will manifest the truth of it unto you, by the power of the Holy Ghost" (Moroni 10:4). ("The Keystone of Our Religion," *Ensign*, Nov. 1983, 9.)

THE IMPORTANCE OF the Book of Mormon in our history and theology cannot be overestimated. The Book of Mormon is the text for this dispensation. Nothing took priority over getting the Book of Mormon translated and published. Everything was held until that was accomplished. There were no apostles until it came into being. Ten days after its publication the Church was organized. It preceded missionary work because Samuel Smith needed to have it in hand before he could go forward as the first missionary of the Church. Both Sections 17 and 20 of the Doctrine and Covenants indicate that the Brethren could not pretend to know the divinity of the latter-day work until the Book of Mormon was translated.

Furthermore, the translation process was the education of Joseph Smith. Like so many of the young missionaries in the field, when the Lord called Joseph Smith, he was a young man, uneducated, unrefined, unremarkable in the eyes of the world. . . .

The doctrines he learned, the truths revealed during translation, and the principles taught in the process of laboring over the book all contributed to his education. Even as the Book of Mormon operates as a "keystone of our religion," so the process of translation was the keystone of the prophet's education.

The Book of Mormon was central to Joseph Smith's coming to an understanding of the doctrines of the restoration and of his role in this mission and of his responsibility to it. Surely the First Vision alerted young Joseph to the fact that he had special responsibilities, but he was not given the fullness of this except through dealing with the Book of Mormon and its translation. The nature of his prophetic responsibilities became clear in the four years before he was allowed even to obtain the plates; the confirmation of his responsibility to translate the record perhaps came only after he had the plates in his possession and was commanded to make it available to this generation. ("Joseph Smith and the Book of Mormon," Mission Presidents Seminar, Provo, Utah, 26 June 1987.)

MOST OBJECTIVE, ANALYTICAL scholars have come to recognize that it would have been impossible for an uneducated boy such as Joseph Smith, reared on the frontiers of America, to write the Book of Mormon. It contains so many exalted concepts, has such different writing styles, and is compiled in such a way that no one person could be its author. The honest inquirer can be led by faith to believe that Joseph Smith did translate the Book of Mormon from ancient plates of gold which were written with engraved characters in the reformed Egyptian language. No other explanations which have seriously challenged Joseph Smith's own account of the Book of Mormon have been able to survive as being factually correct. The evidences of a century and a half continue, and these increasingly affirm that Joseph Smith spoke the truth, completely, honestly, and humbly. ("The Expanding Inheritance from Joseph Smith," *Ensign*, Nov. 1981, 76.)

A KEYSTONE KEEPS an arch in place; without a keystone the whole arch will collapse. Why is the Book of Mormon the keystone of our religion? Because it is central to our history and theology. It is the text for this dispensation. ("Joseph Smith and the Book of Mormon," *Ensign*, Jan. 1996, 7.)

ONE OF THE MOST significant contributions of Joseph Smith is his work in translating and publishing the Book of Mormon, a sacred volume of scripture brought forth from ancient records. When it was first published in 1830, there was little scientific or historical evidence to substantiate the claims of Joseph Smith that the record came from metallic plates and told of ancient civilizations on the North and South American continents. Today such outward evidences have been discovered and help confirm that Joseph Smith was telling the truth about the Book of Mormon. ("The Expanding Inheritance from Joseph Smith," *Ensign*, Nov. 1981, 76.)

TO ME IT IS inconceivable that Joseph Smith, without divine help, could have written this complex and profound book. There is no way that Joseph Smith, an unlearned young frontiersman, could have fabricated the great truths it contains, generated its great spiritual power, or falsified the testimony of Christ that it contains. The book itself testifies that it is the holy word of God. ("The Keystone of Our Religion," *Ensign*, Nov. 1983, 10.)

REFERENCES TO TEACHINGS also taught in the Old Testament and the New Testament are so numerous and overwhelming throughout the Book of Mormon that one can come to a definitive conclusion by logic that a human intellect could not have conceived of them all. But more important than logic is the confirmation by the Holy Spirit that the story of the Book of Mormon is true. ("The Keystone of Our Religion, *Ensign,* Nov. 1983, 10.)

THE TEST FOR understanding [the Book of Mormon] is preeminently spiritual. An obsession with secular knowledge rather than spiritual understanding will make its pages difficult to unlock. ("The Keystone of Our Religion, *Ensign,* Nov. 1983, 10.)

CHASTITY

AS MEMBERS OF the Church and particularly as holders of the priesthood, we believe in being chaste. There is no different or double standard for moral cleanliness for men and women in the Church. In fact, I believe holders of the priesthood have a greater responsibility to maintain standards of chastity before marriage and fidelity after marriage. The Lord has said, "Be ye clean that bear the vessels of the Lord." (D&C 38:42.) This means being pure in thought as well as in deed. The Prophet Joseph Smith stated, "If we would come before God, we must keep ourselves pure, as He is pure." (*Teachings of the Prophet Joseph Smith,* p. 226.) If husband and wife will remain pure and chaste, completely devoted to each other during the storms and sunshine of life, their love for one another will deepen into something of supernal fulfillment. An early LDS Apostle, Parley P. Pratt, said, "From this union of affection, springs all the other relationships, social joys and affections diffused through every branch of human existence." (*Encyclopedia of Mormonism,* vol. 3, "Procreation," pp. 52–54.) ("We Seek After These Things," *Ensign,* May 1998, 44–45.)

SINCE BECOMING A parent is such a transcending blessing, and since each child is so precious and brings so much happiness, a cardinal purpose of marriage and of life itself is to bring forth new life within this partnership with God. Obligations inherent in the creation of precious human life are a sacred trust, which if faithfully kept, will keep us from degenerating into moral bankrupts and from becoming mere addicts of lust.

The responsibilities involved in the divine life-giving process, and the functions of our body, are so sacrosanct that they are to be exercised only within the marriage relationship. Those who do not accept and meet those responsibilities, for any reason, as well as those who do, should never depart from the law of chastity if they wish to be truly happy. All members of this Church seeking eternal joy and peace are expected to and will wish to come to the marriage altar free from sexual transgressions—chaste and pure. Any who fail to do so may find that they have cheated themselves of their own self-respect, dignity, and much of the great joy they seek in marriage. Because of the special inner peace, strength, and happiness it brings, chastity, as the law of God, is and always has been really "in," and unchastity is and always has been really "out." ("The Sanctity of Life," *Ensign,* May 1975, 27–28.)

CHASTITY BEFORE MARRIAGE and faithfulness after marriage are cardinal ingredients for the full flowering of sacred love between husband and wife. Chastity nurtures and builds feelings of self-worth and indemnifies against the destruction of self-image. ("The Dignity of Self," *Ensign,* May 1981, 9.)

BY THE WORD of the Lord, all men and women are to practice chastity before marriage and fidelity after marriage. "Thou shalt not commit adultery," said the Lord (Exodus 20:14), "nor do anything like unto it" (D&C 59:6). The Apostle Paul was more explicit in his epistle to the Corinthians (see 1 Corinthians 6:9), as was Alma in the Book of Mormon (see Alma 39:1–13).

Alternatives to the legal and loving marriage between a

man and a woman are helping to unravel the fabric of human society. That fabric, of course, is the family. These so-called alternative lifestyles cannot be accepted as right because they frustrate God's commandment for a life-giving union of male and female within a legal marriage (see Genesis 1:28). If practiced by all adults, these lifestyles would mean the end of family.

The scriptures clearly and consistently condemn all sex relations outside of legal marriage as morally wrong. Why is this so? It is so because God said so. It is so because we are made in the image of God, male and female (see Genesis 1:27). We are his spirit children (see D&C 76:24). We were with him in the beginning (see D&C 93:23). Bringing to pass our exaltation is his work and glory (see Moses 1:39). We are directed to be the children of light (see D&C 106:5). We are heirs to eternal life. The Spirit gives light to every man and woman who comes into the world (see D&C 84:46). ("Will I Be Happy?" *Ensign*, May 1987, 81.)

CHILDREN

I WISH TO speak of a hope that children will know a future filled with some happiness and peace. No gift bestowed upon us is so precious as children. They are proof that God still loves us. They are the hope of the future.

In today's world, I cannot help wondering, Who will love them enough to help them be happy? Who will love them enough to teach them faith and moral values? . . .

This teaching of the next generation is not easy in a society where many fundamental beliefs are disappearing. Deadly mass marketing challenges almost every cherished human value. Excessive permissiveness under the banner of individual freedom is one driving force behind this. Reaching a public consensus on what values should be taught to the next generation is almost impossible. People strongly disagree about almost everything. Social restraints are weakened.

This means we will have to teach our children a lifestyle of our own and provide moral anchors in the sea of self-indulgence, self-interest, and self-service in which they float. ("Will I Be Happy?" *Ensign,* May 1987, 80.)

I CANNOT HELP wondering about parents who adopt the attitude with their children, "do as I say, not as I do" with respect to using harmful substances, going to inappropriate movies, and other questionable activities. Children often take license from their parents' behavior and go beyond the values the parents wish to establish. There is one safe parental rule: do not just avoid evil, avoid the very appearance of evil (see 1 Thessalonians 5:22). ("Unwanted Messages," *Ensign,* Nov. 1986, 10.)

WHO DECIDES WHAT is right and wrong in given circumstances? Where does the responsibility for the making of moral judgments rest? With mature individuals, of course, it rests with each individual. In the case of children, the responsibility of giving moral guidance rests with the parents. They know the disposition, understanding, and intelligence of each child. Parents spend a lifetime seeking to establish and maintain good communications with each of their children. They are in the best position to make the ultimate moral decisions as to the welfare and well-being of their offspring. The higher principles of the gospel—justice, mercy, and faith—are very important in all family relationships. ("The Weightier Matters of the Law: Judgment, Mercy and Faith," *Ensign,* Nov. 1997, 54.)

I AM GRATEFUL for people on the earth who love and appreciate little children. Last year I found myself late at night on an airplane bulging with passengers going north from Mexico City to Culiacan. The seats in the plane were close together, and every seat was taken, mostly by the gracious people of Mexico. Everywhere inside the plane there were packages and carry-on luggage of all sizes.

A young woman came down the aisle with four small

children, the oldest of which appeared to be about four and the youngest a newborn. She was also trying to manage a diaper bag and a stroller and some bags. The children were tired, crying, and fussing. As she found her seat in the airplane, the passengers around her, both men and women, literally sprang to her aid. Soon the children were being lovingly and tenderly comforted and cared for by the passengers. They were passed from one passenger to another all over the airplane.

The result was an airplane full of baby-sitters. The children settled down in the caring arms of those who cradled them and, before long, went to sleep. Most remarkable was that a few men who were obviously fathers and grandfathers tenderly cradled and caressed the newborn child without any false, macho pride. The mother was freed from the care of her children most of the flight.

The only thing that I felt bad about was that no one passed the baby to me! I relearned that appreciation for and thoughtfulness and kindness to little children are an expression of the Savior's love for them. ("Gratitude as a Saving Principle," *Ensign*, May 1990, 86–87.)

WITHOUT TURNING BACK to the word of our Creator, no one is wise enough to sort out what ethical, spiritual, and moral values should be taught to the next generation, and to their children, and to their children's children. ("Will I Be Happy?" *Ensign*, May 1987, 82.)

ONE OF THE most difficult parental challenges is to appropriately discipline children. Child rearing is so individualistic. Every child is different and unique. What works with one may not work with another. I do not know who is wise enough to say what discipline is too harsh or what is too lenient except the parents of the children themselves, who love them most. It is a matter of prayerful discernment for the parents. Certainly the overarching and undergirding principle is that the discipline of children must be motivated more by love than by punishment.

Brigham Young counseled, "If you are ever called upon to chasten a person, never chasten beyond the balm you have within you to bind up" (in *Journal of Discourses,* 9:124–25). Direction and discipline are, however, certainly an indispensable part of child-rearing. If parents do not discipline their children, then the public will discipline them in a way the parents do not like. Without discipline, children will not respect either the rules of the home or of society. ("The Greatest Challenge in the World— Good Parenting," *Ensign,* Nov. 1990, 34.)

MAY I . . . SAY a word of comfort for the anguished parents of children who have lost their way and have turned a deaf ear to parental pleading and teaching. While much of the time most children follow in their parents' footsteps—obedient to their teachings, reciprocating their love—a few turn their backs like the prodigal son and waste their lives. The great principle of free agency is essential in fostering development, growth, and progress. It also permits the freedom to choose self-indulgence, wastefulness, and degradation. Children have their agency and often express it when very young. They may or may not follow the teachings and wishes of their parents. . . .

Parents have the obligation to teach, not force, and having prayerfully and conscientiously taught, parents cannot be answerable for all their children's conduct. Obedient children do bring honor to their parents, but it is unfair to judge faithful parents by the actions of children who will not listen and follow. Parents do have the obligation to instruct, but children themselves have a responsibility to listen, to be obedient, and to perform as they have been taught. ("The Works of God," *Ensign,* Nov. 1984, 59–60.)

CHILDREN ARE ALSO beneficiaries of moral agency by which we are all afforded the opportunity to progress, grow, and develop. That agency also permits children to pursue the alternate choice of selfishness, wastefulness, self-indulgence, and self-destruction. Children often express this agency when very young.

Let parents who have been conscientious, loving, and concerned and who have lived the principles of righteousness as best they could be comforted in knowing that they are good parents despite the actions of some of their children. The children themselves have a responsibility to listen, obey, and, having been taught, to learn. Parents cannot always answer for all their children's misconduct because they cannot ensure the children's good behavior. Some few children would tax even Solomon's wisdom and Job's patience. ("The Greatest Challenge in the World—Good Parenting," *Ensign,* Nov. 1990, 34.)

THERE IS OFTEN a special challenge for those parents who are affluent or overly indulgent. In a sense, some children in those circumstances hold their parents hostage by withholding their support of parental rules unless the parents acquiesce to the children's demands. Elder Neal A. Maxwell has said, "Those who do too much for their children will soon find they can do nothing with their children. So many children have been so much done for they are almost done in" (in Conference Report, Apr. 1975, p. 150; or *Ensign,* May 1975, p. 101). It seems to be human nature that we do not fully appreciate material things we have not ourselves earned.

There is a certain irony in the fact that some parents are so anxious for their children to be accepted by and be popular with their peers; yet these same parents fear that their children may be doing the things their peers are doing. ("The Greatest Challenge in the World—Good Parenting," *Ensign,* Nov. 1990, 34.)

GENERALLY, THOSE CHILDREN who make the decision and have the resolve to abstain from drugs, alcohol, and illicit sex are those who have adopted and internalized the strong values of their homes as lived by their parents. In times of difficult decisions they are most likely to follow the teachings of their parents rather than the example of their peers or the sophistries of the media which glamorize alcohol consumption, illicit sex, infidelity, dishonesty, and other vices. They are like Helaman's two thousand young men who "had been taught by their mothers, that if they did not doubt, God would deliver them" from death (Alma 56:47). "And they rehearsed . . . the words of their mothers, saying: We do not doubt our mothers knew it" (56:48).

What seems to help cement parental teachings and values in place in children's lives is a firm belief in Deity. When this belief becomes part of their very souls, they have inner strength. So, of all that is important to be taught, what should parents teach? The scriptures tell us that parents are to teach their children "faith in Christ the Son of the living God, and of baptism and the gift of the Holy Ghost," and "the doctrine of repentance" (D&C 68:25). These truths must be taught in the home. They cannot be taught in the public schools, nor will they be fostered by the government or by society. Of course, Church programs can help, but the most effective teaching takes place in the home. ("The Greatest Challenge in the World—Good Parenting," *Ensign*, Nov. 1990, 34–35.)

THERE ARE SOME great spiritual promises which may help faithful parents in this church. Children of eternal sealings may have visited upon them the divine promises made to their valiant forebears who nobly kept their covenants. Covenants remembered by parents will be remembered by God. The children may thus become the beneficiaries and inheritors of these great covenants and promises. This is because they are the children of the covenant (see Orson F. Whitney, in Conference Report, Apr. 1929, pp. 110–11). ("The Greatest Challenge in the World— Good Parenting," *Ensign*, Nov. 1990, 35.)

CHRISTMAS

CHRISTMAS AND THE holiday season is a wonderful time to help us to forgive and forget. We become our better selves and rise above the shackles that seem to bind us as we meet the concerns of the eternal every day. The holiday season is a wonderful time to find peace. It is a time to make new resolves and to hope for better days. The holiday season is a special time because we make time for family, loved ones, and friends. We seem to turn outward rather than inward. We think more of others, including strangers. We have the spirit of giving. The heavenly hosts who proclaimed the birth of Jesus declared, "Glory to God in the highest, and on earth peace, goodwill toward men" (Luke 2:14). The good tidings of Christmas "shall be to all people" (Luke 2:10). ("Peace There Shall Be No End," Remarks delivered at the Washington, D.C., Temple Visitors Center, 1 Dec. 1993.)

CHRISTMAS IS A time when more Christians take part in religious ceremonies and celebrate the season of peace on earth, goodwill toward men. So much of the celebration of Christmas centers on the wonderful account of the Savior's birth in a manger. The custom of exchanging gifts may have come from the memory of the gifts brought by the Wise Men to give to the baby Jesus. (Matthew 2:11.) . . .

Bringing happiness to others without their knowing the identity of the giver is, as Portia says in *The Merchant of Venice*, "twice blest;/It blesseth him that gives and him that takes." (Shakespeare, *The Merchant of Venice*, iv.i.186–87.) [But] we celebrate Christmas principally to commemorate the birth of our Lord, Redeemer, and Savior, who is the King of Kings and Lord of Lords. In doing so we also open our hearts and souls to show our love for our families, friends, strangers, and all creatures of God. In this way we honor Him in the most important way we can—by keeping his commandment to "love one another" (John 15:12), for He has said, "Inasmuch as ye have done it unto one of the least of these my brethren, ye have done it unto me." (Matthew 25:40.) (First Presidency Christmas Fireside, Salt Lake City, Utah, 8 Dec. 1996.)

CHURCH OF JESUS CHRIST

THE SAVING PRINCIPLES and doctrines of the Church are established, fixed, and unchangeable. Obedience to these absolutes is necessary to enjoy "peace in this world, and eternal life in the world to come." (D&C 59:23.) However, the manner in which the Church administers complex and varied worldwide challenges changes from time to time. Under guidance from living prophets, new guidelines and procedures are put in place. I welcome these inspired changes. They are a proof of the truthfulness of the restored gospel.

I have some fear, however, that some members consider guidelines and procedures to be as important as the timeless, immutable laws of the gospel. ("The Weightier Matters of the Law: Judgment, Mercy and Faith," *Ensign*, Nov. 1997, 53.)

WE SHOULD NOT be preoccupied with the lacquered image of the Church nor worry excessively about what people are going to think. Let us go ahead and do our work. Mostly, let us do what's right—for the right reason.

While serving many years ago as a guide on Temple Square, I found that visitors were unimpressed when I spoke of the holdings of the Church. All of a sudden, it got through to me. Here I have a responsibility to tell them about the beauties and wonders of eternity, and I am spending time talking about bricks and mortar, companies and things.

I think we can properly . . . focus on what we believe, what we try to teach, what we are and what we are trying to be and ought to be. We have the responsibility of saying it right and putting the best face on the Lord's business. But it has to be genuine and it has to be honest.

The Lord said, "By their fruits ye shall know them." We take the apples and we polish them. We wipe off the pears. We wash the grapes. And we put the fruit in the basket so that its natural beauty—its God-given beauty—is obvious and shines. (Address to Public Affairs Directors, 7 May 1991.)

SOME TIME AGO I was walking in the center of Salt Lake City, on my way to City Creek Canyon, where I usually walk every day. A car with an out-of-state license plate was driving by. It pulled over and stopped. The driver asked, "Where is the church of the Mormons?" I assumed they were thinking of some place or building. I took time to point out the Church Office Building, and the Church Administration Building, and the magnificent temple, and the historic tabernacle, most of which were visible from our vantage point. They thanked me and went on their way. . . .

How should I have answered? It has bothered me ever since. If I had pointed to my chest and said that the Church should be first and foremost in my heart, the inquiring travelers surely would have gone away somewhat bewildered. But I would have been more accurate than I was by directing him to our beloved, magnificent, sky-piercing spires; the great majestic dome; and the other world-famous monuments and edifices—wonderful and unique and great as they are. . . .

The Church of Jesus Christ of Latter-day Saints is in our hearts, and when it is in our hearts as individuals, it will also be in our great buildings of worship, in our great educational institutions, in our magnificent temples, and in our homes and families. ("Where Is the Church?" *BYU Speeches*, 24 Sept. 1989, 31, 36.)

THERE IS ONLY one head of this church, and he is the Lord Jesus Christ. (Conference Report, Oct. 1994, 95.)

THE WORLDWIDE MISSION of the Church can be simply stated; it is to perfect the Saints, proclaim the gospel, and redeem the dead in order to bring God's children to Christ. ("An Untroubled Faith," *Ensign*, Mar. 1988, 70.)

A MAJOR REASON this church has grown from its humble beginnings to its current strength is the faithfulness and devotion of millions of humble and devoted people who have only five loaves and two small fishes to offer in the service of the Master. (Conference Report, Apr. 1994, 5.)

CITIZENSHIP

THE DESIRABILITY OF this country will persist so long as its citizenry are a God-fearing people with the integrity to obey the law of the land. This includes the laws we do not like as well as the laws we do like. ("The Integrity of Obeying the Law," Freedom Festival Fireside, Provo, Utah, 2 July 1995.)

AS DEMOCRACIES TEETER around the world, drug cartels take over countries in South America, and the dread disease AIDS destroys the infrastructure of countries in Central Africa, we feel quite smug and secure in the success of our democracy. We say, "It can't fail here." Yet a fair question to ask is whether our citizens are willing to pay the higher price required to preserve a popular sovereignty. Many are disinclined to make the effort to vote, or to serve in the armed forces in an unpopular war. Others are not willing to serve on juries, nor to render public service. Also of concern is the obsession with materialism, the measure of success seeming to be what we have rather than what we are. . . .

Private virtue embodies a nobility of soul based upon the Judeo-Christian values of faith, hope, and charity. Vetterli and Bryner contend that classical public virtues, to which the ancients encouraged even the magistrates to adhere, were "justice," "fortitude," "temperance," and "wisdom." . . . (Richard Vetterli and Gary Bryner, *In Search of the Republic* [Rowman and Littlefield], 1987, p. 20). The founders held these values to be absolutes in the body politic.

The cardinal virtues must be found in the hearts of the citizens, and the public virtue must subordinate individual desires for the greater good of society. ("In Preservation of the Republic," Remarks at the United States Courthouse, Salt Lake City, Utah, 20 Oct. 1988.)

I WONDER HOW this nation will preserve its enduring values. In my view, there is substantial governmental interest within the limits of the religious clauses of the Constitution in public prayer and expressions of all faiths which acknowledge the existence of deity. I believe this because in so doing, the transcendent principles of morality can be reached. Such prayer and expressions accommodate the abiding values shared by a great majority of our citizenry. It gives meaning to a transcendent spiritual reality and idealism which, in the past at least, was quite firmly held by the people of our society. The very essence of our concern for human welfare and alleviation of human suffering lies in our spiritual feelings and expressions.

So, how do we preserve the essence of our humanity? How can we hope to avoid future wars? Perhaps this may not be possible, but try we must; and we must begin in our homes. Our children and our grandchildren must be taught moral responsibility. The moral teachings of all of our churches of every denomination must find an honored place in our society. The general decline in the moral fabric of the citizenry places a greater responsibility on homes and churches to teach values—marriage, morality, decency, family responsibility, respect for others, patriotism and honoring and sustaining the law.

With all other citizens, we also have the right to vote for men and women who reflect our own sense of values. We can also express our views as all other citizens have a right to do in the legislative process of the state and the nation. With all others we can claim our rights of free expression. We can petition for the redress of grievances.

We can help educate the coming generation about their rights but, more importantly, about their duties. ("The Impact of World War II on Utah," World War II Commemoration, Ogden, Utah, 13 Aug. 1995.)

CIVIL DISOBEDIENCE

CIVIL DISOBEDIENCE HAS become fashionable for a few with strongly held political agendas. Even when causes are meritorious, if civil disobedience were to be practiced by everyone with a cause our democracy would unravel and be destroyed. Civil disobedience is an abuse of political process in a democracy. "No one pretends that democracy is perfect or all-wise," as Winston Churchill once said. "Indeed, it has been said that democracy is the worst form of Government except all those other forms that have been tried from time to time" (House of Commons, 11 Nov. 1947, *The Oxford Dictionary of Quotations,* Third Edition, p. 150).

Recently I heard a new convert to our Church urge that the Church resort to civil disobedience and violence because of the moral wrongness of abortion. The position of The Church of Jesus Christ of Latter-day Saints opposing abortion is long-standing and well-known. I told him that it was our belief that even though we disagreed with the law, and even though we counseled our people strongly against abortion, and even though we bring into question the membership of those involved in abortion, we are still obliged to recognize the law of the land until it is changed. His response was, "Even if it is wrong?" I tried to explain that when we disagree with a law, rather than resort to civil disobedience or violence, we are obliged to exercise our right to seek its repeal or change by peaceful and lawful means. ("The Integrity of Obeying the Law," Freedom Festival Fireside, Provo, Utah, 2 July 1995.)

COMMANDMENTS

I WISH TO state unequivocally that the commandments of God must be kept to receive the blessings and promises of the Savior. The Ten Commandments are still a vital thread in the fabric of the gospel of Christ, but with His coming came new light and life which brings a fuller measure of joy and happiness. Jesus introduced a higher and more difficult standard of human conduct. It is simpler as well as more difficult because it focuses on internal rather than external requirements: Do unto others as you would have them do unto you. (See Matt. 7:12.) Love your neighbor as yourself. (Matt. 22:27–39.) When smitten, turn the other cheek. When asked for a coat, give your cloak also. (Matt. 5:40.) Forgive, not just once, but seventy times seven. (Matt. 18:22.) This was the essence of the new gospel. There was more emphasis on do than do not. More moral agency was given to each of us. ("The Weightier Matters of the Law: Judgment, Mercy and Faith," *Ensign*, Nov. 1997, 53.)

CONSCIENCE

THERE IS A defense mechanism to discern between good and evil. It is called conscience. It is our spirit's natural response to the pain of sin, just like pain in our flesh is our body's natural response to a wound—even a small sliver. Conscience strengthens through use. Paul told the Hebrews, "But strong meat belongeth to them that are of full age, even those who by reason of use have their senses exercised to discern both good and evil" (Hebrews 5:14). Those who have not exercised their conscience have "their conscience seared with a hot iron" (1 Timothy 4:2). A sensitive conscience is a sign of a healthy spirit. ("A Crown of Thorns, a Crown of Glory," *Ensign*, May 1991, 68.)

MANY MODERN PROFESSORS of human behavior advocate as a cure to an afflicted conscience that we simply ignore the unwanted messages. They suggest that we change the standard to fit the circumstances so that there is no longer a conflict, thus easing the conscience. The followers of the divine Christ cannot subscribe to this evil and perverse philosophy with impunity. For the troubled conscience in conflict with right and wrong, the only permanent help is to change the behavior and follow a repentant path. ("Unwanted Messages," *Ensign*, Nov. 1986, 10.)

CONSISTENCY

TONIGHT I PLEAD for greater consistency between our beliefs and actions. I take as my text the 13th article of faith. "We believe in being honest, true, chaste, benevolent, virtuous, and in doing good to all men; indeed, we may say that we follow the admonition of Paul—We believe all things, we hope all things, we have endured many things, and hope to be able to endure all things. If there is anything virtuous, lovely, or of good report or praiseworthy, we seek after these things." (Articles of Faith 1:13.) Brethren, does the Spirit of Christ that we have taken upon ourselves spill over into our behavior in the workforce? Brigham Young said: "We want the Saints to increase in goodness, until our mechanics, for instance, are so honest and reliable that this Railroad Company will say, 'Give us a "Mormon" Elder for an engineer, then none need have the least fear to ride, for if he knows there is danger he will take every measure necessary to preserve the lives of those entrusted to his care.' I want to see our Elders so full of integrity that they will be preferred by this Company for their engine builders, watchmen, engineers, clerks, and business managers. If we live our religion and are worthy [of] the name of Latter-day Saints, we are just the men that all such business can be entrusted to with perfect safety; if it can not it will prove that we do not live our religion." (*Discourses of Brigham Young,* 232–33.) What President Young urged of the priesthood holders in his day is just as important in our day. The Spirit of Christ should permeate all we do, whether at work, at school, or at home. ("We Seek After These Things," *Ensign,* May 1998, 43–44.)

CONTENTION

LET US NOT become so intense in our zeal to do good by winning arguments or by our pure intention in disputing doctrine that we go beyond good sense and manners, thereby promoting contention, or say and do imprudent things, invoke cynicism, or ridicule with flippancy. In this manner, our good motives become so misdirected that we lose friends and, even more serious, we come under the influence of the devil. I recently heard in a special place, "Your criticism may be worse than the conduct you are trying to correct." ("The Great Imitator," *Ensign,* Nov. 1987, 35.)

WHEN THERE IS contention, the Spirit of the Lord will depart, regardless of who is at fault. ("What I Want My Son to Know before He Leaves on His Mission," *Ensign,* May 1996, 41.)

CONVERSION

A CONVERT IS converted in the heart. No one can have an understanding of the principles of the gospel except through the Spirit. How is the Spirit generated? It is by fasting, by prayer, and by testimony. . . .

People are converted in their hearts by the Spirit through Joseph Smith. Our message is different. Says the Doctrine & Covenants: This generation shall receive the Lord's word through Joseph Smith (see D&C 5:10). What does that mean? It means exactly what it says. The message is the gospel of Jesus Christ as restored by Joseph Smith, not the *Readers Digest*, not *Time* magazine, nor the Bible alone. It means that we teach and testify to and from the First Vision. It means that we declare the Book of Mormon as the word of God. It means that we declare and testify to the story of Joseph Smith. It means that we teach the restoration of keys, priesthood, sealing power. It means that we teach from the Doctrine and Covenants. It means almost everything we have is different from all other religions, including the so-called Christian churches. . . .

Said Brigham Young concerning his conversion: "But when I saw a man without eloquence or talent for public speaking, who could only say, 'I know, by the power of the Holy Ghost, that the Book of Mormon is true, that Joseph Smith is a prophet of the Lord,' the Holy Ghost proceeding from that individual illuminated my understanding, and light, glory, and immortality were before me. I was encircled by them, filled with them, and I knew for myself that the testimony of the man was true." (*Journal of Discourses*, 1:90). ("The Three Principles of the Conversion Process," Mission Presidents Seminar, June 22, 1984.)

YOU CANNOT CONVERT people beyond your own conversion. ("What I Want My Son to Know before He Leaves on His Mission," *Ensign*, May 1996, 41.)

COVENANTS

ORDINANCES AND COVENANTS help us to remember who we are and our duty to God. They are the vehicles the Lord has provided to conduct us into eternal life. If we honor them, He will give us added strength.

Elder James E. Talmage affirmed that the true believer, "with the love of God in his soul, pursues his life of service and righteousness without stopping to ask by what rule or law each act is prescribed or forbidden." (General Conference, April 1905.)

In a world where we and our families are threatened by evil on every side, let us remember President Hinckley's counsel: "If our people could only learn to live by these covenants, everything else would take care of itself." (*Teachings of Gordon B. Hinckley*, p. 147.)

Faithful members of the Church who are true to their covenants with the Master do not need every jot and tittle spelled out for them. Christlike conduct flows from the deepest wellsprings of the human heart and soul. It is guided by the Holy Spirit of the Lord, which is promised in gospel ordinances. Our greatest hope should be to enjoy the sanctification that comes from this divine guidance; our greatest fear should be to forfeit these blessings. May we so live that we may be able to say, as did the Psalmist: "Search me, O God, and know my heart." (Psalm 139:23.) ("Search Me, O God, and Know My Heart," *Ensign,* May 1998, 19–20.)

CRITICISM

IN THE INFINITE process of accepting and rejecting information in the search for light, truth, and knowledge, almost everyone may have at one time or another some private questions. That is part of the learning process. Many are like the biblical father of the child with the "dumb spirit" who pleaded with the Savior: "Lord, I believe; help thou mine unbelief" (Mark 9:24).

The Church has not and, in my opinion, should not speak on every disputed question. But I cannot help wondering if a member of the Church does not place himself in some spiritual peril when publicly disparaging the prophetic calling of Joseph Smith, or his successors, or any of the fundamental, settled doctrines of the Church.

When a member expresses his private doubts or unbelief as a public chastisement of the leadership or the doctrine of the Church, or as a confrontation with those also seeking eternal light, he has entered upon sacred ground. Those who complain about the doctrine or leadership of the Church but who lack the faith or desire to keep God's commandments risk separating themselves from the divine source of learning. They do not enjoy the same richness of the Spirit that they might enjoy if they proved their sincere love of God by walking humbly before Him, by keeping His commandments, and by sustaining those He has appointed to lead the Church. ("The Abundant Life," *Ensign,* Nov. 1985, 8.)

SINCE THE BEGINNING of the restored Church there have been much opposition and many critics both from within and without. What have been the results of all this opposition and criticism? Some of the spiritually immature, the weak, and incredulous have dropped out. The Church itself, however, not only survives, but it grows and strengthens. In some respects nothing in the world is equal to this work. Despite the many challenges of great growth there are indications of increased faith over much of the earth. For instance, never in the history of the world have so many temples been built.

I do not believe this work will be stopped or seriously injured by its detractors. There are many prophetic statements to the contrary. History has proven quite conclusively that the Church has grown under persecution; it has prospered under criticism. By finding fault with the doctrines, practices, or the leadership of the Church, one can waste much time and effort in a fruitless endeavor. Those who have been washed in the waters of baptism put their eternal soul at risk by carelessly pursuing only the secular source of learning. We believe that The Church of Jesus Christ of Latter-day Saints has the fulness of the gospel of Christ, which gospel is the essence of truth and eternal enlightenment. We hold that the great legacy of this church is that it possesses the only full means for eternal life. ("The Abundant Life," *Ensign,* Nov. 1985, 9.)

DATING

WHEN YOU BOYS become priests and elders and begin to date, you need to know that the best place to date is at Church and Church-related activities. As you date, you will be entrusted by a girl's parents with their most cherished blessing. You will have the responsibility to protect not only her well-being, but also her honor, even above your own safety. One of the duties of manhood is to safeguard womanhood. ("The Highest Place of Honor," *Ensign,* May 1988, 37.)

DEBT

MANY YEARS AGO when I was practicing law, I organized a company for one of the new car dealers in this area. I served as his legal counsel and a corporate officer for many years, and one of my sons has taken over my responsibilities as legal counsel.

Recently we were both at his place of business. I noticed the rows and rows of beautiful, shiny, gleaming, expensive new cars. Out of concern I mentioned to the proprietor that if he did not get those cars sold, the finance charges would be exorbitant and eat up the profits. My son said, "Dad, don't look at it that way. Look at all the profit those cars will bring."

While I think he was more right than I, it suddenly occurred to me that my son had never been through a depression. We looked at the problem through different eyes because I am a child of the Great Depression. I cannot forget what a merciless taskmaster debt is. ("The Blessings of Adversity," *BYU Speeches,* 21 Feb. 1978, 27–28.)

WE MUST BE careful of the misuse of credit. The use of credit cards in many places has increased consumer debt to staggering proportions. I am reminded of the story of "an elderly farmer [who] wrote to a mail order house as follows: 'Please send me one of the gasoline engines you show on page 787, and if it's any good, I'll send you a check.' In time he received the following reply: 'Please send check. If it's any good, we'll send the engine.'" (*Braude's Treasury of Wit and Humor,* Jacob M. Braude, p. 45.)

Contemporary society rushes headlong to accumulate the material goods of this world. This leads many to think they can alter the law of the harvest, reaping rewards without paying the price of honest toil and effort. Wishing to prosper immediately, they speculate in high-risk financial schemes that promote instant wealth. This all too frequently results in economic reverses, sometimes even financial ruin. In Proverbs we read, "A faithful man shall abound with blessings: but he that maketh haste to be rich shall not be innocent." (Proverbs 28:20.) ("We Seek After These Things," *Ensign,* May 1998, 44.)

LIVING OUR LIVES in the Lord's way means that we live providently. It means we live within our means and save a little for a rainy day. It means that we avoid debt as much as possible.

When we borrow we not only have to repay the loan but the interest on the money borrowed. As President J. Reuben Clark, Jr. put it:

"Interest never sleeps nor sickens nor dies; it never goes to the hospital; it works on Sundays and holidays. . . . Once in debt, interest is your companion every minute of the day and night; you cannot shun it or slip away from it; you cannot dismiss it; . . . and whenever you . . . fail to meet its demands, it crushes you." (Conference Report, April 1938, p. 103.)

If we can say that we have managed our stewardship in the Lord's way, both temporally and spiritually, we will be surprised beyond our fondest dreams and expectations by the Lord's generosity as we account to Him for our stewardship. ("In the Lord's Way," Address at Ricks College Commencement, Apr. 28, 1995.)

THERE ARE SOME investment counselors who urge speculative credit practices described as "leverage," "credit wealth," and "borrow yourself rich." Such practices may work successfully for some, but at best they succeed only for a time. An economic reversal always seems to come, and many who have followed such practices find themselves in financial ruin and their lives in shambles.

Elder Ezra Taft Benson stated: "A large proportion of families with personal debt have no liquid assets whatsoever to fall back upon. What troubles they invite if their income should be suddenly cut off or seriously reduced! We all know of families who have obligated themselves for more than they could pay" ("Pay Thy Debt, and Live," *BYU Speeches* [Provo, 28 Feb. 1963], p. 10). ("Responsibility for Welfare Rests with Me and My Family," *Ensign,* May 1986, 20.)

OWNING A HOME free of debt is an important goal of provident living, although it may not be a realistic possibility for some. A mortgage on a home leaves a family unprotected against severe financial storms. Homes that are free and clear of mortgages and liens cannot be foreclosed on. When there are good financial times, it is the most opportune time to retire our debts and pay installments in advance. It is a truth that "the borrower is servant to the lender" (Proverbs 22:7).

Many young people have become so hypnotized by the rhythm of monthly payments they scarcely think of the total cost of what they buy. They immediately want things it took their parents years to acquire. It is not the pathway to happiness to assume debts for a big home, an expensive car, or the most stylish clothes just so we can "keep up with the Joneses." Payment of obligations is a sacred trust. Most of us will never be rich, but we can feel greatly unburdened when we are debt-free.

The Lord said that it is important for the Church to "stand independent above all other creatures beneath the celestial world" (D&C 78:14). Members of the Church are also counseled to be independent. Independence means many things. It means being free of drugs that addict, habits that bind, and diseases that curse. It also means being free of personal debt and of the interest and carrying charges required by debt the world over. ("Responsibility for Welfare Rests with Me and My Family," *Ensign*, May 1986, 21.)

DISABILITIES

I WISH TO say a word of appreciation for those among us who struggle with handicaps, and impart a message of comfort to their families, especially to the parents. Where in all of the world is the son or daughter of God who is totally without blemish? Is life not worth living if it is not perfect? Do not the people with handicaps also bring their own special gifts to life—and to others who are free of those handicaps—in a manner that cannot come in any other way? There is hardly a family without one of its members who might be considered physically or mentally diminished. I have a great appreciation for those loving parents who stoically bear and overcome their anguish and heartbreak for a child who was born with or who has developed a serious mental or physical infirmity. This anguish often continues every day, without relief, during the lifetime of the parent or the child. Not infrequently, parents are required to give superhuman nurturing care that never ceases, day or night. Many a mother's arms and heart have ached years on end, giving comfort and relieving the suffering of her special child. ("The Works of God," *Ensign*, Nov. 1984, 54.)

THE ANGUISH OF parents upon first learning that their child is not developing normally can be indescribable. The tearful concern, the questions about what the child will and will not be able to do are heartrending: "Doctor, will our child be able to talk, walk, care for himself?" Often there are no certain answers but one: "You will have to be grateful for whatever development your child achieves."

The paramount concern is always how to care for the person who is handicapped. The burden of future nurturing can seem overwhelming. Looking ahead to the uncertain years or even to a lifetime of constant, backbreaking care may seem more than one can bear. There are often many tears before reality is acknowledged. Parents and family members can then begin to accept and take the burden a day at a time.

Said one great mother of a severely handicapped child: "I gradually began to take only one day at a time, and it didn't seem so hard. In fact, at the end of each day I would thank the Lord for the strength I had to get through that day and pray that tomorrow would be as good. That way I learned to love him and appreciate his place in our home."

A missionary writing to his parents said of his severely handicapped younger brother: "Mom, kiss Billy every day for me. In one of the discussions we learned that my little brother is an automatic winner of the kingdom of God. I only pray that I too may live with my Heavenly Father and see my little brother and talk and converse with him. He's a special gift, and we are truly blessed." ("The Works of God," *Ensign*, Nov. 1984, 54.)

HOW ARE THE works of God manifest in these, our handicapped brothers and sisters? Surely they are manifested greatly in the loving care and attention given by parents, other family members, friends, and associates. The handicapped are not on trial. Those of us who live free of such limitations are the ones who are on trial. While those with handicaps cannot be measured in the same way as others, many of the handicapped benefit immensely from each accomplishment, no matter how small.

The handiwork of God is manifest with respect to the handicapped in many ways. It is demonstrated in the miraculous way in which many individuals with mental and physical impediments are able to adjust and compensate for their limitations. Occasionally, other senses become more functional and substitute for the impaired senses in a remarkable way. A young friend greatly retarded in speech and movement repaired a complicated clock although she had had no previous training or experience in watch or clock making.

Many of the special ones are superior in many ways. They, too, are in a life of progression, and new things unfold for them each day as with us all. They can be extraordinary in their faith and spirit. Some are able, through their prayers, to communicate with the infinite in a most remarkable way. Many have a pure faith in others and a powerful belief in God. They can give their spiritual strength to others around them. ("The Works of God," *Ensign*, Nov. 1984, 54, 59.)

FOR THE HANDICAPPED, trying to cope with life is often like trying to reach the unreachable. But recall the words of the Prophet Joseph Smith: "All the minds and spirits that God ever sent into the world are susceptible of enlargement" (*Teachings of the Prophet Joseph Smith*, sel. Joseph Fielding Smith [Salt Lake City: Deseret Book Co., 1938], p. 354). Certainly, in the infinite mercy of God, those with physical and mental limitations will not remain so after the Resurrection. At this time, Alma says, "The spirit and the body shall be reunited again in its perfect form; both limb and joint shall be restored to its proper frame" (Alma 11:43). Afflictions, like mortality, are temporary.

Surely more sharing of the burden will contribute to the emotional salvation of the person who is the primary caregiver. Just an hour of help now and then would be appreciated. One mother of a child who is handicapped said, "I could never dream of going to Hawaii on a vacation; all I can hope for is to have an evening away from home." ("The Works of God," *Ensign,* Nov. 1984, 59.)

THE SAVIOR'S TEACHING that handicaps are not punishment for sin, either in the parents or the handicapped, can also be understood and applied in today's circumstances. How can it possibly be said that an innocent child born with a special problem is being punished? Why should parents who have kept themselves free from social disease, addicting chemicals, and other debilitating substances which might affect their offspring imagine that the birth of a disabled child is some form of divine disapproval? Usually, both the parents and the children are blameless. The Savior of the world reminds us that God "maketh his sun to rise on the evil and on the good, and sendeth rain on the just and on the unjust" (Matthew 5:45). ("The Works of God," *Ensign,* Nov. 1984, 59.)

MAY I EXPRESS a word of gratitude and appreciation to those many who minister with such kindness and skill to our handicapped people. Special commendation belongs to parents and family members who have cared for their own children with special needs in the loving atmosphere of their own home. The care of those who are diminished is a special service rendered to the Master himself, for "inasmuch as ye have done it unto one of the least of these . . . , ye have done it unto me" (Matthew 25:40).

Parents of handicapped children are occasionally embarrassed or hurt by others who awkwardly express sympathy but cannot know or appreciate the depth of the parents' love for a handicapped child. Perhaps there is some comparison in the fact that there is no less love in families for the helpless infant who must be fed, bathed, and diapered than for the older but still dependent members. We love those we serve and who need us.

Is it not possible to look beyond the canes, the wheelchairs, the braces, and the crutches into the hearts of the people who have need of these aids? They are human beings and want only to be treated as ordinary people. They may appear different, move awkwardly, and speak haltingly, but they have the same feelings. They laugh, they cry, they know discouragement and hope. They do not want to be shunned. They want to be loved for what they are inside, without any prejudice for their impairment. Can there not be more tolerance for differences— differences in capacity, differences in body and in mind?

Those who are close to the handicapped can frequently feel the nobility of the spirits who are confined in differently shaped bodies or who have crippled minds. ("The Works of God," *Ensign,* Nov. 1984, 59.)

DISCIPLESHIP

IF WE PARTAKE of the sacrament regularly and are faithful to these covenants, the law will be in our inward parts and written in our hearts. Let me illustrate this with a story from the *Church News:*

"A group of religion instructors [were] taking a summer course on the life of the Savior and focusing particularly on the parables.

"When the final exam time came . . . the students arrived at the classroom to find a note that the exam would be given in another building across campus. Moreover, the note said, it must be finished within the two-hour time period that was starting almost at that moment.

"The students hurried across campus. On the way they passed a little girl crying over a flat tire on her new bike. An old man hobbled painfully toward the library with a cane in one hand, spilling books from a stack he was trying to manage with the other. On a bench by the union building sat a shabbily dressed, bearded man [in obvious distress].

"Rushing into the other classroom, the students were met by the professor, who announced they had all flunked the final exam.

"The only true test of whether they understood the Savior's life and teaching, he said, was how they treated people in need.

"Their weeks of study at the feet of a capable professor had taught them a great deal of what Christ had said and done." (*Church News,* "Viewpoint," 1 October 1988, p. 16.)

In their haste to finish the technicalities of the course, however, they failed to recognize the application represented by the three scenes that had been deliberately staged. They learned the letter but not the spirit. Their neglect of the little girl and the two men showed that the profound message of the course had not entered into their inward parts.

We must at times search our own souls and discover what we really are. Our real character, much as we would wish, cannot be hidden. It shines from within us transparently. Attempts to deceive others only deceive ourselves. We are often like the emperor in the fairy tale who thought he was arrayed in beautiful garments when he was in fact unclothed. ("Search Me, O God, and Know My Heart," *Ensign,* May 1998, 18.)

TRUE DISCIPLES ARE those who go beyond simply believing. They act out their belief. Said the Savior, "If any man will do his will, he shall know of the doctrine, whether it be of God, or whether I speak of myself" (John 7:17). Disciples follow the Divine Master. Their actions speak in symphonic harmony with their beliefs. They know who they are. They know what God expects of them. They mirror inner peace and certainty concerning the mission and resurrection of Christ. They hunger and thirst after righteousness. They know they are here on this earth for a purpose. They understand life after death. They believe that the transcendent event in the ministry of the Christ was the Atonement, culminating in the Resurrection.

The prophet Ether says that a disciple may with "surety hope for a better world, . . . which hope cometh of faith, maketh an anchor to the souls of men, which would make them sure and steadfast, always abounding in good works" (Ether 12:4). ("The Resurrection," *Ensign*, May 1985, 30.)

RECENTLY IN SOUTH America, a seasoned group of outstanding missionaries was asked, "What is the greatest need in the world?" One wisely responded: "Is not the greatest need in all of the world for every person to have a personal, ongoing, daily, continuing relationship with the Savior?" Having such a relationship can unchain the divinity within us, and nothing can make a greater difference in our lives as we come to know and understand our divine relationship with God.

We should earnestly seek not just to know about the Master, but to strive, as He invited, to be one with Him (see John 17:21), to "be strengthened with might by his Spirit in the inner man" (Eph. 3:16). ("A Personal Relationship with the Savior," *Ensign*, Nov. 1976, 58.)

THE REPLENISHING OF our inner selves occurs as we come to know the Savior through keeping his commandments and serving him. ("He Restoreth My Soul," *Ensign*, Oct. 1997, 2.)

CHRISTLIKE CONDUCT FLOWS from the deepest well-springs of the human heart and soul. ("Search Me, O God, and Know My Heart," *Ensign*, May 1998, 20.)

DISCIPLINARY COUNCILS

THOSE WHO HAVE keys, which include the judicial or disciplinary authority, have the responsibility for keeping the Church cleansed from all iniquity (see D&C 20:54, 43:11). Bishops, stake presidents, mission presidents, and others who have the responsibility of keeping the Church pure must perform this labor in a spirit of love and kindness. It should not be done in a spirit of punishment, but rather of helping. However, it is of no kindness to a brother or sister in transgression for their presiding officers to look the other way. Some words on this subject come from President John Taylor:

"Furthermore, I have heard of some Bishops who have been seeking to cover up the iniquities of men; I tell them, in the name of God, they will have to bear . . . that iniquity, and if any of you want to partake of the sins of men, or uphold them, you will have to bear them. Do you hear it, you Bishops and you Presidents? God will require it at your hands. You are not placed in a position to tamper with the principles of righteousness, nor to cover up the infamies and corruptions of men" (in Conference Report, Apr. 1880, p. 78).

On this matter we urge you presiding brethren to seek the Spirit of God, to study and be guided by the scriptures and the *General Handbook of Instructions.* Church discipline is not limited to sexual sins but includes other acts such as murder, abortions, burglary, theft, fraud and other dishonesty, deliberate disobedience to the rules and regulations of the Church, advocating or practicing polygamy, apostasy, or any other unchristian conduct, including defiance or ridicule of the Lord's anointed, contrary to the law of the Lord and the order of the Church. ("Keeping Covenants and Honoring the Priesthood," *Ensign,* Nov. 1993, 37.)

DIVERSITY

AS WE MOVE into more and more countries in the world, we find a rich cultural diversity in the Church. Yet everywhere there can be a "unity of the faith." (Eph. 4:13.) Each group brings special gifts and talents to the table of the Lord. We can all learn much of value from each other. But each of us should also voluntarily seek to enjoy all of the unifying and saving covenants, ordinances, and doctrines of the gospel of the Lord Jesus Christ.

In the great diversity of peoples, cultures, and circumstances, we remember that all are equal before the Lord, for as Paul taught, "Ye are all the children of God by faith in Christ Jesus.

"For as many of you as have been baptized into Christ have put on Christ.

"There is neither Jew nor Greek, there is neither bond nor free, there is neither male nor female: for ye are all one in Christ Jesus.

"And if ye be Christ's, then are ye Abraham's seed, and heirs according to the promise." (Gal. 3:26–29.)

We do not lose our identity in becoming members of this Church. We become heirs to the kingdom of God, having joined the body of Christ and spiritually set aside some of our personal differences to unite in a greater spiritual cause. We say to all who have joined the Church, keep all that is noble, good and uplifting in your culture and personal identity. However, under the authority and power of the keys of the priesthood, all differences yield as we seek to become heirs to the kingdom of God, unite in following those who have the keys of the priesthood, and seek the divinity within us. All are welcomed and appreciated. But there is only one celestial kingdom of God.

Our real strength is not so much in our diversity but in our spiritual and doctrinal unity. For instance, the baptismal prayer and baptism by immersion in water are the same all over the world. The sacramental prayers are the same everywhere. We sing the same hymns in praise to God in every country. ("Heirs to the Kingdom of God," *Ensign*, May 1995, 62.)

THE MULTIPLICITY OF languages and cultures is both an opportunity and a challenge for members of the Church. Having everyone hear the gospel in their own tongue requires great effort and resources. The Spirit, however, is a higher form of communication than language. We have been in many meetings where the words were completely unintelligible, but the Spirit bore powerful witness of Jesus Christ, the Savior and Redeemer of the world. Even with language differences, hopefully no minority group would ever feel so unwelcome in the "body of Christ"

(1 Cor. 10:16–17) that they would wish to worship exclusively in their own ethnic culture. We hope that those in any dominant culture would reach out to them in the brotherhood and sister-hood of the gospel, so that we can establish fully a community of Saints where everyone will feel needed and wanted. ("Heirs to the Kingdom of God," *Ensign,* May 1995, 63.)

DIVINE NATURE

IN THE CHURCH that most of us belong to, we do an adequate job of measuring many things. But how can we possibly measure the divine nature and attendant virtues spoken of by Peter (2 Peter 1:4). These qualities are so hard to measure, but they are kindred virtues to gratitude. Peter speaks of faith, virtue, knowledge, temperance, patience, brotherly kindness, charity, and—most important—godliness. What kind of a report could we devise to measure virtue, brotherly kindness, temperance? These high and lofty attitudes defy measurement. They concern the longings of the heart and the depth of the soul more than outward manifes-tations of faithfulness. ("The Law—A Key to Something Greater," J. Reuben Clark Law Society, Washington, D.C., 30 April 1990.)

DIVORCE

SOME YEARS AGO, I was consulted by a woman who desired a divorce from her husband on grounds which, in my opinion, were justified. After the divorce was concluded, I did not see her again for many years. A chance meeting with her on the street was very surprising. The years of loneliness and discour-agement were evident in her once beautiful face.

After passing a few pleasantries, she was quick to say that life had not been rich and rewarding for her and that she was tired of facing the struggle alone. Then came a most startling disclosure, which, with her permission, I share. She said, "Bad as it was, if I had to do it over again, knowing what I do now, I would not have sought the divorce. This is worse." . . .

Divorce can be justified only in the most rare of circumstances, because it often tears people's lives apart and shears family happiness. Frequently in a divorce the parties lose much more than they gain. ("The Enriching of Marriage," *Ensign,* Nov. 1977, 9.)

THERE ARE NO simple, easy answers to the challenging and complex questions of happiness in marriage. There are also many supposed reasons for divorce. Among them are the serious problems of selfishness, immaturity, lack of commitment, inadequate communication, unfaithfulness; and all of the rest, which are obvious and well known.

In my experience there is another reason which seems not so obvious but which precedes and laces through all of the others. It is the lack of a constant enrichment in marriage, it is an absence of that something extra which makes it precious, special, and wonderful, when it is also drudgery, difficult, and dull. ("The Enriching of Marriage," *Ensign,* Nov. 1977, 10.)

I SUGGEST THAT the devil takes some delight every time a home is broken up, even where there is no parent to blame. This is especially so where there are children involved. The physical and spiritual neglect of children is one of the spawning grounds for so many of the social ills of the world. ("Trying to Serve the Lord without Offending the Devil," *BYU Speeches,* 15 Nov. 1994, 62.)

EDUCATION

THE LORD HAS said that "every man [and woman] may give an account unto me of the stewardship which is appointed unto him [or her]" (D&C 104:12). For what will we be required to give a stewardship accounting? "As a steward over earthly blessings, which I have made and prepared" (D&C 104:13). The Lord further explains that as we handle our stewardships "it must needs be done in mine own way" (D&C 104:16). While that scripture is most frequently quoted to refer to temporal things, it also means to me that all knowledge should be acquired and applied, both temporally and spiritually, in the Lord's way.

While [in college], you have spent most of your time on secular learning, and that is appropriate. But that does not mean that your application of that knowledge should be primarily secular rather than spiritual. At your age, one is justified in asking, What is more important in the learning process, the secular or the spiritual? I don't know that the two can be clearly separated, but I suggest that you will learn faster and better and more surely through the spiritual. Through the gift of the Holy Ghost we can "learn all things," and if that is not enough, we are also told that we can learn the truth of all things by that same power (see John 16:13). ("In the Lord's Way," Address at Ricks College Commencement, 28 Apr. 1995.)

LEARNING AND EDUCATION have always been the hallmark of our people. Every president of the Church, beginning with President Joseph Smith, has zealously fostered, encouraged, and supported the cause of education. The reason for this emphasis is that education equates with our eternal well-being. In a First Presidency message dated March 26, 1907, the Brethren said: "To the Latter-day Saints, salvation itself, under the atonement of Christ, is a process of education. That knowledge is a means of eternal progress, was taught by Joseph Smith:—It is impossible for a man to be saved in ignorance.— A man is saved no faster than he gets knowledge."—"The glory of God is intelligence." (*Teachings of Latter-day Prophets, Messages of the First Presidency of The Church of Jesus Christ of Latter-day Saints*, vol. 4 [1901–1915]: 146–47.) ("Learning for Eternity," *BYU Speeches*, 18 Nov. 1997, 76–77.)

IN THE LAW school I attended not far from here, our dean told us we were studying the law so that we could learn to think straight. He said the law would change, but if we could learn to think critically by separating the wheat from the chaff, we would be better qualified to become effective advocates.

Brigham Young stated it better: "Education is the power to think clearly, the power to act well in the world's work, and the power to appreciate life." (Brigham Young, quoted by George H. Brimhall in "The Brigham Young University," *Improvement Era,* vol. 23, no. 9 [July 1920], p. 831.)

Thinking clearly does not mean we can think "by infection, and catch an opinion like a cold." (John Ruskin, *Humorous Quotations,* p. 191.) Thinking clearly is the ability to discern things that matter most and separate them from things of less importance. We can think more clearly when we:

1. Take an interest in current events: listen to the news or read a newspaper.

2. Discuss ideas with one another, even in the courses you are taking! The Internet can be fascinating, but so can a conversation with a live person with whom you can exchange original thoughts.

3. Read good literature. This is, of course, expected of English majors, but for the rest of us good literature improves our vocabularies as well as our minds.

4. Keep our bodies healthy. Go for a walk and look at the trees, the birds, the flowers, the mountains, and the sky. This campus has one of the most beautiful settings in the world. Enjoy the view along with your exercise. A healthy body promotes a healthy mind.

Questions—in the sense of searching, not doubting—seem to be essential for learning. They are a primary means of expressing curiosity, the self-motivation to search for knowledge. Indeed, many of the Prophet Joseph Smith's revelations "came in response to enquiry, in response to prayer. 'Ask and ye shall receive'; 'Seek and ye shall find,' seems to have been the principle on which the Lord has acted with reference to giving revelations." Such inquiries "may be considered as a condition precedent to his receiving revelations." (B. H. Roberts, *History of the Church,* 2:210, ft; 5:34.) ("Learning for Eternity," *BYU Speeches,* 18 Nov. 1997, 76–77.)

DEALING WITH LOFTY issues should not generate pride, which is an enemy to learning spiritual things. The training of the heart comes by and through the Holy Spirit. Reaching for eternity requires an understanding heart. We can all learn from the great Solomon who, when he was made the king of Israel, said, "I am but a little child: I know not how to go out or come in . . .

"Give therefore thy servant an understanding heart to judge thy people, that I may discern between good and bad: for who is able to judge this thy so great a people?" (1 Kings 3:7, 9.)

This so pleased the Lord that he said, "I have given thee a wise and an understanding heart; so that there was none like thee before thee, neither after thee shall any arise like unto thee." (1 Kings 3:12.) ("Learning for Eternity," *BYU Speeches*, 18 Nov. 1997, 77.)

ALL OF US know examples of gospel scholars who have been preoccupied with every jot and tittle of historical fact and gospel scholarship. We wonder if their supposed erudition could in part be an ego trip. Are they looking for motes in another gospel scholar's eyes, while they have great beams in their own? In my experience, a few are often short on the weightier matters of the law: justice, tolerance, mercy, kindness, and forgiveness. ("A Legacy of the New Testament," 12th Annual CES Religious Educators' Symposium, 12 Aug. 1988.)

FOR 25 YEARS I have been privileged to walk with and sit at the feet of the prophets almost daily. Some have excelled academically, or in the business world. Others achieved distinction in medicine, science, or in law. Yet they are all men of great humility and wisdom. They bear witness, as expressed by our late President Howard W. Hunter, that "Belief must be realized in personal achievement. Real Christians must understand that the gospel of Jesus Christ is not just a gospel of belief; it is a plan of action. His gospel is a gospel of imperatives, and the very nature of its substance is a call to action." (Conference Report, Apr. 1967, 118.) Do not become puffed up with pride as you progress in secular learning. ("Learning for Eternity," *BYU Speeches,* 18 Nov. 1997, 78–79.)

MAY I GIVE you four suggestions which might be used to find answers to doctrinal or historical conflicts or doubts?

First, rescue that which is deep down in your soul. Follow that which is intuitive, the purest and most noble feelings of your being.

Second, use the Holy Spirit as a sieve. Employ a spiritual light to read by and interpret everything. Where there is a lapse and gaps and some seeming contradictions, pray diligently and study for answers.

Third, learn to be patient. Not everything can be answered now. In a way, a person must earn the right to enjoy the companionship of the Spirit. Alma reminds us that we must repent, exercise faith, bring forth good works, and pray continually. (Alma 26:22.)

Fourth, it is easy to doubt. It is much more mature and responsible to question and diligently and prayerfully search for the truth. Often, doubters have not paid their dues in terms of work, study, and prayer. ("The Voice of the Spirit," Latter-day Saint Student Association, Salt Lake City, Utah, 27 Oct. 1985.)

FOR MANY STUDENTS in higher education, going to a university is a game, a self-defeating game. To them it is a process of cramming like the seagulls in pioneer times when the crops were threatened by crickets. The gulls came and devoured, then they would fly off to disgorge and return to devour again. Learning is more than cramming for tests. Education is more than bulimia at exam time.

I learned that in my own discipline of the law. Reading the cases and briefing them for possible recitation in the classroom is difficult, arduous, challenging work. You cannot learn the rules of law just by having a good heart. Some found that they could buy canned briefs as a shortcut to the laborious work of reading and briefing the cases. However, in an hour of need in the courtroom, they were apt to find themselves doing a disservice to their clients and embarrassing themselves. There is no simple substitute for the hard work of learning well the rules of law. And so it is with us. In the courtroom of life we need to have well-honed skills.

President Lorenzo Snow taught that "The whole idea of Mormonism is improvement—mentally, physically, morally, and spiritually. No half-way education suffices for the Latter-day Saint." ("Learning for Eternity," *BYU Speeches*, 18 Nov. 1997, 79.)

EFFORT

WALTER HAGEN, THE great golfer said, "I don't outplay the other players. I outwork them. A small margin makes the difference."

And the same principle applies in happiness, in all success, in church and business. One may be just a little more thoughtful, a little more consistent, loyal, industrious; but it makes a great deal of difference. Think of the magic of 10 percent. An ordinary man is 72 inches. Subtract 10% and you have a man 5' 8." Add 10 percent and you have a giant. There are comparable changes when we add or subtract 10 percent to our own faithfulness and dedication.

Maybe we ought to raise our sights. What if we missed the celestial kingdom by a razor's edge. It may not be far, but oh, what a difference it would make. ("Special Interest Fireside," Salt Lake City, Utah, 29 Jan. 1978.)

WE HAVE ALSO become a generation of critics. I am inclined to be more charitable with those who try but stumble than with those who will not try at all. . . .

I have learned from a lifetime making my living in the arena where I was not shadowboxing with life's problems, that life is fuller and richer and better for those who are not afraid to make a new beginning. My experience has also been that genius is very rare, that life's rich rewards come to those who prepare carefully. Preparation and staying power are more valuable than brilliance. ("Beginnings," University of Utah 2nd Stake Fireside, 27 Sept. 1983.)

ENDURANCE

I WOULD LIKE to say a word to you brethren who are a little older. President J. Reuben Clark, a counselor in the First Presidency, used to say from this pulpit, "Brethren, I hope I can remain faithful to the end." At that time, President Clark was in his eighties. As a young man, I could not understand how this wise, learned, experienced, righteous Apostle of the Lord Jesus Christ could have any concern for his own spiritual well-being. As I approach his age, I now understand. I have the same concern for myself, for my family, and for all of my brethren of the priesthood. Over my lifetime, I have seen some of the most choice, capable, and righteous of men stumble and fall. They have been true and faithful for many years and then get caught in a web of stupidity and foolishness which has brought great shame to themselves, and betrayed the trust of their innocent families, leaving their loved ones a legacy of sorrow and hurt.

My dear brethren, all of us, young and old, must constantly guard against the enticements of Satan. These evil influences come to us like tidal waves. We must choose wisely the books and magazines we read, the movies we see, and how we use modern technology, such as the Internet. ("Pioneers of the Future—Be Not Afraid, Only Believe," *Ensign*, Nov. 1997, 45.)

LIVING THE ETERNAL gospel every day may be harder than dying for the Church and the Lord. ("The Voice of the Spirit," *Ensign*, Apr. 1994, 8.)

IN THE HISTORY of this Church, we have "endured many things." As we look forward to the future, we "hope to be able to endure all things." I am confident that we will do so, even though no one knows fully what may lie ahead. How will we endure all things? The answer is amazingly simple: We shall do so by faith, by unity, and by following the prophets of God. It has been so in the past; it will be so in the future. ("We Seek After These Things," *Ensign,* May 1998, 46.)

EVIL, AVOIDANCE OF

I EMPHASIZE THAT fasting and prayer is a great way to receive the moral strength and spiritual strength to resist the temptations of Satan. But you may say this is hard and unpleasant. I commend to you the example of the Savior. He went into the desert, where he fasted and prayed to prepare himself spiritually for his ministry. His temptation by the devil was great, but through the purification of his spirit he was able to triumph over all evil.

Work is another deterrent to evil. The symbol of this state is the beehive. Our forefathers fostered industry and work. Elder John Longden quoted Herndon as saying: "Satan selects his disciples when they are idle; Jesus selected his when they were busy at their work either mending their nets or casting them into the sea." (John Longden, Conference Report, April 1966, 39.) ("Trying to Serve the Lord without Offending the Devil," *BYU Speeches,* Nov. 15, 1994, 64.)

BELIEVING INVOLVES FAITH and good works. We cannot be passive; we must actively avoid evil. This means that we do not trifle with sacred things. Families in this day and time should not only avoid evil but avoid the very appearance of evil. To combat these influences families must have family prayer, family home evening, and family scripture study.

How corrosive is the daily diet of pornography, immorality, dishonesty, disrespect, abuse, and violence that comes from so many sources. If we are not careful it will shake our spiritual moorings. Once we internalize these evils, it is very difficult to purge ourselves of them. . . .

In some ways we are the most challenged generation in the

history of the world. We seem to be living in a time foreseen by King Benjamin. Said he, "And finally, I cannot tell you all the things whereby ye may commit sin; for there are divers ways and means, even so many that I cannot number them." Now comes this powerful warning: "But this much I can tell you, that if ye do not watch yourselves, and your thoughts, and your words, and your deeds, and observe the commandments of God, and continue in the faith of what ye have heard concerning the coming of our Lord, even unto the end of your lives, ye must perish." (Mosiah 4:29–30.) ("Pioneers of the Future—Be Not Afraid, Only Believe," *Ensign,* Nov. 1997, 45.)

FAITH

I AM PERSUADED that the miraculous and spectacular does not necessarily convert people to the gospel. Miracles are more to confirm a faith already held. After the ten lepers were healed by the Savior, only one even bothered to thank him, and I have found no convincing proof that even that one became a disciple. A quiet witness that Jesus is the Christ is more the product of a committed faith coming from dedication and sacrifice, an effort to keep God's commandments, and following the constituted priesthood authority of the Church. ("A Legacy of the New Testament," 12th Annual CES Religious Educators' Symposium, 12 Aug. 1988.)

IT IS IMPORTANT for us to nurture . . . a simple, untroubled faith. I urge complete acceptance of the absolutes of our own faith. At the same time, I urge you not to be unduly concerned about the intricacies, the complexities, and any seeming contradictions that seem to trouble many of us. Sometimes we spend time satisfying our intellectual egos and trying to find all the answers before we accept any.

We are all in pursuit of truth and knowledge. The nurturing of a simple untroubled faith does not limit us in the pursuit of growth and accomplishment. On the contrary, it may intensify and hasten our progress. This is so because our natural gifts and powers of achievement are increasingly enhanced by the endless growth of knowledge. In our belief, it is possible to be even a helper of the Father and of the Son and to be under their personal tutelage. ("An Untroubled Faith," *BYU Speeches*, 28 Sept. 1986, 46.)

TO HAVE A simple, untroubled faith, you must keep your spiritual innocence. That requires avoiding cynicism and criticism. This is the day of the cynics, the critics, and the pickle-suckers. Said President Hinckley: "Criticism is the forerunner of divorce, the cultivator of rebellion, sometimes a catalyst that leads to failure. In the Church, it sows the seed of inactivity and finally apostasy." (*Church News*, 3 July 1983, p. 10.) ("An Untroubled Faith," *BYU Speeches*, 28 Sept. 1986, 49.)

I HAVE A dear friend with whom I grew up. Although bright and able, he was not a scholarly type. The press of family needs and concerns limited his educational opportunities. He did not graduate from high school. He acquired an old, beat-up truck and began hauling sand and gravel for a few contractors. The work was seasonal and not at all productive. The old truck would frequently break down and need repairs.

In his teenage years he drifted some, but married a good woman and settled down. Their circumstances were economically straitened, but somehow they managed to get a house built on part of the family property. I was the bishop and called him to be the Aaronic Priesthood adviser. He took his calling seriously. He literally wore out the handbook, studying it. He had a notebook filled with dates when all the young men in the ward would reach the age to be advanced in the Aaronic Priesthood. He kept good track of the young men and kept the bishopric informed of their activities.

Some years after I was released, he became a member of our bishopric. He needed a little nudging to become a full tithe-payer, but responded faithfully, as he had done before.

Subsequently, he became our bishop. He served wonderfully and well. In the meantime, he and an associate had learned how to lay bricks and had formed a brick-contracting partnership. The difference between their work and the work of others was in the quality. They did beautiful work. They were in demand. He prospered and became well respected in the community. He also became the president of the local water company. After many successful years as a bishop, he was called to the high council and served well and faithfully. He is now a man of high affairs, respected and honored, although his formal education ended before high school graduation. With the advantage of a college education he no doubt would have achieved even more.

What caused him to succeed? Industry? Thrift? Self-reliance? Yes, but there was more. Conscientiously and untiringly, he sought to know and do the mind and the will of the Lord. He had a simple, untroubled faith. ("An Untroubled Faith," *BYU Speeches,* 28 Sept. 1986, 46–47.)

To HAVE A simple, untroubled faith, we must accept some absolutes. . . . They are to believe:

1. That Jesus, the Son of the Father, is the Christ, and the Savior and Redeemer of the world.

2. That Joseph Smith was the instrument through which the gospel was restored in its fulness and completeness.

3. That the Book of Mormon is the word of God and, as the Prophet Joseph Smith said, is the keystone of our religion.

4. That Ezra Taft Benson is, as were each of his predecessors Presidents of the Church, a successor in holding the keys and authority restored by Joseph Smith.

. . . This untroubled faith can come by prayer, study, and a submissive willingness to keep as many commandments as we can. Let us be more specific.

As to the first absolute, the acceptance of Jesus as the Christ, we have two thousand years of teaching and tradition, which help the inquirer accept him as our Savior and Redeemer. So this absolute, initially, at least, may be the easiest to accept after study, prayer, and trying to follow his teachings.

The second absolute, the calling of Joseph Smith as the Prophet of the Restoration, may be more difficult for the honest seeker to accept. . . . To me, the only logical explanation for the majesty and success of his work is that he saw what he said he saw, and he was what he said he was. What he restored is so complete, so all-encompassing in concept, so majestic and awesome in potential, that only God himself could have been the author and motivating force behind it. The fruits of Joseph Smith's work, so plain for all to see, are also a testimony of the divinity of his work.

The third absolute, namely a testimony of the truthfulness of the Book of Mormon, in my opinion comes exactly as Moroni stated, by the power of the Holy Ghost, by asking God, the Eternal Father, in the name of Christ, if the book is true [see Moroni 10:4].

The fourth absolute is essential to enjoying an untroubled faith. It is the proposition that President Ezra Taft Benson is the inheritor of the restored keys, as was each of his predecessors since Joseph Smith. Some accept the Savior, the divine mission of Joseph Smith, and the Book of Mormon, but then think that after Joseph's time somehow the Brethren went astray. Many who have thought this have taken others with them, and their efforts have not prospered. ("An Untroubled Faith," *BYU Speeches*, 28 Sept. 1986, 50.)

I TAKE AS my text the simple but profound message of the Savior to the ruler of the synagogue. You will recall that the ruler was told that his daughter was dead and that he should not trouble the Master about it. . . .

The Savior's words to the leader of the synagogue capture the essence of this story: "Be not afraid, only believe." (Mark 5:36.) These five words comprise my message to you.

We must believe in God, the Eternal Father, and in His Son, Jesus Christ, and in the Holy Ghost. (See Mosiah 4:9.) We must believe in the Atonement and the Resurrection of the Savior. We must believe in the words of the prophets, both ancient and modern. We should also believe in ourselves.

Believing requires action. If you prepare to walk down the path of life, you can be rewarded beyond your dreams and expectations. But to achieve this, you must work very hard, save, be wise, and be alert. You must learn to deny yourselves of worldly gratification. You must be faithful in paying tithes; you must keep the Word of Wisdom; you must be free from other addictions. You must be chaste and morally clean in every respect. You should accept and be faithful in all of the calls that come to you. Steadiness and toil will serve you better than brilliance. ("Pioneers of the Future—Be Not Afraid, Only Believe," *Ensign*, Nov. 1997, 42–43.)

IF YOU TAKE each challenge one step at a time, with faith in every footstep, your strength and understanding will increase. You cannot foresee all of the turns and twists ahead. My counsel to you is to follow the direction of the Savior of the world: "Be not afraid, only believe." (Mark 5:36.) ("Pioneers of the Future—Be Not Afraid, Only Believe," *Ensign*, Nov. 1997, 43.)

FAITHFULNESS

IN MY LIFETIME I have seen the faithfulness of Church members increase. Measured by fixed standards, there are greater manifestations of faithfulness than ever before. On any given Sunday, percentagewise more than twice as many people partake of the sacrament of the Lord's Supper worldwide than when I was growing up.

We are trying to care for the poor and the needy among us through the generosity of faithful Church members who observe the law of the fast and participate in the inspired welfare program. Humanitarian aid of many kinds worth millions of dollars has been sent to many countries to relieve hunger and suffering. This is administered according to need and without regard for race, color, or religious creed.

More of our people enjoy blessings from living the ancient law of tithing. They voluntarily return to the Lord one-tenth of the increase He has given them. Hundreds of thousands more of our faithful Saints enjoy the privilege of temple worship. We now have 58,000 missionaries serving in the field. I rejoice in this, and I am sure the Lord is pleased. But I wonder if we have become proportionately more Christlike. Does our service come from a pure heart? ("Search Me, O God, and Know My Heart," *Ensign,* May 1998, 18.)

THE GREAT POWERS of the priesthood are beyond our understanding. They are everlasting. Through this power the universe was set in order. I promise you brethren transcendent blessings as you live righteously. I say this without hesitation or equivocation because of the promises from the Lord in the oath and the covenant of the priesthood found in the 84th Section of the Doctrine and Covenants:

"For whoso is faithful unto the obtaining these two priesthoods of which I have spoken, and the magnifying their calling, are sanctified by the Spirit unto the renewing of their bodies.

"They become the sons of Moses and of Aaron and the seed of Abraham, and the church and kingdom, and the elect of God.

"And also all they who receive this priesthood receive me, saith the Lord;

"For he that receiveth my servants receiveth me;

"And he that receiveth me receiveth my Father;

"And he that receiveth my Father receiveth my Father's kingdom; therefore all that my Father hath shall be given unto him." (D&C 84:33–38.)

If we believe and are faithful, we are promised all that the Father has. If we receive all that the Father has, there is nothing more for us to receive in this life or the life to come. We should remember that in our challenges and struggles against the powers of evil and darkness, "they that be with us are more than they that be with them." (2 Kings 6:16.) We belong to the greatest cause on earth. We are the pioneers of the future. Let us go forth like the armies of Helaman and build the kingdom of God. Like the royal army let us be "united, bold, and strong, . . . marching forth to conquer on life's great battlefield." (see *Hymns*, no. 251.) All of these hopes, blessings, and opportunities will come to us if we will only believe, and be not afraid. ("Pioneers of the Future—Be Not Afraid, Only Believe," *Ensign*, Nov. 1997, 45.)

HEBER C. KIMBALL recorded, "The following vision was manifested to him [Joseph Smith] as near as I can recollect:

"He saw the Twelve going forth, and they appeared to be in a far distant land. After some time they unexpectedly met together, apparently in great tribulation, their clothes all ragged, and their knees and feet sore. They formed into a circle, and all stood with their eyes fixed upon the ground. The Savior appeared and stood in their midst and wept over them, and wanted to show Himself to them, but they did not discover Him." (Orson F. Whitney, *Life of Heber C. Kimball*, 2d ed., Salt Lake City: Bookcraft, p. 93; see also *History of the Church*, 2:381.)

The Savior gives us a profound key by which we can cope with and even surmount the debilitating forces of the world. Said the Savior, "I pray not that thou shouldest take them out of the world, but that thou shouldest keep them from the evil." (John 17:15.) This grand key then is that, regardless of the saturation of wickedness around us, we must stay free from the evil of the world. The Savior's prayer both commands us to avoid evil and proffers divine help to do so. Through this effort we become one with our Lord. The prayer of the Savior in Gethsemane was: "That they all may be one; as thou, Father, art in me, and I in thee, that they also may be one in us: that the world may believe that thou hast sent me." (John 17:21.)

To remain true and faithful through this mortal vale of tears, we must love God with all our heart, might, mind, and strength and love our neighbor as ourselves. We must also stand together as families; as members of wards and branches, stakes and districts; and as a people. To our neighbors not of our faith we should be as the good Samaritan who cared for the man who fell among thieves. (Luke 10:29.-37.) We must gather strength from each other. We must also "succor the weak, lift up the hands which hang down, and strengthen the feeble knees." (D&C 81:5.)

Paul taught well on this subject. Said he to the Corinthians, speaking of the body, or Church, of Christ: " . . . that there should be no schism in the body; but that the members should have the same care one for another.

"And whether one member suffer, all the members suffer with it; or one member be honoured, all the members rejoice with it.

"Now ye are the body of Christ, and members in particular." [1 Cor. 12:27.] In this way, as individuals and as a people we may be kept from evil. As we go through travail and difficulty we may feel sorry for ourselves and despair, but with the love of God and the Saints, unitedly bearing each other's burdens, we can be happy and overcome evil. ("Woman, Why Weepest Thou?" *Ensign*, Nov. 1996, 53–54.)

FAMILIES

NO OTHER UNIT of society is an effective substitute for the ties of love and affection inherent in families. The natural leaders of the family unit are the parents, standing side by side as equals in their loving guidance of their children. Each parent brings a separate enriching influence. The power of the priesthood should be the dominant influence in family affairs. Priesthood blessings do not just involve men. They bless equally and fully the women and children of the family. Whatever diminishes family order is destructive to the family unit and to society. ("Priesthood Blessings," *Ensign*, Nov. 1995, 62.)

BECAUSE OF THE erosion of family life and family values, we frequently hear urgent pleas requesting the Church, as an organization, to take over activities formerly considered family activities. An example of this is the super youth activities, some of which have taken the youth at great expense and considerable risk to far distant places. I fear that in more than a few instances, the cost of local Church-sponsored teenage and single adult activities may have prevented some families from having vacations or other activities together.

We also hear requests for a new program for that group or a new organization for this group or a new activity for the other group. We already have the new program. It is called the family. It includes family prayer, family scripture study, family home evening, and family loyalty. I wonder if our maturing youth can hold everything together without daily prayer and daily scripture study. The family is the best environment to encourage both. . . . Family activities can be more effective in fostering the eternal values of love, honesty, chastity, industry, self-worth, and personal integrity than any other institution. ("Where Is the Church?" *BYU Speeches*, 24 Sept. 1989, 32–33.)

MANY YEARS AGO when I was a bishop, a conscientious father came to me for counsel. He felt that the many and frequent activities of the Church made it difficult to have as much family togetherness as he and his wife deemed necessary. The children had the idea that they were not loyal to the Church if they did not participate fully in every recreational activity. I told this caring father that Church activities were to help him and his wife rear their children. They as parents had not only the right but the duty to determine the extent of their family's involvement in social activities. Family unity, solidarity, and harmony should be preserved. After all, a family is the basic, permanent unit of the Church. ("The Weightier Matters of the Law: Judgment, Mercy and Faith," *Ensign*, Nov. 1997, 54.)

A FEW YEARS ago, Bishop Stanley Smoot was interviewed by

President Spencer W. Kimball. President Kimball asked, "How often do you have family prayer?"

Bishop Smoot answered, "We try to have family prayer twice a day, but we average about once."

President Kimball answered, "In the past, having family prayer once a day may have been all right. But in the future it will not be enough if we are going to save our families."

I wonder if having casual and infrequent family home evening will be enough in the future to fortify our children with sufficient moral strength. In the future, infrequent family scripture study may be inadequate to arm our children with the virtue necessary to withstand the moral decay of the environment in which they will live. Where in the world will the children learn chastity, integrity, honesty, and basic human decency if not at home? These values will, of course, be reinforced at church, but parental teaching is more constant. ("The Greatest Challenge in the World—Good Parenting," *Ensign*, Nov. 1990, 33.)

WITH ALL ITS shortcomings, the family is far and away the greatest social unit, the best answer to human problems, in the history of mankind. . . . I would urge over-burdened parents to accept every help. Cannot grandparents, brothers and sisters, aunts, uncles, cousins, and friends also reinforce by example and precept their love and concern for members of the extended family?

My Aunt Angie has hand made 175 quilts for her children, grandchildren, nieces, nephews, and others. They are works of art; but more important, each is a labor of love. She can say to a member of her extended family, as she presents a specially made quilt, "Except when I pricked my finger, with every stitch I thought of my love for you." ("Will I Be Happy?" *Ensign*, May 1987, 82.)

SURELY, THE MOST important ingredient in producing family happiness for members of this Church is a deep religious commitment under wise, mature parental supervision. Devotion to God in the home seems to forge the spiritual moorings and stability that can help the family cope. Some may say this is an oversimplification of a very complex problem, yet I believe the answers lie within the framework of the restored gospel of Christ. ("Enriching Family Life," *Ensign*, May 1983, 40.)

HOW CAN PARENTS and family members introduce and build familial strength? One of my closest boyhood friends recently died of cancer. His family decided he would be happier spending his last days in his own home, so they took him out of the veterans hospital, where the cancer was diagnosed, and cared for him within the familiar walls of his own house. His eighty-one-year-old mother left her home in another state and moved in to supervise the tender, loving care. A sister and a brother left their homes far away several times to help in the emergencies. His children, some of whom also lived away, came and set up a twenty-four-hour vigil so that he would never be alone.

After a few months he passed away, wasted and emaciated, but contented and happy. He had been loved into death. ("Enriching Family Life," *Ensign*, May 1983, 40.)

WE KNOW OF a large, close-knit family that is wonderfully successful in holding everything together. When the parents feel they are losing influence with teenagers, the help of cousins is enlisted to exert some counter peer pressure.

I would urge members of extended families—grandparents, uncles, aunts, nephews, nieces, cousins—to reach out in concern, to succor. Mostly what is needed from grandparents, aunts, and uncles is unreserved love manifest as interest and concern. It builds confidence, self-esteem, and self-worth. . . . But I have [also] been grateful for those in my family who have loved me enough to give me both the gentle and strong reproof on occasion as needed. We read in Proverbs: "He that refuseth reproof erreth." (Prov. 10:17.)

. . . With the increased onslaught of forces that cause families to disintegrate, we ought to dig in our heels to preserve all that is great and good in the family. We are reminded that in times of tribulations, the Nephites were not fighting for a political cause, such as monarchy or power; rather, they "were inspired by a better cause." For "they were fighting for their homes and their liberties, their wives and their children, and their all, yea, for their rites of worship and their church." (Alma 43:45.) ("Where Is the Church?" *BYU Speeches*, 24 Sept. 1989, 33–34.)

MAY I SUGGEST [the following] ways to enrich family life:

1. *Hold family prayer night and morning.* The source of our enormous individual strength and potential is no mystery. It is an endowment from God. . . . It often takes a superhuman effort for parents of a busy family to get everyone out of bed and together for family prayer and scripture study. You may not always feel like praying when you finally get together, but it will pay great dividends if you persevere.

2. *Study the scriptures.* . . . Parents must have a knowledge of the standard works to teach them to their children. A child who has been taught from the scriptures has a priceless legacy. . . .

3. *Teach children to work.* Every household has routine daily chores that children can be responsible for.

4. *Teach discipline and obedience.* If parents do not discipline their children and teach them to obey, society may discipline them in a way neither the parents nor the children will like. . . . Without discipline and obedience in the home, the unity of the family collapses.

5. *Place a high priority on loyalty to each other.* The dictionary defines the word *loyal* as being "constant and faithful in any relation implying trust or confidence; bearing true allegiance to the constituted authority" (*Britannica World Language Dictionary*, s.v. "loyalty"). If family members are not loyal to each other, they cannot be loyal to themselves.

6. *Teach principles of self-worth and self-reliance.* One of the main problems in families today is that we spend less and less time together. . . . Time together is precious time—time needed

to talk, to listen, to encourage, and to show how to do things. Less time together can result in loneliness, which may produce inner feelings of being unsupported, untreasured, and inadequate. . . . When parents say to a son or daughter, leaving the home for some activity, the simple but meaningful words, "Remember who you are," they have helped that child feel important.

7. *Develop family traditions.* . . . The traditions of each family are unique and are provided in large measure by the mother's imprint.

8. *Do everything in the spirit of love.* Elder LeGrand Richards shared with us the tender relationship he had with his father. Said he, "I walked into my father's apartment when he was just about ninety, . . . and as I opened the door, he stood up and walked toward me and took me in his arms and hugged me and kissed me. He always did that. . . . Taking me in his arms and calling me by my kid name, he said, 'Grandy, my boy, I love you.'" (in Conference Report, October 1967, pp. 111–12). ("Enriching Family Life," *Ensign*, May 1983, 40–41.)

Let there be no ill will or anger between parents and children, brothers and sisters, and kinsmen. Lingering feelings of hurt or disagreement should be settled quickly. Why wait until one party is dying or dead? May the rich humanness of warm, loving family life be restored and prevail in all our kinship. ("Enriching Family Life," *Ensign*, May 1983, 42.)

FATHERHOOD

WHEN I HEAR of a family breaking up, I question if family home evening and family prayers have been regularly held in that home and if the law of tithing has been observed. Has that family reverenced the Sabbath day? Have the parents murmured against Church teachings and leaders? I wonder what could possibly justify the forsaking of eternal promises made in the temple, or what could warrant the breaking up of a family with children of tender years.

Why is one family strong, yet another family weak? The problems are infinitely complex. Yet, there are answers. Abundant evidence shows that the presence of a firm, loving father in the home is far more likely to produce responsible, law-abiding children than if the father is not there, or if he does not function as a father at home. In either case it throws a double burden on the mother.

Malachi said the whole world would be smitten with a curse if the hearts of the fathers were not turned to the children, and if the hearts of the children were not turned to their fathers. (See Malachi 4:6.)

The presence of the father in the home, coupled with one or both of the parents being active in Church, and with discipline in the home, seems to produce stable, strong families. ("Enriching Family Life," *Ensign*, May 1983, 40.)

IN THE PAST twenty years, as homes and families have struggled to stay intact, sociological studies reveal this alarming fact: much of the crime and many of the behavioral disorders in the United States come from homes where the father has abandoned the children. In many societies the world over, child poverty, crime, drug abuse, and family decay can be traced to conditions where the father gives no male nurturing. Sociologically, it is now painfully apparent that fathers are not optional family baggage. We need to honor the position of the father as the primary provider for physical and spiritual support. I state this with no reluctance because the Lord has revealed that this obligation is placed upon husbands. "Women have claim on their husbands for their maintenance, until their husbands are taken." (D&C 83:2.) Further, "All children have claim upon their parents for their maintenance until they are of age." (D&C 83:4.) In addition, their spiritual welfare should be "brought to pass by the faith and covenant of their fathers." (D&C 84:99.) As regards little children, the Lord has promised that "great things may be required at the hands of their fathers." (D&C 29:48.) ("Father, Come Home," *Ensign,* May 1993, 35.)

I HOPE YOUR husbands will be more helpful than I have been, but homemaking is whatever you make of it. Every day brings satisfaction along with some work which may be frustrating, routine, drudgery, and unchallenging. But it is the same in the law office, the dispensary, the library, or the store. There is, however, no more important job than homemaking. As C. S. Lewis said, "it is the one for which all others exist." ("Message to Our Granddaughters," *BYU Speeches,* 1984–1985, 81.)

FINANCES

I SHOULD LIKE to now suggest six ways to help us from being overcome by economic stress:

1. *Seek first the kingdom of God.* (See Matthew 6:33.) This seeking includes the payment of our tithes and a generous fast offering and thus being blessed both spiritually and temporally by our obedience. Seeking first the kingdom of God will involve striving to keep the law the Apostle James called "the royal law," which is, "Thou shalt love thy neighbour as thyself" (James 2:8). Seeking first the kingdom of God involves the keeping of the divine commandments. Spiritual strength comes from many sources, including personal prayer, the study of the scriptures, and the willingness to "submit to all things . . . the Lord seeth fit to inflict" (Mosiah 3:19). These measures can give us a certain, peaceful stability.

2. *Solidify family strengths and resources.* Chief among a family's resources are its spiritual strengths, which are enhanced by praying together. Budgeting money together will produce a special unity, as will the holding of family councils. We should work together toward storing a year's supply of food, clothing, and other necessities. In times of stress extra acts of kindness are particularly needed and appreciated. When there is limited money

available, it is easier to teach children the wise use of money, including the need to save for the future. The family can be reminded to maintain an eternal perspective rather than concentrate on worldly possessions and wealth. Family organizations are helpful to render the individual help that may be needed. It is also important to learn how to accept family help graciously.

3. *Exercise faith.* The Savior reminds us, "All things are possible to him that believeth" (Mark 9:23). And again, "All things shall work together for your good" (D&C 90:24). The attitude with which we submit to "all things" is important. Maintaining a positive attitude and being cheerful are helpful. A belief that "all these things shall give thee experience, and . . . be for thy good" is like a spiritual stabilizer (D&C 122:7).

4. *Be adaptable in your work.* . . . In times of economic difficulty it may be necessary to work for less pay. We should be willing to learn new, marketable skills. There are a great many men who have found new joy and satisfaction in having a second career wholly unrelated to the work for which they were originally trained. Family members need to find ways to supplement income through appropriate work opportunities. Being flexible in our approach to our work opportunities may just make it possible to keep afloat financially. Giving a full day's work for a full day's pay has saved many jobs. It will also help us avoid accepting government doles which rob us of our dignity and our self-respect. . . .

5. *Avoid debt.* President J. Reuben Clark, Jr., taught us to "avoid debt as we would a plague" (in Conference Report, Apr. 1937, p. 26). This is particularly sound counsel in these times of exorbitantly high interest rates. Debt and its ever-present offspring, interest, are merciless taskmasters. A year and a half ago in this Tabernacle, President Clark's voice, on a tape, was heard to say, "Whoever borrows should understand what interest is; it is with them every minute of the day and night" (in Conference Report, Apr. 1938, p. 103).

6. *Reduce expense.* When asked how some people in a small farming community in southern Utah got by on their meager

cash income, George Lyman said, "They lived on the absence of expense." . . . Economic wealth does not endow eternal blessings, and financial difficulty does not revoke eternal covenants. ("The Blessings We Receive As We Meet the Challenges of Economic Stress," *Ensign*, Nov. 1982, 89–90.)

ASIDE FROM THE economic tides which run in the affairs of nations, financial hard times can befall any of us at any time. There is no guarantee against personal hard financial times. Financial difficulty may result from several kinds of misfortunes, including all types of natural disasters such as floods, fires, and earthquakes. Accidents and illness can produce unexpected and staggering medical and hospital bills. The misfortunes of other members of our own family may require our help. Unemployment and inflation can quickly wipe away hard-earned savings.

Economic stress can involve personal challenges. Discouragement and frustration are frequent companions to misfortune. Economic problems occasionally put a strain on family relationships. They often require us to do without things we feel we want or need. What can be a calamity for one can be an opportunity for another. Shakespeare, speaking through Duke Senior, said,

> *Sweet are the uses of adversity;*
> *Which, like the toad, ugly and venomous,*
> *Wears yet a precious jewel in his head.*
> (As You Like It, *act 2, sc. 1, lines 12–14.*)

The lasting effects of economic challenges are often determined by our attitude toward life. One writer said, "Out of the same substances one stomach will extract nourishment, and another poison; and so the same disappointments in life will chasten and refine one man's spirit and embitter another's" (William Matthews, *Webster's Encyclopedia of Dictionaries*, New American Edition, Ottenheimer Publishers, Inc., p. 864). ("The Blessings We Receive As We Meet the Challenges of Economic Stress," *Ensign*, Nov. 1982, 88.)

WE REAP THAT which we sow. Latter-day Saints have long been taught to live by the virtues of independence, industry, thrift, and self-reliance. Working for what we receive is a cardinal, timeless principle of self-respect. The whole world admires success. But how each of us defines success and how we seek it is crucial to our happiness.

The fruits of industry and thrift may appropriately be put into sound investments. A good solid investment can equal years of toil, and there is some risk in all we do. But investments that are highly speculative and promoted with unsound, vague promises of inordinate return should be viewed very carefully. The leaders of the Church have long warned against speculation.

Brigham Young said, "If the Lord ever revealed anything to me, he has shown me that the Elders of Israel must let speculation alone and attend to the duties of their calling." (*Journal of Discourses*, 8:179.)

In our time President Nathan Eldon Tanner has said:

"Investment debt should be fully secured so as not to encumber a family's security. Don't invest in speculative ventures. The spirit of speculation can become intoxicating. Many fortunes have been wiped out by the uncontrolled appetite to accumulate more and more. Let us learn from the sorrows of the past and avoid enslaving our time, energy, and general health to a gluttonous appetite to acquire increased material goods." (In Conference Report, Oct. 1979, p. 120; also in *Ensign*, Nov. 1979, p. 82.) ("Integrity, the Mother of Many Virtues," *Ensign*, May 1982, 48.)

FORGIVENESS OF SINS

REPENTANCE AND FORGIVENESS are among the greatest fruits of the Atonement. ("A Crown of Thorns, a Crown of Glory," *Ensign*, May 1991, 70.)

THE HOLY GHOST . . . can help us learn to forgive. There comes a time when people must move on, seeking greater things rather than being consumed by the memory of some hurt or injustice. Dwelling constantly on past injuries is, by its nature, limiting to the Spirit. It does not promote peace. ("The Gift of the Holy Ghost: A Sure Compass," *Ensign*, Apr. 1996, 5.)

EXTENDING FORGIVENESS, LOVE, and understanding for perceived shortcomings and weaknesses in our wives, husbands, children, and associates makes it much easier to say, "God be merciful to me a sinner" (Luke 18:13). ("A Crown of Thorns, a Crown of Glory," *Ensign*, May 1991, 68.)

FREEDOM OF RELIGION

EVERY AMERICAN HAS been taught that "freedom of religion" is the "first freedom" guaranteed by the Bill of Rights. The First Amendment to the Constitution recognizes the "free exercise of religion" as the pre-eminent position among Constitutional rights as intended by the Founding Fathers. Most Americans, however, have seen these principles being eroded.

The twin religious clauses of the Bill of Rights—"Congress shall make no law respecting an establishment of religion nor prohibit the free exercise thereof"—are the golden threads which in the past have permitted those who believe in God to publicly affirm that there is a higher power that "rules in the affairs of men." . . .

In my opinion, the establishment and free exercise clauses should be read together to harmonize the importance of religious liberty with freedom from government regulation. Rather, today in our nation the establishment clause is being used to restrict religious institutions from playing a role in civic issues, and the recent interpolations of the free exercise clause in my opinion denies to some individuals their religious liberty. . . .

The basic concept of Anglo-Saxon-American jurisprudence has held, as affirmed by the Constitution, that God is the source of all of our basic rights, and that the principal function of government is only to secure those rights. May I quote from the Declaration of Independence: "We hold these truths to be self-evident, that all men are created equal, that they are endowed by their Creator with certain unalienable rights. . . . That to secure these rights governments are instituted among Man."

In contrast, the new secular religion of which I speak finds its source of right by invoking the power of the state. It seems to have little purpose, few common values for morality except self-interest. ("The Impact of World War II on Utah," World War II Commemoration, Ogden, Utah, 13 Aug. 1995.)

FRUGALITY

THERE IS A wise old saying: "Eat it up, wear it out, make it do, or do without." Thrift is a practice of not wasting anything. Some people are able to get by because of the absence of expense. They have their shoes resoled, they patch, they mend, they sew, and they save money. They avoid installment buying, and make purchases only after saving enough to pay cash, thus avoiding interest charges. Frugality means to practice careful economy. (See *Webster's New World Dictionary,* 2d. college edition.)

The old couplet "Waste not, want not" still has much merit. Frugality requires that we live within our income and save a little for a rainy day, which always seems to come. It means avoiding debt and carefully limiting credit purchasing. It is important to learn to distinguish between wants and needs. It takes self-discipline to avoid the "buy now, pay later" philosophy and to adopt the "save now and buy later" practice. ("The Responsibility for Welfare Rests with Me and My Family," *Ensign,* May 1986, 20.)

GOD, RELATIONSHIP WITH

ONE OF THIS nation's leading pollsters, Richard Wirthlin, has identified through polls an expression of basic needs of people in the United States. These needs are self-esteem, peace of mind, and personal contentment. I believe these are needs of God's children everywhere. How can these needs be satisfied? I suggest that behind each of these is the requirement to establish one's own personal identity as the offspring of God. All three needs, regardless of ethnic background, culture, or country, can be met if we look to the divinity that is within us. As the Lord himself has said, "And the Spirit giveth light to every man [and woman] that cometh into the world; and the Spirit enlighteneth every man [and woman] through the world, that hearkeneth to the voice of the Spirit." (D&C 84:46.) ("Heirs to the Kingdom of God," *Ensign,* May 1995, 61–62.)

GOVERNMENT

ON THIS [4TH of July] holiday, we celebrate, as we have for 219 years, the establishment of a government in a country unlike any other in the history of the world. It has had at its very heart the concept of a government "instituted of God for the benefit of man" (D&C 134:1). The deepest taproots of our nation and state have lain in the very essence of our humanity, our faith in God. This nation as a democracy has as its basic foundation a government of laws and equality of all before the law. Under the Constitution it has the right and the duty to institute laws to protect its citizenry in their inalienable rights, recognizing that, as the Doctrine and Covenants says, "sedition and rebellion are unbecoming every citizen thus protected, and should be punished accordingly" (D&C 134:5). The government has the right and duty to enact laws within the institutions set up by the Constitution which are best calculated to secure the public interest while at the same time preserving the individual rights of its citizenry. ("The Integrity of Obeying the Law," Freedom Festival Fireside, Provo, Utah, 2 July 1995.)

I HAVE LIVED under military dictatorships for some years of my life. I have a great love for those countries and their people. But in those countries, the principal authority is the man who has the rubber stamp which grants authority and rights. The law is, in large measure, what the man in authority decides it is. The system of law in those countries evolved from the Roman system under which the emperor was above the law, and the state was the source of all individual rights. In some of those countries, inadequate respect was shown for stop signs or traffic lights or even civil authority. These countries were controlled in large measure by bureaucracy. From this experience I have learned that obedience to law must come from one's heart and conscience, reinforced by a patriotic feeling of duty and citizenship. "No man is above the law and no man below it," as Theodore Roosevelt put it. "Nor do we ask any man's permission when we require him to obey it" (*The Story of Theodore Roosevelt and His Influence on Our Times,* Noel F. Busch, Reynal & Company Inc., New York, 1963, p. 305). ("The Integrity of Obeying the Law," Freedom Festival Fireside, Provo, Utah, 2 July 1995.)

IN MY LIFETIME I have seen a decay in the respect for the legal system under which we live, and a disrespect and mistrust of civil authority. In my childhood all police officers were respected and looked up to as friends and protectors, as were judges and congressmen. In the recent bombing explosion in Oklahoma City, some of the heroes who risked their lives were the firemen and policemen who worked round the clock trying to save lives. Yet these same heroes are often defamed and slandered in other circumstances.

Cynicism and distrust of government are abroad in the land. A growing group of our citizenry, including businessmen and professional people, choose not to obey laws they do not like or think are wrong. Like Mr. Bumble in Dickens' *Oliver Twist,* they challenge what they don't like as he did when he said, "If the law supposes that, the law is a ass— a idiot" (*Oliver Twist,* chapter 51). I am quick to admit that some laws seem irrational, but they are the law, and should be changed by orderly process. I again draw from Theodore

Roosevelt: "The best way to get rid of a bad law is to see that it is uniformly enforced" (*The Story of Theodore Roosevelt and His Influence on Our Times,* Noel F. Busch, Reynal & Company Inc., New York, 1963, p. 305). ("The Integrity of Obeying the Law," Freedom Festival Fireside, Provo, Utah, 2 July 1995.)

I BELIEVE THAT most governmental problems can usually be handled best at a level closest to the people. The principal suggestion I have . . . to cure some of the ills and irritations of government is to get personally involved. In a democracy, if we are not involved in our duty as citizens we have the kind of government we deserve. ("The Integrity of Obeying the Law," Freedom Festival Fireside, Provo, Utah, 2 July 1995.)

GRATITUDE

I [WISH] TO speak about gratitude as an expression of faith and as a saving principle. The Lord has said, "And in nothing doth man offend God, or against none is his wrath kindled, save those who confess not his hand in all things, and obey not his commandments" (D&C 59:21). It is clear to me from this scripture that to "thank the Lord thy God in all things" (D&C 59:7) is more than a social courtesy; it is a binding commandment.

One of the advantages of having lived a long time is that you can often remember when you had it worse. I am grateful to have lived long enough to have known some of the blessings of adversity. My memory goes back to the Great Depression, when we had certain values burned into our souls. One of these values was gratitude for that which we had because we had so little. The Great Depression in the United States in the early thirties was a terrible schoolmaster. We had to learn provident living in order to survive. Rather than create in us a spirit of envy or anger for what we did not have, it developed in many a spirit of gratitude for the meager, simple things with which we were blessed, like hot, homemade bread and oatmeal cereal and many other things. ("Gratitude as a Saving Principle," *Ensign,* May 1990, 85.)

ONE OF THE evils of our time is taking for granted so many of the things we enjoy. This was spoken of by the Lord: "For what doth it profit a man if a gift is bestowed upon him, and he receive not the gift?" (D&C 88:33). The Apostle Paul described our day to Timothy when he wrote that in the last days "men shall be lovers of their own selves, covetous, boasters, proud, blasphemers, disobedient to parents, unthankful, unholy" (2 Timothy 3:2). These sins are fellow travelers, and ingratitude makes one susceptible to all of them.

The story of the thankful Samaritan has great meaning [see Luke 17:12–19]. . . .

Leprosy was so loathsome a disease that those afflicted were not permitted under the law to come close to Jesus. Those suffering from this terrible disease were required to agonize together, sharing their common misery (see Leviticus 13:45–46). Their forlorn cry, "Jesus, Master, have mercy on us" must have touched the Savior's heart. When they were healed and when they had received priestly approval that they were clean and acceptable in society, they must have been overcome with joy and amazement. Having received so great a miracle, they seemed completely satisfied. But they forgot their benefactor. It is difficult to understand why they were so lacking in gratitude. Such ingratitude is self-centered. It is a form of pride. ("Gratitude as a Saving Principle," *Ensign,* May 1990, 85.)

IT SEEMS AS though there is a tug-of-war between opposing character traits that leaves no voids in our souls. As gratitude is absent or disappears, rebellion often enters and fills the vacuum. I do not speak of rebellion against civil oppression. I refer to rebellion against moral cleanliness, beauty, decency, honesty, reverence, and respect for parental authority.

A grateful heart is a beginning of greatness. It is an expression of humility. It is a foundation for the development of such virtues as prayer, faith, courage, contentment, happiness, love, and well-being.

But there is a truism associated with all types of human strength: "Use it or lose it." When not used, muscles weaken, skills deteriorate, and faith disappears. President Thomas S. Monson stated: "Think to thank. In these three words are the finest capsule course for a happy marriage, a formula for enduring friendship, and a pattern for personal happiness" (*Pathways to Perfection* [Salt Lake City: Deseret Book Co., 1973], p. 254). Said the Lord, "And he who receiveth all things with thankfulness shall be made glorious; and the things of this earth shall be added unto him, even an hundred fold, yea, more" (D&C 78:19). ("Gratitude as a Saving Principle," *Ensign*, May 1990, 86.)

HERITAGE

THERE COMES DOWN through my family a legacy of testimony concerning the truthfulness of Joseph Smith's work. I learned of this bequest as a small boy at my mother's knee. My great-great-grandfather, Edward Partridge, was intimately associated with the Prophet Joseph for several years prior to his losing his life in consequence of the persecution. (See *History of the Church* 4:132.) He was baptized by Joseph. In a revelation received by the Prophet, he was called as the first bishop of the restored Church. (See D&C 41:9.)

Grandfather was so tortured, humiliated, and suffered so much in his calling from lawless mobs, and was still so steadfast and faithful, that he could not possibly have doubted the genuineness of the revelation that appointed him. Like others who were close to the Prophet, he knew Joseph's heart and soul. Grandfather could not have been deceived. I believe his life and death both prove that he did not lie. His devotion, suffering, and sacrifice eloquently testify that he had implicit faith in Joseph as an inspired servant of God.

In addition to this heritage, I have my own inner witness which confirms to my soul that the Prophet Joseph Smith, as the instrument of God, revealed the greatest body of truth that has come to mankind since the Savior himself walked upon the earth. ("The Expanding Inheritance from Joseph Smith," *Ensign,* Nov. 1981, 77.)

HOW CAN WE pay our debt of gratitude for the heritage of faith demonstrated by pioneers in many lands across the earth who struggled and sacrificed so that the gospel might take root? How is thankfulness expressed for the intrepid handcart pioneers who, by their own brute strength, pulled their meager belongings in handcarts across the scorching plains and through the snows of the high mountain passes to escape persecution and find peaceful worship in these valleys? . . .

Emma Batchelor, a young English girl traveling without family, . . . joined the Paul Gourley family [in the Martin handcart company].

. . . Sister Gourley gave birth to a child, and Emma acted as the midwife and loaded the mother and the child in the cart for two days, which Emma helped pull.

Those who died in the Martin company were mercifully relieved of the suffering of others with frozen feet, ears, noses, or fingers—which maimed them for the rest of their lives. Emma, age twenty-one, however, was a fortunate one. She came through the ordeal whole.

A year later, she met Brigham Young, who was surprised that she was not maimed, and she told him, "Brother Brigham, I had no one to care for me or to look out for me, so I decided I must look out for myself. I was the one who called out when Brother Savage warned us [not to go]. I was at fault in that, but I tried to make up for it. I pulled my share at the cart every day. When we came to a stream, I stopped and took off my shoes and stockings and outer skirt and put them on top of the cart.

Then, after I got the cart across, I came back and carried little Paul over on my back. Then I sat down and scrubbed my feet hard with my woolen neckerchief and put on dry shoes and stockings."

The descendants of these pioneers can partially settle the account by being true to the cause for which their ancestors suffered so much to be part of. ("Gratitude as a Saving Principle," *Ensign*, May 1990, 87.)

THOSE OF YOU who have joined the Church in this generation have acquired fellowship with a people, many of whom have a great heritage of great suffering and sacrifice. Such sacrifice becomes your heritage also, for it is the inheritance of a people who have faults and imperfections but have a great nobility of purpose. That purpose is to help all mankind come to a sweet, peaceful understanding about who they are, and to foster a love for their fellowmen and a determination to keep the commandments of God. This is the gospel's holy call. It is the essence of our worship. ("Gratitude as a Saving Principle," *Ensign*, May 1990, 86.)

IN ADDITION TO the legacy of faith bequeathed by those who crossed the plains, they also left a great heritage of love—love of God and love of mankind. It is an inheritance of sobriety, independence, hard work, high moral values, and fellowship. It is a birthright of obedience to the commandments of God and loyalty to those whom God has called to lead this people. It is a legacy of forsaking evil. Immorality, alternative lifestyles, gambling, selfishness, dishonesty, unkindness, addiction to alcohol and drugs are not part of the gospel of Jesus Christ. ("A Priceless Heritage," *Ensign*, Nov. 1992, 85.)

I CANNOT HELP wondering why these intrepid pioneers had to pay for their faith with such a terrible price in agony and suffering. Why were not the elements tempered to spare them from their profound agony? I believe their lives were consecrated to a higher purpose through their suffering. Their love for the Savior was burned deep in their souls, and into the souls of their children, and their children's children. The motivation for their lives came from a true conversion in the center of their souls. As President Gordon B. Hinckley has said, "When there are throbs in the heart of an individual Latter-day Saint, a great and vital testimony of the truth of this work, he will be found doing his duty in the Church" (Regional Representative Seminar, April 6, 1984). ("A Priceless Heritage," *Ensign,* Nov. 1992, 85.)

ABOVE AND BEYOND the epic historical events they participated in, the pioneers found a guide to personal living. They found reality and meaning in their lives. In the difficult days of their journey, the members of the Martin and Willie Handcart Companies encountered some apostates from the Church who were returning from the West, going back to the East. These apostates tried to persuade some of the companies to turn back. A few did turn back. But the great majority of the pioneers went forward to a heroic achievement in this life, and to eternal life in the hereafter. Francis Webster, a member of the Martin Company, stated, "Everyone of us came through with the absolute knowledge that God lives for we became acquainted with him in our extremities" (*Relief Society Magazine,* Jan. 1948, p. 8). I hope that this priceless legacy of faith left by the pioneers will inspire all of us to more fully participate in the Savior's work of bringing to pass the immortality and eternal life of his children. ("A Priceless Heritage," *Ensign,* Nov. 1992, 85.)

PIONEER MEN WERE strong and courageous, but the pioneer women were stout-hearted and glorious.

Having arrived, they survived and prospered through independence, industry, thrift, self-reliance, and faith. They labored to the exhaustion of their bodies to build, to sow, and to reap. The monuments they built are a testimony of their integrity and their faith in the God they worshiped. There has been no building erected in this state since the Salt Lake Temple which surpasses its quality of superb, loving craftsmanship. It was built over a period of forty years of their extreme poverty. . . .

In the beginning they had to do what had to be done by themselves because there was no government to help them. But they had inspired leaders who were men of vision, faith, and integrity. Their leaders expected of them more than they thought they could possibly do. Somehow, with the help of God, they were able to accomplish it.

They established values of honesty, thrift, faith, common decency, fidelity in marriage, and respect for everyone. At the heart of everything they did was the nurturing of solid families. They voluntarily responded to calls to build their public projects; ditches and canals to carry life-giving water to the parched desert soil; public buildings for worship of the God they served, and for culture and recreation.

Now we are drinking water from wells that we have not dug, but they dug wells where there had not been any wells before. They left us a priceless heritage which blesses us greatly. May we build on their foundation so that we in turn may leave a legacy of industry, trust, and faith for the coming generations. (Remarks at Pioneer Day celebration commemorating the centennial of Utah's statehood, 24 July 1996.)

HOLY GHOST

OF AN INTERVIEW in 1839 between the Prophet Joseph Smith and Martin Van Buren, then president of the United States, the following was reported:

"In our interview with the President, he interrogated us wherein we differed in our religion from the other religions of the day. Brother Joseph said we differed in mode of baptism, and the gift of the Holy Ghost by the laying on of hands. We considered that all other considerations were contained in the gift of the Holy Ghost." (*History of the Church*, 4:42).

One of the reasons the Prophet's response was so inspired is that the right to enjoy the marvelous gifts of the Holy Ghost is conferred upon every member of this Church soon after baptism. This is in fulfillment of the promise of the Savior: "And I will pray the Father, and he shall give you another Comforter, that he may abide with you for ever" (John 14:16).

This powerful gift entitles the leaders and all worthy members of the Church to enjoy the gifts and companionship of the Holy Ghost, a member of the Godhead whose function is to inspire, reveal, and teach "all things" (see John 14:26). The result of this endowment is that for 150 years the leadership and membership of this church have enjoyed, and now enjoy, continuous revelation and inspiration directing them in what is right and good. ("Communion with the Holy Spirit," *Ensign,* May 1980, 12.)

IT WAS A profoundly moving event those centuries ago when the Savior led his beloved disciples into the favored Garden of Gethsemane for the last time. Jesus was mindful of the great ordeal ahead of him. He agonized, "My soul is exceeding sorrowful unto death: tarry ye here, and watch" (Mark 14:34). He was ready for the unspeakable agony. Said he, "The spirit truly is ready, but the flesh is weak" (Mark 14:38).

The eleven Apostles no doubt sensed—but could not understand—that some portentous event would happen. Jesus had spoken of leaving them. They knew that the Master whom they loved and depended upon was going somewhere, but where, they did not know. They had heard him say, "I will not leave you comfortless. . . . But the Comforter, which is the Holy Ghost, whom the Father will send in my name, he shall teach you all things, and bring all things to your remembrance, whatsoever I have said unto you" (John 14:18, 26).

It is of this Comforter that I wish to speak today. I do so because I am persuaded that there is a greater need for divine oversight in our lives today than ever before. I wish to testify that, by the power and gift of the Holy Ghost, we can know what to do and what not to do to bring happiness and peace to our lives. ("The Gift of the Holy Ghost—A Sure Compass," *Ensign*, May 1989, 31.)

THE BOOK OF Mormon, the Bible, and other scriptures, along with the guidance of modern prophets, provide true standards of conduct. In addition, the gift of the Holy Ghost is available as a sure guide, as the voice of conscience, and as a moral compass. This guiding compass is personal to each of us. It is unerring. It is unfailing. However, we must listen to it in order to steer clear of the shoals which will cause our lives to sink into unhappiness and self-doubt.

We need a sure compass because many of the standards, values, vows, and obligations which have helped us preserve our spirituality, our honor, our integrity, our worth, and our decency have little by little been assaulted and discarded. ("The Gift of the Holy Ghost—A Sure Compass," *Ensign*, May 1989, 32.)

I BELIEVE THE Spirit of the Holy Ghost is the greatest guarantor of inward peace in our unstable world. It can be more mind-expanding and can make us have a better sense of well-being than any chemical or other earthly substance. It will calm nerves; it will breathe peace to our souls. This Comforter can be with us as we seek to improve. It can function as a source of revelation to warn us of impending danger and also help keep us from making mistakes. It can enhance our natural senses so that we can see more clearly, hear more keenly, and remember what we should remember. It is a way of maximizing our happiness. ("The Gift of the Holy Ghost—A Sure Compass," *Ensign*, May 1989, 32–33.)

THERE IS ONE unerring voice that is ever true. It can always be relied upon. It should be listened to, although at times this voice too may speak unwelcome warning messages. I speak of the still, small, inner voice which comes from the divine source.

As the prophet Elijah learned, "the Lord was not in the wind: and after the wind an earthquake; but the Lord was not in the earthquake: And after the earthquake a fire; but the Lord was not in the fire: and after the fire a still small voice" (1 Kings 19:11–12).

One single, unwanted message [from the Holy Ghost] may be a call to change our lives; it may lead to the specially tailored opportunity we need. I am grateful that it is never too late to change, to make things right, to leave old activities and habits behind. ("Unwanted Messages," *Ensign*, Nov. 1986, 10.)

I WISH TO say a word about the Holy Spirit of Promise, which is the sealing and ratifying power of the Holy Ghost. To have a covenant or ordinance sealed by the Holy Spirit of Promise is a compact through which the inherent blessings will be obtained, provided those seeking the blessing are true and faithful (see D&C 76:50–54).

For example, when the covenant of marriage for time and eternity, the culminating gospel ordinance, is sealed by the Holy Spirit of Promise, it can literally open the windows of heaven for great blessings to flow to a married couple who seek for those blessings. Such marriages become rich, whole, and sacred. Though each party to the marriage can maintain his or her separate identity, yet together in their covenants they can be like two vines wound inseparably around each other. Each thinks of his or her companion before thinking of self. ("The Gift of the Holy Ghost—A Sure Compass," *Ensign*, May 1989, 33.)

IT IS ALWAYS gratifying to hear of prayers being answered and miracles occurring in the lives of those who need them. But what of those noble and faithful souls who receive no miracles, whose prayers are not answered in the way they wish? What is their solace? From whence will their comfort come? Said the Savior of the world: "I will not leave you comfortless: I will come to you. . . . But the Comforter, which is the Holy Ghost, . . . the Father will send in my name" (John 14:18, 26).

In simple terms, the gift of the Holy Ghost is an enhanced spiritual power permitting those entitled thereto to receive it, to receive a greater knowledge and enjoyment of the influence of Deity. ("The Gift of the Holy Ghost—A Sure Compass," *Ensign*, May 1989, 33.)

HOMOSEXUALITY

THE CHURCH'S STAND on homosexual relations provides another arena where we offend the devil. I expect that the statement of the First Presidency and the Quorum of the Twelve against homosexual marriages will continue to be assaulted. Satan is only interested in our misery which he promotes by trying to persuade men and women to act contrary to God's plan. One way he does this is by encouraging the inappropriate use of sacred creative powers. A bona fide marriage is one between a man and a woman solemnized by the proper legal or ecclesiastical authority. Only sexual relations between husband and wife within the bonds of marriage are acceptable before the Lord.

There is some widely accepted theory extant that homosexuality is inherited. How can this be? No scientific evidence demonstrates absolutely that this is so. Besides, if it were so, it would frustrate the whole plan of mortal happiness. Our designation as men or women began before this world was. In contrast to the socially accepted doctrine that homosexuality is inborn, a number of respectable authorities contend that homosexuality is not acquired by birth. The false belief of inborn sexual orientation denies to repentant souls the opportunity to change, and will ultimately lead to discouragement, disappointment, and despair.

Any alternatives to the legal and loving marriage between a man and a woman are helping to unravel the fabric of human society. I am sure this is pleasing to the devil. The fabric I refer to is the family. These so-called alternative lifestyles must not

be accepted as right because they frustrate God's commandment for a life-giving union of male and female within a legal
marriage as stated in Genesis. If practiced by all adults, these
lifestyles would mean the end of the human family. ("Trying to
Serve the Lord without Offending the Devil," *BYU Speeches*, 15
Nov. 1994, 62.)

HONESTY

IT IS FREQUENTLY astounding to see the dereliction of people in
keeping the standards of ordinary fairness and justice. This
delinquency manifests itself in so many ways. It is sometimes
evident in commercial transactions, as well as in private contacts. Injustice to others is manifest even in the way auto-
mobiles are sometimes driven. This unfairness and injustice
results principally from one person seeking an advantage or an
edge over another. Those who follow such a practice demean
themselves greatly. How can those of us who do not practice
ordinary fairness and justice have serious claim on the blessings
of a just and a fair God?

Do some of us seek to justify our taking of shortcuts and
advantage of others by indulging in the twin sophistries,
"There isn't any justice" and "Everybody does it"? There are
many others who seemingly prosper by violating the rules of
God and the standards of decency and fair play. They appear to
escape the imminent law of the harvest, which states,
"Whatsoever a man soweth, that shall he also reap" (Galatians
6:7). Worrying about the punishment we think ought to come
to others is self-defeating to us. ("Unwanted Messages," *Ensign*,
Nov. 1986, 10.)

HONESTY IS A very important part of character. We have all seen
men who think they are not accountable to the laws of men or
of God. They seem to feel that the rules of human conduct do
not apply to them. A popular philosophy is, "What can I get
away with?" As someone once said, "The difference between a

moral man and a man of honor is that the latter regrets a discreditable act even when it has worked." (H. L. Mencken, *Dictionary of Humorous Quotations,* edited by Evan Esar, New York, 1949, p. 126.)

Honesty begins when we are young. When I was eleven years old, I looked forward eagerly to my magical 12th birthday when I could become a deacon and a Scout. My mother helped me to learn the Articles of Faith, the Scout Law and Motto, and other requirements so that I would have a good start when that special birthday arrived.

. . . One day Mother left me to wash the dishes and clean the kitchen while she attended to a sick neighbor. I agreed to do these duties but put off doing the dishes. Time ran out and they didn't get done. In fact, they didn't even get started. When Mother came home and saw the kitchen, she put on her apron and went to the sink. She spoke only three words, which stung worse than the sting of a dozen hornets. They were the first three words of the Scout Law: "On my honor." That day I resolved that I would never give my mother cause to repeat those words to me again. ("We Seek After These Things," *Ensign,* May 1998, 44.)

WE ALL NEED to know what it means to be honest. Honesty is more than not lying. It is truth telling, truth speaking, truth living, and truth loving. John, a nine-year-old Swiss pioneer child who was in one of the handcart companies, is an example of honesty. His father put a chunk of buffalo meat in the handcart and said it was to be saved for Sunday dinner. John said, "I was so very hungry and the meat smelled so good to me while pushing at the handcart that I could not resist. I had a little pocket knife. . . . Although I expected a severe whipping when father found it out, I cut off little pieces each day. I would chew them so long that they got white and perfectly tasteless. When father came to get the meat he asked me if I had been cutting off some of it. I said, 'Yes. I was so hungry I could not let it alone.' Instead of giving me a scolding or a whipping, father turned away and wiped tears from his eyes.'" (LeRoy R. And Ann W. Hafen, *Handcarts to Zion*, p. 190.) . . .

Honesty is a principle, and we have our moral agency to determine how we will apply this principle. We have the agency to make choices; but ultimately, we will be accountable for each choice we make. We may deceive others, but there is One we will never deceive. From the Book of Mormon we learn, "The keeper of the gate is the Holy One of Israel; and he employeth no servant there; and there is none other way save it be by the gate; for he cannot be deceived, for the Lord God is his name." (2 Nephi 9:41.) ("Honesty—A Moral Compass," *Ensign*, Nov. 1996, 41–42.)

STEALING IS ALL too common throughout the world. For many their reasoning seems to be, "What can I get away with?" or "It's OK to do it as long as I don't get caught!" Stealing takes many forms, including shoplifting; taking cars, stereos, CD players, video games, and other items that belong to someone else; stealing time, money, and merchandise from employers; stealing from the government by the misuse of taxpayers' money or making false claims on our income tax returns; and borrowing without any intention of repayment. No one has ever gained anything of value by theft. . . . The stealing of anything is unworthy of a priesthood holder. ("Honesty—A Moral Compass," *Ensign*, Nov. 1996, 43.)

H U M I L I T Y

NO STONE WALL separates the members of the Church from all of the seductions of the world. Members of the Church, like everyone else, are being surfeited with deceptions, challenges, and temptations. However, to those of enduring faith, judgment, and discernment, there is an invisible wall which they choose never to breach. Those on the safe side of this invisible wall are filled with humility, not servitude. They willingly accept the supremacy of God and rely upon the scriptures and counsel of His servants, the leaders of the Church. These leaders of the Church are men with human frailties, and are imperfect in their wisdom and judgment. Perfection in men is not found on the earth. But almost without exception these leaders sincerely, humbly, and prayerfully render great and dedicated Christian service to the best of their ability. More important, they hold a divine warrant and commission through which great and eternal blessings come to those who sustain and follow them. They are God's servants. ("The Abundant Life," *Ensign,* Nov. 1985, 8.)

THE LORD HAS a great work for each of us to do. You may wonder how this can be. You may feel that there is nothing special or superior about you or your ability. Perhaps you feel, or have been told, that you are stupid. Many of us have felt that and been told that. Gideon felt this when the Lord asked him to save Israel from the Midianites. Gideon said, "My family is poor in Manasseh, and I am the least in my father's house." (Judges 6:15.) He had only three hundred men, but with the help of the Lord, Gideon defeated the armies of the Midianites. (See Judges.)

The Lord can do remarkable miracles with a person of ordinary ability who is humble, faithful, and diligent in serving the Lord and who seeks to improve himself. This is because God is the ultimate source of power. By the gift of the Holy Ghost we can not only "know all things" but even "the truth of all things." (Moroni 10:5.) ("Acting for Ourselves and Not Being Acted Upon," *Ensign,* Nov. 1995, 47.)

IN SPEAKING OF humility I do not refer to the "breast beating," "sackcloth and ashes" kind of humility. I refer to the humility that comes with inner strength and peace. It is the humility that can accept and live with one's own warts without cosmetics to hide them. It is important to learn to live with our incorrectable physical and mental defects without comment and without explanation. ("Self-Esteem: A Great Human Need," Brigham Young University Education Week address, 23 Aug. 1983.)

HUMOR, SENSE OF

AN IMPORTANT PART of the gospel message is that we not be too rigid, that we open up our minds, that we develop some tolerance and not be too quick to render judgment. I learned when I was making my living in the arena of the law that we do not always have all of the facts. There always seemed to be at least two sides to a question. Everything is not just black and white. The counsel of the Savior as he instructed his Twelve was, "Behold, I send you forth as sheep in the midst of wolves: be ye therefore wise as serpents, and harmless as doves" (Matt. 10:16).

It is not always easy to achieve an appropriate balance. In addition to what we read in the newspapers, we can have brought right into our homes in color most of the problems of an entire world. We also have our own personal ups and downs and challenges. The stresses of life are real and rather constant. There is, however, a defense against much of this. A thoughtful man said, "There is no defense against adverse fortune which is, on the whole, so effectual as an habitual sense of humor" (Thomas Wentworth Storrow Higginson, *Dictionary of Thoughts*, J. G. Ferguson Publishing Co., 1969, p. 372). Humor is a defense against adversity.

For many years as I have blessed newborn children, including my own, I have blessed them with a sense of humor. I do this with the hope that it will help guard them against being too rigid, in the hope that they will have balance in their lives, in the hope that situations and problems and difficulties will not be overdrawn. ("The Study and Practice of the Laws of Men in Light of the Laws of God," Address to Brigham Young University law students, 22 Nov. 1987.)

CULTIVATING GOOD humor may be helpful in finding our own identity. Each of you young people are trying to find out who you really are. You can feel your surging powers and strengths, and yet with the many challenges that confront you now and lie ahead of you, you may have some inner concerns as to your ability to meet and cope with them. I wish to assure you that you will ride over the bumps and come quicker to your own identity if you cultivate the good humor which comes naturally. A thoughtful man said: "Humor is an affirmation of dignity, a declaration of man's superiority to all that befalls him." (Romain Gary, in *Dictionary of Thoughts*, J. G. Ferguson Publishing Co., 1969, p. 372). It is important to learn to laugh at yourself and poke fun at yourself. ("The Study and Practice of the Laws of Men in Light of the Laws of God," Address to Brigham Young University law students, 22 Nov. 1997.)

INDUSTRIOUSNESS

To BE INDUSTRIOUS involves energetically managing our circumstances to our advantage. It also means to be enterprising and to take advantage of opportunities. Industry requires resourcefulness. A good idea can be worth years of struggle.

A friend who owned some fertile fields complained to his sister about his lack of means. "What about your crops?" asked the sister. The impoverished man replied, "There was so little snow in the mountains, I thought there would be a drought, so I did not plant." As it turned out, unforeseen spring rains made the crops bountiful for those industrious enough to plant. It is a denial of the divinity within us to doubt our potential and our possibilities. ("Responsibility for Welfare Rests with Me and My Family," *Ensign*, May 1986, 21.)

INSPIRATION

My FIRST RADIO was a crystal set. It was hard to tune to the frequency of a particular radio station. One had to literally scratch the receiving wire whisker over the top of the rough crystal to find the right pin point, a little valley or peak on the crystal, where the signal was received. Just a millimeter off on one side or the other of that point and you would lose the signal and get scratchy static. Over time, with patience and perseverance, good eyesight and a steady hand, you could learn to find the signal point on the crystal without too much difficulty.

So it is in learning to attune ourselves to the inspiration from God and tune out the scratchy static. We have to work at being tuned in. Most of us need a long time to become tuned in most of the time. When I was a young General Authority, President Marion G. Romney, who was in his seventies at the time, told us, "I know when I am working under the Spirit and when I am not." To be able to recognize when one is being guided by the spirit is a supernal gift. ("Personal Epiphanies," Single Adult Fireside, Salt Lake City, Utah, 7 Jan. 1996.)

WHY DOES THIS church grow and flourish? It does so because of divine direction to the leaders and members. This began in our day when God the Father and Jesus Christ appeared to Joseph Smith early in the spring of 1820. However, we claim that God's inspiration is not limited to the members of this church. The First Presidency has stated:

"The great religious leaders of the world such as Mohammed, Confucius, and the Reformers, as well as philosophers including Socrates, Plato, and others, received a portion of God's light. Moral truths were given to them by God to enlighten whole nations and to bring a higher level of understanding to individuals. . . .

"We believe that God has given and will give to all peoples sufficient knowledge to help them on their way to eternal salvation" (*Statement of the First Presidency regarding God's Love for All Mankind,* 15 Feb. 1978). ("Communion with the Holy Spirit," *Ensign,* May 1980, 12.)

LATTER-DAY SAINTS, having received the gift of the Holy Ghost by the laying on of hands, are entitled to personal inspiration in the small events of life as well as when they are confronted with the giant Goliaths of life.

David, the youngest son of Jesse, a mere, stouthearted shepherd boy, volunteered to fight the giant Goliath. David and all of the army of Israel were insulted by the humiliating taunts of this formidable giant, but David knew that inspiration had brought him to save Israel. King Saul was so impressed with the faith and determination of this young boy that he appointed David to fight Goliath.

Goliath made sport of David's youth and lack of armament. David responded that he came in the name of the Lord of Hosts, the God of the armies of Israel, and that the whole assembly would learn that the Lord saveth not by the sword and the spear, "for the battle is the Lord's" (1 Samuel 17:47). Then David threw a rock from his sling with such force and accuracy that the stone sank deep into the forehead of Goliath. Goliath fell to the earth a dying man, and the Philistines fled in fear.

What has happened to David's living God? It is the greatest insult to reason to suggest that God, who spoke so freely to the prophets of the Old Testament including Abraham, Moses, Isaiah, and the other prophets, now stands mute, uncommunicative, and silent.

We may well ask, Does God love us less than those led by the ancient prophets? Do we need his guidance and instruction less? Reason suggests that this cannot be. Does he not care? Has he lost his voice? Has he gone on a permanent vacation? Does he sleep? The unreasonableness of each of these proposals is self-evident. ("Communion with the Holy Spirit," *Ensign*, May 1980, 12–13.)

TO VALIDATE THOSE who have authority, the Lord also stated, "All things shall be done by common consent in the Church, by much prayer and faith." (D&C 26:2.) Yet he also said, "that every man might speak in the name of God." (D&C 1:20.) How can this be? Every man and young man in the Church who lives in accordance with the Savior's teachings is ordained to the priesthood. The use of this power, however, is limited. Every father is to his family a patriarch and every mother a matriarch as co-equals in their distinctive parental roles. Members, men and women, may receive inspiration by the gift of the Holy Ghost for their personal lives and for their areas of responsibility.

Only the Prophet and President, and no one else, can use *all* of the keys of the kingdom of God on earth. In our time that man is President Gordon B. Hinckley. He and his counselors and the Quorum of the Twelve Apostles have delegated specific authority and responsibility to the other General Authorities and to local authorities and auxiliary leaders to direct the work in their own areas of responsibility. ("The Prophetic Voice," *Ensign*, May 1996, 6.)

THERE ARE SOME guidelines and rules necessary for one to be the recipient of revelation and inspiration; they include (1) to try honestly and sincerely to keep God's commandments, (2) to be spiritually attuned as a receiver of a divine message, (3) to ask in humble, fervent prayer, and (4) to seek with unwavering faith.

I testify that inspiration can be the spring of every person's hope, guidance, and strength. It is one of the magnificent treasures of life. It involves coming to the infinite knowledge of God.

How do revelation and inspiration operate? Each person has a built-in "receiving set" which, when fine-tuned, can be a receiver of divine communications. Said Job, "There is a spirit in man: and . . . the Almighty giveth them understanding" (Job 32:8). It is possible, like Nephi, to be led completely by the Spirit, "not knowing beforehand" that which should be done (see 1 Nephi 4:6).

How is inspiration received? Enos stated, "And while I was thus struggling in the spirit, behold, the voice of the Lord came into my mind" (Enos 1:10). One does not necessarily hear an audible voice. The spirit of revelation comes by divine confirmation. "I will tell you in your mind and in your heart, by the Holy Ghost, which shall come upon you and which shall dwell in your heart," says the Lord in the Doctrine and Covenants (D&C 8:2).

How was the voice of the Lord heard by Elijah the Tishbite? It was not the "strong wind [which] rent the mountains, and brake in pieces the rocks," nor "after the wind an earthquake," nor "after the earthquake a fire." It was "a still small voice" (see 1 Kings 19:11–12).

It is the inner voice of the Spirit, which has the capacity to whisper through and pierce all things (see D&C 85:6). Helaman says, "It was not a voice of thunder, neither was it a voice of a great tumultuous noise, but behold, it was a still voice of perfect mildness, as if it had been a whisper, and it did pierce even to the very soul" (Hel. 5:30).

Thus the Lord, by revelation, brings inspiration into one's mind as though a voice were speaking. ("Communion with the Holy Spirit," *Ensign,* May 1980, 14.)

INTEGRITY

THE STANDARD OF the common thief, "What can we get away with?" has become the standard for many in the world rather than what our own integrity ought to demand that we do. What has happened to self-respect and personal integrity, which would not permit even entertaining the idea of doing cheap or small things? An example might be our relationship with the financial credit by which the world's commerce is carried on. Often we forget that those who extend credit to us are also extending trust and confidence in us. Our own integrity is involved. I recall my father speaking with profound respect of a man whom father as a lawyer had taken through bankruptcy. Given time, this man paid in full all of his creditors who had trusted him and extended confidence in him, even though he was legally relieved of paying the debts. Our own integrity is a substantial part of our individual worth. ("The Dignity of Self," *Ensign*, May 1981, 8.)

INTEGRITY IS THE value we set on ourselves. It is a fulfillment of the duty we owe ourselves. An honorable man or woman will personally commit to live up to certain self-imposed expectations. They need no outside check or control. They are honorable in their inner core.

Where does the soul play its part best? Is it in outward show? Or is it within, where no mortal eyes can penetrate and where we have an inner defense against the tragedies of life?

Integrity is the light that shines from a disciplined conscience. It is the strength of duty within us. Moses gave the following counsel: "If a man vow a vow unto the Lord, or swear an oath to bind his soul with a bond; he shall not break his word, he shall do according to all that proceedeth out of his mouth." (Num. 30:2.) ("Integrity, the Mother of Many Virtues," *Ensign*, May 1982, 47.)

BEING TRUE TO oneself at times requires extraordinary strength and courage. For instance, in the early days of the Church it was very unpopular, even dangerous, to uphold Joseph Smith as a prophet of God. Lyman Wight was one of those imprisoned by the leaders of a mob in 1839.

General Wilson advised Brother Wight, "We do not wish to hurt you nor kill you," and then following an oath said, "but we have one thing against you, and that is, you are too friendly to Joe Smith, . . . Wight, you know all about his character."

Brother Wight said, "I do, sir."

"Will you swear all you know concerning him?" said Wilson.

Brother Wight then told Wilson he "believed . . . Joseph Smith to be the most philanthropic man he ever saw, and possessed of the most pure . . . principles—a friend to mankind, a maker of peace."

Wilson then observed, "Wight, I fear your life is in danger, for there is no end to the prejudice against Joe Smith."

"Kill and be damned, sir," was Brother Wight's answer.

Returning later that night, Wilson told Lyman Wight: "I regret to tell you your die is cast; your doom is fixed; you are sentenced to be shot tomorrow morning on the public square in Far West, at eight o'clock."

Brother Wight answered, "Shoot, and be damned."

The decree of execution of the prisoners was revoked the next morning. (See *History of the Church*, 3:446–47.) ("Integrity, the Mother of Many Virtues," *Ensign*, May 1982, 47.)

HOLDERS OF THE priesthood of God should be men of impeccable character. I have always admired the integrity of Father Abraham when he returned from Egypt to Palestine. He came with his nephew, Lot. Soon, there was strife between the herdmen of Abraham's cattle and the herdmen of Lot's cattle. "And Abram said unto Lot, Let there be no strife, I pray thee, between me and thee, and between my herdmen and thy herdmen; for we be brethren." (Genesis 13:8.) Abraham offered Lot his choice of property, either on his left hand or on his right. Lot chose the more productive land to the east, and so Abraham took the land to the west. In course of time, Lot and all his household were captured in battle and taken to Dan, over a hundred miles to the north. When Abraham heard of his fate, he armed 318 of his servants and went in pursuit. He not only rescued Lot and his family but also restored them to their property in Sodom. The King of Sodom returned from exile and, in gratitude, offered Abraham the spoils of victory. But these Abraham declined, saying, "I will not take from a thread even to a shoelatchet . . . I will not take any thing that is thine, lest thou shouldest say, I have made Abram rich." (Genesis 14:23.) In these episodes, Abraham demonstrated his fairness, integrity, and faith. And the Lord rewarded him with both spiritual and earthly blessings so that ultimately he prospered far more than Lot. ("We Seek After These Things," *Ensign*, May 1998, 44.)

NATURAL, INHERENT INTEGRITY is manifested almost every hour of every day of our lives. Those who unjustly profit at the expense of others may gain a fortune, but they forfeit something more important, which is their own integrity. Taking advantage of others is a counterfeit form of true success and honor. ("Integrity, the Mother of Many Virtues," *Ensign,* May 1982, 48.)

COMPLETE AND CONSTANT integrity is a great law of human conduct. There need to be some absolutes in life. There are some things that should not ever be done, some lines that should never be crossed, vows that should never be broken, words that should never be spoken, and thoughts that should never be entertained.

Yet there is a place for mercy, for equity, and for forgiveness. Even the stalwart Peter, the chief Apostle, was forgiven for a moment of weakness (see Luke 22:54–62). . . . I believe this incident strengthened Peter's commitment. He was never to be weak again. The resolve borne of that disappointment in his own temporary weakness tempered his metal into the hardest steel. He proved his devotion every day of his life thereafter, and in his death. So it can be with all of us. When we have been less than we ought to be and have fallen below our own standards, we can have newfound resolve and strength by forsaking our weakness. ("Integrity, the Mother of Many Virtues," *Ensign,* May 1982, 48–49.)

JESUS CHRIST

HOW DO WE accept Jesus of Nazareth?

We joyfully accept him without reservation as the greatest personage who ever lived on the face of the earth.

We believe him to be the Messiah, the Redeemer.

We glory in his mission and his doctrine.

We delight in him as the firstfruits of them that slept.

We worship him as the second member of the Godhead of three.

We humbly come to the Father through him, believing his words. "I am the way, the truth, and the life: no man cometh unto the Father, but by me" (John 14:6).

A hallmark of a disciple is described in the words of the Master: "By this shall all men know that ye are my disciples, if ye have love one to another" (John 13:35).

We can ask, with Job, the age-old question, "If a man die, shall he live again?" (Job 14:14). And the answering testimony is that Jesus Christ made the resurrection possible:

"For I know that my redeemer liveth, and that he shall stand at the latter day upon the earth:

"And though after my skin worms destroy this body, yet in my flesh shall I see God" (Job 19:25–26).

We testify with Isaiah that "his name shall be called Wonderful, Counsellor, The mighty God, The everlasting Father, The Prince of Peace" (Isaiah 9:6). Of the Resurrection we can declare with Paul: "O death, where is thy sting? O grave, where is thy victory?" (1 Corinthians 15:55.) ("The Resurrection," *Ensign*, May 1985, 32.)

THE MESSAGE OF Christ is eternal truth. There is no truth that it is not encompassed within it. But learning the will of the Father and doing it are two different things. ("A Legacy of the New Testament," 12th Annual CES Religious Educators' Symposium, 12 Aug. 1988.)

FOR THOSE WHO have honest doubts, let us hear what eyewitnesses had to say about Jesus of Nazareth. The ancient apostles were there. They saw it all. They participated. No one is more worthy of belief than they. Said Peter: "For we have not followed cunningly devised fables, when we made known unto you the power and coming of our Lord Jesus Christ, but were eyewitnesses of his majesty." (2 Pet. 1:16.) Said John: "For we have heard him ourselves, and know that this is indeed the

Christ, the Saviour of the world." (John 4:42.) Modern-day witnesses, Joseph Smith and Sidney Rigdon, declared: "For we saw
him, even on the right hand of God; and we heard the voice
bearing record that he is the Only Begotten of the Father."
(D&C 76:23.)

Peter counsels us to be "partakers of the divine nature." (2
Pet. 1:4.) The influence and teaching of the Messiah should have
a transcendence over all other interests and concerns in our
lives. We must constantly be reaching upward for the riches of
eternity, for the kingdom of God is within us. (See Luke 17:21.)
("A Personal Relationship with the Savior," *Ensign*, Nov. 1976,
59.)

AS A CARPENTER, Jesus would have been familiar with slivers
and thorny woods. As a child he would have learned that one
rarely gets a sliver when working the wood in the right direction. He would also have known more than any how slivers—-
small and painful—-divert attention from important matters.
The scourging of Jesus took place partly with thorns:

"Then the soldiers of the governor took Jesus into the common hall, and gathered unto him the whole band of soldiers.

"And they stripped him, and put on him a scarlet robe.

"And when they had platted a crown of thorns, they put it
upon his head, and a reed in his right hand: and they bowed
the knee before him, and mocked him, saying, Hail, King of the
Jews!

"And they spit upon him, and took the reed, and smote him
on the head" (Matthew 27:27–30).

Perhaps this cruel act was a perverse attempt to mimic the
placing of an emperor's laurel upon his head. Thus, there was
pressed down upon him a crown of thorns. He accepted the
pain as part of the great gift he had promised to make. How
poignant this was, considering that thorns signified God's dis-
pleasure as he cursed the ground for Adam's sake that hence-
forth it would bring forth thorns. But by wearing the crown,

Jesus transformed thorns into a symbol of his glory. ("A Crown of Thorns, a Crown of Glory," *Ensign,* May 1991, 69.)

IT IS NOT necessary for anyone to depend continually upon the testimony of another regarding the mediation, atonement, and resurrection of Christ as our Redeemer and Savior. Each can savor the sweetness of the truths of the gospel by obedience to the principles, ordinances, and covenants.

One can still go to the Garden of Gethsemane, but the Lord Jesus cannot be found there, nor is He in the Garden Tomb. He is not on the road to Emmaus, nor in Galilee, nor at Nazareth or Bethlehem. He must be found in one's heart. But He left us the great Comforter forever (see John 14:16) and the everlasting power of the priesthood. Of this power, Jacob, the son of Lehi, testified, "We truly can command in the name of Jesus and the very trees obey us, or the mountains, or the waves of the sea" (Jacob 4:6). ("The Supernal Gift of the Atonement," *Ensign,* Nov. 1988, 14.)

JOSEPH SMITH

[UPON THE DEATH of Joseph Smith,] some of [his] enemies exulted in their infamous deeds; and many proclaimed that the Church, which he had restored and for which he had given his life, would die with him.

But, to the surprise of its enemies, the Church did not die nor did the work of Joseph Smith cease with his mortal death. What has transpired in a century and a half bears eloquent testimony to the eternal nature of the work of this singularly remarkable man, Joseph Smith. The Church which he restored has had dramatic growth in many parts of the earth. It has produced an unequaled missionary system and an unmatched welfare program. Its governing system gives priesthood power and authority from God to all worthy male members, at the same time recognizing the exalted status of women as being equal to men. The Church has an inspired law of health and temporal well-being far ahead of its time. By revelation from God, the Church also possesses those keys, saving principles, and ordinances which will bring eternal exaltation to mankind, living and dead.

Because of these and other reasons, millions of people have become members of The Church of Jesus Christ of Latter-day Saints. But to each true believer there must ultimately and finally come a conviction that Joseph Smith was a revealer of truth, a prophet of God. Each must be convinced that God the Father and his Son Jesus Christ did appear to Joseph Smith and did commission him to reestablish the church of Christ upon the face of the earth. ("The Expanding Inheritance from Joseph Smith," *Ensign*, Nov. 1981, 75–76.)

THE EARLY HISTORY of this Church is quite complete, and it has been combed over many times. A search of the history brings little that is new, but the impression that looms largest is the stature of Joseph Smith. Joseph Smith will be discussed, debated, and challenged, but no one can argue about the success of the work which he introduced. There are many distinguishing aspects of The Church of Jesus Christ of Latter-day Saints with its lay priesthood, its unequaled missionary effort, the great welfare program, the women's organization, and all the rest, but that which makes it live is the individual testimony of the members of the Church, which testimony relates back to Joseph Smith as a true prophet. ("Joseph Smith, The Beloved Leader," Logan, Utah, Institute of Religion Fireside, 25 Jan. 1981.)

MANY YEARS AGO, I visited for the first time a wooded area of extraordinary natural beauty near Palmyra, New York. This area is known to members of The Church of Jesus Christ of Latter-day Saints as the Sacred Grove. On the day of our visit, the bees were kissing the wildflowers, and the soft zephyrs gently rustled the leaves of the great trees. It is a place of perfect peace and serenity. It was easy to believe that the heavens were opened and that the magnificent vision took place there.

I refer to the awesome experience of Joseph Smith when he beheld God the Father and his Son, Jesus Christ, in the spring of 1820. There has been no event more glorious, more controversial, nor more important in the story of Joseph Smith than this vision. It is possibly the most singular event to occur on the earth since the Resurrection. Those who do not believe it happened find it difficult to explain away. Too much has happened since its occurrence to summarily deny that it ever took place. Some years later, still suffering under the impact of that happening, Joseph said, "If I had not experienced what I have, I should not have known it myself" (*Millennial Star*, Nov. 1844, p. 93). . . .

Since no one was with Joseph when this great vision took place in the wooded grove near Palmyra, a testimony concerning its reality can come only by believing the truthfulness of Joseph Smith's own account or by the witness of the Holy Ghost, or both. I have such a conviction. It is a sure conviction that lies deep in my soul. As a special witness of the same Christ who appeared with the Father and instructed the boy Joseph Smith, I bear witness of the truthfulness of the magnificent First Vision near Palmyra. ("The Magnificent Vision Near Palmyra," *Ensign*, May 1984, 67, 69.)

NO DOUBT MANY of your investigators will already have heard something of Joseph Smith before they came in contact with the missionaries. We need not claim perfection for Joseph Smith, the way we do for the Savior. His humanity was part of his strength and part of his credibility. He never claimed to be perfect, so we should not try to claim something he did not claim for himself. He claimed only to be a mortal man with human feelings and imperfections, trying honestly to fulfil the divine mission given to him. He so describes himself in recorded counsel given to some of the members of the Church who had just arrived in Nauvoo on October 29, 1842. Said the Prophet: "I told them I was but a man, and they must not expect me to be perfect; if they expected perfection from me, I should expect it from them; but if they would bear with my infirmities and the infirmities of the brethren, I would likewise bear with their infirmities." (*History of the Church*, 5:181.) ("Joseph Smith and the Book of Mormon," Mission Presidents Seminar, Provo, Utah, 26 June 1987.)

JOY AND HAPPINESS

THE ODYSSEY TO happiness seems to depend almost entirely upon the degree of righteousness to which we attain in terms of the degree of selflessness we acquire, the amount of service we render, and the inner peace which we enjoy. It also hangs to some degree on those loved ones and friends on whose smile and welfare our happiness so much depends. ("The Odyssey to Happiness," *BYU Speeches*, 6 Jan. 1974, 326.)

THE JOY WE seek is not a temporary emotional high but a habitual inner joy learned from long experience and trust in God. ("The Voice of the Spirit," *Ensign*, Apr. 1994, 7.)

JOY COMES THROUGH listening to the Spirit. ("The Voice of the Spirit," *BYU Speeches*, 5 Sept. 1993, 2.)

THE KEY TO happiness does not lie alone in gender or marital status or parenthood or being free of physical challenges. Happiness comes from living the teachings of the Savior and having the vision to see what He would have us become. Remember what He said: "He that findeth his life shall lose it: and he that loseth his life for my sake shall find it" (Matt. 10:39). ("A Vision of What We Can Be," *Ensign,* Mar. 1996, 12.)

WORLDLY PLEASURES DO not match up to heavenly joy. ("The Voice of the Spirit," *Ensign*, Apr. 1994, 10.)

MANY YEARS OF listening to the tribulations of man have persuaded me that the satisfaction of all desires is completely

counterproductive to happiness. Instant and unrestrained gratification is the shortest and most direct route to unhappiness.
("The Odyssey to Happiness," *BYU Speeches*, 6 Jan. 1974, 319.)

SOME PEOPLE ARE seeking to find the abundant life. Paul made it
clear that it is "the spirit [that] giveth life" (2 Corinthians 3:6).
Indeed, the Savior said, "The words that I speak unto you, they
are spirit, and they are life" (John 6:63).

You may ask, then, "What are the fruits of the Spirit?" Paul
answered this by saying they are "love, joy, peace, longsuffer-
ing, gentleness, goodness, faith, meekness, temperance"
(Galatians 5:22–23). The joy we seek is not a temporary emotional high, but a habitual inner joy learned from long experience and trust in God. . . .

Lehi's teaching to his firstborn son Jacob declares: "Men are,
that they might have joy" (2 Nephi 2:25). To achieve this great
objective, we must "Give ear to the voice of the living God"
(D&C 50:1).

I wish to testify as a living witness that joy does come
through listening to the Spirit, for I have experienced it. Those
who live the gospel learn to live "after the manner of happiness," as did the Nephites (see 2 Nephi 5:27). All over the
world, in the many countries where the Church is established,
members could add their testimonies to mine. Abundant evidence verifies the promise of peace, hope, love, and joy as gifts
of the Spirit. Our voices join in a united petition for all of God's
children to partake of these gifts also. ("The Voice of the Spirit,"
Young Adult Fireside Satellite Broadcast, 5 Sept. 1993.)

MAY I SUGGEST a few things which might be done to prepare us
for a time when we are less affluent and possibly happier.

1. Wean ourselves away from dependence for our happiness upon mere material and physical things. This could mean
a bicycle instead of a car, and walking instead of a bicycle. It
may mean skim milk instead of cream.

2. Learn to do without many things and have some reserve

to fall back on. A recent article in Indiana concerning the present coal crisis and telling of a member of the Church there, a coal miner with a year's supply, brought much publicity and attention in the newspapers.

3. Develop an appreciation for the great gifts of God as found in nature, in the beauty of the seasons: the eloquent testimony of God in the sunrise and the sunsets, the leaves, the flowers, the birds, and the animals.

4. Engage in more physical activity that does not employ the use of hydrocarbons, including walking, jogging, swimming, and bicycling.

5. Have a hobby that involves your mind and your heart and can be done at home.

6. Pay your tithes and offerings. The keeping of this commandment will not insure riches—indeed, there is no assurance of being free from economic problems—but it will smooth out the rough spots, give the resolution and faith to understand and accept, and create a communion with the Savior which will enhance the inner core of strength and stability. . . .

7. Develop the habit of singing or, if this is not pleasant, whistling. . . . My father one time came home from a deer hunt empty-handed, but his heart was renewed and his spirit lifted. He recounted with great appreciation that one of his companions had frightened the deer away because he was always singing trumpet-voiced to himself as he walked through the pines and the quaking aspen. Father was more enriched by the mirth of the song than by the meat of the venison. ("The Blessings of Adversity," *BYU Speeches*, 21 Feb. 1978, 29.)

DURING THE PAST two years, and indeed for about five years of my life, I have lived in countries where most of the people are far below the poverty level of the United States. During this last period of time, . . . we made our home in São Paulo, Brazil. During most of that time our neighbor to the north was constructing a new home. The carpenters, the tile setters, the plumbers, and the cabinet workers on that house received far below what we know as the minimum wage. In fact, some lived in a shack on the site. There was cold running water available from the end of a hose, but no warm or hot water. Their work day was from 6:00 A.M. till about 5:30 P.M. This meant that at about 5:00 in the morning they would begin to prepare their meals and get ready for work.

My college-age daughter, Lisa, could not help complaining that she was awakened almost every morning by their clarion-voiced singing. They sang, they laughed, they chattered—only occasionally unpleasantly—the whole day through. When I explained to Lisa how little money they made and how little they had she made an interesting observation, "But Dad, they seem so happy." And happy they were. Not one owned an automobile, nor even a bicycle—just the clothes on their backs—but they found life pleasant and fulfilling. We were reminded again how little it takes to make some people happy. ("The Blessings of Adversity," *BYU Speeches,* 21 Feb. 1978, 27.)

[FACING THOSE TIMES that challenge our quality of life,] may mean that to be happy we are not going to be able to rely upon physical comforts and to satisfy our whims, but must learn to draw upon inner strengths and inner resources. It will likely mean that we will find our entertainment and pleasure in simpler things that do not cost money and are closer to home. Hopefully, it will mean the development of untapped inner strengths and resources that will bring an inner peace and a self-understanding so articulately explained by Anwar Sadat in a recent essay which no doubt many of you read in *Time* magazine. He related his experience of being confined in a British jail. Like Sadat, hopefully we will find ourselves and like ourselves better, be more at peace with our surroundings, and appreciate more our fellowmen. We will become less sated with the material and the mechanical and learn to cultivate a taste for bread and milk. ("The Blessings of Adversity," *BYU Speeches,* 21 Feb. 1978, 28–29.)

THE ODYSSEY TO happiness lies in the dimension of the heart. Such a journey is made on stepping-stones of selflessness, wisdom, contentment, and faith. The enemies of progress and fulfillment are self-doubt, a poor self-image, self-pity, bitterness, and despair. By substituting simple faith and humility for these enemies we can move rapidly in our journey to true felicity. ("The Odyssey to Happiness," *BYU Speeches*, 6 Jan. 1974, 323.)

JUDGING

MANY OF YOU [missionaries] are going to the poor of the earth. You will live among them. You will eat their food. You will learn to love them. Please don't judge them by our measurements of success. That is, materialism. You will find that they will take their humble provender out of their own mouths, and out of the mouths of their children, to give it to you. Always be grateful and appreciative for whatever they have to offer. Don't be critical of their customs and their country. Please judge them by what is in their hearts rather than by what they own. (Christmas fireside address, Missionary Training Center, Provo, Utah, 24 Dec. 1992.)

JUDGMENT

ALL OF US have made wrong turns along the way. I believe the kind and merciful God, whose children we are, will judge us as lightly as He can for the wrongs that we have done and give us the maximum blessing for the good that we do. Alma's sublime utterance seems to me to be an affirmation of this. Said Alma, "And not many days hence the Son of God shall come in his glory; and his glory shall be the glory of the Only Begotten of the Father, full of grace, equity, and truth, full of patience, mercy, and long-suffering, quick to hear the cries of his people and to answer their prayers." (Alma 9:26.) ("Woman, Why Weepest Thou?" *Ensign*, Nov. 1996, 53.)

KNOWLEDGE

THE ABUNDANT LIFE involves an endless search for knowledge, light, and truth. ("The Abundant Life," *Ensign,* Nov. 1985, 7.)

QUESTIONS—IN THE sense of searching, not doubting—seem to be essential for learning. They are a primary means of expressing curiosity, the self-motivation to search for knowledge. ("Learning for Eternity," *BYU Speeches,* 18 Nov. 1997, 3.)

WE ARE ALL in pursuit of truth and knowledge. The nurturing of a simple, untroubled faith does not limit us in the pursuit of growth and accomplishment. On the contrary, it may intensify and hasten our progress. This is so because our natural gifts and powers of achievement are increasingly enhanced by the endless growth of knowledge. ("An Untroubled Faith," *Ensign,* Mar. 1988, 69.)

THINKING CLEARLY DOES not mean we can think "by infection, catching an opinion like a cold" (John Ruskin, in *Dictionary of Humorous Quotations,* ed. Evan Esar [New York: Paperback Library, Inc., 1949], p. 154). Thinking clearly is the ability to discern things that matter most and separate them from things of less importance. ("Learning for Eternity," *BYU Speeches,* 18 Nov. 1997, 3.)

IN THE INFINITE process of accepting and rejecting information in the search for light, truth, and knowledge, almost everyone may have at one time or another some private questions. That is part of the learning process. Many are like the biblical father of the child with the "dumb spirit" who pleaded with the Savior: "Lord, I believe; help thou mine unbelief." (Mark 9:24.) ("The Abundant Life," *Ensign,* Nov. 1985, 8.)

SOME PEOPLE IN their searching . . . are not seeking for truth but are given to contention. They do not sincerely seek to learn; rather they desire to dispute, to show their supposed learning and thus cause strife. ("The Truth Shall Make You Free," *Ensign*, Sept. 1998, 5.)

I URGE YOU not to be unduly concerned about the intricacies, the complexities, and any seeming contradictions that seem to trouble many of us. Sometimes we spend time satisfying our intellectual egos and trying to find all the answers before we accept any. ("An Untroubled Faith," *Ensign*, Mar. 1988, 69.)

LEADERS, SUSTAINING OF

THERE IS A certain arrogance in thinking that any of us may be more spiritually intelligent, more learned, or more righteous than the Councils called to preside over us. Those Councils are more in tune with the Lord than any individual persons they preside over, and the individual members of the Councils are generally guided by those Councils. In this church, where we have lay leadership, it is inevitable that some will be placed in authority over us who have a different background from our own. This does not mean that those with other honorable vocational or professional qualifications are any less entitled to the spirit of their office than any other. Some of the great bishops of my lifetime include a brick mason, a grocer, a farmer, a dairyman, and one who ran an ice cream business. What any may have lacked in formal education was insignificant. They were humble men, and because they were humble they were taught and magnified by the Holy Spirit. Without exception they were greatly strengthened as they learned to labor diligently to fulfill their callings and to minister to the Saints they were called to preside over. So it is with all of the callings in the Church. President Thomas S. Monson teaches us, "Whom the Lord calls, the Lord qualifies" (in Conference Report, Apr. 1988, p. 52; or *Ensign*, May 1988, p. 43). ("Keeping Covenants and Honoring the Priesthood," *Ensign*, Nov. 1993, 38.)

I STRONGLY COUNSEL all who have membership in this Church to follow the teachings and counsel of those who now have the keys as prophets, seers, and revelators. They are the ones who will inspire us to deal with the vicissitudes of our time. I plead with all not to try to selectively invoke gospel principles or scripture to wrongly justify spiritual disobedience, or to separate themselves from the responsibilities of covenants and ordinances contrary to the counsel of those who have the prophetic voice in the Church. The scriptures and doctrines of the Church are not, as Peter warned, "of any private interpretation." (2 Pet. 1:20.)

Great temporal and spiritual strength flows from following those who have the keys of the kingdom of God in our time. Personal strength and power result from obedience to eternal principles taught by the living legates of the Lord. May the Spirit of God rest upon us as we follow the living oracles. ("The Keys That Never Rust," *Ensign*, Nov. 1994, 74.)

LEADERSHIP

THE MOST ENCOMPASSING short course on leadership was given by the Savior himself: "And he saith unto them, Follow me" (Matt. 4:19). A leader cannot ask of others what he is not willing to do himself. Our safest course is to follow the example of the Savior, and our security is to listen to and follow the direction of his prophet, the President of the Church. ("These I Will Make My Leaders," *Ensign*, Nov. 1980, 35.)

SOME YEARS AGO I was traveling in the Rosario Argentina Mission up in the northern part of Argentina. As we were traveling along the road, we passed a large herd of cattle being moved. The herd was moving peaceably and without difficulty. The herd was quiet. There were no dogs. Out in front leading the herd were three gauchos on horseback, each about fifteen or twenty yards apart. These three horsemen were slumped forward in their saddles, completely relaxed, confident that the herd would follow them. At the rear of the herd was a single rider bringing up the rear. He, too, was slumped forward in his saddle as if he were sleeping. The whole herd moved peacefully, quietly, and was subdued. From that experience it seemed obvious to me that leadership is about three-fourths show-the-way and about one-fourth follow-up.

The leader himself, when directing, does not have to be bombastic and loud. Those who are called to lead in the ministry of the Master are not called to be chiefs or dictators. They are called to be good shepherds. ("These I Will Make My Leaders," *Ensign,* Nov. 1980, 35.)

EVER SINCE I was first in Egypt in World War II, I have been interested in ancient ruins. There is a fascination in observing why some columns still stand and others have toppled over. Very frequently those still standing do so because they bear a weight on top. There is, I believe, a parallel principle in leadership. Those who stand faithful to their priesthood are often those who bear some weight of responsibility. Those involved are those most likely to be committed. So a successful quorum leader will want all of those in his quorum to have an opportunity to serve with some kind of calling appropriate to the circumstances. ("These I Will Make My Leaders," *Ensign,* Nov. 1980, 35.)

MOST OF US who are called to leadership in the Church feel that we are inadequate because of inexperience, lack of ability, or meager learning and education. Of the many descriptions of Moses is the following: "Now the man Moses was very meek, above all the men which were upon the face of the earth" (Num. 12:3).

Years ago I recall President John Kelly, who was then presiding over the Fort Worth Texas Stake, called Brother Felix Velasquez to be the president of the Spanish branch. This good man worked, as I recall, as a car inspector on the railroad. When President Kelly called him to this service, he responded, "President, I cannot be the president of the Spanish branch. I cannot read." President Kelly then promised him that if he would accept the calling and labor diligently to magnify it, he would be sustained and blessed. With the help of the Lord, this humble man, through his diligent efforts, became able to read. He served well as branch president and for many years subsequent and now is serving in the high council of that stake. The Lord blesses his servants in many ways. ("These I Will Make My Leaders," *Ensign*, Nov. 1980, 36.)

A LEADER MUST be a good listener. He must be willing to take counsel. He must show a genuine concern and love for those under his stewardship. No priesthood leader can ever be effective unless he has firmly in mind the transcending keys of leadership found in section 121 of the Doctrine and Covenants:

"No power or influence can or ought to be maintained by virtue of the priesthood, only by persuasion, by long-suffering, by gentleness and meekness, and by love unfeigned;

"By kindness, and pure knowledge, which shall greatly enlarge the soul without hypocrisy, and without guile—

"Reproving betimes with sharpness, when moved upon by the Holy Ghost; and then showing forth afterwards an increase of love toward him whom thou hast reproved, lest he esteem thee to be his enemy" (D&C 121:41–43).

In my experience, the Holy Ghost moves to reprove with sharpness only very rarely. Any reproving should be done gently in an effort to convince the one being reproved that it is done in his own interest. ("These I Will Make My Leaders," *Ensign*, Nov. 1980, 35.)

SOMETIMES LEADERS hold the reins too tightly, often limiting the natural talents and gifts of those who are called to labor at their sides.

Leadership does not always produce a harmonious symphony of faith, skills, and talents of the group, producing maximum effectiveness and power. It is sometimes a loud solo. President Lee taught a fuller meaning of the scripture, "Wherefore, now let every man learn his duty, and to act in the office in which he is appointed, in all diligence" (D&C 107:99). In addition to having all of us learn our duties, leaders should let, or permit, their associates to be fully effective within their own office and callings, and helpers should be fully clothed with appropriate authority.

Recently Elder Howard W. Hunter effectively taught the Regional Representatives on this subject: "The story is told of how in ancient Greece, Alexander the Great went to the brilliant Diogenes who was busy doing some research. Alexander hovered about Diogenes anxiously and asked: 'How can I help you?' Diogenes replied simply: 'Please stand out of my light!'" ("These I Will Make My Leaders," *Ensign*, Nov. 1980, 37.)

A YEAR OR so ago I sat in an elders quorum meeting. The members of the presidency were fine, capable young men; but when they got around to sharing the quorum responsibilities and getting the work done, they limited it to those who were present and who would volunteer. Not one assignment was given.

One of the first principles we must keep in mind is that the work of the Lord goes forward through assignments. Leaders receive and give assignments. This is an important part of the necessary principle of delegating. No one appreciates a willing volunteer more than I, but the total work cannot be done as the Lord wants it done merely by those doing the work who may be present at meetings. I have often wondered what the earth would look like if the Lord in the Creation had left the work to be done only by volunteers.

If we look upon fulfilling of assignments as building the kingdom of God and as being an opportunity as well as a privilege and an honor, then assignments and challenges should certainly be given to every member of the quorum. Such involvement should include, with appropriate wisdom and discretion, those who perhaps need them the most—the inactive and the partially active brethren. Assignments always should be given with the greatest love, consideration, and kindness.

Those asked to respond should be treated with respect and appreciation.

General Authorities regularly receive assignments from the First Presidency and the President of the Council of the Twelve. Whether such assignments come in writing, as most do, or are personally given, they are always couched with "if you please" or "if it is convenient" or "Would you kindly attend to this or to that." Never are these assignments framed in terms of a command or a demand. ("These I Will Make My Leaders," *Ensign*, Nov. 1980, 34.)

MARRIAGE

YOU MIGHT WONDER, "How can a marriage be constantly enriched?" Adam, speaking of Eve, said, "This is now bone of my bones, and flesh of my flesh." (Gen. 2:23.)

We build our marriages with endless friendship, confidence, integrity, and by administering and sustaining each other in our difficulties.

There are a few simple, relevant questions which each person, whether married or contemplating marriage, should honestly ask in an effort to become "one flesh." They are:

First, am I able to think of the interest of my marriage and partner first before I think of my own desires?

Second, how deep is my commitment to my companion, aside from any other interests?

Third, is he or she my best friend?

Fourth, do I have respect for the dignity of my partner as a person of worth and value?

Fifth, do we quarrel over money? Money itself seems neither to make a couple happy, nor the lack of it, necessarily, to make them unhappy, but money is often a symbol of selfishness.

Sixth, is there a spiritually sanctifying bond between us?

I commend to all the excellent discussion by President Kimball, "Marriage and Divorce," in which he reminds us,

"[There are] no combination[s] of power [which] can destroy [a] marriage except the power within either or both of the spouses themselves." (*Marriage and Divorce*, Deseret Book, p. 17.) ("The Enriching of Marriage," *Ensign*, Nov. 1977, 10.)

I URGE THE husbands and fathers of this church to be the kind of a man your wife would not want to be without. I urge the sisters of this church to be patient, loving, and understanding with their husbands. Those who enter into marriage should be fully prepared to establish their marriage as the first priority in their lives.

It is destructive to the feeling essential for a happy marriage for either party to say to the other marriage partner, "I don't need you." This is particularly so because the counsel of the Savior was and is to become one flesh: "For this cause shall a man leave father and mother, and shall cleave to his wife: and they twain shall be one flesh[.]

"Wherefore they are no more twain, but one flesh." (Matt. 19:5–6.) It is far more difficult to be of one heart and mind than to be physically one. This unity of heart and mind is manifest in sincere expressions of "I appreciate you" and "I am proud of you." Such domestic harmony results from forgiving and forgetting, essential elements of a maturing marriage relationship. Someone has said that we should keep our eyes wide open before marriage and half shut afterward. (Magdeleine Scudéry, as cited in *The International Dictionary of Thoughts*, Chicago: J. G. Ferguson Publishing Co., 1969, p. 472.) True charity ought to begin in marriage, for it is a relationship that must be rebuilt every day. ("Father, Come Home," *Ensign*, May 1993, 36.)

THERE IS NO great or majestic music which constantly produces the harmony of a great love. The most perfect music is a welding of two voices into one spiritual solo. Marriage is the way provided by God for the fulfillment of the greatest of human needs, based upon mutual respect, maturity, selflessness, decency, commitment, and honesty. Happiness in marriage and parenthood can exceed a thousand times any other happiness. ("The Enriching of Marriage," *Ensign,* Nov. 1977, 11.)

IT MUST BE recognized that some marriages just fail. To those in that circumstance, I extend understanding because every divorce carries heartache with it. I hope what I say will not be disturbing. In my opinion, any promise between a man and a woman incident to a marriage ceremony rises to the dignity of a covenant. The family relationship of father, mother, and child is the oldest and most enduring institution in the world. It has survived vast differences of geography and culture. This is because marriage between man and woman is a natural state and is ordained of God. It is a moral imperative. Those marriages performed in our temples, meant to be eternal relationships, then, become the most sacred covenants we can make. The sealing power given by God through Elijah is thus invoked, and God becomes a party to the promises.

What, then, might be "just cause" for breaking the covenants of marriage? Over a lifetime of dealing with human problems, I have struggled to understand what might be considered "just cause" for breaking of covenants. I confess I do not claim the wisdom nor authority to definitely state what is "just cause." Only the parties to the marriage can determine this. They must bear the responsibility for the train of consequences which inevitably follow if these covenants are not honored. In my opinion, "just cause" should be nothing less serious than a prolonged and apparently irredeemable relationship which is destructive of a person's dignity as a human being.

At the same time, I have strong feelings about what is not provocation for breaking the sacred covenants of marriage. Surely it is not simply "mental distress," nor "personality differences," nor "having grown apart," nor having "fallen out of love." This is especially so where there are children. Enduring divine counsel comes from Paul: "Husbands, love your wives, even as Christ also loved the church, and gave himself for it." (Eph. 5:25.) ("Father, Come Home," *Ensign,* May 1993, 36–37.)

MARRIAGE RELATIONSHIPS CAN be enriched by better communication. One important way is to pray together. This will resolve many of the differences, if there are any, between the couple before sleep comes. I do not mean to overemphasize differences but they are real, and make things interesting. Our differences are the little pinches of salt which can make the marriage seem sweeter. We communicate in a thousand ways, such as a smile, a brush of the hair, a gentle touch, and remembering each day to say "I love you" and the husband to say "You're beautiful." Some other important words to say, when appropriate, are "I'm sorry." Listening is excellent communication. ("The Enriching of Marriage," *Ensign,* Nov. 1977, 10.)

COMPLETE TRUST IN each other is one of the greatest enriching factors in marriage. Nothing devastates the core of mutual trust necessary to maintain a fulfilling relationship like infidelity. There is never a justification for adultery. Despite this destructive experience, occasionally marriages are saved and families preserved. To do so requires the aggrieved party to be capable of giving unreserved love great enough to forgive and forget. It requires the errant party to want desperately to repent and actually forsake evil.

Our loyalty to our eternal companion should not be merely physical, but mental and spiritual as well. Since there are no harmless flirtations and no place for jealousy after marriage, it is best to avoid the very appearance of evil by shunning any questionable contact with another to whom we are not married.

Virtue is the strong glue which holds it all together. Said the Lord, "Thou shalt love thy wife with all thy heart, and shalt cleave unto her and none else." (D&C 42:22.) ("The Enriching of Marriage," *Ensign,* Nov. 1977, 10.)

OF ALL THAT can bless marriages, there is one special enriching ingredient, which above all else will help join a man and a woman together in a very real, sacred, spiritual sense. It is the presence of the divine in marriage. Shakespeare, speaking in

Henry the Fifth, said, "God, the best maker of all marriages, combine your hearts in one." (*Henry V,* 5:2.) God is also the best keeper of marriages.

There are many things which go into making a marriage enriching, but they seem to be of the husk. Having the companionship and enjoying the fruits of a Holy and Divine Presence is the kernel of a great happiness in marriage. Spiritual oneness is the anchor. Slow leaks in the sanctifying dimension of marriage often cause marriages to become flat tires. ("The Enriching of Marriage," *Ensign,* Nov. 1977, 10–11.)

IN THE ENRICHING of marriage the big things are the little things. It is a constant appreciation for each other and a thoughtful demonstration of gratitude. It is the encouraging and the helping of each other to grow. Marriage is a joint quest for the good, the beautiful, and the divine. ("The Enriching of Marriage," *Ensign,* Nov. 1977, 11.)

MEDITATION

[SOME TIME] AGO, Elder and Sister F. Arthur Kay and I arrived on the beautiful and exotic island of Tahiti. Our flight arrived at the Papeete airport at about four in the morning. We were met at the airport by a group of local Church leaders headed by our Regional Representative, Victor Cave. We quickly assembled our bags and headed for the hotel to get what rest we could before the day's activities began.

Our route took us through the deserted, dimly lighted streets of Papeete. In the dark, we saw the faint figure of a man crossing the street in front of Brother Cave's car. Brother Cave gave the man a lot of room and said to Brother and Sister Kay: "That man is Brother So-and-so. He is hurrying to get to the temple. The first session of the temple doesn't begin until nine o'clock, but he wants to be there well in advance."

"How far away does he live?" asked Brother Kay. The answer: "Two or three blocks." Brother Cave indicated that the caretakers open the temple gates early and that this man comes in and watches the day begin within the sacred precincts of the beautiful temple in Papeete.

I marveled at the faith of that man, who is willing to forgo his sleep and other activities in order to follow this ritual of meditation and contemplation. Some would no doubt say, "How foolish! How wasteful of time that could be spent sleeping or studying." I choose to hope that in those programmed hours of meditation and contemplation that faithful man is coming to know himself and his Creator. ("An Untroubled Faith," *BYU Speeches*, 28 Sept. 1986, 46.)

MERCY

MORAL STANDARDS MUST be maintained. In large measure, those who are disobedient punish themselves. As the Lord said through Jeremiah: "Thine own wickedness shall correct thee, and thy backslidings shall reprove thee." (Jeremiah 2:19.) Those entrusted with judicial responsibility in the Kingdom of God must see that the Church remains clean so that the living waters of life flow unimpeded.

However, true religion is not looking primarily for weaknesses, faults, and errors. It is the spirit of strengthening and overlooking faults even as we would wish our own faults to be overlooked. When we focus our entire attention on what may be wrong rather than what is right, we miss the sublime beauty and essence of the sweet gospel of the Master. ("The Weightier Matters of the Law: Judgment, Mercy and Faith," *Ensign*, Nov. 1997, 54.)

I AM FRANK to admit that when I say my prayers I do not ask for justice; I ask for mercy. ("The Weightier Matters of the Law: Judgment, Mercy and Faith," *Ensign*, Nov. 1997, 54.)

MISSIONARY WORK

WE ARE ANNOUNCING no new missionary programs. . . . We do not have any new organization to announce. The manuals, the guidelines, and the instructions are unchanged. Certainly, there is nothing new in the doctrine, nor in the covenants.

. . . What we seek to do is to join with you in calling forth the Spirit of God upon our work. The priesthood quorums, the auxiliary organizations, the stake missions, the member-missionary class are available. Everything is in place. It is felt at this time that no new changes in programs or organizations are needed. Perhaps the only change that is really needed is to change ourselves. Missionary work begins with each of us at home. It ought to be motivated more by fresh faith and conviction rather than obligation. It involves quiet living. If we do this, missionary work in the stakes and the wards will be fruitful.

How can I change? I can certainly change my attitude. I can change *my* commitment. I can change my approach. Hopefully, with diligent study of the scriptures and obedience to saving principles, I can expand my soul. Missionary work is a natural manifestation of the pure love of Christ. We need to learn and teach the gospel doctrines—the requirements, principles and promises. Hopefully, like the sons of Mosiah, we will become "instruments in the hands of God in bringing many to a knowledge of truth" and "to the knowledge of their Redeemer" (Mosiah 27:36.) (Address to Regional Representatives and Mission Presidents, Salt Lake City, Utah, 5 Apr. 1985.)

THE FIRST PRESIDENCY have the opportunity to meet with many ambassadors, prime ministers, rulers, and prominent public and political figures from all over the world. Frequently they say, "We have met your missionaries. We have seen them in many places." Sometimes these prominent people visit the Missionary Training Center in Provo and see the thousands of missionaries there. These officials always seem to be greatly impressed. The missionaries appear well groomed and dignified. Sometimes they say, "We would like our children to be associated with your young people at one of your schools."

Being a missionary is a continuing responsibility. Returned missionaries need to be exemplary in living the principles which they taught to others in the mission field. President Spencer W. Kimball said, "Please, you returned missionaries . . . , please do not abandon in appearance or principle or habit the great experiences of the mission field when you were like Alma and the sons of Mosiah, as the very angels of God to the people you met and taught and baptized. We do not expect you to wear a tie, white shirt, and a dark blue suit every day now that you are back in school. But surely it is not too much to ask that your good grooming be maintained, that your personal habits reflect cleanliness and dignity and pride in the principles of the gospel you taught. We ask you for the good of the kingdom and all those who have done and yet do take pride in you." (*The Teachings of Spencer W. Kimball,* edited by Edward L. Kimball, p. 593.) ("We Seek After These Things," *Ensign,* May 1998, 45.)

WHEN I WAS a boy, I remember attending the homecoming of Ames Bagley who came home from a mission in a distant land across the sea. His mother, Sister Amanda Bagley, had been a wise Stake Relief Society President. Sister Bagley was invited to speak at her son's homecoming sacrament meeting. In her response, she wondered why we send our missionaries so far, spend so much time, effort, and money to support missionaries so far away, when our next-door neighbors and friends at home have souls just as important and precious as those in distant lands. We may have a tendency to think if we are sending missionaries that we are taking care of our responsibilities for this important work. If we feel we are relieved of our duty to our nonmember neighbors because full-time missionaries happen to be working in our neighborhoods, it is most unfortunate. All of us have neighbors, all of us have friends, and many of us have kinsmen who are not members. (Address to Regional Representatives and Mission Presidents, Salt Lake City, Utah, 5 Apr. 1985.)

I DO NOT believe that we need to be bombastic, loud, pushy, or insensitive in our approach [to missionary work]. Our personal missionary work should not be so threatening as to destroy our personal friendships and good will. There should be nothing approaching even a hint of a threat or ultimatum of any kind. Alma said we should "use boldness, but not overbearance." (Alma 38:12) The light of the gospel should show in our countenances as well as our actions. I do, however, believe that we need to be courageous, resourceful, and sensitive. The Lord counsels us, "And let your preaching be the warning voice, every man to his neighbor in mildness and in meekness." (D&C 38:41.) (Address to Regional Representatives and Mission Presidents, Salt Lake City, Utah, 5 Apr. 1985.)

DESPITE THE SUCCESS we are enjoying [in our missionary efforts], no doubt we can improve. We hope for steady growth and activity in all phases of missionary work, including among the members. Hopefully this increase will be based upon our increasing knowledge of God and his holy word on the earth. We would rather not have a great spurt or surge which dies out after a time. We don't need a quick fix. We need fathers and families. Steady, sustained efforts will bring great results. (Address to Regional Representatives and Mission Presidents, Salt Lake City, Utah, 5 Apr. 1985.)

WE HAVE NOTED in this conference that the Spirit of the Lord must be present if investigators are to be converted to the gospel. The same is true if members are to be converted to their missionary responsibilities. Quorum leaders have the responsibility to prepare members to feel the Spirit of the Lord so that their missionary actions will be prompted by inner conviction rather than a mere sense of obligation or duty. (Address to Regional Representatives and Mission Presidents, Salt Lake City, Utah, 5 Apr. 1985.)

As THE HUMBLE servants of God—the General Authorities, the missionaries, and others—travel throughout the world, we are compelled to ask: What can we do for the peoples of the earth? What can we give that no one else can? What can justify the great expenditure of effort, time, and means to "go . . . into all of the world" (Mark 16:15), as the Savior commanded. We cannot change the economy of countries. We do not seek to change governments. The answer is simple. We can offer the hope promised by the Savior: "Peace in this world and eternal life in the world to come." (D&C 59:23.) Lives are changed as the servants of God teach God's children everywhere to accept and keep the commandments of God. Anyone, regardless of culture or economic circumstance, can go to the depths of his spiritual wells and drink of that water. He that partakes of this water, as the Savior said, "shall never thirst; but . . . shall be in him a well of water springing up unto everlasting life." (John 14:40.) The basic needs of mankind identified by Dr. Wirthlin—self-esteem, peace of mind, and personal contentment—can be fully satisfied by faithful obedience to the commandments of God. This is true of any person in any country or culture.

Though many lack the necessities of life, I take comfort in the words of Nephi. "But they were . . . one, the children of Christ, and the heirs to the kingdom of God." (4 Ne. 1:17.) ("Heirs to the Kingdom of God," *Ensign*, May 1995, 62.)

MODESTY

UPON RETURNING FROM living in South America I was struck by the lack of self-esteem revealed in the manner by which so many people now clothe themselves in public. To attract attention or in the name of comfort and informality, many have sunk not only to immodesty but to slovenliness. Against their own self-interest, they present themselves to others in the worst possible way.

In forsaking the great principle of modesty, society has paid a price in the violation of a greater but related principle—that of chastity. The purveyors of the concept of irresponsible sexual relations that degrade and brutalize the participants have grossly masqueraded and completely missed the purpose of these divine gifts. ("The Dignity of Self," *Ensign*, May 1981, 9.)

MORALITY

THERE IS A popular notion that doing our own thing or doing what feels good is our own business and affects no one but us. The deadly scourges that are epidemic all over the world have flourished in the context of this popular notion. But this is simply not true.

All immoral behavior directly impacts society. Even innocent people are affected. Drug and alcohol abuse have public consequences, as do illegitimacy, pornography, and obscenity. The public cost in human life and tax dollars for these so-called private choices is enormous: poverty, crime, a less-educated work force, and mounting demands for government spending to fix problems that cannot be fixed by money. It simply is not true that our private conduct is our own business. Our society is the sum total of what millions of individuals do in their private lives. That sum total of private behavior has worldwide public consequences of enormous magnitude. There are no completely private choices. ("Will I Be Happy?" *Ensign*, May 1987, 80.)

YOU YOUNG, SINGLE men who hold the priesthood and are dating the splendid young ladies of the Church have a duty to do everything you can to protect their physical safety and virtue. The Priesthood you hold gives you the greater responsibility to see that the high moral standards of the Church are always maintained. The Lord knows that you know better than to approach the edge of sexual enticement. You will lose part of that which is sacred about you if you go beyond the edge and abuse the great powers of procreation. Each of us is accountable for his own actions. How can any of us hope to play a great role in time or eternity if we have no power of self-control? ("Acting for Ourselves and Not Being Acted Upon," *Ensign,* Nov. 1995, 47.)

ADULTS AND CHILDREN need to know that public and private morality is not outmoded. We need to love our children enough to teach them that laws, policies, and public programs with a moral and ethical basis are necessary for the preservation of a peaceful, productive, compassionate, and happy society. Without the qualities and characteristics of integrity, honesty, commitment, loyalty, respect for others, fidelity, and virtue, a free and open society cannot endure. ("Will I Be Happy?" *Ensign,* May 1987, 80.)

In our society many sacred values have been eroded in the name of freedom of expression. The vulgar and the obscene are protected in the name of freedom of speech. The mainstream of society has become more tolerant, even accepting, of conduct that Jesus, Moses, the Prophet Joseph Smith, and other prophets have warned against since the beginning of human history.

We should not allow our personal values to erode, even if others think we are peculiar. We have always been regarded as a peculiar people. However, being spiritually correct is much better than being politically correct. ("Search Me, O God, and Know My Heart," *Ensign,* May 1998, 18–19.)

MOTHERHOOD

IT IS MY feeling that we grossly underestimate the sacred nature of motherhood. Psychiatric experts remind us that there are certain fundamental, biological facts which influence the psyche of those who bring new life into the world. One says, "The ability of mothers to accept infants after they are born is underrated and underestimated." (Dr. S. Bolter, *American Journal of Psychiatry*, Oct. 1962. pp. 312–16.) Childbearing is a basic biological and psychological, privileged function of womankind. ("The Sanctity of Life," *Ensign*, May 1975, 28.)

OBEDIENCE

A FEW MAY lack understanding of the real commitment of the faithful. For instance, a critic [of the Church] recently wrote that obedience to commandments such as tithing is mandatory. In order to claim certain blessings, obedience is certainly obligatory, but compliance is never mandatory—that is, forced. Nothing is mandatory in this church. Free agency is a cardinal principle of obedience. Obedience comes from love of God and a commitment to his work. The only punishment for serious transgression or apostasy is the removal of members from the society and fellowship of the Church. (See D&C 134:10.) ("The Abundant Life," *Ensign*, Nov. 1985, 8–9.)

IS PERSONAL SELF-SUFFICIENCY one of the reasons men and women may lack faith? Some seem afraid to look to any source of wisdom and knowledge above themselves. They rely only on the secular source of learning.

A small number may claim fealty and loyalty to the Church but think it smart, sophisticated, or trendy to be a little rebellious, a little bit independent, and to disparage some of the traditional doctrines handed down by the Prophet Joseph Smith and his successors. This may result from a lack of divine knowledge. When I was a boy, one frequently maligned doctrine was the Word of Wisdom. Some took offense when Church leaders taught it. Now scientific proof, unknown in my youth, has established the Word of Wisdom to be a great law of physical health, even though, in my opinion, its greatest benefits are spiritual.

I have heard some say, "Well, I can believe all of the revelations but one." It is hard to understand this logic. If one believes that revelations come from a divine source, how can one pick and choose? Acceptance of the gospel should be complete and absolute, with full heart and soul. ("The Abundant Life," *Ensign*, Nov. 1985, 9.)

ORDINANCES

WE ALL RECALL the statement of Brigham Young, "We never began to build a temple without the bells of hell beginning to ring." (*Discourses of Brigham Young*, p. 410.) Elder W. Grant Bangerter has taught us that the reason for this devilish activity is that every ordinance of the gospel further restricts the adversary. He is thereby bound against intruding into the lives and conduct of those who have kept their covenants faithfully. It is true of those who have made the baptismal covenant. It is true of those who are ordained to the priesthood. It is especially true in relation to those who have gone to the temple to make covenants and have their families organized through the sealing ordinances of the holy priesthood.

Those who are faithful to these covenants are better able to avoid divorces, temptations, immoralities, drug problems, disobedience and waywardness, and problems with paying tithing. Children from these families are better able to cope. They are more likely to serve missions and be married in the temple. ("The Key to Activity and Retention," Regional Representatives' Seminar, 31 Mar. 1989.)

PARENTING

WHILE FEW HUMAN challenges are greater than that of being good parents, few opportunities offer greater potential for joy. Surely no more important work is to be done in this world than preparing our children to be God-fearing, happy, honorable, and productive. Parents will find no more fulfilling happiness than to have their children honor them and their teachings. It is the glory of parenthood. John testified, "I have no greater joy than to hear that my children walk in truth" (3 John 1:4). In my opinion, the teaching, rearing, and training of children requires more intelligence, intuitive understanding, humility, strength, wisdom, spirituality, perseverance, and hard work than any other challenge we might have in life. This is especially so when moral foundations of honor and decency are eroding around us. To have successful homes, values must be taught, and there must be rules, there must be standards, and there must be absolutes. Many societies give parents very little support in teaching and honoring moral values. A number of cultures are becoming essentially valueless, and many of the younger people in those societies are becoming moral cynics.

As societies as a whole have decayed and lost their moral identity and so many homes are broken, the best hope is to turn greater attention and effort to the teaching of the next generation—our children. In order to do this, we must first reinforce the primary teachers of children. Chief among these are the parents and other family members, and the best environment should be in the home. Somehow, some way, we must try harder to make our homes stronger so that they will stand as sanctuaries against the unwholesome, pervasive moral dry rot around us. Harmony, happiness, peace, and love in the home can help give children the required inner strength to cope with life's challenges. ("The Greatest Challenge in the World—Good Parenting," *Ensign*, Nov. 1990, 32–33.)

THOSE WHO HAVE children and are involved in doing something less than they should may be involved in a double evil, for in addition to the inherent wrong they commit, they also teach another generation to do wrong. There seems to be an immutable law that children may take license from what their parents do and expand upon it, confirming the old adage that the chickens not only come home to roost, but they bring their chicks with them. ("Integrity, the Mother of Many Virtues," *Ensign*, May 1982, 48.)

WHEN PARENTS TRY to teach their children to avoid danger, it is no answer for parents to say to their children, "We are experienced and wise in the ways of the world, and we can get closer to the edge of the cliff than you." Parental hypocrisy can make children cynical and unbelieving of what they are taught in the home. For instance, when parents attend movies they forbid their children to see, parental credibility is diminished. If children are expected to be honest, parents must be honest. If children are expected to be virtuous, parents must be virtuous. If you expect your children to be honorable, you must be honorable.

Among the other values children should be taught are respect for others, beginning with the child's own parents and family; respect for the symbols of faith and patriotic beliefs of others; respect for law and order; respect for the property of others; respect for authority. Paul reminds us that children should "learn first to shew piety at home" (1 Timothy 5:4). ("The Greatest Challenge in the World—Good Parenting," *Ensign*, Nov. 1990, 33–34.)

THE WORKS OF God are manifest in so many ways in the challenges of parents and children, especially to those who are handicapped and to those who have lost their way. For those who have asked, "Why did this happen to me?" or, "Why did this happen to my child?" there is assurance that the difficulty will not last forever. Life on this earth is not long. Caring for the unfortunate and laboring with the wayward is a manifestation of the pure love of Christ. For those who carry such a challenge in this life, God himself provides a response. That response is patience and the strength to endure. It lies, as Paul and Job testify, "in hope of eternal life, . . . promised before the world began" (Titus 1:2), "when the morning stars sang together, and all the sons of God shouted for joy" (Job 38:7). ("The Works of God," *Ensign*, Nov. 1984, 60.)

TO BE A good father and mother requires that the parents defer many of their own needs and desires in favor of the needs of their children. As a consequence of this sacrifice, conscientious parents develop a nobility of character and learn to put into practice the selfless truths taught by the Savior Himself. ("The Greatest Challenge in the World—Good Parenting," *Ensign,* Nov. 1990, 33.)

PARENTS, HONORING OF

[A] TRANSCENDENT BUT often unheeded message which peals down from Sinai is "Honour thy father and thy mother" (Exodus 20:12). I have frequently walked by a rest home that provides excellent care. But it is heartrending to see so many parents and grandparents in that good care facility so forgotten, so bereft of dignity, so starved for love. To honor parents certainly means to take care of physical needs. But it means much, much more. It means to show love, kindness, thoughtfulness, and concern for them all of the days of their lives. It means to help them preserve their dignity and self-respect in their declining years. It means to honor their wishes and desires and their teachings both before and after they are dead. . . .

Besides being one of God's commandments, the kind, thoughtful consideration of parents is a matter of common decency and self-respect. On their part, parents need to live so as to be worthy of the respect of their children. ("Unwanted Messages," *Ensign,* Nov. 1986, 9, 10.)

PATRIARCHAL BLESSINGS

WE ARE MOST fortunate some men are specifically ordained and authorized by their priesthood office and calling to give blessings and declare our lineage in the house of Israel. The inspired declaration of lineage is an integral part of the blessing. I pay honor and tribute to the noble, faithful men who are our ordained patriarchs. They have not sought this heavy and lonely responsibility. They are often among the most humble and devoted of our brethren. These chosen men live worthy of the inspiration of heaven. Patriarchs are privileged to bestow blessings for they are entitled to speak authoritatively under the inspiration of the Lord. . . .

The patriarch has no blessing of his own to give. We heard Elder LeGrand Richards tell of a patriarch who once said to a woman, "I have a wonderful blessing for you." But when the patriarch laid his hands on the head of the recipient his mind went completely blank. He apologized. "I was mistaken. I do not have a blessing for you. It is the Lord who has the blessing for you." The woman came back the next day and, after the patriarch had prayerfully importuned the Lord, a blessing came that made mention of concerns known only to this good sister. All blessings come from God. Our Heavenly Father knows his children. He knows their strengths and weaknesses. He knows their capabilities and potential. Our patriarchal blessings indicate what He expects of us and what our potential can be.

Patriarchal blessings should be read humbly, prayerfully, and frequently. A patriarchal blessing is very sacred and personal but may be shared with close family members. It is a sacred guideline of counsel, promises, and information from the Lord; however, a person should not expect the blessing to detail all that will happen to him or her or to answer all questions. The fact that one's patriarchal blessing may not mention important events in life, such as a mission or marriage, does not mean that they will not happen. In order to receive the fulfillment of our patriarchal blessings we should treasure in our hearts the precious words they contain, ponder them, and so live that we will obtain blessings in mortality and a crown of righteousness in the hereafter.

My own blessing is short, and it is limited to perhaps three quarters of a page on one side, yet it has been completely adequate and perfect for me. I received my patriarchal blessing as I entered my early teenage years. The patriarch promised that my blessing would "be a comfort and a guide" to me throughout my life. As a boy I read it over and over again. I pondered each word. I prayed earnestly to understand fully the spiritual meaning. Having that blessing early in my life guided me through all of the significant events and challenges of my life. I did not fully understand the meaning of my blessing until I gained more maturity and experience. This blessing outlined some of the responsibilities I would have in the Kingdom of God on earth.

President Heber J. Grant told of the patriarchal blessing he received, "That patriarch put his hands upon my head and bestowed upon me a little blessing that would perhaps be about one-third of a typewritten page. That blessing foretold my life to the present moment." ("Priesthood Blessings," *Ensign,* Nov. 1995, 62, 63–64.)

THE OFFICE OF patriarch is an office of the Melchizedek Priesthood. It is one of blessing, not of administration. It is a sacred and spiritual revelatory calling which will usually continue for much of the patriarch's life. Our patriarchs devote themselves fully to their callings and do all they can to live in faith and worthiness so that each blessing is inspired. The patriarch's calling becomes a beautiful, sacred, spiritual, and fulfilling experience. As moved upon by the Holy Spirit, the patriarch declares by inspiration the lineage in the house of Israel of the recipient, together with such blessings, spiritual gifts, promises, advice, admonition, and warnings the patriarch feels inspired to give. The patriarchal blessing is, in essence, a prophetic blessing and utterance.

A patriarchal blessing from an ordained patriarch can give us a star to follow, which is a personal revelation from God to each individual. If we follow this star, we are less likely to stumble and be misled. Our patriarchal blessing will be an anchor to our souls, and if we are worthy, neither death nor the devil can deprive us of the blessings pronounced. They are blessings we can enjoy now and forever. . . .

Elder John A. Widtsoe said, "It should always be kept in mind that the realization of the promises made may come in this or the future life. Men have stumbled at times because promised blessings have not occurred in this life. They have failed to remember that, in the gospel, life with all of its activities continues forever and that the labors of earth may be continued in heaven. Besides, the Giver of blessings, the Lord, reserves the right to have them become active in their life as suits His divine purposes. We and our blessings are in the hands of the Lord. But, there is a general testimony that when the gospel law has been obeyed, the promised blessings have been realized." (*Evidences and Reconciliations*, p. 329.)

This was well illustrated in my father's patriarchal blessing. He was told in his blessing that he would be blessed with "many beautiful daughters." He and my mother became the parents of five sons. No daughters were born to them, but they treated the wives of their sons as daughters. Some years ago when we had a family gathering, I saw my father's daughters-in-law, granddaughters, and great-granddaughters moving about tending to the food, ministering to the young children and the elderly, and the realization came to me that Father's blessing literally had been fulfilled. He has, indeed, many beautiful daughters. The patriarch who gave my father his blessing had spiritual vision to see beyond this life. The dividing line between time and eternity disappeared. ("Priesthood Blessings," *Ensign*, Nov. 1995, 63–64.)

AS WITH MANY other blessings, patriarchal blessings should ordinarily be requested by the one desiring the blessing. Responsibility for receiving a patriarchal blessing rests primarily upon the individual when he or she has sufficient understanding of the significance of a patriarchal blessing. I encourage all members of the Church, having this maturity, to become worthy and obtain their blessings. By their very nature, all blessings are conditional upon worthiness regardless of whether the blessing specifically spells out the qualifications. The patriarchal blessing is primarily a guide to the future, not an index to the past. Therefore, it is important that the recipient should be young enough that many of the significant events of life are in the future. I recently heard of a person over ninety years of age who received his patriarchal blessing. It would be interesting to read that blessing. ("Priesthood Blessings," *Ensign*, Nov. 1995, 63.)

SOME MIGHT BE disturbed because members of the same family have blessings declaring them to be of a different lineage. A few families are of a mixed lineage. We believe that the house of Israel today constitutes a large measure of the human family. Because the tribes have intermixed one with another, one child may be declared to be from the tribe of Ephraim, and another of the same family from Manasseh or one of the other tribes. The blessings of one tribe, therefore, may be dominant in one child, and the blessings of another tribe dominant in yet another child. So, children from the same parents could receive the blessings of different tribes. ("Priesthood Blessings," *Ensign*, Nov. 1995, 64.)

PERSEVERANCE

WHEN I WAS your age and in college, I was a member of the track team. On our team was one of the most gifted athletes I ever knew. He could do everything. He had grace and timing and strength. But he lacked staying power. He was a sprinter. To stretch the sprinters and the quarter-milers, we would all race together for three hundred yards to train. The gifted athlete would lead the whole group until he reached about two hundred and thirty yards, and then he would quit. He would just pull up and stop! He held a conference record for the hurdles, but he wouldn't run three hundred yards! He became a professional football player and then he got on drugs and alcohol and died as a relatively young man. Like the old fable of the tortoise and the rabbit, the plodders who make a contribution every day are the ones who, after years of labor, are able to achieve. The workhorses, not the show horses, seem to get the work done in the end. ("If You Are Starting at the Bottom, Then Reach for the Stars," Ricks College Devotional, 17 Apr. 1990.)

POOR, CARING FOR THE

THE CURTAINS ARE opening up to more and more of the non-industrialized nations. In some of these countries a large percentage of the population is poor. Many have much less opportunity than others to acquire the comforts of life and even some of the necessities. We have seen men and women working to exhaustion from sunrise to sundown for a pittance. Yet their ready smiles and cheerful countenances indicated that they had found some happiness with their lot in life.

Some might say, "Where is the justice in the fact that some of God's children have so much of health and this world's goods and others so very little?" So many of those who have in abundance seem unappreciative of what they have. But we also see the generosity of members of this Church who have great concern for those worldwide who lack the necessities of life. They generously contribute to help the poor in many countries, even though we have no members there. Humanitarian help has been given in 114 countries since 1985. ("Helping Hearts and Hands Span the Globe," *Church News*, 11 Feb. 1995, pp. 8–10.)

I have learned to admire, respect, and love the good people from every race, culture, and nation that I have been privileged to visit. In my experience, no race or class seems superior to any other in spirituality and faithfulness. Those who seem less caring spiritually are those individuals—regardless of race, culture, or nationality—spoken of by the Savior in the parable of the sower who are "choked with the cares and riches and pleasures of this life, and bring no fruit to perfection." (Luke 8:14.) ("Heirs to the Kingdom of God," *Ensign*, May 1995, 61.)

P R A Y E R

THE GREAT ENERGIZER of the true Christian, the battery which generates the starter of our inner strengthening motors, is prayer. ("Christianity—Repression or Liberation?" *BYU Speeches,* 10 June 1975, 142.)

OF ALL THAT we might do to find solace, prayer is perhaps the most comforting. ("He Healeth the Broken in Heart," in *Finding Light in a Dark World* [Salt Lake City: Deseret Book, 1995], 30.)

AN IMPORTANT PART of the spiritual being of all of us is the quiet and sacred part from which we may feel a sanctification in our lives. It is that part of us wherein no other soul intrudes. It is that part of us that permits us to come close to the divine, both in and out of this world. This portion of our beings is reserved only for ourselves and our Creator; we open the portals thereof when we pray. ("Strengthening the Inner Self," in *To Reach Even unto You* [Salt Lake City: Deseret Book, 1980], 14.)

A FERVENT, SINCERE prayer is a two-way communication which will do much to bring His Spirit flowing like healing water to help with the trials, hardships, aches, and pains we all face. What is the quality of our secret prayers when only He listens? As we pray, we should think of Him as being close by, full of knowledge, understanding, love, and compassion, the essence of power, and as having great expectations of each of us. ("A Personal Relationship with the Savior," *Ensign,* Nov. 1976, 58.)

P R E P A R E D N E S S

SOME OF US are children of the Great Depression in the United States over fifty years ago. Most of us who passed through that period will never forget the difficult economic times almost everyone experienced. At that time many banks failed; people lost their life's savings; a great many were unemployed, and some of them lost their homes because they could not pay the mortgage. Many went hungry. If we didn't eat our oatmeal cereal for breakfast, we would often have it fried for lunch or dinner. Such widespread economic problems could come again. But any of us, at any time, could meet with a personal calamity, such as sickness or an accident, which could limit or destroy our income. . . . Let us examine ourselves and, like pilots in the sky, take our bearings to see if we are on course financially. We must build upon sound principles. The bedrock principle of which I speak is that the responsibility for welfare rests with me and my family. In 1936 the First Presidency said in a great statement of purpose, "The aim of the Church is to help the people to help themselves" (in Conference Report, Oct. 1936, p. 3). ("Responsibility for Welfare Rests with Me and My Family," *Ensign*, May 1986, 20.)

THE COUNSEL TO have a year's supply of basic food, clothing, and commodities was given fifty years ago and has been repeated many times since. Every father and mother are the family's storekeepers. They should store whatever their own family would like to have in the case of an emergency. Most of us cannot afford to store a year's supply of luxury items, but find it more practical to store staples that might keep us from starving in case of emergency. Surely we all hope that the hour of need will never come. Some have said, "We have followed this counsel in the past and have never had need to use our year's supply, so we have difficulty keeping this in mind as a major priority." Perhaps following this counsel could be the reason why they have not needed to use their reserve. By continued rotation of the supply it can be kept usable with no waste.

The Church cannot be expected to provide for every one of its millions of members in case of public or personal disaster. It is therefore necessary that each home and family do what they can to assume the responsibility for their own hour of need. If we do not have the resources to acquire a year's supply, then we can strive to begin with having one month's supply. I believe if we are provident and wise in the management of our personal and family affairs and are faithful, God will sustain us through our trials. He has revealed: "For the earth is full, and there is enough and to spare; yea, I prepared all things, and have given unto the children of men to be agents unto themselves" (D&C 104:17). ("Responsibility for Welfare Rests with Me and My Family," *Ensign*, May 1986, 22.)

PRIDE

THE EGO INTERFERES with husbands and wives asking each other for forgiveness. It prevents the enjoyment of the full sweetness of a higher love. The ego often prevents parents and children from fully understanding each other. The ego enlarges our feelings of self-importance and worth. It blinds us to reality. Pride keeps us from confessing our sins and shortcomings to the Lord and working out our repentance. ("Five Loaves and Two Fishes," *Ensign*, May 1994, 6.)

PRIESTHOOD

THE OBJECT OF God's work is "to bring to pass the immortality and eternal life of man" (Moses 1:39). God has given the priesthood to man at various times since Adam's day to bring about the great plan of salvation for all mankind. Through our faithfulness, the transcendent blessings of eternal life flow from this priesthood authority.

For these priesthood blessings to flower, there is a constant need for unity within the priesthood. We must be loyal to the leadership who have been called to preside over us and hold the keys of the priesthood. The words of President J. Reuben Clark, Jr., still ring loudly in our ears: *"Brethren, let us be united."* He explained:

"An essential part of unity is loyalty. . . . Loyalty is a pretty difficult quality to possess. It requires the ability to put away selfishness, greed, ambition and all of the baser qualities of the human mind. You cannot be loyal unless you are willing to surrender. . . . [A person's] own preferences and desires must be put away, and he must see only the great purpose which lies out ahead" *(Immortality and Eternal Life* [Melchizedek Priesthood Course of Study, 1968–69], p. 163). . . .

In some legislative assembles of the world, there are some groups termed the "loyal opposition." I find no such principle in the gospel of Jesus Christ. The Savior gave us this solemn warning: "Be one; and if ye are not one ye are not mine" (D&C 38:27). The Lord made it clear that in the presiding quorums every decision "must be by the unanimous voice of the same; that is, every member in each quorum must be agreed to its decisions" (D&C 107:27). This means that after frank and open discussion, decisions are reached in council under the direction of the presiding officer, who has the ultimate authority to decide. That decision is then sustained, because our unity comes from full agreement with righteous principles and general response to the operation of the Spirit of God. ("Keeping Covenants and Honoring the Priesthood," *Ensign,* Nov. 1993, 36–38.)

POWER IS HIGHLY attractive. It can be both good and bad. In your formative years, you young men are attracted to power figures of one kind or another. These often include sports idols, entertainers, people of wealth, and those who have political power. Unfortunately, some young men, particularly those who fall short scholastically, who don't make the team, or who are not chosen to sing in a specially selected choir may feel rejected and be lured into groups that they think will compensate for their inadequacies. This hunger for acceptance or power draws them like a moth to a flame to street gangs and other associations that can be violent and encourage habits which are dangerous to the body and to the soul.

You young holders of the priesthood have access to the greatest power source in the world. It is the priesthood of God. In complete contrast to other power sources, the holy priesthood, through its proper exercise, continues to build spiritual and physical strength which endures through the eternities. It is "inseparably connected with the powers of heaven" and can be "handled only upon the principles of righteousness." (D&C 121:36.) Regarding the priesthood, the Prophet Joseph Smith stated: "[It] is the channel through which all knowledge, doctrine, the plan of salvation and every important matter is revealed from heaven. . . . It is the channel through which the Almighty . . . has continued to reveal Himself to the children of men to the present time, and through which He will make known His purposes to the end of time." (*History of the Church*, 4:39.) ("By What Power Have Ye Done This?" *Ensign*, Nov. 1998, 45.)

[PRIESTHOOD] POWER COMES in proportion to our faithfulness in fulfilling our duties. As the Prophet Joseph observed, "The Lord gave us power in proportion to the work to be done, and strength according to the race set before us, and grace and help as our needs required." (*History of the Church*, 1:175.) As an example, the prophet Elijah, using his priesthood, was able to call forth fire from heaven to demonstrate the power of God.

Before President Hugh B. Brown was a General Authority, he served in England as an officer in the Canadian army and had great power. Men stood at attention before him and called him "sir." One day Brother Brown received a message that he was wanted in the hospital. When he got there, someone directed him to a little room where a sick young man lay. Brother Brown remembered that he had once been that young man's Sunday School teacher. "Brother Brown," said the young man, "would you use your authority in my behalf? The doctors say I cannot live. Will you give me a blessing?" All the pride Brother Brown felt in wearing the uniform of the king disappeared as he laid his hands upon the boy's head and gave him a blessing. The help that the boy needed was not from any authority of an officer in the king's army but from the authority of the priesthood. (Adapted from Hugh B. Brown, "Be What You Will to Be," *Brigham Young University Speeches of the Year* [14 Feb. 1967], 8–9.) ("By What Power Have Ye Done This?" *Ensign*, Nov. 1998, 45–46.)

MANY PEOPLE DO not understand our belief that God has wisely established a guiding authority for the most important institutions in the world. This guiding authority is called the priesthood. The priesthood is held in trust to be used to bless all of God's children. Priesthood is not gender; it is blessings from God for all at the hands of the servants He has designated. Within the Church this authority of the priesthood can bless all members through the ministration of home teachers, quorum presidents, bishops, fathers, and all other righteous brethren who are charged with the administration of the affairs of the kingdom of God. Priesthood is the righteous power and influence by which boys are taught in their youth and throughout their lives to honor chastity, to be honest and industrious, and to develop respect for, and stand in the defense of, womanhood. Priesthood is a restraining influence. Girls are taught that through its influence and power to bless, they can fulfill many of their desires.

Holding the priesthood means following the example of Christ and seeking to emulate his example of fatherhood. It means constant concern and caring for one's own flesh and blood. The man who holds the priesthood is to honor it by eternally cherishing, with absolute fidelity, his wife and the mother of his children. He is to extend lifelong care and concern for his children, and their children. ("Father, Come Home," *Ensign,* May 1993, 36.)

YOU YOUNG MEN of the Aaronic Priesthood have only glimpsed the satisfaction that comes through the righteous exercise of your priesthood. This priesthood holds "the key of the ministering of angels." (D&C 84:26.) Priests may be permitted to perform the sacred ordinance of baptism in order to have our sins removed. The Aaronic Priesthood administers and passes the sacred emblems of the sacrament. Both ordinances relate directly to the Savior's Atonement. In addition, as home teaching companions you are to help watch over the Church, urging members "to pray . . . and attend to all family duties." (D&C 20:51.)

Another duty particularly pertains to you wonderful young men. That is the duty to follow the counsel of those in authority over you. Listen to your parents. Be obedient to them whether you agree with them or not. They love you more than anyone else and have your best interests at heart. Listen to your quorum president, your bishop, your stake president, the apostles, seers, and revelators, and especially President Hinckley, as well as the other General Authorities of the Church. They will lead you into the ways of righteousness. ("By What Power Have Ye Done This?" *Ensign,* Nov. 1998, 47.)

ISN'T IT REMARKABLE that we do not have to understand all of the intricate laws of physics, chemistry, and medicine to experience the power of the priesthood? To control the great physical laws by the power of the priesthood, we need to understand and invoke the greater spiritual laws of faith, righteousness, and obedience. Often the humblest and meekest among us have great spiritual gifts and powers. ("The Priesthood of God," Priesthood Fireside, 6 May 1990.)

IT IS IMPORTANT to remember that in this Church, the husbands and fathers, and members of the family through them, enjoy a power and influence in their lives, far beyond the natural gifts of intellect and character of the father. I refer to the priesthood of God, which every worthy man and boy over 12 years of age enjoys.

A prominent Church and business leader in this community was born without life. His father, exercising his priesthood, made a promise that if his firstborn could live, that he, the father, would do all in his power to provide the proper example and teachings for his son. After a few minutes his infant son began to breathe and is well and vigorous to this day. ("Happiness Is Having a Father Who Cares," *Ensign,* Jan. 1974, 23.)

THE PRIESTHOOD OF God is a shield. It is a shield against the evils of the world. That shield needs to be kept clean; otherwise, our vision of our purpose and the dangers around us will be limited. The cleansing agent is personal righteousness, but not all will pay the price to keep their shields clean. The Lord said, "For many are called, but few are chosen" (Matt. 22:14). We are called when hands are laid upon our heads and we are given the priesthood, but we are not chosen until we demonstrate to God our righteousness, our faithfulness, and our commitment. ("The Priesthood of God," Priesthood Fireside, 6 May 1990.)

JUST A FEW weeks ago, in a stake conference, one gracious mother joyously recounted a marvelous experience of being in one of the temples with her husband and with all of her children but one and being sealed together as husband and wife and family for time and all eternity. Her husband, newly involved in the priesthood, sat in the conference audience a few rows back. For a moment she seemed to forget all of the rest of us and spoke only to him. Over the pulpit, and through the loudspeaker, with over 1,000 people in tears watching and listening, she said, "John, the children and I don't know how to tell you what you mean to us. Until you honored the priesthood, the greatest blessings of eternity would not open up for us. Now they have. We all love you very much and we thank you with all our hearts for what you have made possible for us." ("Happiness Is Having a Father Who Cares," *Ensign,* Jan. 1974, 23–24.)

THE CHURCH CANNOT cloak a man in medieval robes and give him a parchment saying that he is fully ready and worthy to use all of the powers of the priesthood. The authority of the priesthood is not manifest in such outward symbols. But as a worthy man grows in strength and spiritual righteousness, he can receive a warm, spiritual cloak. ("The Priesthood of God," Priesthood Fireside, 6 May 1990.)

BRETHREN, WE ARE the authorized servants of the risen Christ. With this authority comes the duty to move this holy work forward across the world. We are part of the greatest brotherhood in all the world. We will be held accountable for what we do with the keys, power, and authority granted to us. We must be true to this great trust in every way.

As we look to the future, we will continue to have obstacles, difficulties, challenges, and opposition. Satan has more tools at his disposal than ever before to deceive, distract, and corrupt our people. We will continue to be winnowed. One day in the future, we will have to account through President Gordon B. Hinckley to the Prophet Joseph for what we have done with this great power which the Lord has invested in us.

We are grateful that the work of God moves forward as powerfully as it does under the leadership of President Gordon B. Hinckley. After the death of the Savior, his apostles did great and marvelous things in His name. Peter and John were asked by Caiaphas and the high priests, "By what power . . . have ye done this?" (Acts 4:7.) Like Peter, we declare to the world that all this happens by and through the power of the holy priesthood and in the "name of Jesus Christ of Nazareth." (Acts 4:10.) ("By What Power Have Ye Done This?" *Ensign,* Nov. 1998, 47.)

MORE THAN FIFTY years ago a patriarch indicated that I would be called to preside among the people. The blessing does not say preside "over," it says preside "among." I have always thought this was significant. . . .

One does not have to hold an administrative calling in the Church, such as bishop or stake president or General Authority, to receive all of the blessings of the priesthood. The promise of the oath and covenant of the priesthood to His worthy holders is that through their faithfulness they may be sanctified by the Spirit and may become the elect of God (see D&C 84:33–34). The further promise is that "all that my Father hath shall be given unto him" (D&C 84:38). If therefore the worthy holders of the priesthood receive all that the Father hath, by giving "diligent heed to the words of eternal life" (D&C 84:43), then there is nothing more to receive. ("The Priesthood of God," Priesthood Fireside, 6 May 1990.)

PRIESTHOOD BLESSINGS

A PRIESTHOOD BLESSING is sacred. It can be a holy and inspired statement of our wants and needs. If we are in tune spiritually, we can receive a confirming witness of the truth of the promised blessings. Priesthood blessings can help us in the small and great decisions of our lives. If, through our priesthood blessings, we could perceive only a small part of the person God intends us to be, we would lose our fear and never doubt again.

As a small boy, I remember being intrigued by my grandmother's magnifying glass which she used in her old age to read and do needlework. When the glass was in focus everything I looked at was greatly magnified. But I was most intrigued by what happened when the lens concentrated the sunlight on an object. When it passed through the magnifying glass the sunlight's power was absolutely amazing.

This great magnifying effect can be compared to a profound blessing that came to Jacob who wrestled most of the night for a blessing [see Gen. 32:24–28]. . . .

Unlike Jacob, we do not need to wrestle physically much of the night for blessings to strengthen and magnify us. In the Church, blessings are available to all who are worthy through those authorized and even appointed to give priesthood blessings. Stake presidents, bishops, quorum presidents, and home teachers are authorized to give blessings. Worthy fathers and grandfathers, as well as other Melchizedek Priesthood holders, may give blessings to members in times of sickness and when important events occur. Such individual blessings are part of the continuous revelation that we claim as members of The Church of Jesus Christ of Latter-day Saints. ("Priesthood Blessings," *Ensign*, Nov. 1995, 62.)

PRIESTHOOD LEADERS

HOW CAN OUR priesthood leaders, already administratively bur-
dened, be helpful to parents in order to help their children? I
believe the answer is basic. In the last days of the Savior's ministry he said to Peter: "Simon, Simon, behold, Satan hath
desired to have you, that he may sift you as wheat:

"But I have prayed for thee, that thy faith fail not: and when
thou art converted, strengthen thy brethren" (Luke 22:31–32).

There needs to be a converting and a strengthening of parents. This comes about by the teaching, the understanding, and
the applying of gospel principles. It is a great challenge to the
priesthood leaders to have everyone in our wards, branches,
and quorums be strengthened in their understanding of the
gospel. Priesthood leaders are clothed with great authority.
When bishops and other priesthood leaders are needed for specific family or personal reasons, their availability is a great
strength and comfort. Their genuine interest and concern for us
as individuals is a vital support mechanism. ("Enriching Family
Life," *Ensign,* May 1983, 42.)

PRIORITIES

MEMBERS OF THIS Church, professional and otherwise, have a
balancing act to perform. How much time and effort should be
devoted and dedicated to one's temporal calling as against the
responsibility to one's family and the Church? This depends in
part on what make of car we wish to drive, how large a home
we wish to live in, and how big of a bank account to enjoy. In
my life, my family and my Church callings came first. We lived
carefully and I tried not to become obsessed with financial gain.
These conflicting interests were accommodated and, I can
honestly say, if I had to do it over, I would do it the same way.
("The Law: Calling or Trade?" address given to law firm, Salt
Lake City, Utah, August 1988.)

SOME YEARS AGO I was assigned by the brethren to attend a stake

conference in one of the most remote areas of Idaho. The stake
president is a cattle rancher on a ranch that is up high in the
mountains. In this family was a mother who had thirteen children and had [endured many] natural miscarriages. We arrived
after our evening meeting. Their home was not luxurious, but
comfortable and heated by a wood stove. . . . In the morning we
got up and came to breakfast. The little boy, who has a different kind of a spirit, came in and the stake president said, "This
is Johnny." A few minutes later, we heard somebody sawing on
the front door with a saw. The stake president, without raising
his voice, simply said, "Johnny, come in." He came in and the
evidence was in his hand—the saw. Apparently this was not an
unusual occurrence. Then came little Mary. Mary had a harelip.
And they brought a little baby in, maybe six months old. This
great woman had raised this family.

That morning we called on her in stake conference. She
said, "We heard about Mary and nobody wanted her. We need
a new truck, but when we saw her, we knew we needed her
more than we needed the new truck. And then we heard
about Johnny who kind of listens to a different voice. I needed
a new range in the kitchen, but when we met Johnny we knew
we needed him more than we needed a new range in the
kitchen. And I wanted a new love seat, but we heard about the
baby and we knew we needed the baby more than the love
seat."

Then she went on to say, "The other evening I finished my
work about midnight and my husband and all my children
were asleep and I was tired. I should have gone to bed. But I sat
down in the rocker and thought about my childhood dreams.
When I was a young girl I wanted to be rich and famous. And
then I thought about all of my children asleep and my husband
and how hard he has to work to be a good father to all of these
children and a good spiritual father to all of the people in the
stake. And how his calling as a stake president doesn't take
away from the family; it adds to it."

Then she said, "I realized that I was married to the finest

man in all the world. And as I counted my children, I realized then that I wouldn't trade places with my childhood dreams of being rich and famous." (Special Interest Fireside, Salt Lake City, Utah, 29 Jan. 1978.)

WE ARE NOT only to avoid evil, not only to do good but, most importantly, to do the things of greatest worth. We are to focus on the inward things of the heart, which we know and value intuitively but often neglect for that which is trivial, superficial, or prideful. ("The Weightier Matters of the Law: Judgment, Mercy and Faith," *Ensign*, Nov. 1997, 53.)

THINKING CLEARLY IS often characterized as "prioritizing." But clear thinking means more than that: it is choosing the better part, not the one that will bring the most money or fame. It also means making the best use of our time. ("Learning for Eternity," *BYU Speeches*, 18 Nov. 1997, 3.)

PROPHETS

ALTHOUGH EVERY FAITHFUL member of the Church is entitled to receive personal revelation, there is only one man upon the earth who receives revelation for the whole Church.

Beginning with Joseph Smith, the Prophet of the Restoration, there have been living oracles of God designated to communicate minute by minute, day by day, and hour by hour, as needed, to the leaders of the Church.

President Wilford Woodruff, fourth president of the Church, said: "The Church of God could not live twenty-four hours without revelation" (*Discourses of Wilford Woodruff*, p. 61). ("Communion with the Holy Spirit," *Ensign*, May 1980, 14.)

NO ONE CAN fully understand how and why the Church has come "out of obscurity" (D&C 1:30) and blossomed without knowing some of the fundamental prophetic truths on which the Church rests. . . .

First, the keys and authority of God have been given by

Him to Joseph Smith and to each of his successors who have
been called as Presidents of the Church.

Second, those keys and authority are never to be given to
another people, and those who have such authority are to be
"known to the Church."

Third, continuing revelation and leadership for the Church
comes through the President of the Church, and he will never
mislead the Saints.

Fourth, individual members of the Church may receive revelation for their own callings and areas of responsibility and for
their own families. They may not receive spiritual instruction
for those higher in authority.

Fifth, those who claim direct revelation from God for the
Church outside of the established order and channel of the
priesthood are misguided. This also applies to any who follow
them.

If any find themselves in this position, please know there is
always an open door in the Church for those who wish to
return to full fellowship with the sisters and the brethren of the
priesthood. The welcome will be with open arms.

My testimony of the divinity of the callings of the presiding
Brethren as the representatives of the Lord Jesus Christ flows
from the deepest wellspring of my soul. For many years, I have
watched the process of continuous revelation which emanates
from God through the keys, authority, and under the direction
of the President of the Church. I testify that this revelatory
power has directed this work since April 6, 1830. That confirmation is the source of the greatest knowledge I have. ("The
Prophetic Voice," *Ensign*, May 1996, 7.)

HOW CAN WE be so sure that, as promised, the prophets, seers,
and revelators will never lead this people astray? (see Joseph
Fielding Smith, in Conference Report, Apr. 1972, p. 99;
or *Ensign*, July 1972, p. 88). One answer is contained in the
grand principle found in the 107th section of the Doctrine
and Covenants: "And every decision made by either of these

quorums must be by the unanimous voice of the same" (107:27). This requirement of unanimity provides a check on bias and personal idiosyncrasies. It ensures that God rules through the Spirit, not man through majority or compromise. It ensures that the best wisdom and experience is focused on an issue before the deep, unassailable impressions of revealed direction are received. It guards against the foibles of man. ("Continuous Revelation," *Ensign*, Nov. 1989, 10.)

PROPHETS, FOLLOWING THE

YOU MAY ASK, "How can I discern which of the prophetic utterances of this conference have a particular message for me?" My answer is, you can know. You can know by the whisperings of the Holy Spirit if you righteously and earnestly seek to know. Your own inspiration will be an unerring vibration through the companionship of the Holy Ghost. As the Lord spoke to Elijah, this will come, not in the great strong wind, nor in the earthquake, nor in the fire, but in a still, small voice. (See 1 Kings 19:11–12.) This will help us, if necessary, to make the required change in our lives and lifestyles to get onto a sure course. ("Responsibility for Welfare Rests with Me and My Family," *Ensign*, May 1986, 22.)

WHEN I WAS first named as a General Authority many years ago, I went to see President Hugh B. Brown, then in the First Presidency, and asked him, "President Brown, what advice have you got for a new, young, inexperienced General Authority?" This wise and venerable man responded simply and directly, "Stick with the Brethren." Who are the Brethren? The Brethren are those who hold the keys of the kingdom of God on earth. They are the First Presidency and the Quorum of the Twelve Apostles, each of whom is an apostle and prophet; the Seventy, to whom apostolic authority is given; and, in temporal matters, the Presiding Bishopric. ("The Prophetic Voice," *Ensign*, May 1996, 4.)

SOME HAVE SAID, "My integrity will not permit me to yield my conscience to anyone." A clear conscience is a very precious spiritual endowment when it is guided by the Holy Ghost. Ultimately, everyone has the responsibility of making their own moral decisions. However, the Prophet Joseph Smith stated that "it is contrary to the economy of God for any member of the Church . . . to receive instruction for those in authority, higher than themselves." (*Teachings of the Prophet Joseph Smith,* p. 21; see also D&C 28:12.)

In addition, some have claimed higher spiritual gifts or authority outside the established priesthood authority of the Church. They say that they believe in the principles and ordinances of the gospel and accept the President of the Church as the legal administrator thereof, but claim that they have a higher order which the President does not have. This is often done to justify an activity which is not in accordance with the doctrines of the Church. There can be no higher order, however, because the President of the Church both holds and exercises all of the keys of the kingdom of God on earth. The Lord has said of the President of the Church "that none else shall be appointed [to receive commandments and revelations] except it be through him." (D&C 43:3–4.) ("The Prophetic Voice," *Ensign,* May 1996, 6–7.)

RELIEF SOCIETY

I REVERE THE influence and accomplishments of the Relief Society. It is the greatest women's organization in the world. You are especially privileged to belong to this wonderful organization. My life has been richly blessed because of Relief Society. My great-grandmother was a ward Relief Society president for thirty-three years. I have been married to both the stake and ward Relief Society president! Both the same woman! Our eldest daughter now serves as ward Relief Society president. One of our daughters-in-law is a stake Relief Society president. As my dear Ruth faithfully attended Relief Society over the years, our home and family was blessed with more spirituality and peace. Things seemed to go smoother because of the spiritual enrichment she received. I feel well-schooled in the benefits of Relief Society. I learned long ago to sustain the priesthood and not get in the way of the Relief Society. ("The Grand Keys of the Relief Society," *Ensign,* Nov. 1996, 94.)

REPENTANCE

THE DENIAL OF our own sins, of our own selfishness, of our own weakness is like a crown of thorns which keeps us from moving up one more step in personal growth. Perhaps worse than sin is the denial of sin. If we deny that we are sinners, how can we ever be forgiven? How can the atonement of Jesus work in our lives if there is no repentance? If we do not promptly remove the slivers of sin and the thorns of carnal temptation, how can the Lord ever heal our souls? The Savior said, "Repent of your sins, and be converted, that I may heal you" (3 Nephi 9:13). It is most difficult for us to pray for those who hate us, who despitefully use us, who persecute us. But by failing to take this vital extra step, however, we fail to remove some of the festering briars in our souls. Extending forgiveness, love, and understanding for perceived shortcomings and weaknesses in our wives, husbands, children, and associates makes it much easier to say, "God be merciful to me a sinner" (Luke 18:13). ("A Crown of Thorns, a Crown of Glory," *Ensign,* May 1991, 68.)

ONE OF THE members of our family has a remarkable dog named Ben. A few years ago, on a beautiful fall day, some of us were walking in the fields. Ben was going back and forth in front of us, sniffing the ground, tail wagging, and obviously enjoying himself. After a while we sat down on a ditch bank to rest and could feel the warmth of the autumn sun caressing us. Ben came limping up to his master and, with a pained look in his eye, held up his front paw. Ben's master gently took his paw into his hands and examined it carefully. Between two of his toes was a thorn. The thorn was carefully removed, and Ben stayed long enough to wag his tail a little more vigorously and receive a few pats on his head. He then ran off, no longer limping nor bothered by the pain. I was amazed that Ben instinctively seemed to know that the thorn needed to come out to relieve the pain and to know where to go to have it removed. Like Ben, we also seem to instinctively look for relief from the thorns of sin that inflict us. In contrast, however, we do not always seek our Master for relief; and many do not yet know who their Master is. . . .

All irritants of the flesh and the soul should be removed before they fester. However, though they ulcerate and though they torment, they can still be removed, and the healing process will take place. When the infection is healed, the soreness will leave. That process is known as repentance. Repentance and forgiveness are among the greatest fruits of the Atonement. It is not easy to remove the thorns of pride, the thistles of selfishness, the slivers of ego, and the briars of appetite. ("A Crown of Thorns, a Crown of Glory," *Ensign*, May 1991, 69, 70.)

SURELY, REPENTANCE IS one of the great principles of the gospel. No one is perfect, and we all have need to invoke this principle. For those who have been involved in serious transgressions, however, it is a lifesaving principle. The longer we go down the wrong road, the harder it is to come back and get on the right road. ("Beginnings," Training Film Lecture Series, 29 Jan. 1982.)

THERE IS HOPE for all to be healed through repentance and obedience. The prophet Isaiah verified that "though your sins be as scarlet, they shall be as white as snow" (Isaiah 1:18). The Prophet Joseph Smith stated, "There is never a time when the spirit is too old to approach God. All are [in] reach of pardoning mercy" (*Teachings of the Prophet Joseph Smith*, p. 191).

After full repentance, the formula is wonderfully simple. Indeed, the Lord has given it to us in these words: "Will ye not now return unto me, and repent of your sins, and be converted, that I may heal you?" (3 Nephi 9:13). In so doing, we have his promise that "He healeth the broken in heart, and bindeth up their wounds" (Psalm 147:3). ("Spiritual Healing," *Ensign*, May 1992, 8.)

FOR THE TROUBLED conscience in conflict with right and wrong, the only permanent help is to change the behavior and follow a repentant path. ("Unwanted Messages," *Ensign*, Nov. 1986, 10.)

RESURRECTION

THE RESURRECTION OF Jesus is one of the greatest messages of all Christianity. It is a divine gift of the Atonement for all mankind. The idea that one who has died can live again was so unprecedented, so foreign to all human experience, that even the Apostles, who had been told it would happen, could hardly believe it. . . . Latter-day Saints have additional witnesses of the reality of the resurrection of Jesus Christ and of the certainty of life after death. One of these witnesses is the Book of Mormon, a record containing the ministry of the resurrected Christ upon the American continent after his death and resurrection in Jerusalem. The appearance was preceded by a voice as if it came out of heaven: "And it was not a harsh voice, neither was it a loud voice; nevertheless, and notwithstanding it being a small voice it did pierce them that did hear to the center . . . ; yea, it did pierce them to the very soul, and did cause their hearts to burn" (3 Nephi 11:3). . . .

Joseph Smith also testified of the appearance of the Father and the Son to him as a young boy.

With the abundance of testimony, both ancient and modern, sealed by the witness of the Holy Spirit of God, we stand firm and unequivocating in our knowledge that Jesus of Nazareth is the resurrected Savior. His arms are stretched forth to all men, including my native friend in Africa, who, by accepting Him in His appointed way, may become not just believers but true disciples and with Paul hope to "obtain a better resurrection" (Hebrews 11:35). ("The Resurrection," *Ensign*, May 1985, 30–31, 32.)

DURING THE FORTY days that the Savior spent with the Apostles and others, they heard and saw many unspeakable things. This special ministry changed the Apostles from an uncertain, confused, divided, and weak group into powerful witnesses of the Lord. Mark records that the Savior upbraided the eleven "because they believed not them which had seen him after he was risen" (Mark 16:14).

Perhaps the Apostles should not be unduly criticized for not believing that Jesus, having been crucified and buried in a tomb, had come back to earth as a glorified being. In all human experience, this had never happened before. It was completely unprecedented. This was a different experience than the raising of Jairus' daughter (see Mark 5:22, 24, 35–43), the young man of Nain (see Luke 7:11–15), or Lazarus (see John 11:1–44). They all died again. Jesus, however, became a resurrected being. He would never die again. So it was that to the Apostles the story of Mary Magdalene and the other women who witnessed the Resurrection "seemed to them as idle tales, and they believed them not" (Luke 24:11). . . .

Like the Apostles of old, this knowledge and belief should transform all of us to be confident, settled, unafraid, and at peace in our lives as followers of the divine Christ. It should help us carry all burdens, bear any sorrows, and also fully savor all joys and happiness that can be found in this life. The disciples who walked with the Savior on the road to Emmaus said to one another, "Did not our heart burn within us, while he talked with us by the way, and while he opened to us the scriptures?" (Luke 24:32). No wonder they entreated him, "Abide with us: for it is toward evening," and he "sat at meat with them" (Luke 24:29–30). They sought to savor those precious moments and feelings.

The vacating of the tomb transcended all other events in the history of the world, for it attested that Jesus had not died, but that death itself had been overcome. ("The Supernal Gift of the Atonement," *Ensign,* Nov. 1988, 13–14.)

REVELATION

PERSONAL REVELATION COMES as a testimony of truth and as guidance in spiritual and temporal matters. Members of the Church know that the promptings of the Spirit may be received upon all facets of life, including daily, ongoing decisions (see D&C 42:61). How could anyone think of making an important decision such as "Who is to be my companion?," "What is my work to be?," "Where will I live?," and "How will I live?" without seeking the inspiration of Almighty God. ("Communion with the Holy Spirit," *Ensign,* May 1980, 13.)

THE NINTH ARTICLE of faith [states, in part], "We believe . . . all that [God] does now reveal." For some strange reason it seems easier for many to believe the words of dead prophets rather than those of living prophets. The greatest revelator in our time has been Joseph Smith. In the difficult period between 1823 and 1843, just twenty years, 134 revelations were received, printed, and made public. . . .

. . . Line upon line and precept upon precept, new knowledge and direction have been given to the Church. . . .

. . . Much revelation received, in this time as well as anciently, has been doctrinal. Some of it has been operational and tactical. Much of it is not spectacular. President John Taylor reminds us: "Adam's revelation did not instruct Noah to build his ark; nor did Noah's revelation tell Lot to forsake Sodom; nor did either of these speak of the departure of the children of Israel from Egypt. These all had revelations for themselves" (*Millennial Star,* 1 Nov. 1847, p. 323).

In our time God has revealed how to administer the Church with a membership of over six million differently than when there were just six members of the Church. These differences include the use of modern technology such as films, computers, and satellite broadcasts to teach and communicate new ways to conduct missionary work in various nations; the location and building of temples; and many others.

This process of continuous revelation comes to the Church very frequently. President Wilford Woodruff stated, "This power is in the bosom of Almighty God, and he imparts it to his servants the prophets as they stand in need of it day by day to build up Zion" (in *Journal of Discourses*, 14:33). This is necessary for the Church to fulfill its mission. Without it, we would fail. ("Continuous Revelation," *Ensign*, Nov. 1989, 9–10.)

REVELATION WAS REQUIRED to establish this church. Revelation has brought it from its humble beginnings to its present course. Revelation has come like flowing, living water. Continuing revelation will lead it forward to the windup scene. But as President Clark told us, we do not need more or different prophets. We need more people with "a listening ear" (in Conference Report, Oct. 1948, p. 82).

We make no claim of infallibility or perfection in the prophets, seers, and revelators. Yet I humbly state that I have sat in the company of these men, and I believe their greatest desire is to know and do the will of our Heavenly Father. Those who sit in the highest councils of this church and have participated as inspiration has come and decisions have been reached know that this light and truth is beyond human intelligence and reasoning. These deep, divine impressions have come as the dews from heaven and settled upon them individually and collectively. So inspired, we can go forward in complete unity and accord. ("Continuous Revelation," *Ensign*, Nov. 1989, 11.)

THERE IS SO much continuous, ongoing revelation that comes to this people that the extent of it cannot be fully appreciated. It does not ever, however, become commonplace. As one who is involved in the calling of stake presidents, patriarchs, and other

Church officers, from my own experience I think perhaps Enos said it well: "And while I was thus struggling in the spirit, behold, the voice of the Lord came into my mind." (Enos 1:10.) (Untitled address delivered at the Sidney B. Sperry Symposium on the Scriptures, Brigham Young University, 28 Jan. 1984.)

SABBATH OBSERVANCE

I CONFESS THAT as a young boy, Sunday was not my favorite day. Grandfather shut down the action. We didn't have any transportation. We couldn't drive the car. He wouldn't even let us start the motor. We couldn't ride the horses or the steers or the sheep. It was the Sabbath, and by commandment the animals also needed rest. We walked to Church and everywhere else we wanted to go. I can honestly say that we observed both the spirit and the letter of Sabbath worship.

By today's standards, perhaps Grandfather's interpretation of Sabbath day activities seems extreme, but something wonderful has been lost in our lives. To this day, I have been pondering to try to understand fully what has slipped away. Part of it was knowing that I was well on the Lord's side of the line. Another part was the feeling that Satan's influence was further away. Mostly it was the reinforcement received by the spiritual power which was generated. We had the rich feeling that the spiritual "fulness of the earth" (D&C 59:16) was ours, as promised by the Lord in section 59 of the Doctrine and Covenants. ("The Lord's Day," *Ensign*, Nov. 1991, 33.)

THE SABBATH WAS referred to in the Old Testament days as a blessed and hallowed day (see Exodus 20:11), as a symbol of a perpetual covenant of faithfulness (see Exodus 31:16), as a holy convocation (see Leviticus 23:3), as a day of spiritual celebration (see Leviticus 23:32).

Jesus reaffirmed the importance of the Sabbath day devotion, but he introduced a new spirit into this part of worship (see Matthew 24:20). Rather than observe the endless technicalities and prohibitions concerning what should and should not be done on the Lord's day, he affirmed that it is lawful to do well on the Sabbath (see Matthew 12:12). He taught us that "the Son of man is Lord even of the sabbath day" (Matthew 12:8) and introduced the principle that "the sabbath was made for man, and not man for the sabbath" (Mark 2:27). He performed good deeds on the Sabbath, such as healing the man with palsy (see Mark 2:1–12) as well as the man with the paralyzed hand (see Matthew 12:10–13). So the divine mandate of Sabbath day observance in our day is now more of a manifestation of individual devotion and commitment rather than a requirement of civil law. ("The Lord's Day," *Ensign*, Nov. 1991, 33.)

WHY HAS GOD asked us to honor the Sabbath day? The reasons I think are at least threefold. The first has to do with the physical need for rest and renewing. Obviously God, who created us, would know more than we do of the limits of our physical and nervous energy and strength.

The second reason is, in my opinion, of far greater significance. It has to do with the need for regeneration and the strengthening of our spiritual being. God knows that, left completely to our own devices without regular reminders of our spiritual needs, many would degenerate into the preoccupation of satisfying earthly desires and appetites. This need for physical, mental, and spiritual regeneration is met in large measure by faithful observance of the Sabbath day.

The third reason may be the most important of the three. It has to do with obedience to commandments as an expression of our love for God. Blessed are those who need no reasons other than their love for the Savior to keep his commandments. The response of Adam to the angel who asked Adam why he made a sacrifice unto the Lord is a model for all. Responded Adam, "I know not, save the Lord commanded me" (Moses 5:6).

The prophet Samuel reminds us, "To obey is better than

sacrifice, and to hearken than the fat of rams" (1 Samuel 15:22). ("The Lord's Day," *Ensign*, Nov. 1991, 35.)

WHILE THE SAVIOR himself cautioned against extreme forms of Sabbath day observance, it is well to remember whose day the Sabbath is. There seems to be an ever-increasing popularity in disregarding the centuries-old commandment to observe and respect the Sabbath day. For many it has become a holiday rather than a holy day of rest and sanctification. For some it is a day to shop and buy groceries. The decision of those who engage in shopping, sports, work, and recreation on the Sabbath day is their own, for which they alone bear responsibility.

The Lord's commandment about the Sabbath day has not been altered, nor has the Church's affirmation of the commandment to observe the Sabbath day. Those who violate this commandment in the exercise of their agency are answerable for losing the blessings which observance of this commandment would bring. The Lord has spoken in our day concerning the Sabbath day. We are to keep ourselves "unspotted from the world" and "go to the house of prayer." We are to rest from our labors and pay our "devotions unto the Most High" (D&C 59:9–10). The Doctrine and Covenants reminds us: "And on this day thou shalt do none other thing, only let thy food be prepared with singleness of heart that thy fasting may be perfect, or, in other words, that thy joy may be full" (D&C 59:13). The blessings for those who do righteousness are supernal. They shall enjoy "peace in this world, and eternal life in the world to come" (D&C 59:23). ("Unwanted Messages," *Ensign*, Nov. 1986, 9.)

THE MOSAIC INJUNCTIONS of Sabbath day observance contained many detailed do's and don'ts. This may have been necessary to teach obedience to those who had been in captivity and had long been denied individual freedom of choice. Thereafter, these Mosaic instructions were carried to many unwarranted extremes which the Savior condemned. In that day the technicalities of Sabbath day observance outweighed the "weightier matters of the law" (Matthew 23:23) such as faith, charity, and the gifts of the Spirit.

In our time God has recognized our intelligence by not requiring endless restrictions. Perhaps this was done with a hope that we would catch more of the spirit of Sabbath worship rather than the letter thereof. In our day, however, this pendulum of Sabbath day desecration has swung very far indeed. We stand in jeopardy of losing great blessings promised. After all, it is a test by which the Lord seeks to "prove you in all things" (D&C 98:14) to see if your devotion is complete.

Where is the line as to what is acceptable and unacceptable on the Sabbath? Within the guidelines, each of us must answer this question for ourselves. While these guidelines are contained in the scriptures and in the words of the modern prophets, they must also be written in our hearts and governed by our conscience. Brigham Young said of the faithful, "The spirit of their religion leaks out of their hearts" (in *Journal of Discourses,* 15:83). It is quite unlikely that there will be any serious violation of Sabbath worship if we come humbly before the Lord and offer him all our heart, our soul, and our mind (see Matthew 22:37).

What is worthy or unworthy on the Sabbath day will have to be judged by each of us by trying to be honest with the Lord. On the Sabbath day we should do what we have to do and what we ought to do in an attitude of worshipfulness and then limit our other activities. ("The Lord's Day," *Ensign,* Nov. 1991, 35.)

OVER A LIFETIME of observation, it is clear to me that the farmer who observes the Sabbath day seems to get more done on his farm than he would if he worked seven days. The mechanic will be able to turn out more and better products in six days than in seven. The doctor, the lawyer, the dentist, the scientist will accomplish more by trying to rest on the Sabbath than if he tries to utilize every day of the week for his professional work. I would counsel all students, if they can, to arrange their schedules so that they do not study on the Sabbath. If students and other seekers after truth will do this, their minds will be quickened and the infinite Spirit will lead them to the verities they wish to learn. This is because God has hallowed his day and blessed it as a perpetual covenant of faithfulness (see Exodus 31:16). ("The Lord's Day," *Ensign*, Nov. 1991, 34.)

A . . . MIRACLE OCCURRED at the Wells Stake Welfare Tannery some years ago where hides of animals were tanned into leather. On regular workdays, the hides were removed from the vats and fresh lime placed in the vats, after which the hides were returned to the lime solution. If the hides were not turned on holidays, they would spoil. But the change was never made on Sunday, and there were no spoiled hides on Monday. Explained J. Lowell Fox, the supervisor of the tannery at the time:

"This brought a strange fact to our minds: holidays are determined by man, and on these days just as on every week day, the hides need to have special care every twelve hours. Sunday is the day set aside by the Lord as a day of rest, and He makes it possible for us to rest from our labors as He has commanded. The hides at the tannery never spoil on Sundays. This is a modern-day miracle, a miracle that happens every weekend!" (*Handbook for Guide Patrol Leaders* [Salt Lake City: The Church of Jesus Christ of Latter-day Saints, 1964], p. 37). ("The Lord's Day," *Ensign*, Nov. 1991, 35.)

SACRIFICE

THE WORK OF God is moving forward in many parts of the world like it never has before, particularly in countries where the economic standards are not high and new members are still learning the principle of faith and how it relates to blessings. To be faithful members of this Church requires sacrifice and consecration. It means that worldly pleasures and earthly possessions should not be our principal aim in life, because the gift of eternal life requires a willingness to sacrifice all we have and are in order to obtain it.

In Old Testament times the Lord sent a pestilence upon Israel, and many people died. He commanded David to offer a sacrifice at the threshing floor of Araunah the Jebusite. When David went to see Araunah, and Araunah found out why he had come, he generously offered to give him whatever was needed for the sacrifice. David's response was profound: "I will surely buy it of thee at a price: neither will I offer burnt offerings unto the Lord my God of that which doth cost me nothing." (2 Samuel 24:24.) He bought the threshing floor, offered the sacrifice, and the plague ceased.

In our time we are surfeited with a pestilence of violence, evil, and wickedness in so many forms. Those who keep their covenants and pay their tithes and offerings will have some extra defense against these virulent modern-day forms of evil. But this protection will not come with a sacrifice which costs us nothing. ("Opening the Windows of Heaven," *Ensign*, Nov. 1998, 60.)

THE WORLD'S RELIGIOUS drift is obvious. If something can be had cheaply, without exertion or sacrifice, people do not mind having a little bit of it. In contrast, the blessings of membership in The Church of Jesus Christ of Latter-day Saints require both exertion and sacrifice. Receiving the blessings requires the payment of tithes and offerings. Ours is not a Sunday-only religion. It demands exemplary conduct and effort every day of the week. It involves accepting calls and serving with fidelity in those callings. It means strength of character, integrity, and honesty to the Lord and our fellowmen. It means that our homes need to be places of sanctuary and love. It means a relentless battle against the bombardment of worldly evils. It means, at times, being unpopular and politically incorrect. . . .

The ultimate offering was that offered by the Savior Himself in giving His very life. It causes each of us to wonder, How many drops of blood were shed for me? ("Opening the Windows of Heaven," *Ensign*, Nov. 1998, 60.)

LIVING A CHRISTLIKE life every day may, for many, be even more difficult than laying down one's life. (Stockholm Sweden Area Conference, Aug. 1974, 113.)

SATAN

SOMEONE SAID IN these few words: "I have heard much about the devil. I have read a great deal about the devil. I have even done business with the devil, but it didn't pay." Your generation lives in a day when many things are measured against the standard of social or political correctness. Today I challenge that false doctrine of human behavior. The influence of Satan is becoming more acceptable. Elizabeth Barrett Browning said, "The devil is most devilish when respectable." (*Aurora Leigh*, book VII.) However, as Shakespeare said, "He's mad that trusts in the tameness of a wolf." (Shakespeare, *King Lear*, vi. 20.)

It is not good practice to become intrigued by Satan and his mysteries. No good can come from getting close to evil. Like playing with fire, it is too easy to get burned: "The knowledge of sin tempteth to its commission." (Joseph F. Smith, *Gospel Doctrine* [Salt Lake City: Deseret Book Co., 1939], p. 373.) The only safe course is to keep well distanced from him and from any of his wicked activities or nefarious practices. The mischief of devil worship, sorcery, casting spells, witchcraft, voodooism, black magic, and all other forms of demonism should be avoided like the plague.

However, Brigham Young said that it is important to "study . . . evil, and its consequences." (*Discourses of Brigham Young*, comp. John A. Widtsoe [Salt Lake City: Deseret Book Co., 1941], p. 257.) Since Satan is the author of all evil in the world, it would therefore be essential to realize that he is the influence behind the opposition to the work of God. Alma stated the issue succinctly: "For I say unto you that whatsoever is good cometh from God, and whatsoever is evil cometh from the devil." (Alma 5:40.)

My principal reason for choosing this subject is to help young people by warning them, as Paul said, "lest Satan should get an advantage of us: for we are not ignorant of his devices." (2 Cor. 2:11.) ("Trying to Serve the Lord without Offending the Devil," *BYU Speeches*, 15 Nov. 1994, 59.)

SATAN HAS HAD great success with this gullible generation. As a consequence, literally hosts of people have been victimized by him and his angels. There is, however, an ample shield against the power of Lucifer and his hosts. This protection lies in the spirit of discernment through the gift of the Holy Ghost. This gift comes undeviatingly by personal revelation to those who strive to obey the commandments of the Lord and to follow the counsel of the living prophets.

This personal revelation will surely come to all whose eyes are single to the glory of God, for it is promised that their bodies will be "filled with light, and there shall be no darkness" in them (D&C 88:67). Satan's efforts can be thwarted by all who come unto Christ by obedience to the covenants and ordinances of the gospel. . . .

I wish to testify that there are forces which will save us from the ever-increasing lying, disorder, violence, chaos, destruction, misery, and deceit that are upon the earth. Those saving forces are the everlasting principles, covenants, and ordinances of the eternal gospel of the Lord Jesus Christ. These same principles, covenants, and ordinances are coupled with the rights and powers of the priesthood of Almighty God. We of this church are the possessors and custodians of these commanding powers which can and do roll back much of the power of Satan on the earth. We believe that we hold these mighty forces in trust for all who have died, for all who are now living, and for the yet unborn. ("The Great Imitator," *Ensign*, Nov. 1987, 35–36.)

YOGI BERRA IS reported to have said, "If you come to a fork in the road, take it." But it doesn't work that way. The Savior said, "No man can serve two masters: for either he will hate the one, and love the other; or else he will hold to the one, and despise the other. Ye cannot serve God and mammon." (Matthew 6:24.) Today many of us are trying to serve two masters: the Lord and our own selfish interests, without offending the devil. The influence of God, our Eternal Father, urges us, pleads with us, and inspires us to follow him. In contrast the power of Satan urges us to disbelieve and disregard God's commandments. ("Trying to Serve the Lord without Offending the Devil," *BYU Speeches*, Nov. 15, 1994, 60.)

I WONDER HOW much we offend Satan if the proclamation of our faith is limited only to the great humanitarian work this Church does throughout the world, or our beautiful buildings, or this great university, marvelous as these activities are. When we preach the gospel of social justice, no doubt the devil is not troubled. But I believe the devil is terribly offended when we boldly declare by personal testimony that Joseph Smith was a prophet of God and that he saw the Father and the Son; when we preach that the Book of Mormon is another witness for Christ; when we declare that there has been a restoration of the fullness of the gospel in its simplicity and power in order to fulfill the great plan of happiness.

We challenge the powers of darkness when we speak of the perfect life of the Savior and of his sublime work for all mankind through the Atonement. This supernal gift permits us, through repentance, to break away from Satan's grasping tentacles.

We please the devil when we argue that all roads lead to heaven; therefore, it does not matter which road we take, we will all end up in God's presence. And when we contend that "we are all God's children; therefore, it makes no difference to which church a person belongs; we are all working for the same place."

This man-made philosophy—for such it is—sounds good, but the scriptures do not support it. I assure each of you that the road to God's presence is not that easy. It is strait and narrow. Elder Delbert L. Stapley said, "I feel certain that the devil chuckles whenever this false opinion is expressed, for it pleases him that the minds of men have been so blinded to revealed truth by his cunning craftiness and deceit that they will believe any religion to be acceptable to God regardless of its tenets and ordinances or how or by whom those ordinances are administered." (Delbert L. Stapley, Conference Report, April 1958, 115.) ("Trying to Serve the Lord without Offending the Devil," *BYU Speeches,* 15 Nov. 1994, 63.)

WE NEED NOT become paralyzed with fear of Satan's power. He can have no power over us unless we permit it. He is really a coward, and if we stand firm, he will retreat. The Apostle James counseled: "Submit yourselves therefore to God. Resist the devil, and he will flee from you." (James 4:7.) He cannot know our thoughts unless we speak them. And Nephi states that "he hath no power over the hearts" of people who are righteous. (1 Nephi 22:26.)

We have heard comedians and others justify or explain their misdeeds by saying, "The devil made me do it." I do not really think the devil can make us do anything. Certainly he can tempt and he can deceive, but he has no authority over us which we do not give him.

The power to resist Satan may be stronger than we realize. The Prophet Joseph Smith taught: "All beings who have bodies have power over those who have not. The devil has no power over us only as we permit him. The moment we revolt at anything which comes from God, the devil takes power." (*Teachings of the Prophet Joseph Smith,* sel. Joseph Fielding Smith [Salt Lake City: Deseret Book Co., 1938], p. 181.)

He also stated, "Wicked spirits have their bounds, limits, and laws by which they are governed." (*History of the Church,* 4:576.) So Satan and his angels are not all-powerful. ("Trying to Serve the Lord without Offending the Devil," *BYU Speeches,* 15 Nov. 1994, 64.)

WE HOPE THAT young people, unfamiliar with the sophistries of the world, can keep themselves free of Satan's enticements and deceitful ways. I personally claim no special insight into Satan's methods, but I have at times been able to identify his influence and his actions in my life and in the lives of others. When I was on my first mission, Satan sought to divert me from my future path and, if possible, to destroy my usefulness in the Lord's work. That was almost fifty years ago, and I still remember how reasonable his entreaties seemed.

Who has not heard and felt the enticings of the devil? His voice often sounds so reasonable and his message so easy to justify. It is an enticing, intriguing voice with dulcet tones. It is neither hard nor discordant. No one would listen to Satan's voice if it sounded harsh or mean. If the devil's voice were unpleasant, it would not entice people to listen to it. ("The Great Imitator," *Ensign,* Nov. 1987, 34.)

WE ALL HAVE an inner braking system that will stop us before we follow Satan too far down the wrong road. It is the still, small voice which is within us. But once we have succumbed, the braking system begins to leak brake fluid and our stopping mechanism becomes weak and ineffective. ("The Great Imitator," *Ensign,* Nov. 1987, 34.)

WE JUST RECENTLY heard President Ernest LeRoy Hatch of the Guatemala City Temple say, "The devil is not smart because he is the devil; he is smart because he is old." Indeed, the devil is old, and he was not always the devil. Initially, he was not the perpetrator of evil. He was with the hosts of heaven in the beginning. He was "an angel of God who was in authority in the presence of God" (D&C 76:25). He came before Christ and proposed to God the Father, "Behold, here am I, send me, I will be thy son, and I will redeem all mankind, that one soul shall not be lost, and surely I will do it; wherefore give me thine honor" (Moses 4:1). This he proposed to do by force, destroying the free agency of man. Does his statement "Give me thine

honor" mean that he wanted to mount an insurrection to sup-
plant even God the Father?

Satan became the devil by seeking glory, power, and dominion by force (see Moses 4:3–4). But Jesus, "chosen from the
beginning" (Moses 4:2), said unto God, "Father, thy will be
done, and the glory be thine forever" (Moses 4:2). What a contrast in approaches! Wrong as his plan was, Satan was persuasive enough to entice one-third of the hosts of heaven to follow
him (see D&C 29:36, Revelation 12:4). He practiced a great
deception by saying, "I am also a son of God" (Moses 5:13).
("The Great Imitator," *Ensign,* Nov. 1987, 35.)

SEALING POWER

PERHAPS WE REGARD the power bestowed by Elijah as something
associated only with formal ordinances performed in sacred
places. But these ordinances become dynamic and productive of
good only as they reveal themselves in our daily lives. Malachi
said that the power of Elijah would turn the hearts of the fathers
and the children to each other. The heart is the seat of the emotions and a conduit for revelation. (See Mal. 4:5–6.) This sealing
power thus reveals itself in family relationships, in attributes
and virtues developed in a nurturing environment, and in loving service. These are the cords that bind families together, and
the priesthood advances their development. In imperceptible
but real ways, the "doctrine of the priesthood shall distil upon
thy soul [and thy home] as the dews from heaven." (D&C
121:45.) ("Father, Come Home," *Ensign,* May 1993, 37.)

SECULARISM

MY FATHER, WHO fought in World War I, used to tell his sons, three
of whom fought in World War II and one in the Korean War, that
World War I was fought as the war to end all wars. He saw his
sons go and come back from the other wars. Since that time,
there has been in some ways a lessening of respect for human

life. There is also a developing disrespect for the sacred in our society. The constitutionality of public reference to deity and prayer to God is in controversy. There seems to be developing a secular faith or religion with no moral absolutes. It is non-theistic and non-denominational. It is antagonistic to religion and rejects the religious tradition of this nation. This secular religion is not a faith or church or synagogue that worships all-mighty God or adheres to a code of moral conduct for its followers. In fact, this secular religion is in opposition to traditional religion.

The long history and tradition of this nation, which had in its roots petitions for divine guidance and its coinage stamped *In God We Trust,* is being challenged. Appeals for divine guidance, forgiveness, and approbation have been part of the fabric of this nation from the beginning. The first prayer in Congress was offered September 17, 1774. In his farewell address, George Washington acknowledged that "of all the dispositions and habits which lead to political prosperity, religion and morality are indispensable supports. Reason and experience both forbid us to expect that national morality can prevail in exclusion of religious principle." . . .

Thomas Jefferson, in his first inaugural address, prayed, "May that infinite power which rules the destinies of the universe lead our councils to do what is best and give them a favorable issue for your peace and prosperity." ("The Impact of World War II on Utah," World War II Commemoration, Ogden, Utah, 13 Aug. 1995.)

THE RECENT CONTROVERSY in the state and the nation regarding the constitutionality of certain public prayers casts a serious cloud over the reality and meaning of the sacred in our society.

There seems to be developing a new civil religion. The civil religion I refer to is a secular religion. It has no moral absolutes. It is non-denominational. It is non-theistic. It is politically focused. It is antagonistic to religion. It rejects the historic religious traditions of this nation. It feels strange. If this trend continues, non-belief will be more honored than belief. While all beliefs must be protected, are atheism, agnosticism, cynicism, and moral relativism to be more safeguarded and valued than Christianity, Judaism, and the tenets of Islam which hold that there is a Supreme Being and that mortals are accountable to him? If so, this would, in my opinion, place this nation in great moral jeopardy. ("A New Civil Religion," Pioneer Day Fireside, Ogden, Utah, 19 July 1992.)

SELFISHNESS

I BELIEVE THAT earthly crowns such as power, the love of money, the preoccupation with material things, the honors of men are a crown of thorns because they are based upon obtaining and receiving rather than giving. So selfishness can make what we think is a noble crown into a crown of thorns beyond our power to endure. When I first started my professional career, one of the senior members in our office asked another senior member for some help on a legal matter. The other man who was asked to help was gifted and able but also selfish. He replied, "What's in it for me?" The "what's in it for me" philosophy is basically what's wrong with the world. It is surely one of the sharpest points in a crown of thorns.

The call of Jesus Christ to each of us is, "If any man will come after me, let him deny himself, and take up his cross, and follow me" (Matthew 16:24). Is it not time that we begin denying ourselves, as the Savior counseled, and surrender and master ourselves rather than indulge ourselves in a "do my own thing" selfish little world? The question is not so much what we can do, but what God can do through us. Paul said, "If a man therefore purge himself . . . , he shall be a vessel unto honour, sanctified, and meet for the master's use, and prepared unto every good work" (2 Timothy 2:21). ("A Crown of Thorns, a Crown of Glory," *Ensign*, May 1991, 70.)

S E L F - W O R T H

I AM AT once humbled and challenged in trying to speak of a great human need, self-esteem. I refer to what we think of ourselves, how we relate to what others think of us and the value of what we accomplish. Shakespeare in Othello said, "I have never found a man that knew how to love himself." (*Othello,* act I, scene 3.)

The consequences of falling in love with oneself generally continue as an extended romance. This is what Thomas Carlyle, the famous Scottish writer referred to as "the sixth insatiable sense." And the English author Browning said self-esteem is "an itch for the praise of fools." The self-esteem that I speak of today is something different. It is not blind, arrogant, vain, self-love, but self-respecting, unconceited, honest self-esteem. It is born of inner peace and strength. . . .

Self-esteem goes to the very heart of our personal growth and accomplishment. Self-esteem is the glue that holds together our self-reliance, our self-control, our self-approval or disapproval, and keeps all self-defense mechanisms secure. It is a protection against excessive self-deception, self-distrust, self-reproach, and plain old-fashioned selfishness. ("Self-Esteem: A Great Human Need," Brigham Young University Education Week address, 23 Aug. 1983.)

HOW CAN CHRISTIAN belief and morality translate more completely into Christian action? Does our commitment fall short of being a consecration? The doubting Thomas wanted to believe; he believed part way. It is my firm persuasion that building self-esteem sufficiently to forsake all evil requires a consecration to the saving principles and ordinances of the gospel under divine priesthood authority. It must be consecration to simple, basic Christian principles, including honesty to self and others, forgetting of self, integrity of thought and action. The principles of the restored gospel are so plain, so clear, so compassionate, so endowed with beauty, so graced with love unfeigned, as to be imprinted with the indisputable impress of the Savior himself.

There also needs to be a confrontation with and mastery of life's challenges, especially those that come with temptation. Instead of squarely and honestly meeting the problems of life, many negotiate their way through difficulties, rationalizing their departure from the great truths which bring happiness and justifying the leaving of their sacred promises and holy commitments for seemingly logical but fragile and unjustifiable reasons.

I cannot help wondering if we have not fallen short of the mark. Have we been measuring by standards that are too short and unworthy of those in the pursuit of holiness? Have we taken too much comfort in feeling that we have qualified through our attendance at meetings or through minimal involvement in a conscience-easing effort? Have our guidelines been a ceiling instead of a floor? ("The Dignity of Self," *Ensign,* May 1981, 8–9.)

ONE OF THE root social problems of our day concerns the lack of self-esteem.

A shallow self-image is not reinforced by always letting others establish our standards and by habitually succumbing to peer pressure. Young people too often depend upon someone else's image rather than their own.

Insecurity and lack of self-esteem may be related to lack of self-respect. Can we respect ourselves when we do things that we do not admire and may even condemn in others? Repenting of transgressions and forsaking of weaknesses represent, however, a great restorative salve for the strengthening of human worth and dignity. ("The Dignity of Self," *Ensign,* May 1981, 9.)

WHEN I WAS growing up in the Cottonwood area of Salt Lake County, it was the rural part of the valley. One of the men who had the greatest dignity and commanded the greatest respect was an old Scandinavian brother who, after walking a couple of miles, traveled by streetcar to work at the Salt Lake City Cemetery and back every day. His work was to water and mow the grass, tend the flowers, and dig the graves. He said little because he did not speak English well, but he was always where he should be, doing what he should do in a most dignified, exemplary way. He had no problems with ego, or with faith, for while he dug graves for a living, his work was to serve God. He was a man of little status, but of great worth.

Not far away from his humble home was where the more affluent people of our community lived. Many of the well-to-do were fine, honorable people; but some of them who had much status lived lives of debauchery and drunkenness but little worth.

When the Savior called his disciples he was not looking for men and women of status, property, or fame. He was looking for those of worth and potential. They were an interesting group, those early disciples: the fishermen, the tax gatherer, and the others. On one occasion, after some of the apostles were beaten, they went "rejoicing that they were counted worthy to suffer shame for his name." (Acts 5:41).

Worth has little to do with age. It has everything to do with service. The Lord has made it clear that worthiness is built upon service, not just to family and friends, but also to strangers and even enemies. ("Self-Esteem: A Great Human Need," Brigham Young University Education Week address, 23 Aug. 1983.)

SINCE VIRTUE AND faith too often do not readily trade in the marketplace, some may feel that they can live by whatever standards their whim or fancy suggest. In a value-free society—free of morals, free of standards—many also live free of feelings of self-worth, self-respect, and dignity. Far too many young people, and older ones, too, fail to realize, as the motto of the city of Nottingham, England, affirms: *Vivet post funera virtus* ("Virtue lives on after death").

In the intellectual approach to human worth, the values of

faith in God and virtuous behavior cannot be quantitatively proven or measured, and so faith and virtue are often rejected by many as worthless. This is a route destined to failure because it does not take into account the powerful importance of the subjective things we can know but not measure. For instance, I love my wife and family, and I feel their love for me. You cannot measure how deep our feelings of love are for each other, but that love is very real to us. Pain is also difficult to measure, but it is real. The same is true of faith in God. We can know of his existence without being able to quantitatively measure it. Paul states, "The Spirit itself beareth witness with our spirit, that we are the children of God." (Romans 8:16 .) ("The Dignity of Self," *Ensign,* May 1981, 9–10.)

THE DIGNITY OF self is greatly enhanced by looking upward in the search for holiness. Like the giant trees, we should reach up for the light. The most important source of light we can come to know is the gift of the Holy Ghost. It is the source of inner strength and peace.

I have seen human dignity and self-worth expressed eloquently in the lives of the humblest of the humble, in the lives of the poor as well as in the lives of the formally educated and the affluent. The fruits of the search for holiness in their lives have been transparent, expressed through their inner dignity, their feelings of self-respect and personal worth. ("The Dignity of Self," *Ensign,* May 1981, 10.)

SERVICE

I DON'T THINK our motivation [for service and community relations] ought to be proselyting—I think it ought to be trying to make the world a better place in which to live. Or course, we are happy to share the gospel with anyone who is sincerely interested. But it ought to be a happy consequence of what we're doing, not a primary motivation for it. (Address to Public Affairs Directors, Salt Lake City, Utah, 7 May 1991.)

TAKING UP ONE'S cross and following the Savior is always a commitment to service. When going to school I was very poor. I worked long hours in a canning factory catching steaming-hot cans for twenty-five cents an hour. I learned that selfishness has more to do with how we feel about what we have than how much we have. A poor man can be selfish and a rich man generous, but a person obsessed only with getting will have a hard time to find God. I have come to know that with any privilege comes responsibility. Most privilege carries with it the responsibility to serve, to give, and to bless. God can take away any privilege if it is not used under his omnipotent will. Meeting that challenge to give, to serve, to bless in faithfulness and devotion is the only way to enjoy the crown of glory spoken of by the original Apostles. It is the only way true meaning comes to life. We will be able to receive honors or scorn with equal serenity. ("A Crown of Thorns, a Crown of Glory," *Ensign*, May 1991, 70.)

SOME MONTHS AGO, as Elder Spencer J. Condie and I were in the Salt Lake airport, we unexpectedly met a devoted and faithful couple who have been friends for long years. This couple have spent a lifetime of service, meekly, faithfully, and effectively trying to build up the Church in many places in the world. Elder Condie noted, "Isn't it remarkable what people with five loaves and two fishes do to build up the kingdom of God." This kind of quiet, devoted service is surely a fulfillment of the word of God "that the fulness of my gospel might be proclaimed by the weak and the simple unto the ends of the world, and before kings and rulers" (D&C 1:23). . . .

It has been said that this church does not necessarily attract great people but more often makes ordinary people great. Many nameless people with gifts equal only to five loaves and two small fishes magnify their callings and serve without attention or recognition, feeding literally thousands. In large measure, they make possible the fulfillment of Nebuchadnezzar's dream that the latter-day gospel of Christ would be like a stone cut out of the mountain without hands, rolling forth until it fills the whole earth (see Daniel 2:34–35; D&C 65:2). These are the hundreds of thousands of leaders and teachers in all of the auxiliaries and priesthood quorums, the home teachers, the Relief Society visiting teachers. These are the many humble bishops in the Church, some without formal training but greatly magnified, always learning, with a humble desire to serve the Lord and the people of their wards. ("Five Loaves and Two Fishes," *Ensign,* May 1994, 4, 5.)

ANY MAN OR woman who enjoys the Master's touch is like potter's clay in his hands. More important than acquiring fame or fortune is being what God wants us to be. Before we came to the earth, we may have been fashioned to do some small good in this life that no one else can do. The Lord said to Jeremiah, "Before I formed thee in the belly I knew thee; and before thou camest forth out of the womb I sanctified thee, and I ordained thee a prophet unto the nations" (Jeremiah 1:5). If God has a work for those with many talents, I believe he also has an important work for those of us who have few. ("Five Loaves and Two Fishes," *Ensign,* May 1994, 5–6.)

THERE IS [A] . . . matter which impacts both single and married members of the Church that I will briefly discuss. As we serve others, we must always be conscious of the principle of agency and the need to teach and foster self reliance. . . .

As we serve we must be careful not to create an unnecessary or unwise dependency on the part of others. Render appropriate assistance, but also teach correct principles and allow others "to act for themselves."

Please do not misunderstand. I am not suggesting that we back away from service to those in need. The Lord will hold us accountable if we do not obey His injunction that the "widows and orphans shall be provided for, as also the poor" (D&C 83:6). Surely there are many single parent homes today, created by death and divorce, where the spirit of this divine declaration applies.

The mark of discipleship is service to and love for our fellowman. Recall the words of King Benjamin that "when ye are in the service of your fellow beings ye are only in the service of your God" (Mosiah 2:17).

Paul taught the ancient Saints "to bear the infirmities of the weak, and not to please ourselves" (Romans 15:1).

In modern days, the Lord Himself instructed His Saints to "succor the weak, lift up the hands which hang down, and strengthen the feeble knees" (D&C 81:5).

The challenge is to know which hands are hanging down and which knees need strengthening. ("The Responsibility of Church Leaders to Members of the Church Who Are Single," Church Satellite Broadcast, 23 Feb. 1992.)

SIN

SO-CALLED SMALL sins include the challenge to the "sin laws" which seek to control forms of gambling, alcohol, and drug consumption. Some who wish to appear broad-minded say, under the guise of not imposing religious belief, "I don't drink or gamble, but I don't think we ought to have any laws to control others that wish to." This completely ignores the health and social costs to society of the vices. They foolishly argue that laws cannot control human behavior. My long legal career has led me to conclude that all criminal laws have a moral basis. ("Trying to Serve the Lord without Offending the Devil," *BYU Speeches*, 15 Nov. 1994, 63.)

IT SEEMS THAT no matter how carefully we walk through life's paths, we pick up some thorns, briars, and slivers. As a young boy, when school was out for the summer and we went to the farm, off came our shoes. The shoes stayed off all summer long except for special occasions. For the first week or two, when our feet were tender, the smoothest pebble or stick would be painful. But as the weeks came and went, the soles of our feet toughened so that they could withstand almost anything in the path except thistles, of which there seemed to be more than any other weed. And so it is with life: as we grow and mature and keep close to Him who was crowned with thorns, our souls seem to get stronger in withstanding the challenges, our resolve hardens, our wills become firmer, and our self-discipline increases to protect us from the evils of this world. These evils are so omnipresent, however, that we must always walk in the paths which are the most free of the thistles of earthly temptation.

As children we used to delight in waving thistledown stalks to watch the seeds float on the wind. Only later did we realize the effects that this had on our own and neighboring gardens. Many of us delight in flirting with temptation, only later to learn how we and others have sown the seeds of our own unhappiness and how we can also affect our neighbor's happiness. ("A Crown of Thorns, a Crown of Glory," *Ensign*, May 1991, 68.)

I WARN YOU of a pervasive false doctrine. For want of a better name, I call it "premeditated repentance," by which I mean consciously sinning with the forethought that afterwards repentance will permit the enjoyment of the full blessings of the gospel, such as temple marriage or a mission. In an increasingly wicked society, it is harder to toy with evil without becoming contaminated. This foolish doctrine was foreseen by Nephi.

"And there shall also be many which shall say: Eat, drink, and be merry; nevertheless, fear God—he will justify in committing a little sin; yea, lie a little, take the advantage of one because of his words, dig a pit for thy neighbor; there is no harm in this; and do all these things, for tomorrow we die; and if it so be that we are guilty, God will beat us with a few stripes, and at last we shall be saved in the kingdom of God" (2 Nephi 28:8).

Of all those who teach this doctrine the Lord says, "The

blood of the saints shall cry from the ground against them" (2 Nephi 28:10). ("The Voice of the Spirit," Young Adult Fireside Satellite Broadcast, 5 Sept. 1993.)

REGARDLESS OF THE saturation of wickedness around us, we must stay free from the evil of the world. ("Woman, Why Weepest Thou?" *Ensign,* Nov. 1996, 53.)

I FEAR THAT some of our greatest sins are sins of omission. These are some of the weightier matters of the law the Savior said we should not leave undone. These are the thoughtful, caring deeds we fail to do and feel so guilty for having neglected them. ("The Weightier Matters of the Law: Judgment, Mercy and Faith," *Ensign,* Nov. 1997, 59.)

TRANSGRESSION IS DEVASTATING to self-esteem, and after transgression usually comes rationalization, and often lying. This is what makes justice so violent to the offending. ("Self-Esteem: A Great Human Need," Brigham Young University Education Week address, 23 Aug. 1983.)

PERHAPS WORSE THAN sin is the denial of sin. If we deny that we are sinners, how can we ever be forgiven? How can the atonement of Jesus work in our lives if there is no repentance? If we do not promptly remove the slivers of sin and the thorns of carnal temptation, how can the Lord ever heal our souls? ("A Crown of Thorns, a Crown of Glory," *Ensign,* May 1991, 68.)

SINGLE ADULTS

IN SPEAKING OF adult members of the Church who are single, we are reminded of Paul's counsel to the Corinthians (1 Corinthians 12):

"For the body is not one member, but many" (vs. 14).

" . . . there should be no schism in the body; but that the members should have the same care one for another" (vs. 25).

Each member, regardless of marital status, age, sex, race, or color is important to the body of the Church.

While we have Church programs based on age (Primary), gender (Young Women and Relief Society), and marital status (Young Single Adults, Single Members), these are designed to meet special needs. They are to foster faith and fellowship, not to create fixed categories of people who are separated from the body of the Church.

Single members are "fellow citizens . . . of the household of God" (Ephesians. 2:19). ("The Responsibility of Church Leaders to Members of the Church Who Are Single," Church Satellite Broadcast, 23 Feb. 1992.)

MOST OF THE single adult members are well adjusted to life and its problems, but they still need the loving attention from the Church and its members to reaffirm their usefulness and the love that God has for each of them. They are not problem people, but many have problems, often not of their own making. A choice friend reminds us, "If you don't have any problems, just wait awhile." ("Reaching the One," *Ensign*, July 1973, 86.)

THE PROPER AND rightful focus of the Church on the home and the family frequently causes the single members who have no companion and family to feel left out. One writes, "Many members of the Church treat a divorcee as if she had leprosy. I have lived in a certain LDS ward in Salt Lake for several years, where they had a widows' and widowers' party every year at Christmas time. I was never invited. I have always lived a good life and believe the Savior would have invited me. I am acquainted with some who have experienced both death and divorce, and they say that divorce is worse than death."

Still another writes, "Believe me, with the Church emphasis on families and children, we are already thoroughly aware that we are 'oddballs.' It has been a real pleasure to be accepted as a normal person."

We must begin by trying to reach the one—every single individual. We want all to feel that they belong to the Church in the context of Paul's message to the Ephesians: " . . . ye are no more strangers and foreigners, but fellowcitizens with the saints, and of the household of God." (Eph. 2:19.) ("Reaching the One," *Ensign,* July 1973, 86.)

I SAY TO you single brethren, do not take too much counsel from your fears. Marriage is in large measure an act of faith—faith in yourself, faith in your eternal companion, and faith in God. While the sublime happiness I have known in marriage is not guaranteed, if you marry, you will more likely be happier, live longer, be healthier, live better, and make more money!

The answer lies in finding out what God expects of each of us in our circumstances—single, widowed, divorced, husband, wife, father, or mother. Let us not grope blindly for fulfillment without the vision of who we are and what we can become. ("A Vision of What We Can Be," Singles Satellite Broadcast, 12 Nov. 1995.)

YOU PRIESTHOOD AND women leaders who are gathered together tonight are among those who have been called to nurture, fellowship, and serve with the single members of the Church. . . .

Each of you has a specific responsibility to reach out in love and fellowship to the members of the Church who are single. However, as with all members of the Church—married or single—needs will vary according to individual circumstances. Look at each person individually. ("The Responsibility of Church Leaders to Members of the Church Who Are Single," Church Satellite Broadcast, 23 Feb. 1992.)

TOO OFTEN WE are thoughtless and insensitive to the feelings of these choice souls among us. One well-meaning priesthood leader, concerned about one of these choice single women, whose heart was aching for companionship and a more fulfilling life, asked, "Why don't you get a husband?" She replied in good humor, "Brother, I would love to, but I can't go pick one off a tree." ("Reaching the One," *Ensign*, July 1973, 87.)

OUR SISTERS, THE beloved handmaidens of God, approach the throne of the Almighty as often and surely as closely as men. We realize that there are many who are noble and faithful among us who have not all of the blessings they would wish. We should like to reassure the adult singles of the Church that they can and will, through their faithfulness, enjoy the love of God reserved for his faithful, especially for those who through no fault of their own these blessings have not been realized. Some of our most faithful members are single and unsealed. However, all of us are a part of a family unit past, present or future. Personal sanctification is available to all God's children. Our judgment will be based on our own personal righteousness; how fully we made our tithes and offerings; how faithfully we attended to our duties and how effectively we rendered personal service to our fellow beings.

All womankind can have a second birth. They can call forth that portion of divinity which is within them and bring it to its full potential. They can have their souls renewed and sanctified, and come to know and feel that they are "chosen vessels unto the Lord," even as the Lord said of Paul. (Remarks delivered at the dedication of the Eliza R. Snow Center for the Performing Arts, Ricks College, 9 Dec. 1980.)

SINS OF OMISSION

I FEAR THAT some of our greatest sins are sins of omission. These are some of the weightier matters of the law the Savior said we should not leave undone. (Matt. 23:23.) These are the thoughtful, caring deeds we fail to do, and feel so guilty for having neglected them.

As a small boy on the farm during the searing heat of the summer, I remember my grandmother, Mary Finlinson, cooking our delicious meals on a hot wood stove. When the wood box next to the stove became empty, Grandmother would silently pick up the box, go out to refill it from the pile of cedar wood outside, and bring the heavily laden box back into the house. I was so insensitive and so interested in the conversation in the kitchen, I sat there and let my beloved grandmother refill the kitchen wood box. I feel ashamed of myself and have regretted my omission for all of my life. I hope someday to ask for her forgiveness. ("The Weightier Matters of the Law: Judgment, Mercy and Faith," *Ensign*, Nov. 1997, 59.)

SPIRIT, LISTENING TO THE

PAUL SAID, "THERE are . . . so many kinds of voices in the world" (1 Corinthians 14:10) that compete with the voice of the Spirit. We have come here to hear just one voice. I have humbly prayed that I will speak by the power of the Holy Ghost so that my message may be carried into your hearts by that same power (see 2 Nephi 33:1). Imagine, however, what would happen if all of a sudden a heckler in the back of this hall started to yell obscenities; another on my left began to contend with him; another on my right began to debate with his neighbor; someone in the center turned on a recording of some loud music. Soon a chorus of raucous, rival voices would smother my voice, and it would be difficult, if not impossible, to deliver a spiritual message to you.

Such is the situation in the world. The Spirit's voice is ever-present, but it is calm. Said Isaiah, "And the work of righteousness shall be peace; and the effect of righteousness quietness and assurance for ever" (Isaiah 32:17). The Adversary tries to smother this voice with a multitude of loud, persistent, persuasive, and appealing voices. . . .

In your generation you will be barraged by multitudes of voices telling you how to live, how to gratify your passions, how to have it all. You will have up to five hundred television channels at your fingertips. There will be all sorts of software, interactive computer modems, data bases, and bulletin boards;

there will be desktop publishing, satellite receivers, and communications networks that will suffocate you with information. Local cable news networks will cover only local news. Everyone will be under more scrutiny. There will be fewer places of refuge and serenity. You will be bombarded with evil and wickedness like no other generation. As I contemplate this prospect, I am reminded of T. S. Eliot's words, "Where is the wisdom we have lost in knowledge? Where is the knowledge we have lost in information?" ("Choruses from 'The Rock,'" *The Complete Poems and Plays,* New York: Harcourt, Brace & World, Inc., 1930, p. 96.) ("The Voice of the Spirit," Young Adult Fireside Satellite Broadcast, 5 Sept. 1993.)

SPIRITUAL GIFTS

BEING THOUGHTFUL STUDENTS, you are all aware of the cynical statement of Karl Marx, "Religion is the sign of the oppressed creature, the feeling of a heartless world, just as it is the spirit of unspiritual conditions. It is the opium of the people." Rather than being like a drug, these gifts of the spirit work differently. They do not excite, they calm. They do not hallucinate, they strengthen. They do not weaken, but make more powerful. They are not mere escape hatches from responsibilities, but instruments of insight into what life really means. The spiritually liberating life proves itself by moral responsibility, by an awareness of human fallibility, yet reserves, indeed teaches the ultimate majesty and meaning of life. It is that which spans our horizons, our feelings, our senses, rather than limiting and inhibiting them. It is the learning of the vast difference between saying prayers and praying. Our prayers, like lightning, go into the unseen and the responses that we receive give us the safest course which can be found. ("Christianity—Repression or Liberation?" *BYU Speeches,* 10 June 1975, 143–44.)

NOT EVERYONE . . . has a talent for the arts. Some may have a gift to make others feel important, happy, and special. This gift should also be developed and strengthened.

The spiritual gifts likewise can be refined and enlarged by attentive application to righteous living, to prayer, to study of the scriptures, and to obedience. ("Self-Esteem: A Great Human Need," Brigham Young University Education Week address, 23 Aug. 1983.)

SPIRITUAL SICKNESS

ONE REASON FOR the spiritual sickness of our society is that so many do not know or care about what is morally right and wrong. So many things are justified on the basis of expediency and the acquiring of money and goods. In recent times, those few individuals and institutions that have had the courage enough to stand up and speak out against adultery, dishonesty, violence, and gambling, and other forms of evil are often held up to ridicule. Many things are just plain and simply wrong, whether they are illegal or not. Those who persist in following after the evil things of the world cannot know the "peace of God, which passeth all understanding" (Phil. 4:7). ("Spiritual Healing," *Ensign*, May 1992, 6.)

SPIRITUALITY

NOT MANY MONTHS ago we were in one of the oldest cities on earth. Some of the greatest wonders of the world are there; so are crime, squalor, poverty, and filth. Our kind hosts observed as we were making our way through the teeming masses—past the overloaded donkeys, the filth, the smells—that everything was beautiful in that city if you would raise your sights and only look a foot or more above the ground.

In recent times the price of oil, gold, and other precious minerals has greatly increased. These treasures are all obtained by looking down. They are useful and necessary, but they are tangible riches. What of the treasures that are to be found by raising our vision? What of the intangible riches which come from the pursuit of holiness? Stephen looked upward: "Being full of the Holy Ghost, [he] looked up steadfastly into heaven, and saw the glory of God, and Jesus standing on the right hand of God." (Acts 7:55.) ("The Dignity of Self," *Ensign,* May 1981, 8.)

WITHOUT QUESTION, WE need to be informed of the happenings of the world. But modern communication brings into our homes a drowning cascade of the violence and misery of the worldwide human race. There comes a time when we need to find some peaceful spiritual renewal.

I acknowledge with great gratitude the peace and contentment we can find for ourselves in the spiritual cocoons of our homes, our sacrament meetings, and our holy temples. In these peaceful environments, our souls are rested. We have the feeling of having come home. ("Gratitude as a Saving Principle," *Ensign,* May 1990, 86.)

THE SPIRITUAL RICHNESS of our meetings seems to have little to do with the buildings or country in which we meet. Many years ago, we went to Manaus, Brazil, a city far upstream on the Amazon River, surrounded by jungle, to meet with the missionaries and the handful of Saints who were then in that area. We met in a very humble home with no glass panes in the windows. The weather was excessively hot. The children sat on the floor. The mission president, President Helio da Rocha Camargo, conducted the meeting and called on a faithful brother to give the opening prayer. The humble man responded, "I will be happy to pray but may I also bear my testimony?" A sister was asked to lead the singing. She responded, "I would love to lead the singing, but please let me also bear my testimony." And so it was all through the meeting with those who participated in any way. All felt impelled to bear their profound witness of the Savior and his mission and of the restoration of the gospel of Jesus Christ. All who were there reached deep down in their souls to their spiritual taproots, remembering the Savior's words that "where two or three are gathered together in my name, there am I in the midst of them." (Matt. 18:20.) This they did more as heirs to the Kingdom of God than as Brazilian members of the Church. ("Heirs to the Kingdom of God," *Ensign*, May 1995, 63.)

SOMEHOW, SOME WAY, we must find the healing influence that brings solace to the soul. Where is this balm? Where is the compensating relief so desperately needed to help us survive the world's pressures? The offsetting comfort in large measure can come through increased communion with the Spirit of God. This can bring spiritual healing. . . .

The sixth Article of Faith states that, among other spiritual gifts, we believe in the gift of healing. To me, this gift extends to healing of both the body and the spirit. The Spirit speaks peace to the soul. This spiritual solace comes by invoking spiritual gifts, which are claimed and manifested in many ways. They are rich, full, and abundant in the Church today. They flow from the humble and proper use of a testimony. They also come through administering to the sick following an anointing with consecrated oil. Christ is the great Physician, who rose from the dead "with healing in his wings" (2 Nephi 25:13), while the Comforter is the agency of healing.

The Lord has provided many avenues by which we receive this healing influence. . . . Our temples provide a sanctuary where we go to lay aside many of the anxieties of the world. Our temples are places of peace and tranquillity. In these hallowed sanctuaries God "healeth the broken in heart, and bindeth up their wounds" (Psalm 147:3). ("Spiritual Healing," *Ensign*, May 1992, 6–7.)

FOR MANY OF US, . . . spiritual healing takes place not in great arenas of the world, but in our sacrament meetings. It is comforting to worship, partake of the sacrament with, and be taught in a spirit of humility by neighbors and close friends who love the Lord and try to keep his commandments. . . .

Our sacrament meetings should be worshipful and healing, restoring those who attend to spiritual soundness. . . .

Spiritual healing also comes from bearing and hearing humble testimonies. A witness given in a spirit of contrition, thankfulness for divine providence, and submission to divine guidance is a powerful remedy to help relieve the anguish and concerns of our hearts.

I doubt that sincere members of this church can achieve complete spiritual healing without our being in harmony with the foundation of the Church, which the Apostle Paul stated is, "the apostles and prophets" (Ephesians 2:20). It is also essential for us to be found sustaining our bishops and stake presidents. ("Spiritual Healing," *Ensign*, May 1992, 7–8.)

OF ALL THAT we might do to find solace, prayer is perhaps the most comforting. . . . The very act of praying to God is satisfying to the soul, even though God, in his wisdom, may not give what we ask for. . . . Prayer is most helpful in the healing process. . . .

We find solace in Christ through the agency of the Comforter, and he extends this invitation to us: "Come unto me, all ye that labour and are heavy laden, and I will give you rest" (Matthew 11:28). The Apostle Peter speaks of "casting all your care upon him; for he careth for you" (1 Peter 5:7). As we do this, healing takes place, just as the Lord promised through the Prophet Jeremiah when he said, "I will turn their mourning into joy, and will comfort them, and make them rejoice from their sorrow. . . . I have satiated the weary soul, and I have replenished every sorrowful soul" (Jeremiah 31:13, 25). ("Spiritual Healing," *Ensign*, May 1992, 8.)

IN ROSELANDIA, BRAZIL, outside the great city of São Paulo, there are many acres of beautiful roses. When one stands on a small hill above the rose fields, the aroma is delightful and the beauty is exhilarating. The thorns on the bushes are there, but they in no way lessen the enjoyment of the sight and the smell. I would challenge all to put the thorns, slivers, and thistles we encounter in life in proper perspective. We should deal with them but then concentrate on the flowers of life, not on the thorns. We should savor the smell and beauty of the flower of the rose and the cactus. To savor the sweet aroma of the blossoms, we need to live righteous and disciplined lives in which the study of the scriptures, prayer, right priorities, and right attitudes are integrated into our lives. For members of this church, that focus sharpens inside of our temples. We will all surely encounter some of the thorns, but they are only incidental to the sweet fragrances and exquisite beauty of the blooms. ("A Crown of Thorns, a Crown of Glory," *Ensign,* May 1991, 70.)

STANDARDS

MANY IN SOCIETY, and even some in this university, expend far too much precious energy in protesting the rules. Since they did not make the rules, some feel that they should not be restricted by them. Others make a game of testing the fences to see what they can get away with. Some think that by breaking the rules somehow they become stronger or independent. Those who fight the rules spend much time and energy trying to express independence in their attempted quest to find some identity.

Talents, gifts of expression, and precious time are exhausted in swimming against too many tides. I have no hesitancy to suggest that young men . . . can learn to express themselves better through excellence in the classroom or on the playing field than in the length of their hair. Young ladies can obtain a better identity and receive a better notice by their academic excellence and artistic expression rather than through an immodesty of dress. ("The Study and Practice of the Laws of Men in Light of the Laws of God," Address to Brigham Young University law students, 22 Nov. 1987.)

S U C C E S S

WHAT IS SUCCESS? Is it money? Is it achievement? Is it fame? Is it position? Is it dominion? The prophet Micah defined success as follows: "He hath shewed thee, O man, what is good; and what doth the Lord require of thee, but to do justly, and to love mercy, and to walk humbly with thy God?" (Micah 6:8.) ("Integrity, the Mother of Many Virtues," *Ensign,* May 1982, 48.)

THE WHOLE WORLD admires success. But how each of us defines success and how we seek it is crucial to our happiness. ("Integrity, the Mother of Many Virtues," *Ensign,* May 1982, 48.)

SUCCESSES SHOULD BE obtained . . . through integrity in all transactions. Success has a price, and the price has to be paid. ("Doing the Best Things in the Worst Times," *Ensign,* Aug. 1984, 43.)

HARD WORK IS more important than intellect. ("What I Want My Son to Know Before He Leaves on His Mission," *Ensign,* May 1996, 40.)

T E A C H I N G

PRESIDENT [J. REUBEN] Clark . . . told [a group of educators] in such a gathering as this that you are walking on sacred ground as you teach our young people. I tell you that it is also like walking on wet cement. What kind of footprints will you leave? Will you be flitting across with flights into esoteric mysteries? Or will you be leaving solid, well-placed footprints that can be followed with eternal life? ("A Legacy of the New Testament," 12th Annual CES Religious Educators' Symposium, 12 Aug. 1988.)

T E M P L E   W O R K

WE DO CHERISH our temple buildings, but the buildings alone do not bless. In the history of the Church it has been necessary to leave two beautiful temples built at great sacrifice. But when the saints left, they did not leave the keys, the authority, the covenants, and the blessings; these were taken with them. It is what takes place inside of the buildings through the keys, the covenants, the ordinances, and the spirit of Elijah working under the Spirit of the Lord that blesses the Saints. ("The Covenant People of the Lord," Address to Regional Representatives, Salt Lake City, Utah, 3 Apr. 1987.)

THE DUTY, FUNCTION, and mission of the greater priesthood in relation to the ordinances of the temple was stated by the Lord:

"And this greater priesthood administereth the gospel and holdeth the key of the mysteries of the kingdom, even the key of the knowledge of God.

"Therefore, in the ordinances thereof, the power of godliness is manifest.

"And without the ordinances thereof, and the authority of the priesthood, the power of godliness is not manifest unto men in the flesh." (D&C 84:19–21.)

Of course, going to the temple is a matter of choice, but many do not realize that in order to come unto Christ receiving the ordinances of the temple is not optional, it is essential. No one will be able to come unto Christ without these steps and ordinances. ("The Key to Activity and Retention," Regional Representatives' Seminar, 31 Mar. 1989.)

THE REQUIREMENTS FOR temple attendance do not change from place to place. Where a temple is available, priesthood authority gives no greater or lesser blessings in one place than another. Temple worship is a perfect example of our unity as Church members. All of us answer the same questions of worthiness to enter the temple. All the men dress alike. All the women dress alike. We leave the cares of the world behind us as we enter the temple. Everyone receives the same blessings. All make the same covenants. All are equal before the Lord. Yet within our spiritual unity there is wide room for everyone's individuality and expression. In that setting, all are heirs to the kingdom of God. President Hunter said it well: "The key to a unified church is a unified soul, one that is at peace with itself and not given to inner conflicts and tensions." (*That We Might Have Joy*, p. 50.) ("Heirs to the Kingdom of God," *Ensign*, May 1995, 62–63.)

QUORUM LEADERS SHOULD encourage quorum members to do all [the temple work] they can without placing an unreasonable burden upon them or sending them on a guilt trip. Some may only be able to do as little as occasionally attending the temple and assisting or contributing to a family organization. Most members of the Church, however, can attend the temple regularly and identify one deceased ancestor for whom they can perform vicarious temple endowments and/or sealings. Some will be able to do much more. ("The Key to Activity and Retention," Regional Representatives' Seminar, 31 March 1989.)

RECENTLY AN OUT-OF-STATE journalist used the phrase that there were appearing "cracks in the walls of the temple," figuratively speaking, of course. By this I suppose he meant that the moorings of the Church were being shaken by a very few who do not fully sustain the leaders of the Church or keep their covenants. To dispel this perception of cracks in our members' faith, we need only to observe the joyful people who worship in any of our forty-five temples worldwide. Many are couples clutching their little bags and holding hands, and many are the unmarried, seeking the peaceful blessings of the house of the Lord. Their countenances reflect much joy and satisfaction in their lives. ("Five Loaves and Two Fishes," *Ensign*, May 1994, 6.)

IT WAS IN the temple that Jesus received much of his early education. It was there he revealed the spiritual insight he had received to be about his Father's business. In the temple the Savior announced his Messianic mission. Simeon came by the Spirit to the temple and there had fulfilled for him the promise by the Holy Ghost that he would not die until he had seen "the Lord's Christ" (see Luke 2:18–29). The last verse of Luke's gospel states that after the ascension the apostles "returned to Jerusalem . . . and were continually in the temple, praising and blessing God" (Luke 24:52–53). Why were the apostles continually in the temple if it was not an important part of what Christ taught? ("Coming unto Christ through the Ordinances and Covenants of the Temple," Temple Presidents Seminar, Salt Lake City, Utah, 19 Aug. 1987.)

TESTIMONY

THE THINGS OF the Spirit are most to be treasured because from these spiritual reassurances come the sacred inner peace and strength, as was the testimony of John the Baptist: "A man can receive nothing, except it be given him from heaven" (John 3:27). ("A Testimony of Christ," *BYU Speeches*, 13 Mar. 1979, 66.)

THIS MORNING I want to speak about the importance of each of us bearing our testimony. We bear testimony, not only through our words, but also through our lives. I take as my text Paul's message to the Romans, "For I am not ashamed of the gospel of Christ: for it is the power of God unto salvation to every one that believeth; to the Jew first, and also to the Greek" (Romans 1:16). . . . Some of us are naturally reserved and timid about bearing our testimony with words. Perhaps we should not be so timid. The Doctrine and Covenants tells us, "But with some I am not well pleased, for they will not open their mouths, but they hide the talent which I have given unto them, because of the fear of man" (D&C 60:2) We should testify with a spirit of humility. Section 38 of the Doctrine and Covenants reminds us, "And let your preaching be the warning voice, every man to his neighbor, in mildness and in meekness" (D&C 38:41). . . . All my life I have tried not to hide who I am and what I believe in. I cannot recall a single instance when it hurt my career or I lost valued friends by humbly acknowledging that I was a member of this Church. ("The Importance of Bearing Testimony," Frankfurt Area Conference, 28 May 1988.)

TITHING

As A BOY I learned a great lesson of faith and sacrifice as I worked on my grandfather's farm during the terrible economic depression of the 1930s. The taxes on the farm were delinquent, and Grandfather, like so many, had no money. There was a drought in the land, and some cows and horses were dying for lack of grass and hay. One day when we were harvesting what little hay there was in the field, Grandfather told us to take the wagon to the corner of the field where the best stand of hay stood and fill the wagon as full as we could and take it to the tithing yard as payment of his tithing in kind.

I wondered how Grandfather could use the hay to pay tithing when some of the cows that we were depending upon to sustain us might starve. I even questioned if the Lord expected that much sacrifice from him. Ultimately, I marveled at his great faith that somehow the Lord would provide. The legacy of faith he passed on to his posterity was far greater than money because he established in the minds of his children and grandchildren that above all he loved the Lord and His holy work over other earthly things. He never became wealthy, but he died at peace with the Lord and with himself. ("Opening the Windows of Heaven," *Ensign*, Nov. 1998, 54.)

PAYMENT OF OUR tithes and offerings can help us become independent. President Nathan Eldon Tanner said: "Paying tithing is discharging a debt to the Lord. . . .

"If we obey this commandment, we are promised that we will 'prosper in the land.' This prosperity consists of more than material goods—it may include enjoying good health and vigor of mind. It includes family solidarity and spiritual increase" (in Conference Report, Oct. 1979, p. 119; or *Ensign*, Nov. 1979, p. 81). It is my firm belief, after many years of close observation, that those who honestly pay their tithes and offerings do prosper and get along better in almost every way. It is my testimony that in discharging this debt to the Lord, one enjoys great personal satisfaction. Unfortunately this great satisfaction will be known only by those who have the faith and strength to keep this commandment. ("Responsibility for Welfare Rests with Me and My Family," *Ensign*, May 1986, 21.)

THE LAW OF tithing is simple: we pay one-tenth of our individual increase annually. (See D&C 119:4.) Increase has been interpreted by the First Presidency to mean income. (See Church Handbook of Instructions, Book 1: Stake Presidencies and Bishoprics (1998), 134.) What amounts to 10 percent of our individual income is between each of us and our Maker. There are no legalistic rules. As a convert in Korea once said: "With tithing, it doesn't matter whether you are rich or poor. You pay 10 percent, and you don't have to be ashamed if you haven't earned very much. If you make lots of money, you pay 10 percent. If you make very little, you still pay 10 percent. Heavenly Father will love you for it. You can hold your head up proud." (Letter from D. Brent Clement, president of the Korea Seoul Mission, 1981.)

Why should members worldwide, many of whom may not have enough for their daily needs, be encouraged to keep the Lord's law of tithing? As President Hinckley said in Cebu in the Philippine Islands, if members "even living in poverty and misery . . . will accept the gospel and live it, pay their tithes and offerings, even though those be meager, . . . they will have rice in their bowls and clothing on their backs and shelter over their heads. I do not see any other solution." ("Opening the Windows of Heaven," *Ensign*, Nov. 1998, 59.)

SOME MAY FEEL they cannot afford to pay tithing, but the Lord has promised that He would prepare a way for us to keep all of His commandments. (See 1 Ne. 3:7.) To pay tithing takes a leap of faith in the beginning, but as Jesus said, "If any man will do his will, he shall know of the doctrine." (John 7:17.) We learn about tithing by paying it. Indeed, I believe it is possible to break out of poverty by having the faith to give back to the Lord part of what little we have. ("Opening the Windows of Heaven," *Ensign*, Nov. 1998, 59.)

I LEARNED IN serving almost twenty years as bishop and stake president that an excellent insurance against divorce is the payment of tithing. Payment of tithing seems to facilitate keeping the spiritual battery charged in order to make it through the times when the spiritual generator has been idle or not working. ("The Enriching of Marriage," *Ensign*, Nov. 1977, 11.)

MEMBERS OF THE Church who do not tithe do not lose their membership; they only lose blessings. Through Malachi the Lord asks: "Will a man rob God? . . . But ye say, Wherein have we robbed thee? In tithes and offerings." (Malachi 3:8.) If we will trust in the Lord, He will open the windows of heaven to us as we give back to Him the one-tenth He asks of us. His promise is sure: "I will . . . pour you out a blessing, that there shall not be room enough to receive it." (Malachi 3:10.) Although tithing carries with it both temporal and spiritual blessings, the only absolute promise to the faithful is "ye shall have the riches of eternity." (D&C 38:39.) ("Opening the Windows of Heaven," *Ensign*, Nov. 1998, 59.)

THE LORD SPEAKS of offerings in the plural. He expects us, as a condition of faithfulness, to pay our tithing and our fast offerings to help the poor and the needy. But we are privileged to make other offerings, not by way of assignment, assessment, or ecclesiastical direction. Among these are donations to the General Missionary Fund, Humanitarian Aid Fund, and the Book of Mormon Fund. We are also privileged to voluntarily contribute to building the new temples President Hinckley has announced.

Recently I received an anonymous letter from a person who

made a substantial sacrifice for the General Temple Fund of the Church. She said: "I decided when I wanted to spend any money on myself I would forgo it and put the money into the temple fund. This meant no new clothes or shoes, books, hair appointments, necklaces, or anything of a personal nature until I reached my goal. I thought this would be a sacrifice, but instead I have found joy in it. It has been a rewarding and fulfilling experience."

The Prophet Joseph Smith once said, "A religion that does not require the sacrifice of all things never has power sufficient to produce the faith necessary unto life and salvation." He continues, "Those who do not make the sacrifice cannot enjoy this faith, because men are dependent upon this sacrifice in order to obtain this faith." (*Lectures on Faith* [1985] 69–70.) ("Opening the Windows of Heaven," *Ensign*, Nov. 1998, 59–60.)

UNITY

As A YOUNG man I recall President J. Reuben Clark pleading time after time in general priesthood meetings that there be unity in the priesthood. He would quote frequently the message of the Lord, "I say unto you, be one; and if ye are not one ye are not mine" (D&C 38:27). . . . If we are united and go forward under the leadership of those who have the keys to the kingdom of God on earth, our homes will be enriched, our lives purified, and the gates of hell will not prevail against us. ("Enriching Family Life," *Ensign*, May 1983, 40, 42.)

THE MULTIPLICITY OF languages and cultures is both an opportunity and a challenge for members of the Church. . . . Even with language differences, hopefully no minority group would ever feel so unwelcome in the "body of Christ" that they would wish to worship exclusively in their own ethnic culture. We hope that those in any dominant culture would reach out to them in the brotherhood and sisterhood of the gospel so that we can establish fully a community of Saints where everyone will feel

needed and wanted. ("Heirs to the Kingdom of God," *Ensign,*
May 1995, 63.)

WE DO NOT lose our identity in becoming members of this
church. We become heirs to the kingdom of God, having joined
the body of Christ and spiritually set aside some of our personal differences to unite in a greater spiritual cause. ("Heirs to
the Kingdom of God," *Ensign,* May 1995, 62.)

OUR REAL STRENGTH is not so much in our diversity but in our
spiritual and doctrinal unity. ("Heirs to the Kingdom of God,"
Ensign, May 1995, 62.)

WITHIN OUR SPIRITUAL unity there is wide room for everyone's
individuality and expression. ("Heirs to the Kingdom of God,"
Ensign, May 1995, 62.)

VALUES

I SPEAK OF the importance of keeping covenants because they
protect us in a world that is drifting from time-honored values
that bring joy and happiness. In the future this loosening of
moral fiber may even increase. The basic decency of society is
decreasing. In the future our people, particularly our children
and grandchildren, can expect to be bombarded more and more
by the evils of Sodom and Gomorrah.

Too many families are being broken up. Good is called evil,
and evil is called good. (See Isaiah 5:20.) In our present "easi-
ness of the way" (Alma 37:46), have we forgotten the elements
of sacrifice and consecration that our pioneer forebears demonstrated so well for us? It may be that, as Wordsworth suggested:

> *The world is too much with us; late and soon,*
> *Getting and spending, we lay waste our powers: . . .*
> *We have given our hearts away, a sordid boon! . . .*
> *For this, for everything, we are out of tune.*
> (The Oxford Book of English Verse [London:
> Oxford University Press, 1949], p. 626.)

Perhaps in our day and time it is more difficult to maintain moral strength and stand against the winds of evil that blow more fiercely than ever before. It is a sifting process. Today the modern counterparts of Babylon, Sodom, and Gomorrah are alluringly and explicitly displayed on television, the Internet, in movies, books, magazines, and places of entertainment. ("Search Me, O God, and Know My Heart," *Ensign,* May 1998, 18.)

IN OUR SOCIETY many sacred values have been eroded in the name of freedom of expression. The vulgar and the obscene are protected in the name of freedom of speech. The mainstream of society has become more tolerant, even accepting, of conduct that Jesus, Moses, the Prophet Joseph Smith, and other prophets have warned against since the beginning of human history.

We should not allow our personal values to erode, even if others think we are peculiar. We have always been regarded as a peculiar people. However, being spiritually correct is much better than being politically correct. Of course, as individuals and as a people we want to be liked and respected. But we cannot be in the mainstream of society if it means abandoning those righteous principles which thundered down from Sinai, later to be refined by the Savior, and subsequently taught by modern prophets. We should only fear offending God and His Son, Jesus Christ, who is the head of this Church. . . .

Paul spoke of those in his day who demonstrated that "the work of the law [was] written in their hearts, their conscience also bearing witness." (Romans 2:15.) For members of this Church to enjoy the blessings of a covenant people, the law of the Lord must be written in their hearts. . . .

Joshua spoke unequivocally when he said: "But as for me and my house, we will serve the Lord. . . .

"And the people said unto Joshua, The Lord our God will we serve, and his voice will we obey." (Joshua 24:15, 24.) ("Search Me, O God, and Know My Heart," *Ensign,* May 1998, 18–19.)

THERE IS A widespread feeling that the honored values of this nation are eroding and must be re-enthroned. When someone in good conscience tries to say this, invariably someone else raises the voice, "Whose values?" My answer to that is, everybody's values: Time-honored values such as absolute honesty, complete integrity, decency and civility, marriage, independence, industry, thrift, self-reliance, respect for law and order, and hard work. These are human values. ("The Integrity of Obeying the Law," Freedom Festival Fireside, Provo, Utah, 2 July 1995.)

WELFARE

HUNDREDS OF MILLIONS of our Father's children face poverty and illiteracy and other problems—both temporal and spiritual— that are almost beyond our comprehension. Of such people President Kimball stated: "Give these people to us and we'll open their eyes to a vision of eternity and show them how to reach up to the stars" (Dec. 1974).

We recognize that the process of establishing the Lord's church encompasses much more than baptizing people. In the first chapter of Alma in the Book of Mormon we find an instructive sequence of events outlining the way by which the Lord's church is established. Beginning with verse 26 we read:

"The priests left their labor to impart the word of God unto the people. . . . And when the priest had imparted unto them the word of God they all returned again diligently unto their labors; . . . and thus they were all equal, and they did all labor, every man according to his strength.

"And they did impart of their substance, every man according to that which he had, to the poor, and the needy, and the sick, and the afflicted; and they did not wear costly apparel, yet they were neat and comely" (Alma 1:26–27).

Let us take note of this process:

First, the doctrines are taught (see v. 26).

Second, members esteem each other as themselves (see v. 26).

Third, they all labor; they work and earn that which they receive (see v. 26).

Fourth, they impart of their substance to the less fortunate; they serve one another (see v. 27).

Fifth, they discipline their own appetites while at the same time caring appropriately for their own needs (see v. 27).

Now listen to the declaration of the prophet:

"And thus they did establish the affairs of the church. . . .

"And now, because of the steadiness of the church they began to be exceeding rich, having abundance of all things whatsoever they stood in need" (Alma 1:28–29).

This mighty change happened, not because the people were given things, but rather because they were taught and began to help themselves and to care for those who were less fortunate. It was when they gave of themselves in the Lord's way that their circumstances began to improve. ("Establishing the Church," *Ensign*, Nov. 1979, 91.)

I HAVE BEEN wondering where the Lord's storehouse really is. The bishops' storehouse is certainly the Lord's storehouse, but I think the Lord's storehouse is much more. President Monson indicated to us what the Lord's storehouse includes, and I quote: "The Lord's storehouse includes the time, talents, skills, compassion, consecrated material and financial means of faithful Church members. These resources are available to the bishop in assisting those in need." Our new Leaders Guide to Welfare provides a beautiful definition of what the Lord's storehouse is: "In form and operation, the storehouse is as simple or sophisticated as circumstances require. It may be a list of available services, money in an account, food in a pantry, or commodities in a building. A storehouse is established the moment faithful members give to the bishop of their time, talents, skills, compassion, materials and financial means in caring for the poor and the building up of the Kingdom of God on earth."

But where is the Lord's storehouse? I believe that in a sense, ultimately and finally, the Lord's storehouse must be in our hearts. Our hearts must be full of compassion for our fellow men and women. In that spirit, all who administer and serve in this building will want to do so in a spirit of kindness and in the pure love of Christ. (Remarks at dedication of Welfare Center in Ogden, Utah, 21 Nov. 1991.)

PARTICIPATING IN THE activities of basic welfare gives members the opportunity to incorporate fundamental gospel principles into their lives.

For example, by living the law of the fast members learn of love and selflessness. As home teachers help a family mend a fence, or as Relief Society sisters prepare food for a neighbor who is ill, they experience the meaning of service. In seeking to be prepared individually and as a family, members practice self-reliance and work. ("Establishing the Church," *Ensign*, Nov. 1979, 92.)

I HOPE NONE of our people will be too proud to accept help when they are in need. I am grateful for an experience in my life which taught me this great principle. My father was a successful lawyer, but not many years after the Depression he had two sons on a mission at the same time, my older brother, Gus, and me. He fell ill and was hospitalized and financially things became difficult. Our good bishop went to him and said, "George, this month the ward is going to send the money to your two missionary sons while you get back on your feet." I did not learn of this until some years later, but I was grateful that my father, who gave generously to the Church all of his life, in a moment of need was not too proud to accept the help of the loving brothers and sisters in the ward. After all, that is the spirit of the gospel. In order to have the blessing of giving, one needs to receive. (Remarks at dedication of Welfare Center in Ogden, Utah, 21 Nov. 1991.)

RECENTLY IN THE small village of Ubon, Thailand, a member family by the name of Tan was beset with what seemed to be insurmountable problems. The father had lost his job, they had no money, the children were sick and malnourished. They were being forced to remove their humble home from the government land upon which it was built, and they had no place to go.

At this point a fine priesthood leader, who had been using welfare services missionaries as a resource, stepped in and averted what could otherwise have been a tragic situation. Under his guidance and with the assistance of all the branch members, a piece of land was obtained, and the Tan family home was dismantled, transported, and rebuilt. Brother Tan began farming the land and started a family produce business which is now flourishing. Some hard work, dedication, and love from local leaders and members, aided by the suggestions of welfare services missionaries, caused a miracle for one family and a great learning and growing experience for a whole branch. ("Establishing the Church," *Ensign,* Nov. 1979, 93.)

WISDOM

WHAT IF THE Lord appeared to each of us, as he did to Solomon, and said, "Ask what I shall give thee"? How would you answer? Would you ask for a new car? A new home? A blessing of health? Or a station in life? Solomon asked for none of these. He did not ask for fame or for fortune. He asked, "Give therefore thy servant an understanding heart." This reply pleased the Lord.

"And God said unto him, Because thou hast asked this thing, and has not asked for thyself long life; neither hast asked riches for thyself, nor hast asked the life of thine enemies; but hast asked for thyself understanding to discern judgment;

"Behold, I have done according to thy words: lo, I have given thee a wise and an understanding heart; so that there was none like thee before thee, neither after thee shall any arise like unto thee.

"And I have also given thee that which thou hast not asked, both riches, and honour: so that there shall not be any among the kings like unto thee all thy days." (1 Kings 3:5, 9, 11–13.) ("Where Is the Church?" *BYU Speeches*, 24 Sept. 1989, 35–36.)

W O M E N

IT HAS BEEN my great blessing to know three perfect women. I speak of my wife, my mother, and my mother-in-law. I would like to tell you of my mother-in-law. . . . Her name was Elizabeth Hamilton Wright. She was a twin, born into a family of fourteen children. . . . She was taken out of school after the third grade and given the necessary task of tending the younger children. . . . But she was liberated and fully emancipated because she had graduated summa cum laude in spirituality. She knew things beyond the understanding of those of us who were merely college trained. She knew them by the Spirit of God. She was the humblest of the humble, the wisest of the wise, because she was simple enough to be able to accept a complete belief in God. She knew that the best religion is humanity and the best divine service is to love thy neighbor as thyself. ("Christianity—Repression or Liberation?" *BYU Speeches*, 10 June 1975, 143.)

HOW CAN ANY faithful sister in this Church feel that she is unimportant if she is to do the work which the Savior did? Inherent in this is the forgetting of self and the serving of others.

A . . . friend of ours who lives alone broke her shoulder and needed help. Word soon spread throughout her ward, and ward members brought dinners by the dozen so that she had to tell them to stop because her refrigerator was overflowing. One of them was a nearly blind sister who crossed a busy street with a hot dinner on a tray. Another sister volunteered to help clean her apartment. Seeing our friend's reluctance she countered, "How else can I show you that I love you?" Another sister who helped with grocery shopping saw the bright side of our friend's accident as she pointed out, "This opportunity has brought us close to each other again!" These sisters all had the vision of the work the Savior had in mind for them to do. ("The Grand Key-words for the Relief Society," *Ensign*, Nov. 1996, 95.)

SOME WOMEN, FOR reasons beyond their control, have to work and leave their young children in the care of others. At the press conference on March 13, 1995, when the new First Presidency was announced, reporters asked about working mothers. President Hinckley responded, "Do the best you can and remember that the greatest assets you have in this world are those children whom you have brought into the world and for whose nurture and care you are responsible" (Press Conference, March 13, 1995). (Address at Ricks College Commencement, 28 Apr. 1995.)

THE STRUGGLE TO improve the place of women in society has been a noble cause, and I sincerely hope the day will come when women with equal skills will be fully equal with men in the marketplace. However, this is an issue of equality, not sameness, and does not mean that women should be the same as men or try to do things the way men do them. Although some jobs that are traditionally masculine are now being done by women, it is possible for them to be done in a feminine way, and yet be done equally as well, or possibly even better.

Over a hundred years ago, in 1872, Eliza R. Snow said that some women "are so radical in their extreme theories that they would set for her an antagonism to man, [and] . . . make her adopt the more reprehensible phases of character which men present and which should be shunned or improved by them instead of being copied by women." Becoming like men is not the answer; being who you are and living up to your potential and commitment is. ("Message to Our Granddaughters," *BYU Speeches*, 12 Feb. 1985, 78.)

You say, "Where do I begin?" Rather than beginning with a wish list of all the things you want in life, the real question may be what you are not willing to do without. Select two or three of life's experiences you are absolutely sure you want to have. Do not leave important things to chance. Then think about what you can contribute to society by serving your family, the Church, and the community. Also think of what life will demand from you. Everything has a price. Much is expected of us. Becoming like men is not the answer. Rather, the answer lies in being who you are and living up to your divine potential by fulfilling eternal commitments.

You cannot trust the many conflicting voices that clamor about what women should or should not do in today's society. Some of the loudest voices are echoes of those others who are out of harmony with themselves and out of tune with life in general rather than being unhappy with their role as women.

Do not be deceived in your quest to find happiness and an identity of your own. Entreating voices may tell you that what you have seen your mothers and grandmothers do is old-fashioned, unchallenging, boring, and drudgery. It may have been old-fashioned and perhaps routine; at times it was drudgery. But your mothers and grandmothers have sung a song that expressed the highest love and the noblest of womanly feelings. They have been our nurturers and our teachers. They have sanctified the work, transforming drudgery into the noblest enterprises. ("How Near to the Angels," *Ensign*, May 1998, 96.)

Surely the secret citadel of women's inner strength is their spirituality. In this they equal and even surpass men, as they do in faith, morality, and commitment when truly converted to the gospel. They have "more trust in the Lord [and] more hope in his word" ("More Holiness Give Me," *Hymns* [1985], no. 131). This inner spiritual sense seems to give them a certain resilience to cope with sorrow, trouble, and uncertainty. ("The Highest Place of Honor," *Ensign*, May 1988, 37.)

YOU ARE APPRECIATED and valued far more than you realize. We are mindful of your many challenges, which are often overwhelming and exhausting in this unsettled world. . . .

Despite all of this, greater blessings are coming to women than ever before. In my lifetime, the drudgery of caring for a home and family has been greatly reduced. I remember my grandmother's old washboard, which was used to scrub clothes by hand. She cooked hot meals winter and summer on a wood-burning stove. I remember the coming of electricity to our small town and all the marvelous advantages that it brought. Women now have never had greater opportunities for education and travel. But in the eternal scheme of things, your role is infinitely more vital, and it carries the promise of spiritual blessings greater than these temporal benefits. ("The Grand Key-words for the Relief Society," *Ensign,* Nov. 1996, 95–96.)

IT MAY NOT be possible for economic reasons, but if you have the choice, do not abandon too quickly the full-time career of marriage and mothering. Some may criticize you and say that you have no gumption, that you lack brains, that you have no ambition, or even that you are seeking to get your fulfillment from others. As you go forward with a professional career, remember that no one will love you more than those in your own home. In the business or scientific world, probably no one would consider you to be perfect. But your little ones, for a time, will think that you are perfect. If you are wise, they will adore you for eternity. No one will need more of your time and energy and attention on a twenty-four hour basis than your family. Their needs will not go away during the daytime working hours. There is the advantage that in working twenty-four hours a day on family relations, you are working on eternal relations. Thus you will also have more time for service in the administration of the Lord's church on earth where your service is valued and needed. You don't have to earn money to be important. You may choose not to sell your time. ("Message to Our Granddaughters," *BYU Speeches,* 12 Feb. 1985, 80–81.)

YOU WILL HAVE to answer to your natural womanly instincts which the Prophet Joseph said are according to your natures. You should respond generously to these instincts and promptings to do good. With your very being held still, you should listen to the whisperings of the Holy Spirit. You should follow the noble, intuitive feelings planted deep within your soul by Deity in the previous world. In this way you will be responding to the Holy Spirit of God, and will be sanctified by truth. By so doing, you will be eternally honored and loved. Much of your work is to enrich mankind. Care and mercy seem to be a dominant refrain of the song you have the opportunity to sing. I hope you will not leave any of the melody unsung. ("Message to Our Granddaughters," *BYU Speeches*, 12 Feb. 1985, 82.)

PART OF THE problem is for us to live eternal principles faithfully every day. . . .

To meet the challenges of the eternal every day, every sister will be strengthened by daily communion with our Heavenly Father through prayer. Scripture study will be beneficial in bringing spiritual reassurances. Attending sacrament meeting, partaking of the sacred emblems, and the renewal of our covenants will be a weekly source of strength.

The sisters who try to cope with the myriad challenges of our complex times can benefit from the sisterhood of the Church more than ever before. The words of Sister Lucy Mack Smith in one of the first meetings of the Relief Society are as relevant today as when first spoken. She said, "We must cherish one another, watch over one another, comfort one another, and gain instruction, that we may all sit down in heaven together." (Relief Society Minutes of Nauvoo, 24 March 1842.) . . .

The bearing of testimony benefits both the one testifying as well as the one listening. Regular temple attendance will help us meet all our challenges. Accepting calls from priesthood leaders as well as visiting teaching assignments from the Relief Society president will be a great strengthening experience. In rendering compassionate service individually and as a group you lose sight of your own problems and do the work the Savior did. ("The Grand Key-words for the Relief Society," *Ensign*, Nov. 1996, 96.)

IF WE [WHO hold the priesthood] could recognize the true greatness of . . . women, we would not treat them as we sometimes do. The world often uses and abuses women. We holders of the priesthood should honor good women in and out of the Church as true sisters, not as objects and sources of service or pleasure. Our consideration for women should spring from esteem for the daughters of Zion and an awareness of their true identity more than from a concern with their functions and roles. ("The Highest Place of Honor," *Ensign*, May 1988, 36.)

WOMEN AND THE PRIESTHOOD

THERE ARE COEQUAL blessings and opportunities for both men and women in the Lord, neither having a superiority nor inferiority in eternal promises, commitments and faithfulness. They are different, however, in eternal assignments. In a far distant time perhaps God said to you beloved sisters, "You are best adapted to be a woman. You have special gifts, sensitivities of the spirit, faith and talents which particularly endow you for the exalting role of womanhood."

Your role is not an accident nor a mistake. No doubt all of you were pleased and happy with your being a woman—a very special and unique being. Motherhood is a very special calling, as is fatherhood for men. It is a great privilege for you with your husband to be involved together in the greatest of all works—that of rearing and teaching his children.

The priesthood leader, be he father, bishop or stake president, is not necessarily greater or better or smarter than his followers. Someone has to be appointed to be the focal point of responsibility and receive inspiration to give priesthood direction in the kingdom and "get on with the war" against Satan. It does not follow that because our sisters are not priesthood leaders that they are spiritually inferior or that their work in the kingdom is in any sense less important. The role of womankind as followers of the Savior is not limiting or confining, but liberating. God expects in his economy that his daughters will use all of the gifts and talents which he gave to them to be as fully flowered as his sons in their own spheres of influence and activity. (Remarks delivered at the dedication of the Eliza R. Snow Center for the Performing Arts, Ricks College, 9 Dec. 1980.)

FOR THE DAUGHTERS of God, doing the Savior's work does not, of course, include the use of priesthood keys, authority, or powers. But it does include building faith by testimony and example. It includes teaching the doctrines of salvation. It includes following the Savior's example of love for all mankind. It includes ministering to others for, as the Prophet Joseph said when the Relief Society was organized, "This is a charitable Society, and according to your natures; it is natural for females to have feelings of charity and benevolence." (*Teachings of the Prophet Joseph Smith* [1976], p. 226.) "Let the weight of your innocence, kindness and affection be felt . . . ; not war, not jangle, not contradiction, or dispute, but meekness, love, purity—these are the things that should magnify you in the eyes of all good men." (Ibid., p. 227.)

This charge to the women of the Church carries a promise. Said the Prophet Joseph: "If you live up to these principles, how great and glorious will be your reward in the celestial kingdom! If you live up to your privileges, the angels cannot be restrained from being your associates." (Ibid., pp. 226–27.) ("The Grand Key-words for the Relief Society," *Ensign*, Nov. 1996, 94.)

I BELIEVE THAT we, as . . . holders of the priesthood, will never achieve our potential without having in our lives the blessings of the unique qualities of our mothers, wives, sisters, daughters, and all of the good women of the Church.

Perhaps you have all heard the story, and it is just a story, of the insensitive man who held two season tickets to the basketball games at the local university. His wife died, and a day or two later he went to the game. The seat previously occupied by his wife was empty. Someone said, "Those seats of yours must be very expensive. Couldn't you find a member of the family to come and sit in your wife's seat?" The man answered, "No, they couldn't come. They've all gone to her funeral."

I fear that we brethren often get far too engrossed in the apparent importance of our own activities and relegate the less visible contributions of the sisters to a lesser role. They serve very quietly and effectively, often unnoticed, unrecognized, and unappreciated. ("The Highest Place of Honor," *Ensign*, May 1988, 36.)

BECAUSE YOU DESCENDED from great women, each of you has the potential to become a great woman.

Now you need to know that to me great does not necessarily mean your becoming a great doctor, lawyer, or business executive. You may, of course, become any of these if you so desire, and if you work hard enough, and I would be proud of such an achievement. However, to me greatness is much, much more. I hope that each of you girls will become an individual of significant worth and a person of virtue so that your contributions are maintained in both human and eternal terms. ("Message to Our Granddaughters," *BYU Speeches*, 12 Feb. 1985, 77–78.)

THE SISTERS HERE have something very special. It is their great femininity—part of the divinity of God which is in you. The men have masculinity, also part of divinity. Sister Faust, from this pulpit some years ago, reminded us that you women are very special because all life begins with you. And you have a direct pipeline with God because of your great capacity to love. Because of your great capacity to love; therefore, to bless. (Special Interest Fireside, Salt Lake City, Utah, 29 Jan. 1978.)

YOU SISTERS WHO sit in the ward and stake councils should feel free to share your special wisdom and experience in those councils. Then, when the bishop or stake president makes a decision, all will wish to support it. ("The Grand Key-words for the Relief Society," *Ensign,* Nov. 1996, 95.)

THE PRIESTHOOD PLACES upon the fathers the responsibility of being the head of the family and the home. What does being the head of the family mean? It is a priesthood power, and the Doctrine and Covenants, section 121, makes it clear that all priesthood responsibilities must be exercised "only by persuasion, . . . by gentleness and meekness, and by love unfeigned" (D&C 121:41). Holding the priesthood does not mean that a man is a power-broker, or that he sits on a throne, dictating in macho terms, or that he is superior in any way. Rather, he is a leader by authority of example. Paul's counsel to the Ephesians included, "Husbands, love your wives, even as Christ also loved the church, and gave himself for it" (Ephesians 5:25). As Christ lifts us all, so must we, rather than put down women or anyone.

Nowhere does the doctrine of this Church declare that men are superior to women. Paul said to the Corinthians, "Nevertheless neither is the man without the woman, neither the woman without the man, in the Lord" (1 Corinthians 11:11). Each brings his or her own separate and unique strengths to the family and the Church. Women are not just cooks, stewards of our homes, or servants. They are much more. They are the enrichment of humanity. ("The Highest Place of Honor," *Ensign,* May 1988, 36.)

HOW SHOULD THE holders of the priesthood treat the women of the Church? The sisters of this church since the beginning have always made a great and marvelous contribution to the work of the Lord. They have added so very much of intelligence, work, culture, and refinement to the Church and our families. The contributions of the sisters as we move into the future are needed more than ever to help establish the values, the faith, and the future of our families and the well-being of our society. They need to know they are valued, honored, and appreciated. The sisters who serve as leaders need to be invited to participate and to be listened to and included in our stake and ward council meetings, particularly concerning matters involving sisters, youth, and children.

How should those who bear the priesthood treat their wives and the other women in their family? Our wives need to be cherished. They need to hear their husbands call them blessed, and the children need to hear their fathers generously praise their mothers (see Proverbs 31:28). The Lord values his daughters just as much as he does his sons. In marriage, neither is superior; each has a different primary and divine responsibility. Chief among these different responsibilities for wives is the calling of motherhood. I firmly believe that our dear faithful sisters enjoy a special spiritual enrichment which is inherent in their natures. ("Keeping Covenants and Honoring the Priesthood," *Ensign*, Nov. 1993, 38–39.)

SOME WOMEN MAY feel it is subversive to their free agency to be directed by the power of the priesthood. This feeling comes from misunderstanding. There should be no compulsion, duress, or unrighteous dominion involved in priesthood authority. President Stephen L Richards stated: "Our accord comes from universal agreement with righteous principles and common response to the operation of the Spirit of our Father. It is actuated by no fear except one. That is the fear of offending God, the Author of our work" (Conference Report, Oct. 1938, p. 116). ("Message to Our Granddaughters," *BYU Speeches*, 12 Feb. 1985, 81.)

IT IS MOST important that you Aaronic Priesthood holders learn what strengths you have as men. Possibly you were foreordained to great priesthood callings. You need to learn that these masculine strengths are great, noble, and God-given; however, they also have some limitations. Because of these limitations, it is equally important to learn how the influence of good women in our lives can complement these strengths and overcome these limitations. As you walk on the way to eternity, it is important to gain some understanding and appreciation for the wonderful endowments and callings God has given uniquely to women. ("The Highest Place of Honor," *Ensign*, May 1988, 36.)

YOU YOUNG MEN who hold the Aaronic Priesthood need to know that you cannot achieve your potential without the influence of good women, particularly your mother and, in a few years, a good wife. But it is too soon for you deacons and teachers to think seriously about dating. Dating, along with temple marriage, will come at the appropriate season in your life. You have to be elders to go to the temple.

In preparation for that surpassing experience, it is important for you to learn now to appreciate the special gifts of the good sisters of the Church, whom God has so abundantly endowed with talents. Your eternal helpmate will gently hold you to your potential. She will give loving and thoughtful encouragement, as well as comfort and discipline. She will also lift you up when you are down and bring you back to earth when you are puffed up. She will bless your life in countless ways. As President Kimball said, "Brethren, we cannot be exalted without our wives. There can be no heaven without righteous women" (in Conference Report, Oct. 1979, p. 7; or *Ensign*, Nov. 1979, p. 5). ("The Highest Place of Honor," *Ensign*, May 1988, 37.)

WORK

AN ESSENTIAL PART of teaching children to be disciplined and responsible is to have them learn to work. As we grow up, many of us are like the man who said, "I like work; it fascinates me. I can sit and look at it for hours" (Jerome Klapka Jerome, in

The International Dictionary of Thoughts, comp. John P. Bradley, Leo F. Daniels, and Thomas C. Jones [Chicago: J. G. Ferguson Publishing Co., 1969], p. 782). Again, the best teachers of the principle of work are the parents themselves. For me, work became a joy when I first worked alongside my father, grandfather, uncles, and brothers. I am sure that I was often more of an aggravation than a help, but the memories are sweet and the lessons learned are valuable. Children need to learn responsibility and independence. Are the parents personally taking the time to show and demonstrate and explain so that children can, as Lehi taught, "act for themselves and not . . . be acted upon"? (2 Nephi 2:26). ("The Greatest Challenge in the World—Good Parenting," *Ensign,* Nov. 1990, 34.)

WORKING FOR WHAT we receive is a cardinal, timeless principle of self-respect. ("Integrity, the Mother of Many Virtues," *Ensign,* May 1982, 48.)

YOUTH

YOU HAVE FEARS about being accepted. You worry about being popular in your age-group. It is natural to want to belong.

Recently I heard of a good man who, after being married in the temple and having four children, fell away from the Church. His physical appearance became shabby and his demeanor sad, as he became a drug addict, an alcoholic, and then a chain-smoker. He continued in this destructive lifestyle for many years. However, in time, with the help of a good wife, home teachers, a caring bishop, and our loving Heavenly Father, he eventually started on the long road back. One of the proudest days in his life came when he once again qualified for a temple recommend. Looking back on those bad years he later admitted, "All I ever wanted was to belong." Seeking acceptance from the wrong source brought untold misery and pain.

Please be assured, brethren, that we all belong. Nothing is more important or precious to any of us than belonging to The

Church of Jesus Christ of Latter-day Saints. We belong to the greatest cause on earth—that of our Lord and Savior, Jesus Christ. We have been endowed with the greatest power on earth—that of the holy priesthood. ("Pioneers of the Future— Be Not Afraid, Only Believe," *Ensign,* Nov. 1997, 43.)

RECENTLY I ASKED some special young people what I should know about your generation. One young man spoke for the group and said, "We live on the edge." Since that time I have thought a lot about what it means to live on the edge. Of course it can mean many things. I think my fine young friend was referring to hazardous motor cycling, cliff climbing, and other forms of recreation, which may involve taking unnecessary risks to produce a challenge or a thrill.

Some years ago Elder Marion D. Hanks told about a group of Boy Scouts who went cave exploring. The narrow trail was marked with white stones and lighted in sections as they went. After about an hour they came to a huge, high dome. Below it lay an area called the Bottomless Pit, so called because the floor of the cave had collapsed leaving a deep, gaping hole. It was hard not to jostle each other on that narrow path. Pretty soon, one of the bigger boys accidentally pushed a smaller boy into a muddy area away from the light. Terrified as he lost his footing, he screamed in the darkness. The ranger heard his cry of terror and came quickly. The boy let out another cry as the beam of the ranger's light showed he was right at the very edge of the pit.

In this story, the boy was rescued. But this does not always happen. So many times young people are enticed to go to the very edge or even beyond it. With only a precarious toehold, it is easy to be seriously injured or even die. Life is too precious to throw away in the name of excitement, or as Jacob said in the Book of Mormon, "looking beyond the mark." (Jacob 4:14.)

You young people may think that you are indestructible and that you are going to live forever. In a few years you will learn that this is not so. Living on the edge can also mean being perilously close to the Bottomless Pit. ("Acting for Ourselves and Not Being Acted Upon," *Ensign*, Nov. 1995, 45–46.)

THE MESSAGE I wish to speak today is one of hope. It concerns a conviction as well as a challenge that the youth, young adults, and young marrieds of this Church who believe in and follow its lofty purposes as a part of [a] new aristocracy will, by their influence and example, begin to reverse this spreading moral dry rot the world over.

In a letter to John Quincy Adams in 1813, Thomas Jefferson said: "There is a natural aristocracy among men. The grounds of this are virtue and talents. There is also an artificial aristocracy founded on wealth and birth, without either virtue or talents."

How is this new aristocracy distinguished? . . .

First, by their example of obedience to the commandments of God, thus enjoying the personal guidance of his Holy Spirit.

Second, by sharing their special knowledge as missionaries.

Third, by responding to the high level of expectancy of their parents and Church leaders.

Fourth, through the giving of themselves. A very special young friend of mine served as a missionary of this Church in Japan. His dedication to missionary work and the Japanese people was so complete and full that, rather than spend all of the money his parents sent to him, he unselfishly made a regular contribution of part of his money to help another local Japanese missionary. His parents sent him extra money so that he could buy some camera equipment available in Japan to record in pictures a few of the great experiences he was having. Rather than buy the camera equipment, which would have served him well for a lifetime, he chose rather to send the money back to his parents. In time, as with most missionaries, the clothes of my young friend became threadbare and thin. In order for him to be able to come home, it was necessary for him to buy a second-hand suit from one of the other elders. His regular denial of himself, in order to share his substance with the local Japanese missionary, was a very closely guarded secret. He is a good example of the young elect of God of this Church, as are hundreds of thousands of others. ("A New Aristocracy," *Ensign,* Nov. 1974, 59, 60.)

EXERCISE YOUR MORAL agency wisely. Omni tells us how we can make the proper channel selections. "There is nothing which is good save it comes from the Lord; and that which is evil cometh from the devil" (Omni 1:25). Every moment demands that we choose, over and over again, between that which comes from the Lord and that which comes from the devil. As tiny drops of water shape a landscape, so our minute-by-minute choices shape our character. Living the eternal gospel every day may be harder than dying for the Church and the Lord. ("The Voice of the Spirit," Young Adult Fireside Satellite Broadcast, 5 Sept. 1993.)

IF I WERE to ask you young people, "How is your testimony?" I suppose that many of you would say, "I don't know." But if I asked you some specific questions, the result would be different. For instance, if I asked you, "Do you believe that God lives and we are His children?" I think most of you would answer this question quickly and affirmatively.

And if I asked, "Do you believe and have faith in the Lord Jesus Christ as our Savior and Redeemer?" I think most of you would hasten to say yes.

And if I then asked, "Do you believe that Joseph Smith was the prophet of the Restoration?" I think most of you have a belief concerning this. Some of you would already be familiar with the 135th Section of the Doctrine and Covenants which states that "*Joseph Smith, the Prophet and Seer of the Lord, has done more, save Jesus Christ only, for the salvation of men in this world, than any other man that ever lived in it*" (D&C 135:3).

If I were to ask you, "Do you believe the Book of Mormon is the word of God?" I think many of you already have acquired a testimony concerning the truthfulness of the Book of Mormon.

Lastly, if I were to ask you, "Do you believe that President Benson and his counselors and the members of the Quorum of the Twelve Apostles are the prophets, seers, and revelators of our day?" I think most of you have formed a respect for the leaders of this Church.

Having answered these five questions in the affirmative, you already have a foundation of a testimony. As you acquire knowledge of the plan of salvation and learn why you are here and where you are going, your testimony will be strengthened. In addition, as you walk by faith you will have confirmed in your young hearts spiritual experiences which will strengthen your faith and testimony. You of this generation are a chosen generation. ("The Voice of the Spirit," Young Adult Fireside Satellite Broadcast, 5 Sept. 1993.)

STAY MORALLY CLEAN. You must believe that it is worth it in the end to be true and faithful. Worldly pleasures do not match up to heavenly joy. It may not be "cool" to avoid certain things, or "rad" to do other things, but it is better to be alone and to be right than to be eternally wrong. We counsel you to associate with those who can help you maintain your standards rather than tear them down. You must learn to be your own person and to live by your own standards. Even though you may have become somewhat desensitized or made some mistakes, you must not let Satan reduce your self-esteem to the point that you become discouraged. We urge you to carry and frequently read your *For the Strength of Youth* booklet and to listen to your parents and your leaders. As a chosen generation there is not a problem that you cannot handle with the help of the Lord. We counsel you not to grow up too fast. Do not miss the joy of being a righteous young adult. Enjoy your dating years. Have many friends. Have confidence in yourselves and in your future. You must learn to labor and you must learn to wait. ("The Voice of the Spirit," Young Adult Fireside Satellite Broadcast, 5 Sept. 1993.)

I HAVE SUGGESTED a simple solution for selecting the channel to which you will attune yourselves: Listen to and follow the voice of the Spirit.

•This is an ancient solution, even eternal, and may not be popular in a society that is always looking for something new.

•This solution requires patience in a world that demands instant gratification.

•This solution is quiet, peaceful, and subtle in a world enamored by that which is loud, incessant, fast-paced, garish, and crude.

•This solution requires you to be contemplative while your peers seek physical titillation.

•This solution requires the prophets to "put you always in remembrance of these things, though ye know them, and be established in the present truth" (2 Peter 1:12). This may seem foolish in a time when it is not worth remembering much of the trivial tripe to which we are exposed.

•This solution is one unified, consistent, age-old message in a world that quickly becomes bored in the absence of intensity, variety, and novelty.

•This solution requires you to walk by faith in a world governed by sight (see 2 Corinthians 4:18; 5:7). You must see with the eye of faith eternal, unseen, spiritual verities, while the masses of mankind depend solely on temporal things, which can be known only through the physical senses.

•In short, this solution may not be popular, it may not get you gain, or worldly power. But "our light affliction, which is but for a moment, worketh for us a far more exceeding and eternal weight of glory" (2 Corinthians 4:17).

•Learn to ponder the things of the Spirit and to respond to its promptings; filter out the static generated by Satan. As you become attuned to the Spirit, "thine ears shall hear a word behind thee, saying, This is the way, walk ye in it" (Isaiah 30:21).

•Hearkening to the "voice of the living God" will give you—

"Peace in this world, and

"Eternal life in the world to come" (D&C 59:23).

These are the greatest of all the gifts of God (see D&C 14:7). ("The Voice of the Spirit," Young Adult Fireside Satellite Broadcast, 5 Sept. 1993.)

INDEX